METAPHYSICAL ANIMALS

METAPHYSICAL ANIMALS

How Four Women Brought Philosophy Back to Life

Clare Mac Cumhaill
and Rachael Wiseman

Chatto & Windus

LONDON

1 3 5 7 9 10 8 6 4 2

Chatto & Windus, an imprint of Vintage, is part of the Penguin Random House group
of companies whose addresses can be found at global.penguinrandomhouse.com

Penguin
Random House
UK

Copyright © Clare Mac Cumhaill and Rachael Wiseman 2022

Clare Mac Cumhaill and Rachael Wiseman have asserted their right to be identified as the
author of this Work in accordance with the Copyright, Designs and Patents Act 1988

First published by Chatto & Windus in 2022

penguin.co.uk/vintage

A CIP catalogue record for this book is available from the British Library

ISBNs
9781784743284 (hardback)
9781784743291 (trade paperback)

Lines on p. 35 ('Oh where is Iris Murdoch, tell me where? tell me where?') © David Midgley;
p. 40 ('Between line eighty three and line a thousand') © Audi Bayley; p. 58 ('If you should hear
my name among those killed) © Kate Thompson; p. 126 ('Few could long withstand your haggard
beauty') reproduced by kind permission of Routledge & Kegan Paul; p. 274 ('Dieses weinglas schenk
ich dir') © J. D. Adler / ('This wine glass I present to thee') © Mara-Daria Cojocaru.

Typeset in 10.7/13.5pt Goudy Old Style by Jouve (UK), Milton Keynes
Printed and bound in Great Britain by Clays Ltd, Elcograf S.p.A.

The authorised representative in the EEA is Penguin Random House Ireland,
Morrison Chambers, 32 Nassau Street, Dublin D02 YH68

Penguin Random House is committed to a sustainable future
for our business, our readers and our planet. This book is made
from Forest Stewardship Council® certified paper.

To our grandmothers, mothers and daughters:
Alice, Joan, Rose, Christina, Paula, Lynda, Penelope and Ursula

Contents

Preface

The history of European philosophy is usually the story of the ideas, visions, hopes and fears of men. It is also the story of the ideas, visions, hopes and fears of men who have – in the main – lived unusually isolated lives, away from women and children. 'Practically all the great European philosophers have been bachelors,' wrote the philosopher Mary Midgley in 1953.[1] This was the first line of a script for a radio talk commissioned by the BBC but rejected: Mary's observation concerning the marital status of philosophers was a 'trivial, irrelevant intrusion of domestic matters into intellectual life', said the producer.[2] But Mary argued that the solipsism, scepticism and individualism that is characteristic of the Western philosophical tradition would not feature in a philosophy written by people who had shared intimate friendships with spouses and lovers, been pregnant, raised children, and enjoyed rich and full and varied human lives.

This book tells a history with four women philosophers and their friendship at its centre. Mary Midgley (née Scrutton), Iris Murdoch, Elizabeth Anscombe and Philippa Foot (née Bosanquet) came of age during some of the most tumultuous events of the twentieth century. Born just after the First World War, they began their philosophical studies at Oxford University shortly after Hitler's troops entered Austria. In fact, Mary was staying in Vienna when the troops arrived – she had embarked on a trip to improve her German before going up to college, reassured by her schoolteacher that the trouble in Europe would blow over. She returned home after signs went up in the shop windows: 'If you come in here as a true German, let your greeting be "Heil Hitler"'.[3] The events that unfolded over the coming years would change the human scene – Nazism, the Holocaust, Total War, Hiroshima and Nagasaki. This generation was brought face to face with acts of depravity and disorder that those who lived before them would hardly have thought possible.

Iris Murdoch observed that French and British philosophers seemed to respond very differently to post-Nazi reality. The French experience of Occupation infused French post-war philosophy and literature.[4] While Jean-Paul Sartre's philosophy explored the moral and political implications of freedom, and attempted to understand whether authenticity and sincerity were possible for those who had lived through Vichy France, the British had suffered no such crisis. Instead, in 1945 Oxford's men returned from their war work, rolled up their sleeves, and picked up where they had left off.

The task that the young men had begun, before the interruption of the war, was a bold one: to kill off the subject formerly known as 'philosophy' and to replace it with a new set of logical, analytic and scientific methods known as logical positivism. Speculative metaphysical enquiry – the pursuit of knowledge of human nature, morality, God, reality, truth and beauty – was to give way to clarification and linguistic analysis in the service of science. The only questions permitted were those that could be answered by empirical methods. 'What is the meaning of human life?', 'How ought we to live?', 'Does God exist?', 'Is time real?', 'What is truth?', 'What is beauty?' Metaphysical questions like these go beyond the limits of what we can measure and observe, and so they were designated 'Nonsense'. Banished too was the old philosophical picture of man as a spiritual creature whose life is oriented toward God or the Good, and for whom philosophy is the attempt to contemplate the fundamental structure of reality. In its stead: a vision of human beings as 'efficient calculating machines',[5] individuals whose intellectual powers enable them to move beyond their messy animal nature so as to organise and rationalise an otherwise brute and formless world. It was declared that there were no genuine philosophical problems; questions that were not amenable to scientific investigation were embarrassing muddles or linguistic confusions.

Had it not been for the interruption of war, Mary, Iris, Elizabeth and Philippa may well have joined the men in the effort to usher in the brave new world of a philosophy divested of poetry, mystery, spirit and metaphysics. Or, more likely, they would have finished their degrees and left philosophy behind them, convinced, as so many young women still are, that the subject was not for them. What happened instead was that the young men and the 'Big Beasts' of British philosophy (A. J. Ayer, Gilbert Ryle and J. L. Austin) were uprooted from Oxford and replanted in Whitehall and the War Office. Our four friends were left behind to finish their degrees in a disrupted Oxford, full of evacuees from London and refugees from Europe. And philosophy began to come back to life. The old metaphysicians were free once again to speak of poetry, transcendence, wisdom and truth. The conscientious objectors asked what God and duty required of them. The refugee academics, speaking in a language that was not their own, shared scholarship and learning of a kind Oxford had never seen before. And the women, no longer in classrooms full of clever young men who liked winning arguments, turned their attention, together, on to the world.[6] They were interested in 'the reality that surrounds man – transcendent or whatever', said Iris.[7] And they had questions. Lots of them.

This is how it was that these four women learnt to see philosophy as they did. As an ancient form of human enquiry, kept alive through thousands of years of conversation, the task of which is to help us, collectively, to find our way about in a vast reality that transcends any one of us. When the young men returned from war, with their analytic methods and their disdain for mystery and metaphysics, our four friends were ready with a joint 'No!'

We began our own philosophical conversation in the summer of 2013. We met in Geneva, two of a small cluster of philosophers gathered to try to understand the nature of dreaming. Each of us saw in the other a fellow philosopher who loved the obscure, ephemeral and tangential and had a tendency to ask weird questions. We soon discovered that we shared a common despair at the state of academic philosophy, a discipline that we were both trying to make our way in. We knew that if we were to keep going we would need to find a way to do philosophy in a more engaged, creative and open way. We were bored of listening to men talk about books by men about men. And we wanted to philosophise together, as friends. We were looking for a story that could help us. Then, on 28 November, a letter appeared in the Guardian, under the heading 'The Golden Age of Female Philosophy'. It was from 'Mary Midgley', a name we recognised but not a philosopher whose work appeared on university syllabuses or was discussed in the major professional journals. In that letter she set out the bare bones of the narrative you are about to read. She explained how she and her friends, Iris, Elizabeth and Philippa, had flourished in philosophy, a subject famously inhospitable to women, because at the crucial moment, the men had been called away to war.[8] 'The trouble is not, of course, men as such,' the letter went on, '– men have done good enough philosophy in the past.' She appeared to be suggesting, with a wink, that it was about time to consider what kind of philosophy women had done – and would do. The cosmos seemed to have delivered us just what we had asked for: and right on our doorstep. Before we knew it, we were frequent visitors at a retirement home in a Newcastle suburb just a few miles from our own homes, and in regular conversation with Mary Midgley. Sunk into her armchair, she spoke of the authors of the books on her shelves as if they had just left the room, passing us papers, notes and clippings from little heaps that covered sills, surfaces and carpet in her tiny living room: Collingwood, Joseph, Price, Wittgenstein, Austin, Ayer, Hare. She told us about her friends, all now dead: Iris, Philippa and Elizabeth.

One thing Mary wanted us to understand was 'what it is like to be literally "at war"'. This was at a time when we had been told, for over a decade, that we were at 'war on terror'; Mary insisted that we know the difference. *You are not doing what you would normally be doing; you are not where you would normally be; you are sent about, redirected, restricted. Your family and friends have been moved about too; or killed or injured or are in danger. It is hard to find out what is happening; the newspapers are not reliable, the radio is propaganda, the letters are censored. Food is scarce, petrol is rationed, travel is restricted. The future is uncertain. You are afraid. It is dark.*[9] When she told us these things, they were not recollections of a fixed and changeless past, but a living background to the philosophy she wanted to give us. Philosophy is needed in times of chaos, she said, and here was a theory about human life worked out by her and her friends, smoking cigarettes to dull the hunger, while air-raid sirens wailed and the blackout curtains shut out the light.

As the world tries to recover from a pandemic, and wakes up to the reality of the climate crisis, it is perhaps time to ask again, as these women did after the Second World War: What sort of animal is a human being? What do we need to live well? Is philosophy of any use?

After the war, the men on both sides of the English Channel shared a 'picture of man' that still dominates our collective imagination. The 'hero' of modern philosophy is, Iris wrote, the 'offspring of the age of science'. He is 'free, independent, lonely, powerful, rational, responsible, brave, the hero of so many novels and books of moral philosophy'.[10] But he is alienated from his own nature, from the natural world that is his home and from other humans. For us, now, loneliness and alienation have a distinctive twist. The technological development of the last few decades creates the impression of a world that lies wholly open to view – in a matter of seconds our computers show us the surface of Mars, the inside of a wasps' nest, the plans for a nuclear reactor. Yet in the face of the overwhelming complexity of human life, and increasingly happy with ersatz virtual versions of friendship, play, love and human contact, we are collectively reneging on the task that confronts us. We instead prefer fantasies in which some future generation, or AI, or scientific innovation, will take up the burden for us. But as Mary put it, '[w]hat actually happens to us will surely still be determined by human choices. Not even the most admirable machines can make better choices than the people who are supposed to be programming them'.[11]

What we need now is a picture that can help us to understand ourselves in a way that will show us how to go on. We need to be able to see the patterns of action and thought that characterise our lives today and in the past, and to understand the possibilities for changing those patterns and the mechanisms by which such change can be wrought. 'I have listed "men" with such objects as "cats" and "turnips",' Elizabeth Anscombe wrote in 1944, insisting that any attempt to understand ourselves must begin from the fact that we are living creatures.[12] But while we can study the life of turnips and cats only objectively, from the outside, the life of humans must, for humans, be studied from within. And if the task is to discover what *we* are, then it is one that we must attempt in company, as these women did; in college rooms and dining halls, tea shops and living rooms, by post and in pubs, among nappies and babies. Their habitat a patchwork of walled gardens, rivers, art galleries, refugee camps and bombed-out buildings.

Seen through the eyes of these friends, a new picture emerges. Our familiar world is transformed into a rich tapestry of interlocking patterns, studded with cultural objects of metaphysical power, teeming with plant, animal and human life. And we, the human individuals whose lives help to create and sustain those patterns and objects, are seen afresh as the kind of animal whose essence it is to question, create and love. We are *metaphysical animals*. We make and share pictures, stories, theories, words, signs and artworks that help us to navigate our lives together. These creations are immensely powerful, because they at once show us what is and was the case, and at the same time suggest new ways of going on. They show us that what becomes our shared past is always provisional; the past is kept alive through testimony and preservation and, as such, is mutable and easily elided or lost. But because the past is a living thing, discoveries we make now can affect our history. We can see our past differently – and we can rewrite what we understand to have happened. Different pasts await us.

We have reconstructed this past by joining together fragments from letters, journals, photos, conversations, notebooks, reminiscences and postcards, to make pictures. Those pictures make patterns, held in place by the most important one of all: the unfolding interweaving lives of four startlingly brilliant women. We meet them as teenagers on the cusp of a war and follow them as they struggle to find their way in a changing intellectual and political scene. We leave them in their late thirties, stepping on to the world stage; their names in print and their voices on the radio. Each woman suggests a different way to live a life dedicated to the task of making sense of the world. Each found different solutions to the practical, intellectual and psychological problems of philosophising while female. And all drew strength from their friendships with each other.

The lives of these women in turn illuminate a counter-narrative to the prevailing history of twentieth-century philosophy. Its heroes are not A. J. Ayer, J. L. Austin and R. M. Hare, but characters you may not know: H. H. Price, H.W.B. Joseph, Susan Stebbing, R. G. Collingwood, Dorothy Emmet, Mary Glover, Donald MacKinnon and Lotte Labowsky. This counter-narrative connects contemporary philosophy with the great speculative metaphysicians of the nineteenth and early twentieth centuries, Idealists and Realists, who struggled to understand the nature of truth, reality and goodness before the turn to linguistic analysis saw philosophy lower its sights to the meaning of the words 'true', 'real' and 'good'. It shows that asking, and seeking to answer, metaphysical questions is a natural and essential part of human life. It connects seemingly abstract and esoteric enquiries with the urgent and real ethical, practical and spiritual questions that confront each of us in our day-to-day lives. Cutting across this story are the grand historical arcs of Western philosophical thought: Plato, Aristotle, Aquinas; Descartes, Hume, Kant, Hegel; Frege, Wittgenstein; Moore. And of course, disrupting all these lives and patterns is the great chaos of the twentieth century: of refugees and migrants, murder and war, death and confusion.

The book begins with a scene that poses a philosophical question. It is 1956 and Elizabeth Anscombe stands before the dons of Oxford University and declares that the former president of the United States, Harry S. Truman, the man who ordered the bombing of Hiroshima and Nagasaki, is a mass murderer and must not be given an honorary degree. Almost unanimously, the dons disagree and Truman is feted. Elizabeth is puzzled: what does she see that they do not? If they are inclined to honour a man famous for the merciless killing of tens of thousands of innocent people, she says, they have lost their way. The philosophy of this book is a map back from that place.

You can read it as a story and take away from it a picture of human life that will help you to see our everyday world as these women did: as something astonishing and fragile and in need of constant care and attention. And you can read it as a philosophical argument, one that brings philosophy back to life. If you can, you should read it with friends.

Players

Elizabeth
Anscombe

Philippa Foot
(née Bosanquet)

Mary Midgley
(née Scrutton)

Iris
Murdoch

WOMEN PHILOSOPHERS

Alice Ambrose
Dorothy Emmet
Mary Glover
Martha Kneale
Margaret Masterman
Susan Stebbing
Mary Warnock (née Wilson)

COLLEGE WOMEN

Myra Curtis
Helen Darbishire
Vera Farnell
Barbara Gwyer
Mildred Hartley
Isobel Henderson
Carlotta Labowsky
Lucy Sutherland
Janet Vaughan

IDEALISTS &
THE BOARS HILL SET

E. F. & Winifred Carritt
H.W.B. Joseph
Sandie & Erica Lindsay
Gilbert Murray & Lady
Mary
E. J. & Theo Thompson

THE REALISTS

G. E. Moore
H. A. Prichard
W. D. Ross

'OLD MEN' &
CONSCIENTIOUS
OBJECTORS

R. G. Collingwood
E. R. Dodds
Peter Geach
Donald MacKinnon
H. H. Price
Victor White
Oscar Wood

REFUGEE SCHOLARS	THE WITTGENSTEINEANS	THE EXISTENTIALISTS
Heinz & Eva Cassirer	Ludwig Wittgenstein	Martin Buber
Eduard Fraenkel	Wasfi Hijab	Katharine Farrer
Fritz Heinemann	Georg Kreisel	Gabriel Marcel
Raymond Klibansky	Rush Rhees	Jean-Paul Sartre
Franz Steiner	Kanti Shah	
Friedrich Waismann	Yorick Smythies	
Richard Walzer	John Wisdom	

THE METAPHYSICALS	'YOUNG MEN' IN WAR SERVICE	THE SOCRATIC CLUB
Ian Crombie	*The dons*	Stella Aldwinkle
Austin Farrer	J. L. Austin	C. S. Lewis
Michael Foster	A. J. Ayer	
Basil Mitchell	Isaiah Berlin	
Eric Mascall	Gilbert Ryle	
Dennis Nineham		
	The students	
	Nick Crosbie	
	Richard Hare	
	David Hicks	
	M.R.D. Foot	
	Geoffrey Midgley	
	Frank Thompson	
	Geoffrey Warnock	

Mr Truman's Degree

Elizabeth Anscombe Takes a Stand – Philippa Foot Is on to Something

Elizabeth Anscombe Takes a Stand

Just after lunch, on 1 May 1956, the tolling of the treble bell of St Mary's church summoned Oxford University's dons to the Old Bodleian Library,[1] a site of male learning and clerical endeavour for four centuries, now, suddenly and inexplicably, said to be under threat from 'the women'.[2] From St John's, New College and Worcester, the dons made their way south down St Giles', west along Holywell Street, and east along Broad Street, gowns, habits and hoods flapping.[3] As they gathered in the courtyard outside Convocation House, rumours were circulating. 'The women are up to something in Convocation; we have to . . . vote them down.'[4]

Some things were known. The Vice Chancellor, Alic Halford Smith, had proposed to the Hebdomadal Council that Oxford University award an honorary degree to the former US president Harry S. Truman.[5] Tradition dictated that the nomination be waved through at Convocation (the governing body composed of all the doctors and masters of the university) and the award given the following month at the ancient ceremony of Encaenia. And yet . . . Here the facts gave out and the rumours began, pieced together in half-sentences. The nomination, it was said, was to be challenged by 'the women'.

Dons from St John's had arrived under a simple imperative: 'vote them down'.[6] Now they milled around trying to discover *which* women. No surprise to find Somerville at the centre of things. Godless Somerville, a college for brains (or, some said, 'freaks').[7] In All Souls, consciences had been roused by a sense of injustice: Surely it '*would be wrong to try to PUNISH Mr Truman!*'; 'Hang it all, you can't make a man responsible just because "his is the signature at the foot of the order".' At the New College dining tables, it had been agreed that though 'the action' was a '*mistake*', it was just 'an incidental, as it were, in a career'.[8] Though, some reflected, little

2

else was known of Mr Truman's career. Hearing the word 'Truman', one's mind could not help but run on: 'Hiroshima', 'Nagasaki'.

Now in Convocation House, the dons filed into the chamber – a medieval courtroom set out rather like a miniature House of Commons. All eyes scanned the benches near the entrance (by custom occupied by women) for the trouble-maker. There she was, still and silent and seated: Miss Elizabeth Anscombe.

Behind the scenes, the university's proctors and wardens, deans and censors, were ruffled. Had she 'got up a party'? She said not, but could she be trusted?[9] University officials had been sedulously consulting statute books and examining past precedents as the procedure for handling such protests was unknown; no one could remember a past occasion. Vice Chancellor Alic Halford Smith was on the verge of retirement and had asked his replacement, John Masterman, to preside over the meeting in his stead.[10] Masterman was still learning the ropes and as he straightened the hood of his gown and prepared to take his seat, he remained a little unsure of the procedure. There was a heavy agenda; the status of the Greek New Testament in the Theology degree was to be discussed. The Hebdo-madal Council was impatient to push through its proposal to honour Truman, already a year delayed, and now 'Miss Anscombe' was an irritation that had the potential to become an embarrassment.[11] She had confused things further by requesting permission to address the meeting in English rather than Latin (despite the fact that her Latin was perfect).[12]

Masterman's priority was that 'as little mud as possible should be stirred up'.[13] Journalists were hanging around, eager for information. No question, a 'scene' was in the offing. As for the proctors, Miss Anscombe had long been a thorn in their side. She was renowned for turning up at lectures in trousers: forbidden attire for women under the university statutes. There was great relief all round when she rose to her feet and a skirt and stock-inged legs were visible beneath her gown.[14]

Something resembling silence descended as Miss Anscombe made her way to the lectern, muffled comments of amusement or derision petering out to nothing as she began to speak. Her somehow disreputable appearance (hair long and unset, clean face, no cosmetics, shapeless clothes) was offset by the beauty of her low and sonorous voice. 'I am determined to oppose the proposal to give Mr Truman an honorary degree here at Oxford.'[15] She was nervous, but her speech was clear and slow.

'Now, an honorary degree is not a reward of merit: it is, as it were, a reward for being a very distinguished person, and it would be foolish to enquire whether a candidate deserves to be as distinguished as he is. That is why, in general, the question whether so-and-so should have an honorary degree is devoid of interest.' There was perhaps a visible relaxing of tension as she spoke these apparently placatory words. 'A very distinguished person will hardly be also a notorious criminal,' she continued, 'and if he should chance to be a non-notorious criminal it would, in my opinion, be improper to bring the matter up.' A few of those gathered perhaps allowed themselves to share her smile. 'It is only' [*Oh dear*] 'in the rather rare case in which a man is known everywhere for an action, in face of which it is sycophancy to honour him, that the question can be of the slightest interest.' Her words, their meaning, sank in.

As Miss Anscombe continued to speak, the assembled dons struggled to follow her argument. She did not want to dispute that Truman's action 'pretty certainly saved a huge number of lives'. Nor that it averted a terrible prospect: '[v]ery many soldiers on both sides would have been killed; the Japanese . . . would have massacred the prisoners of war; and large numbers of their civilian population would have been killed by "ordinary" bombing'. She thinks pacifism 'is a false doctrine'. She is not against the death penalty. And yet, she insists: Truman's action 'is murder'; he has 'a couple of massacres' to his name.

At times she appeared to throw outrageous insults at the former head of state: 'a quite mediocre person can do spectacularly wicked things without thereby becoming impressive'; 'every fool can be as much of a knave as suits him'; 'you cannot be or do any good where you are stupid'.[16] She compared him to history's greatest villains: 'If you do give this honour, what Nero, what Genghis Khan, what Hitler, or what Stalin will not be honoured in the future?'[17] At some point she used the word 'butcher'.[18]

John Masterman became increasingly 'incensed' as the 'woman member' made her 'intemperate speech'. As he looked across the house, he felt confident that 'the women' would be defeated in a vote. But could it be handled with the minimum of mud? The press would 'quite properly, have seized on the incident', and he and Oxford would be guilty of 'an act of discourtesy' to President Truman, who was to be an honoured guest. Masterman toyed with the idea of adjourning the assembly before a vote could be called.[19]

Miss Anscombe began to wind up her address. 'Protests by people who have not power are a waste of time', she said. She was still speaking slowly and calmly. 'I am not seizing an opportunity to make a "gesture of protest" at atomic bombs; I vehemently object to *our* action in offering Mr Truman honours, because one can share in the guilt of a bad action by praise and flattery.'[20] There was silence as she returned to her seat. 'Not a murmur, not a rustle, not a change of countenance.'[21]

It fell to the historian Alan Bullock, as a member of the Hebdomadal Council, to speak on behalf of the nomination. The assembled company appeared utterly imperturbable;[22] still, Bullock's strong male voice and Yorkshire accent would have been reassuring. 'We do not approve the action', he said, with his 'we' gathering in the sober committee men around him, restoring comfortable order; 'no, we think it was a *mistake*.'[23] Nevertheless, he continued, there are many mitigations; 'Mr Truman did not make the bombs by himself, and decide to drop them without consulting anybody.' Bullock spoke with the authority of an historian; he had recently written the first book-length biography of Hitler.[24] No, Truman 'was only responsible for the decision'. His was only 'the signature at the foot of the order'.[25] Mr Truman's action, he seemed to suggest, was just a matter of completing the paperwork. Bullock concluded – he kept things short – 'an action of this sort is, after all, only one episode: an incidental, as it were, in a career. Mr Truman has done some good.'[26]

In the end, and despite his reservations, Masterman did what he ought. He put the motion to the house by saying, '*Placet ne vobis, Domini Doctores? Placet ne vobis, Magistri?*' Had anyone called, 'Non placet', he would have been obliged to take a formal vote, but to his relief there were no shouts – at least none that he chose to hear. Miss Anscombe, and any supporters she might have had, must have been ignorant of the procedure, he thought with relief. After a second or two of silence, he recorded the decree as unanimously passed.[27]

After the meeting adjourned, there was confusion among witnesses as to what precisely had happened. Was Miss Anscombe a pacifist in disguise? Was it some sort of Roman Catholic protest? What sort of 'high-minded' nonsense was this?[28] Had 'the women' set the whole thing up for purposes as yet unknown? Didn't the 'intemperate woman' understand how far the Japanese were willing to fight?[29] Some were certain that Miss Anscombe had stood completely alone, but others were sure they had heard or seen supporters. Didn't (the vaguely disgraceful) Miss Hubbard of St Anne's raise a hand? Mrs Foot of Somerville: some swore she made a sound.[30] 'Solitary

Opponent', read the headline in the *Manchester Guardian* the next day –
despite Masterman's best efforts, the press had after all got hold of it.[31]
There was no other opposition, ran the story; but the following week a
contradictory letter to the editor was printed from an M.R.D. Foot.[32] Miss
Anscombe had not been alone. A few voices, conveniently missed by
Masterman, had said, 'Non placet', it insisted.

News of the 'one-woman campaign' made it across the Atlantic on to
the pages of the *New York Times* and prompted a journalist to ask Harry
Truman what he thought of Miss Anscombe's intervention. Truman
answered: 'I made the decision on the facts as they existed at that time,
and if I had to do it again I would do it all over again.'[33] Nevertheless,
on the eve of the Potsdam Conference, having seen the 'absolute ruin of
conquered Berlin', he had written in the privacy of his diary: 'I thought
of Carthage, Baalbek, Jerusalem, Rome, Atlantis, Peking . . . [of] Scipio,
Rameses II . . . Sherman, Jenghiz Khan . . . I fear that machines are ahead
of morals by some centuries and when morals catch up there'll be no
reason for any of it.'[34]

By 20 June, the incident in Convocation was barely a memory as Mr and
Mrs Truman were feted with peaches and champagne in the Founder's
Library of New College. Later, Truman, resplendent in a black velour bonnet and scarlet robe, proceeded to Christopher Wren's Sheldonian Theatre
for the award-giving ceremony. Twelve hundred people crowded in. Applause
lasted three minutes as the Earl of Halifax, the university Chancellor,
proclaimed, 'Harricum Truman, Doctoris in Iure Civili' (Doctor of Civil
Law). All six bells of St Mary's rang out.

That evening, Truman took his place at the High Table at Christ
Church's annual white-tie 'Gaudy' Dinner (an all-male affair named
after the Latin word *gaudium* or 'joy'), a string of bishops, knights and
lords, ambassadors and earls to his left and right. They feasted on seven
courses: *Pâté Maison, Tortue Claire, Escalopes de Saumon Granville, Mousse
de Caneton Aylesbury, Selle d'Agneau, Coupe Hélène*, followed by *Pailles
au Parmesan*.[35] Up from the cellars: *Sercial Madeira, Bernkasteler Lay 1953,
Château Certan de May, Louis Roederer N.V., Cockburn 1935, Segonzac
Fine Champagne 1924*.[36] Afterwards, as he passed through the quad on his
way out, undergraduates called to him from their windows, 'Give 'em
hell, Harricum!'[37]

6

Philippa Foot Is on to Something

Seventeen months later, in October 1957, the whole of Somerville College came down with flu. Philippa Foot, the college's philosophy lecturer, took to her bed in 16 Park Town, a hot-water bottle, a heap of handkerchiefs and a box of expensive chocolates (part of her staple diet) close at hand.[38] She was used to working under the eiderdown, having spent most of her final year as the undergraduate Miss Bosanquet confined to bed through the recurrence of a childhood illness. Now, she set to work on a very important letter.[39] 'Dear Janet', she began.

The addressee was Mrs Janet Vaughan, a haematologist and Principal of Somerville College. The week that President Truman had been told of the existence of the atomic bomb,[40] Janet Vaughan had been, in her own words, 'trying to do science in hell'. She had been sent by the Medical Research Council to the newly liberated Bergen-Belsen concentration camp to advise on the safest way to feed people on the verge of dying from starvation.[41] Now she had returned to Oxford to research the effects of radiation on the human skeleton. She would soon be recognised as a world authority.[42]

'When the flu has abated,' wrote Philippa, 'may I come to talk to you about Elizabeth Anscombe's future?' She tried to keep her spidery handwriting legible, but the flu and the pillows were against her. She was feeling rather weak. But she continued. Miss Anscombe is in need of a job and 'Somerville is obviously the place for her.' She is 'probably the best all round philosopher (although not the best logician) in the University, at the present time. I doubt if there is anyone better in the country – not counting Russell and G. E. Moore who are no longer working. There has never been a woman who could do philosophy as she can.'

Elizabeth's current fellowship at Somerville was about to end. Along with Isobel Henderson, the college's Ancient History fellow, Philippa had been working on a scheme that would keep Elizabeth at Somerville despite there being no available post, and no money to pay for a new one. She rearranged the pillows before sharing her idea.

'This seems to lead to only one conclusion; either we manage to split the job, or else I have to resign. But I don't want to resign. I've never wanted to resign less than at the moment when I <u>think</u> I've got onto a fruitful line in moral philosophy.' However fond she is of Somerville, she continued, 'If there is no other way out I shall have to resign, because to stay on keeping

Elizabeth out would be a thing which would leave one without a shred of self respect.'

The letter ran on, ten sides in all, as she attempted to make things clear through the fug of her illness. 'One point I want to get quite straight. None of this is for Elizabeth's sake. I want her in Somerville . . . She has always helped me with my philosophy and if I am on to something in ethics I shall want her more than ever.'[43]

By the time this letter was written, Elizabeth and Philippa had spent half of their lives growing up together in philosophy, along with Iris Murdoch and Mary Midgley. In the decade that had passed since President Truman had signed his name and released a 'rain of ruin' on Hiroshima and Naga-saki,[44] they had worked together to get 'onto a fruitful line in moral philosophy'. Now, their conversations in cafés, bedrooms, living rooms, pubs, lecture halls and classrooms, on floors, chairs, divans and bicycles, had brought them back to the beginning. In philosophy, 'one must start from scratch', Elizabeth had told Iris after the war, '– & it takes a very long time to reach scratch'.[45]

The events of 1 May 1956 confirmed what they had discovered: that moral philosophy too must start from scratch. It must begin much further back than questions like 'What is the morally right thing to do?' or 'Which moral principles should I choose?' or 'Which outcomes are morally better?' Elizabeth had seen that something had happened to the concept of *murder*, so that it was possible for a room full of theologians, philosophers and historians – educated and humane men and women at Oxford University – to honour a man who had ordered two of the greatest massacres in human history. To get dressed in the morning in their academic finery, and drink champagne with him on a college lawn.

The men and women who filed into the hall that day had witnessed the same events as Elizabeth but they did not see what she saw. Unlike Eliza-beth, they could not hold what Truman did – a tiny physical act, pen on paper – in the same frame as those awesome and terrible scenes that were later reported in the newspapers: 80,000 or 140,000 or 200,000 dead. They did not see Miss Anscombe and her protest clearly either. In their eyes she was 'rude', 'high-minded', 'naive', 'pacifist', 'Catholic', 'woman'. Truman by contrast was 'brave', 'decisive', 'statesmanlike'. Ten years had passed, the fog of war had cleared, and yet . . .

*

When human actions happen on a grand scale and people make choices in disrupted and difficult circumstances, we cannot take it for granted that we will see clearly what is done, or understand easily what it means. When the background to our lives changes, our words may no longer work as they used to, and possibilities for seeing and understanding each other and the world may be lost. Sometimes, when it matters most, what another person is doing (what *we* are doing) can be obscure and dark. This is when philosophy comes into its own.

CHAPTER 1

On Probation

OXFORD

OCTOBER 1938–SEPTEMBER 1939

Miss Mary Scrutton & Miss Iris Murdoch of Somerville College – Miss Elizabeth Anscombe of St Hugh's College – Mary & Iris Join the Political Scene & We Meet the Inhabitants of Boars Hill – The Agamemnon Class – A Revolution in Philosophy: Freddie Ayer Declares War on Metaphysics & Ethics – A Last Word from the Idealists

Miss Mary Scrutton & Miss
Iris Murdoch of Somerville College

Early in her schooldays Mary Scrutton had an experience of seeing pure sense data. It happened like this. 'I was bending over a bath, stirring the water before getting into it, when I felt a light tap on the back of my head and the world before me suddenly turned into an expanse of white triangles.' As she looked in wonder, the triangles began to move and turn blue at the edges. Finally, things began to reassemble. The white patches were not tiny sensory objects, fragments of private experience, but small pieces of the plaster ceiling, gently shattering as they tapped her on the head on their downward flight into the bath. Later, when she started studying philosophy, she remembered this scene, in which she had experienced pure colour and shape. Is it possible that the stable world of baths and ceilings can be assembled out of such ephemeral fragments? she wondered. Are baths and ceilings no more than constellations of appearances?[1] Mary was thinking thoughts that had troubled the mind of the ancient philosopher Protagoras, on an island in the Aegean Sea, 450 years before the birth of Christ.

Now, in the mild, breezy autumn of 1938, she was on Oxford's busy Woodstock Road, facing the arched entrance of Somerville College, her back to the low morning sun and a pair of perfectly circular glasses perched high on her nose. As she stepped through, her childhood folded silently behind her: the garden walls of her girlhood home, a rectory in Greenford in Middlesex with its chestnut and ilex trees;[2] her teenage bedroom, book-strewn, in the new house in Kingston-upon-Thames; herself and her mother, Lesley, smiling in matching chinoiserie dresses;[3] an impractically shaped dachshund singing by the gramophone;[4] her father's car, the starting-handle of which was kept not by the bonnet but by the driver's seat so he didn't have to run around to the side in the rain before leaping in when the engine started.[5] Her hair may have been temporarily in an adult roll, but more often it was braided like a Girl Guide's.[6] As a child, she preferred collecting newts to dolls, whose stiff perms when replicated in living women unnerved her. She vigorously resisted her mother's attempts to put her hair in a Marcel wave – 'it's far too stiff. I don't believe in it.'[7] At nearly six foot, she could not see a way to be 'dainty'. Her shoelaces were often undone, broken or replaced with string.[8] She was more likely to find a fountain pen leaking in her pocket than a glove or compact, or anything betokening a grown-up female life. Mary took some pride in her ability – which she retained – to be vaguely exasperating to her peers and elders. A letter from her father pointed the way forward: 'The great thing is, to clear one's mind and REFUSE TO ACCEPT OUTWORN PRESUP-POSITIONS. Form a picture of mankind as it should be and think out the path to that state.'[9]

By the time Mary stood at Somerville Lodge, Prime Minister Neville Chamberlain had declared 'peace for our time'; but trenches were already being dug in London parks. Most could see that Europe was now heading inexorably towards a second war. Many of the young men who found them-selves, as Mary did, at the gates of Oxford colleges and on the threshold of adulthood, did not expect to finish their degrees.

If things had gone to plan, Mary would have arrived at Somerville fresh from Vienna, her German fluent, her conversation studded with casual references to Viennese culture and art. But her Austrian adventure had been cut short: she had arrived in the capital a fortnight before the country ceased to exist. Mary's teacher, Jean Rowntree (granddaughter of the Quaker philanthropist, Joseph Rowntree), had reassured her concerned parents that it would be safe and that any dangers posed by fascism would be balanced by improvements in Mary's German.[10] Jean had spent a sabbatical term in Vienna in 1935, working alongside other Quakers to assist fleeing civilians, and was shortly off to Prague to do the same there, so she knew more than most about the situation in Europe.[11] But on 12 March, Mary watched from the window as Nazis marched through the city, lacing the Ringstrasse lamp posts with swastikas sewn on to billowing red banners. Blonde German girls handed out flowers and beamed as Jewish shops were ransacked and their owners rounded up. Professor Jerusalem, Mary's Jewish host, was among those arrested, and Mary picked her way through the broken glass on the pavement to join a frantic queue at the Quaker meeting house, hoping the Society of Friends could help. They couldn't – Professor Jerusalem was an Austrian citizen – and she cried all the way through the interview.[12]

Mary returned to England before the month was out, and her hosts were, thankfully, not far behind her. On Professor Jerusalem's release, he, Frau Jerusalem and their fourteen-year-old daughter Leni managed to escape Austria to join Mary and her family at their home. They would stay with the Scruttons until April, when they received permits for a new life in Palestine.[13]

Mary had been offered the Deakin Scholarship (£50 per year, for three years)[14] after a panicked attempt at an entrance exam in Autumn 1937, from which she expected nothing but disaster. She was a product of Downe House, a school that had begun life in Charles Darwin's home before moving to The Cloisters, the former home of a female religious community in Berkshire. The school's founder and headmistress, Olive Willis, took inspiration from the American pragmatist philosopher John Dewey.[15] The fundamental task for an educator was to curate her pupils' experiences, cultivating impressions that will 'live fruitfully and creatively in subsequent experiences'.[16] As the child grows, 'life-space and life-durations are expanded',[17] he explained, and a school must lay down a store of experiences that will allow her to navigate this expanding future with well-tempered curiosity.[18] Olive Willis fostered non-autocratic relationships between teacher and student. Young and old were to be real friends.[19] Reform would be gentle. Mary had been excited at her election to Form Captain, until she discovered it was part of the 'Tidier Scrutton Campaign', launched after the loss of a bicycle, music case, three screw-pencils, a badminton racket and the Book of Judges roused her classmates to action.[20] At Downe there were no prizes, no Head Girl and no houses. Tests and competitions were not part of Mary's childhood. But despite her misgivings about the Somerville examination, her General Paper had impressed.

At the request of the college, Mary had spent the year before going up having coaching in Latin and Greek from Mrs Zvegintzov (formerly Miss Diana Lucas), a tall masterful ex-Somervillian, married to the son of Russian émigrés, to whom the college regularly referred prospective students.[21] Mrs Z's methods were severe and surprising. Prudence Smith, another Somervillian sent to Mrs Z, complained to her boyfriend: 'she suggests in all sobriety that I lie in a cold bath . . . and sing the declensions and conjugations'. Despite Prue's scepticism, the unusual method proved so successful that she feared that in her dying moments she would find Goodwin's 'Greek Moods and Tenses' marching through her head.[22] Mrs Z was astounded by Mary's ignorance – but also by her success. 'Well, well,' she said, on hearing of Mary's scholarship to Somerville, 'I'd rather lose my reputation as a prophet than my reputation as a coach.'[23]

Mrs Z had another tutee that year, on whom she might well have risked a forecast, Miss Iris Murdoch. Iris was once said to be a 'poor girl who only just made it into a rich girls' school'.[24] The only daughter of Irish Protestant immigrants, Iris was born on 15 July 1919 at 59 Blessington Street, Dublin – a down-at-heel Georgian terrace on the north side of the River Liffey. The family had crossed the Irish Sea to settle in London a year later; part of a mass upheaval of people around the time of the partition of Ireland in 1921. Iris said her father had come to England to find his fortune, but her parents did not assimilate, making few, or maybe no, friends in suburban west London. When Hughes Murdoch died after forty-five years in England, there were only six people at his funeral.[25]

In 1932, twelve-year-old Iris had won one of the first two available open scholarships to Badminton, an exclusive girls' school in the suburbs of Bristol. Miss Colebrook, the school secretary, wrote to Iris's delighted parents that her scholarship had been announced in *The Times*, the *Manchester Guardian* and the local newspapers: 'It looks very well'.[26] Badminton's principal, Miss Beatrice May Baker (alias BMB), was a progressive woman with an international outlook – pupils between the wars were told: 'You must not expect jam for tea while German children are starving'.[27] When Iris had first arrived at the school, she suffered from terrible homesickness. She cried so much during her first weeks that one of the older pupils formed the Society for the Prevention of Cruelty to Iris (SPCI), the sole activity of which was being nice to her.[28] BMB sent Iris to 'work in the garden under the care of the lady head gardener', in the hope that the 'less stimulating' atmosphere would calm her. The young Iris could be found in the greenhouse, dressed in the fawn-coloured tunic and woollen blouse that was the school's uniform, 'pricking out seedlings . . . quietly and painstakingly'.[29]

The combined efforts of BMB and the SPCI paid off and Iris soon 'stopped crying and started to write colourful, imaginative and brilliant essays', a classmate recalled.[30] As Iris progressed through the school, BMB made her a favourite and the odd pair would be seen in BMB's drawing room deep in philosophical conversation.[31] Younger girls remembered Iris as a good hockey player and a well-liked head prefect who everyone knew 'was very clever'.[32]

'Iris was a remarkable girl, who already had a philosophy of life', BMB told the girls in the year below.[33] Iris 'was one of the kindest people that I have ever met', recalled her Latin teacher, Miss Jeffery.[34] In 1938 she was awarded an Open Exhibition of £40 a year by Somerville College.

Mary may have dodged past Iris in Mrs Z's hallway that summer, belongings and shoelaces trailing, head buzzing with Greek declensions. But it was only once inside the walls of Somerville College that the pair met properly. With a blunt fringe and dirndl-ish clothes, Iris was now artsy, assured and immediately at ease in her new habitat and role – there was no repeat of her Badminton homesickness.[35] Though Mary was by far the taller, when people saw her and Iris together, crossing the Somerville College lawn, it was Iris they remembered – her 'corn-hair' and confidence caught the eye.[36] 'She's like a little bull!' observed a friend's mother.[37] Fellow undergraduate Carol Stewart thought Iris 'aboriginal': 'simplicity, naiveté, power, and space'.[38] In that year's matriculation photo, Mary, wearing a dark woollen suit, sits awkwardly on the front row (fourth from left); Iris, in a light cotton blouse, stands behind (second row, fourth from right).

There were forty-three Somerville entrants that year and, Mrs Z's astonishment notwithstanding, Iris and Mary were the only two up to read Honour Moderations and Literae Humaniores.[39] More commonly known as 'Mods and Greats', the four-year degree had two parts. 'Mods' would last five terms and culminate in twelve three-hour examinations across seven consecutive days. Candidates would be required to translate unseen passages of Greek and Latin poetry and prose with seamless facility. Success would see them progress to seven terms of 'Greats', which took in Greek and Roman history, archaeology and art, as well as philosophy.[40] They would tackle a little modern philosophy up to and beyond Kant (including Hegel and Marx), as well as some logic, ethics and political philosophy. But the largest part of their studies would be devoted to Ancient Philosophy, along with its reception in Christian thought in the Middle Ages. Plato's *Republic* and Aristotle's *Nicomachean Ethics*, which they would read in Greek, would be their main diet. In their first year of Greats, Iris and Mary would have the pick of fourteen lecture courses dedicated to works over 2,000 years old.

All this was ahead of them as Mary sat cross-legged on Iris's floor that first term, Iris lying on her bed surrounded by books and flowers, penning an enthusiastic letter to a schoolfriend. She was delighted that the dons called her 'Miss Murdoch'; at school she'd been only 'Iris'.[41] The change of name signified a change of state. Iris had a sunny room in East, Somerville's new front quadrangle, while Mary's was dark and at the other end of the oldest building, West.[42] Anyone who had any money went out at once to buy a comfortable chair for their room, and from Iris's first-floor window, above the archway overlooking the small front quad, a parade of armchairs could be seen crossing the lawn, moving in and out of doorways, as the new undergraduates settled in.[43] Iris settled instead for a striped aquamarine art deco cushion.[44]

Iris and Mary, along with the other new arrivals – fledgling zoologists, linguists, mathematicians and historians – were soon summoned to the Junior Common Room by Somerville's French tutor, Vera Farnell. Speaking as Dean, she warned that any misstep, any rule-breaking or scandal, would injure not only themselves but future generations of aspirant women scholars. She told them sternly: 'You must seriously realise that you have to be careful how you behave. It isn't a joking-matter, the women are still very much on probation in this University. You may think that it doesn't matter if you do something a little wild, but I can tell you that it will.'[45] Within months, she had her eyes trained on Miss Scrutton's academic dress (the clothing worn under the scholar's long black gown).[46]

Mary found a caution in her pigeonhole.[47]

> From THE DEAN, SOMERVILLE COLLEGE, OXFORD.
>
> Dear Miss Scrutton
> I must draw your attention to
> the rule that 'slacks are not
> recognised as a part of
> Women's Academic Dress.
> Yours sincerely
>
> Vera Farnell.
>
> Feb. 24

Miss Scrutton was not the first undergraduate to receive sartorial correction from Miss Farnell. As an undergraduate Vera had conveyed a message from the then Principal Emily Penrose to fellow undergraduate (and future novelist) Dorothy Sayers: earrings featuring 'scarlet and green parrots in pendent gilt cages' amounted to 'unnecessarily, even outrageously, conspicuous behaviour and attire'.[48]

Vera Farnell spoke from experience when she issued her warning. She had arrived at Somerville to read modern languages in 1911, almost a decade before women were permitted to take degrees. The fight had been hard won and many in the wider community, including many women, remained unconvinced. Who could tell what new forms of female life were taking shape within the walls of the women's colleges, and what the effect might be on the world outside? In 1926, Countess Bathurst (an anti-suffrage campaigner and former owner of the right-wing and anti-Semitic Morning Post)[49] complained: 'I am of the opinion that women have completely spoilt Oxford as it is, and to build more women's colleges would achieve its ruin. I have a son there, and he is obliged to attend the lectures of 3 lady dons. I consider this ridiculous – humiliating. I wish we had sent our sons to Cambridge, where the atmosphere is still virile.'[50] In 1897, a vote in Cambridge to recognise women's degrees had ended in a riot, with male undergraduates burning bicycle-riding effigies of Anne Clough (Newnham's first Principal) and classicist Katharine Jex-Blake (niece of Sophia, Scotland's first female doctor).[51] The matter had not been raised again, and it would be 1948 before women were granted degrees at Cambridge. In Oxford, women were blamed for the new tendency of men to drink morning coffee; since the 1920s tea rooms had been providing what Vice Chancellor Lewis Farnell (Vera Farnell's paternal uncle) called 'unnecessary and unmanly food'.[52] The whole atmosphere was *'bewomaning'*.[53]

Oxford's women had made considerable progress in the decade before Mary and Iris's arrival. Until 1925, girls needed chaperones to go anywhere, including lectures. Vera Farnell recalled that in her student days 'nearly every one of the lecturers insisted that the two or three women in his audience should be chaperoned for fear they should cause him acute embarrassment by a faint or a fit or some other feminine fuss'.[54] For a small 'chaperonage fee', older ladies would be ushered into lecture theatres where they knitted through 'The History of British Idealism from 1863'.[55] But Iris and Mary were free to attend their lectures unchaperoned, and even to accept invitations from young men to visit their rooms, unaccompanied, for cinnamon toast.[56] In return, young men were permitted to enter the college on Saturdays for tea. Miss Martha Hurst had just become the second female philosopher to retain her fellowship (at Lady Margaret Hall) after marriage, when she became Mrs Kneale. Still, when a mysterious questionnaire was sent to some of the girls in Iris and Mary's first year – 'Do you aim at marriage or a career?' – something resembling panic engulfed the Somerville dining hall. 'The trouble was, of course, that we didn't want to face this question,' Mary later recalled. The speculation was that 'the authorities were somehow trying to winkle out their secrets'.[57] 'What business is it of theirs?' one of the recipients asked Mary, indignant but also a little thrilled at having been asked. Mary, who hadn't received the survey, felt left out: she held a secret fear that her appearance and brains rendered her unlovable.[58] Was this why the authorities hadn't even bothered to enquire? In the end, it transpired that the survey was the work of a fellow undergraduate, the young (Miss) Peter Ady. She would choose a career, going on to become an eminent economist, and perhaps already knew that marriage was not for her: later we will find her sharing passionate kisses with Iris in the back seat of a car.

While Mary hoped it would be possible to eat her cake and have it,[59] Iris seemed to know her priorities. 'I *long* to get married, I'd do *anything* to get married,' she declared at the end of their first year, on a summer punt up the River Cherwell to the Victoria Arms public house. Mary's fingers trailed in the water as one of the Williams-Ellis sisters (Charlotte or Susie) propelled them along the river past a family of moorhens, chicks in tow. 'But you've had six proposals this term alone,' cried one of the sisters, perhaps momentarily rocking the boat. 'Oh, they don't count', said Iris.[60]

Of the four women's colleges, all but Somerville were Church of England and each came with its own reputation: Lady Margaret Hall (for rich girls), St Hilda's (for poor girls), St Hugh's (for pious girls), Somerville (for clever girls). Or, as the proverb went: 'LMH for Young Ladies, St Hilda's for Games, St Hugh's for Religion and Somerville for Brains.'[61] The men's colleges had their reputations too, among them: Christ Church (grand and liberal), Keble (weedy priests), Magdalen (clever progressives), Trinity (hearties or sporty types), Balliol (brain-powered, egalitarian, world-influencing), Wadham (witty), New College (for the earnestly rational).[62] Finer gradations could be made at the level of the college kitchens: venison at Magdalen, wildfowl at Christ Church, fondues at Brasenose and dressed crab and hare soup at Merton.[63] The colleges differed too in wealth. Though Somerville was richer than the other women's colleges, St John's, the wealthiest college, was as much as 100 times richer.[64] Women's colleges were kept poor by the university's Limitation Statute, which guaranteed five male undergraduates for every female, thus capping income, depriving numerous girls of the opportunity of a place, and ensuring neither venison nor dressed crab made it on to the menu.[65]

The poorer colleges had fewer fellows, so the women's colleges routinely shared their undergraduates; a St Hugh's student might go to Somerville for her History tutorials. The girls were also, on occasion, tutored by dons from the male colleges, but precautions were taken. Male tutors were usually required to come into the women's colleges to give their tutorials, rather than teaching in their own rooms. In 1921, the then Principal of Somerville, Margery Fry, granted a young philosopher called John Mabbott special dispensation to tutor her girls in St John's. He had been tutoring Somerville girls for five years 'without disaster': 'Well, you didn't have to marry any of them, did you?' she clarified.[66] Her fears of a 'disaster' were not ungrounded. Many of the wives of dons who handed out sandwiches on crimped plates in North Oxford drawing rooms had been tutored by their much older husbands. Alice Cameron, a student before the First World War, generously attributed the male dons' predilection for their female undergraduates to 'the chivalrous, almost romantic, spirit' with which young men viewed the fledgling women's colleges.[67] But by the late 1930s, when Mary and Iris were at university, the women's colleges were quite grown up, and yet the 'romantic spirit' continued. In her first term of Greats, Somervillian Jean Coutts – a promising philosopher one year ahead of Mary and Iris – took John (J. L.) Austin's sparsely attended class on Aristotle. Four days after the first meeting, she received an evidently brand-new handkerchief from her tutor, along with a note:

18 vi 40

Dear Miss Coutts,
I wonder if this is your handkerchief? I found it on my sofa last Friday. Only it isn't your name on it. Some verbal confusion.
Yours sincerely,
John Austin[68]

Jean received at least three proposals of marriage from her tutor over the next six months, before eventually accepting. By special permission of the governing body of Somerville, she was married before her finals and sat her exams pregnant with her first child.

Anxieties about the future of Europe and Empire had been the background to Mary and Iris's teenage years, and both arrived in Oxford well prepared to enter into the political conversation that would be the backdrop to their early friendship at Somerville.

As a child Mary had enjoyed easy access to the latest left-wing and progressive views. She took political life for granted, regarding it 'as unavoidable like the weather'.[69] Copies of the *New Statesman* were, like the wallpaper, part of the fabric of the Rectory. On arrival at Downe House she distinguished herself by writing a poem, now lost, on the war-guilt clause in the Versailles peace treaty. A delighted Olive Willis published it in the school magazine. (Mary's ear for a pithy turn of phrase and startling image would stay with her.)

'We're all left-wing here, you know,' BMB reminded prospective Badminton teachers.[70] The year before Iris arrived at the school, BMB explained to a journalist: 'Our aim is to inculcate an ideal of Service . . . A school can no longer be a self-contained little community . . . It should be related to the world outside, if girls are to face modern problems courageously and sensibly'.[71] When the school's debating society considered the proposition that 'The Woman's Place is In the Home', it was defeated by twelve votes to none – one of those votes was Iris's.[72] As a member of the League of Nations Junior Branch, the teenage Iris (along with six other pupils) spent ten days in Geneva at the League summer school, swimming in Lac Léman and admiring the private telephone in her balconied hotel room, an astonishing luxury for a schoolgirl.[73] The League occupied a large part of BMB's political imagination, to the extent that she once attended the school's Christmas fancy-dress party dressed as it.[74] Photographs, sadly, do not survive.

Iris won a League of Nations essay competition for two years running. The first, on the choice between democracy and dictatorship in relation to the Spanish Civil War, earned her a prize of £2 12s 6d. 'We are told that to-morrow's world will be ours to do what we like with. But it will be an extra-ordinarily difficult world, and the question is, what are we to do with it?' begins the essay.[75] A second, titled 'If I were Foreign Secretary', argued that if fascist countries persevered with their expansionism they should be brought around by the threat of severe sanctions. If they could be tempted to join the democratic community by economic advantage alone, the 'world would be calmed and reassured, and the menace of war would gradually disappear'.[76] This tells us something of Iris's girlish confidence; the League of Nations had looked on as Hitler and Mussolini united in aid of Francisco Franco's Nationalists and the Soviet Union lent support to the Republicans. For many in Britain, the Spanish conflict was an ideological showdown in blood and arms. Some 2,500 British and Irish volunteers, most just a few years older than Iris and Mary, went to join the fight, and one fifth did not return. Two sons of the socialist philosopher Edgar Frederick Carritt (known for giving Oxford University's first lectures on both Aesthetics and Dialectical Materialism) had joined the International Brigade; only one came home.[77]

While Mary was pragmatic and attentive, Iris was impatient and restless, and she charged into the role of grown-up undergraduate. She was soon first-year representative on the Junior Common Room Committee and on the staff of two university papers, the *Cherwell* and *Oxford Forward*. In a missive for the Badminton School magazine, she described a 'hurricane of essays and proses and campaigns and committees and sherry parties and political and aesthetic arguments'.[78] A great fear of not being there when Something Was Happening necessitated a frenetic pace to her social life. In flagrant contravention of college rules, she had her first alcoholic drink in the Royal Oak pub right opposite Somerville, with the 'very dashing' Carol Stewart, whom she admired for having 'more of the jungle animal' in her than other peers (Mary Scrutton certainly included).[79] Carol ordered them gimlets.[80] They weren't the only escapees. Despite Miss Farnell's warning, at night from her room in West, Mary would occasionally glimpse girls overleaping the college's Walton Street wall. Such wayward bits of living could often be tolerated – the only punishment meted out to one Somervillian caught out of bounds was a bath, lest she develop a chill.[81] But some rules would not bend, especially when they contributed to the life and community of the college. Over at St Hugh's, one mile up the Banbury Road, Miss Elizabeth Anscombe had to be reined in after she skipped dinner three times in one week without permission. To make amends for her waywardness, the Principal, Miss Barbara Gwyer, required Elizabeth to dine five nights the following week and specify any future absences in advance. 'Can't I leave it to the time? Mostly, when I go out it's on casual invitations from people I meet,' Elizabeth implored. 'Do not tell me, Miss Anscombe, that you are as flotsam and jetsam on the waves of circumstance,' said Miss Gwyer.[82]

Iris displayed her own flotsam-and-jetsam character as she navigated the dining hall. At the High Table sat the dons. Vera Farnell was usually to be seen in conference with Principal Helen Darbishire (the pair were close friends and later set up home together); classicist Mildred Hartley perhaps chatting to Isobel Henderson, the glamorous tutor in Ancient History, or to the historian Lucy Sutherland. The third-years sat at the three long tables by the windows, the second-years on the middle tables, and the freshers on those nearest the serving hatch. This was the cross-ways, customary reading. But looking at the situation askance, longways, a more subtle system prevailed. The top tables – the ones nearest the dons – were occupied by anxious girls, dressed mostly in navy and beige, who would troop in *en bloc* from the library when a meal began, and troop back when it ended. These specimens were sometimes called 'bunnies'. The bottom tables, lying beyond Miss Farnell's immediate field of vision, 'harboured a mix centring on long-haired doe-eyed lovelies, variously but always intriguingly dressed and often late for meals'. Here sat Princess Natalya Galitzine, who eloped

in the first term;[83] Léonie Marsh, a flamboyant and highly fashionable Communist – she dressed 'like a bolshevik . . . in her warm woollen jerkin, her blue serge skirt, red belt, sandals and red mittens', her hair a 'black defiant lion's mane';[84] Lucy Klatschko, a beautiful half-Latvian and Jewish senior Somervillian, once caught scaling the college wall, who later became a nun and great friend of Iris's;[85] Anne Cloake, who liked to shock – she later claimed to have taught Iris the 'facts of life';[86] and Zuzanna Przeworska, a Polish undergraduate and member of the Communist Party. And 'in the middle things were pretty much intermediate'.[87] Bunnies, intermediate, lovely. Or, as Iris cast it, 'stodgy, middling, and wild'.[88]

Mary settled in the middle, together with Charlotte, the punting zoology student (as a small child, Charlotte had asked her mother: 'What are birds for?'),[89] and Greta Myers, who was responsible for inserting the first bit of biology into Mary's mental map. Worldly wise, Greta also told her to stop wearing her hair like a Girl Guide and do something about her shoes.[90] Iris, who was friends with all sorts without necessarily wanting to introduce them, drifted to top and bottom, but was usually found in the middle with Mary.[91]

It is in this dining hall that Iris and Mary will first meet the third of our heroines, Miss Elizabeth Anscombe of St Hugh's – but not just yet.

Miss Elizabeth Anscombe of St Hugh's College

Miss Elizabeth Anscombe had won the Clara Evelyn Mordan Scholarship to St Hugh's College in the summer of 1937, with a £60 emolument.[92] Clara Mordan, a suffragist and supporter of women's education, established the scholarship in 1897 with a single condition: that its holder 'shall not perform or witness any experiment or demonstration on a living animal during her tenure of the scholarship'.[93] Elizabeth arrived at Oxford to study Mods and Greats a year ahead of Iris and Mary, and two years ahead of the war. At the end of her second term, St Hugh's Classics tutor Dorothea Gray listed 'logic and humour' as 'Miss Anscombe's most marked virtues'.[94]

Lewisham's Sydenham School had been sad to wave off their talented pupil. The secretary of the school's Political Society reported on a 'Mock trial', held in Elizabeth's final term:

> The chief honours for the success of the meeting must go to Elizabeth Anscombe, who not only planned the whole trial most admirably, but also played her part as the judge excellently. She had exactly the right judicial air, made dry comments at appropriate moments (adding much to the mirth of the proceedings) and gave a masterly and witty summing up. We were very sorry to say goodbye to Elizabeth at the end of the term; she has always been one of the keenest members of the Political Society, and has shown herself eager to take part in all its activities and to make its meetings successful.[95]

There had been no need for Elizabeth to be sent to Mrs Z. 'Our congratulations are due to Elizabeth Anscombe for her signal success in winning three of the prizes awarded by the trust,' declared her school magazine in 1935. '[T]he George Hallam Senior Prize for Greek, the Mary Gurney Senior Prize for Latin, and also the Assistant Mistresses' Jubilee Essay Prize'.[96] Elizabeth, alongside her older brothers, twins John and Tom, had been taught Greek from a young age by her mother, Gertrude Thomas. The trio had their first brush with Plato under her tuition.[97] Unusually, Gertrude had herself been home-schooled by male tutors – her parents resorted to the arrangement after they found themselves unable to protect a string of female governesses from the arduous attentions of her uncle. So, instead of learning French and needlework, she learnt Latin and Greek, going on to study Classics at university in Aberystwyth before becoming a headmistress. It was only when she married, late at thirty-nine, that she gave up her career. When Elizabeth entered Sydenham School, Gertrude insisted that her Greek education continue: she told Miss Edith Turner, the headmistress, that she intended her daughter to go to university.[98]

St Hugh's (for Religion) is set in a beautiful 14-acre garden; in spring and summer, girls would criss-cross the grand lawn, loll on rugs or occasional deckchairs, drinking black coffee and reading. It was a prospicient setting for Miss Anscombe, standing on the right below.

Rowena Trevaldwyn, Anscombe,
Winifred Law, Diggy, Elizabeth Elliott
Jean Crumb, Freda Cranley
Nan Gamon, Margaret Gyde.
1938

Miss Gwyer, the Principal, believed the college to have been 'called into being by God'.[99] In reality, it was the work of Dame Elizabeth Wordsworth. In 1886, Wordsworth (who had ignored her brother's declaration that to educate women was 'beastly' to become Principal) oversaw the extension of LMH to create a new hall to cater for girls from more 'modest homes', chiefly the daughters of parsons.[100] St Hugh's Hall, later St Hugh's College, quickly gained a reputation as *the* place to produce headmistresses.[101]

While Miss Gwyer ruled the college, the magnificent garden was the province of Miss Annie Rogers, Oxford's first female tutor, and the

chronicler of women's fight for full membership of the university.[102] Born
in 1857, a child model of Lewis Carroll,[103] Annie Rogers knew the struggle
first hand. At seventeen, she had been the top candidate in the county
exams (the Senior Locals) and was offered exhibition scholarships at Worcester College and Balliol. The fellows had not considered the possibility
that such grades belonged to a female student, and the offer had to be
withdrawn when 'A.M.A.H. Rogers' was revealed to be 'Annie'. (Balliol
consoled her with four volumes of Homer.)[104] When Annie Rogers retired
as tutor in Classics in 1921, St Hugh's created for her the office of *Custos
Hortulorum*. The early minutes of her garden committee meetings reflect
post-First World War exhortations to grow more food: potatoes, rhubarb,
plum and apple trees were planted as well as currant and gooseberry bushes.
But Miss Rogers's greatest expertise was the cultivation of flowering plants,
for which the St Hugh's garden was perfectly suited. Passionflower, myrtle,
loquat and pomegranate flourished under the shelter of the south-facing
front of the main building. Ferns thrived in the shade of the dell. On the
terrace she chose plants for their colour: an abundance of helianthemums,
alpine phloxes and saxifrages.[105] She was often to be found in the herbaceous
border: on a camp stool, tending the plants in an ancient black velvet hat,
still following the old-fashioned habit of never appearing in public, even
in the garden, bareheaded.

Elizabeth arrived in Oxford having already made 'strenuous' efforts in philosophy. It had not been the dialogues of Plato chosen by her mother that
first captured her curiosity, but a nineteenth-century Jesuit tome on *Natural
Theology*. Around the age of thirteen, the religious writings of G. K. Ches-
terton had drawn Elizabeth away from the Anglicanism of her family towards
the Catholic faith.[106] Ignoring her parents' attempts to prevent her from
converting, the teenage Elizabeth embarked on a programme of enthusiastic
reading, during which she had picked up the Jesuit text. She devoured it,
page after page – but there were two points that puzzled her. The first was
the idea that God could infallibly see what any human individual would
freely choose at every future time.[107] This seemed to involve a contradiction: how, for example, could her mother's marriage to Allen Wells Anscombe
have been freely chosen if God saw infallibly that it would happen?

The second puzzle got her *doing* philosophy. The book contained a pur-
ported proof of the principle that every event must have a cause. Elizabeth
thought she saw an error in the reasoning, and set to work to fix it. She

tried this way and that, jotting down new versions only to find the same flaw reappearing in a different guise. She tore up her efforts, and tried again. Perhaps inspired by Plato's depiction of his teacher Socrates, she went around interrogating people. 'Why, if something happened, would you be sure it had a cause?'[108] Why? Why? Why? No one had a good answer and she kept it up. After two or three years of effort, she had produced 'five versions of a would-be proof', but each was 'found guilty of the same error, though each time it was more cunningly concealed'.[109] All this while devoting her schoolgirl energies to the activities of the Political Society, and her spare time to a protracted (and at times murderous) sibling battle against The Twins. (She would later confess to Mary that she had once crouched in their play-tent with a stick, intent on doing them in the moment their heads poked through the fabric.)[110]

Once at Oxford, Elizabeth set about making her conversion official. She went to a Dominican priest, Father Richard Kehoe, with her questions. While amused by her precocious difficulties, he sympathised: she had hit upon a heated doctrinal debate between Dominicans and Jesuits. But he assured her that she could be a Catholic even if she didn't believe those things. And so, she broke off a long line of Anglican vicars' wives and daughters and converted to Roman Catholicism. Miss Anscombe was received into the Church on Easter Day 1938, a few months before Iris and Mary's arrival at Oxford.[111] St Aloysius church, its yellow bell tower visible, and its bells audible, from their Somerville rooms, will be her place of worship for the remainder of our narrative. She is to be found there at early matins.

In 1938, Elizabeth took logic tutorials from the married philosophy don, Martha Kneale. The new, if lone, appearance of 'Mrs' on the philosophy lecture lists may have given some comfort to Miss Anscombe who, before Iris had received any of her (six) proposals of marriage, had accepted her first and was engaged. Just a few months after Elizabeth formally joined the Catholic Church, she attended the Corpus Christi procession at the priory in Begbroke, a small village five miles north-west of Oxford. The thanksgiving service celebrates the Real Presence of the Body, Blood, Soul and Divinity of Jesus Christ, and at the end of Holy Mass the Servite Friars, dressed in their dark grey habits, carried the Sacrament, in a cloud of incense and Latin, through the church and up to the altar. It was there

that she met Peter Geach, a fellow Catholic convert and philosopher at
Balliol, three years older than her.

Peter's unhappy childhood had been a cross between those of Oliver
Twist and John Stuart Mill. His mother, Eleonora Sgonina, the daughter
of Polish immigrants, had studied literature at Cambridge University.[112]
There she met his father, George Hender Geach, and once they were married followed him to Lahore, Punjab, where he was to teach philosophy
with the Indian Educational Service. The marriage was unhappy and when
she travelled to England in 1916 to give birth to Peter, instead of returning
to her husband she returned to her studies. She spent three terms at Somerville, tutored by Dorothy Sayers, and began publishing poetry.[113] Peter's
toddler years were spent with his Polish-speaking grandparents in Cardiff,
while Eleonora continued her studies and edited *Oxford Poetry 1918* (along
with Dorothy Sayers and Thomas Wade Earp).

In 1920, Peter's life abruptly changed. George, still in Lahore, secured
a court order to make Peter a ward of Miss Tarr, an elderly woman who
had once been George's own guardian. Peter was taken from his mother,
to whom he never spoke again, and sent to boarding school. Four years
later, his father returned from Lahore and, unable to secure a university
post in England, began to school his son. George had read Moral Sciences at Cambridge, and by the age of thirteen Peter had mastered
Neville Keynes's *Formal Logic*, studied Russell and Whitehead's *Principia
Mathematica* and made a survey of the logical fallacies contained in
Berkeley's *Dialogues*, Mill's *Utilitarianism* and McTaggart's *Some Dogmas
of Religion*.[114]

Peter escaped his father's relentless training when he went up to Oxford
in 1934. George would have much preferred a Cambridge education for his
child – 'what they call logic at Oxford, Peter, is just a bad joke'[115] – but
financial considerations precluded it. Even with a Balliol scholarship, George
was unable to pay Peter's remaining college fees. After a year or two the
college agreed to fund Peter fully, on one striking condition: that he take
the advice of his psychiatrist and agree never to see his father again.[116]
He did so and, a de facto orphan at eighteen, converted to Roman
Catholicism.

According to Peter, his religious rebirth had left him 'in love with love'
and desperately in need of 'a girl to love and woo and marry'.[117] Seeing a
young woman after the service at Begbroke he, under the impression she

was someone else, proposed to her.[118] Elizabeth's account differs. She recalls Peter approaching her after the procession and, beginning to massage her shoulder, saying, 'Miss Anscombe, I like your mind.'[119] Maybe the blend of incense and spiritual elevation muddled their memories, but as neither tale is especially plausible they are more likely in-jokes between two philosophers interested in personal identity. Depending on whose story you prefer, Elizabeth either said 'yes' or 'And I, yours'. Soon, she was studying Thomas Aquinas and the new logic of Gottlob Frege with her fiancé. Together they read Ludwig Wittgenstein's *Tractatus Logico-Philosophicus*. Written in the trenches during the First World War, this short but elusive book contained Wittgenstein's first attempt to place a limit on thought by means of a description of the structure of language. 'Elizabeth had a lot of philosophical teaching from me,' Peter would later boast, 'I could see she was good at the subject.'[120]

Mary & Iris Join the Political Scene & We Meet the Inhabitants of Boars Hill

Iris's Greek was better than Mary's, but both were far behind the public-school boys with whom they came up – no amount of time in Mrs Z's front room could make up for the fact that the formative education of such boys was organised around an early mastery of Greek and Latin. So, no sooner had they unpacked their cases than they plunged together into 'a desperate race to catch up'.[121] Mildred Hartley, their exacting Somerville tutor, thought their ignorance an inconvenience, but she was determined that her undergraduates should do just as well as the men, judged by exactly the same standards. They bonded over the misery produced by her idea of equality – she seemed to them oblivious to the fact that they were not leaping the same hurdles as the men but ones 'grotesquely higher'. On her instruction they chose 'Latin and Greek composition in verse as well as in prose',[122] a masochistic choice that denied them access to any illuminating secondary literature. Mildred's demand for excellence flowed from her love of Greek, and she was happy to run the race with them. She overlooked Iris's rather idiosyncratic attire ('she always seemed to be in fancy dress') in light of her extraordinary energy: 'she didn't know what idleness was', Mildred recalled.[123] High praise from a woman of remarkable drive who did not permit herself to relax until the end of term, when she donned trousers, thriller in one hand and pipe in the other.[124]

In Iris's sunny room, the new friends struggled together over Greek verse and prose, every week turning out reams of mistranslations and sub-par exercises. But in 1938, the urgent call of the political stage could hardly be ignored, and the friends were drawn into a frenzy of political campaigning: Greek composition could wait but canvassing could not. The British public had been bitterly divided when Prime Minister Neville Chamberlain returned from Munich in September 1938 and declared 'peace for our time'. Somervillian Beatrix Walsh recalled the 'flourish of paper fresh from Herr Hitler's hand', that marked Chamberlain as a saviour to some and a traitor to others.[125] For many of the European refugees already on the pavements of British cities, the betrayal was devastating. The Kantian scholar Heinz Cassirer, who had travelled from Germany to England with his father Ernst, presented himself a few days later at Mildred Hartley's college room. A rumour had reached him that friendship and common cause could be found among the women within Somerville's walls and he arrived in search of reassurance that he was still among people ready to stand firm against the Nazi threat.[126]

A month after Munich, there was an opportunity for the city of Oxford to take a stand against Chamberlain's action in a by-election. Roy Harrod, a Christ Church economist, published an open letter to Labour and Liberal candidates in the *Oxford Mail*: would they step aside and unite behind an independent candidate on an anti-appeasement ticket? Just nine days before polling the two parties reached an agreement.[127] Two Oxford dons stood for the vacant seat. In favour of appeasement was the Conservative candidate Quintin Hogg, fellow of All Souls. Against was the political philosopher and Master of Balliol College, Sandie (A. D.) Lindsay.

Mary and Iris joined the conveyor belt of undergraduates stuffing envelopes in Lindsay's campaign headquarters, hastily assembled in a room opposite St Peter's Hall.[128] Mary 'ran errands and addressed envelopes'.[129] Alongside them was Somerville's brilliant Ancient History tutor, Isobel Henderson, with whom Iris, Mary and Elizabeth were all to study. They would have surveyed the Socialist League pamphlets that littered the rooms of this 'decidedly political animal' as they tried to follow her obscure but ingenious reconstructions of Roman politics, which she created from primary sources.[130] When Franco had come to power, Isobel, 'a passionate

Hispanophile, vowed never to set foot in Spain again until he had fallen'.[131] Outside politics and tutorials, 'Music, racing, poetry, cricket and the Mediterranean were essential parts of her life'.[132] She was a buoyant entertainer; one snapshot memory has her in full-length evening gown, a fur stole and elbow-length white gloves stacked with diamond bracelets, plunging a carving knife into chicken *en croute*.[133] And a tragic history lent her extra glamour. As Miss Munro, she had become the first woman to be elected to a fellowship while engaged to be married. The wedding took place in Oxford in June 1933, with the daughter of her former tutor, the philosopher R. G. Collingwood, as bridesmaid.[134] Husband and wife left for Italy on a honeymoon, but Isobel returned alone as the widow Mrs Henderson, after Charles Henderson died of heart failure during a visit to the Sanctuary of Monte Sant'Angelo.[135]

Lindsay's supporters were a broad church, encompassing Communists, Labour and Liberal voters and some dissident Conservatives. Harold Macmillan, Conservative MP for Stockton, rallied for Sandie Lindsay at a meeting in the Town Hall. Oxford zoologist Solly Zuckerman held out a telephone receiver in his rooms to his friend Randolph Churchill: 'LINDSAY MUST GET IN,' boomed the voice of Randolph's father, Winston.[136] Ted Heath (the future Conservative prime minister) careered around Oxford on a bike, campaigning with the left-wing Denis Healey. Both men were Lindsay's tutees, and as likely to have Søren Kierkegaard or the mystic Pyotr Uspensky in their blazer pockets as John Locke.[137] Even the Oxford Anarchists pledged their non-support to the Master of Balliol:

> Dear Sir,
> The Anarchists of the University find it impossible to support your parliamentary campaign. In fact we are preparing a campaign against voting in any election. As, however, you are prepared to oppose Chamberlain, we would like you to know that we will attempt to dissuade from voting only the supporters of Q. Hogg.[138]

Hogg's supporters warned that Lindsay had received telegrams from Stalin,[139] but for many of the young women of Somerville, dropping Lindsay's pamphlets through letterboxes on the Iffley Road, this only provided further encouragement.

WHO IS DR. LINDSAY?

D R. LINDSAY, the Progressive Independent candidate in the Oxford by-election, is 59 years old. His father was a professor of Theology in Scotland, and his mother was Chairwoman of the Scottish Liberal Women's Federation : she also founded the first women's Trade Union in Glasgow.

Dr. Lindsay first came to Oxford in 1898; he has lived here ever since, except for two years in Glasgow, one other year away, and the duration of the War.

He has been a member of the Fabian Society since 1899, and a member of the Labour Party since it was founded.

War Service

H E was 35 when the War began. When he volunteered for service he was sent out to join the Intelligence Staff in France. There, a friend who was starting a Labour Corps found him and got him transferred to the job of directing the technical side of it.

He describes his job as 'a cushier job than a great many'; but it took him into the Ypres district and he was nearly every day in the firing line. He confesses that he was 'very, very frightened'. *He never wants another war.*

Three Children

D R. Lindsay is married and has three children.

His eldest son Michael is now in Pekin where he is introducing some of the Oxford methods of teaching to the Chinese Universities.

His daughter Drusilla, has married a man in the Indian Political Service in India, and is now living on the North-West Frontier.

Iris and Mary both joined the university's Labour Club, said to have the 'best girls' (in 1936, a group of them had burnt their silk stockings to protest against Japanese aggression in China).[140] A few risked Miss Farnell's displeasure and wore red lipstick to go with their red commitment. Reportedly some men joined only to get 'lined up with women', which perhaps accounts for the fact that among the membership were two who sat on the Conservative Club's committee. But the serious question for the membership was not how far will you go, but how far left will you go? Labour pink or, like Iris and Léonie Marsh, full-blown Communist Party red? 'The very first thing I did when I arrived at Oxford was to join the CP,' Iris recounted, many years later.[141] (This was not quite true: she went first to the yellow-towered St Aloysius' church, perhaps passing Elizabeth en route. When she knocked there was no answer.)[142]

Iris's letter to a Badminton friend, Ann Leech, during her second term at Somerville offers a glimpse of her youthful fanaticism. 'I thank God that I have the party to direct and discipline my previously vague and ineffective idealism,' she explained. 'I feel now that I am doing *some* good, and that life has a purpose and that the history of civilisation is not just an interesting series of unconnected muddles, but a comprehensible development towards the highest stage of society, the Soviet world state.' In an attempt to pre-empt Ann's concerns about bloodshed, she offered reassurance: 'a Bolshevik revolution is not a wild emotional business of random bomb-throwing – it's a carefully planned, scientific affair, which occurs at a moment when there will be a minimum of people to be dealt with violently'.[143] As she waited for that glorious and efficient day, she went with 'some nice Oxford reds' to the Festival of Music for the People at the Royal Albert Hall. She stood as the Spanish national anthem played, and the Dean of Canterbury in red robes exalted the 'fullness of life in the Soviet Union'.[144]

Mary, perhaps feeling that even a 'minimum' number of violent deaths was too many, remained pink. The volumes of the Left Book Club on the occasional tables in her parents' house cast the Soviet Union in an ambivalent light. Stories circulated about the Moscow trials, and while the socialist intellectual Beatrice Webb was 'pleased that Stalin had "cut the dead wood"',[145] many were disillusioned. In April 1937, John Dewey – the philosopher who had inspired Olive Willis's vision for Downe House – led a delegation to Mexico to interview the exiled Trotsky. The Dewey Commission's 400-page report revealed its conclusions in the title: *Not Guilty*.[146] The Moscow trials, Dewey concluded, were 'frame-ups'. There was much disenchantment in the Scrutton household.

As they progressed through their studies, Mary found it increasingly hard to make sense of her friend's fervent attachment to the Communist Party. When the student Labour Club split, with the moderates forming the breakaway Democratic Socialist Club (DSC), Mary and Iris found themselves on opposite sides. Mary surprised herself by giving a 'fiery speech' at the initial meeting of the DSC, and was elected to its committee; Iris held a counterpart role in the Marxist-leaning Labour Club.[147] Iris's political enthusiasm was unstoppable and, as she made clear to Mary, far surpassed her interest in philosophy.

The mood in Oxford, at least beyond the Junior Common Rooms, was more with Mary: pink rather than red. Mary gifted Iris a poem after her friend had joined a May Day march that was pelted with tomatoes by an apparently ungrateful local proletariat:

Oh where is Iris Murdoch, tell me where? tell me where?
She has gone to help the workers demonstrate!
Plutaristocrat tomatoes in her hair, in her hair
Cannot wean her from the proletariate.
Though the gilded youth are baying in the High, in the High,
And the Bullingdon are calling for her head,
Crowned with gory drops and golden, in her heart she is beholden
Shown at last in her true colours as a Red![148]

During the by-election, however, everyone on the left, red and pink, young and old, united behind Lindsay. Isaiah Berlin, a philosopher and fellow of All Souls, swapped stickers on cars pledging support to Hogg for ones celebrating Lindsay.[149] Maurice Bowra, Wadham's (witty) Warden, who otherwise lamented the fact that all young men are interested in politics ('Where are the aesthetes of yesteryear?'),[150] got behind the campaign. J. L. Austin, bearer of handkerchiefs, coined the unofficial campaign slogan, 'A Vote for Hogg is a Vote for Hitler', and trailed Hogg from meeting to meeting to heckle him. 'Hogg had a nimble mind,' recalled E. R. Dodds, the Regius Professor of Greek, 'but Austin's was nimbler. Repartees flashed from him like rapier thrusts; he rarely missed an opening and never gave one.'[151]

The votes were cast on 27 October. Lindsay stopped campaigning early: he was revolted by Austin's slogan. Hogg won by a small margin, with the usual Tory majority halved. The results were announced from the balcony of the Town Hall.[152]

Hogg 15,797
Lindsay 12,363

For those nine days of campaigning, all youthful energy had converged on the fifty-nine-year-old Sandie Lindsay. Lindsay moved in an elevated enclave of high-class internationalists, Idealists, Fabian socialists, versifying Communists and poets laureate, a world that occupied Boars Hill, a village atop one of the Cumnor Hills to Oxford's north. In *Brideshead Revisited*, conservative Evelyn Waugh has Charles Ryder receive from his cousin Jasper the curt imperative: 'Keep clear of Boars Hill.'[153] Mary, Iris and Philippa would all be regular visitors.

At the heart of Boars Hill life were classicist Gilbert Murray and his wife Lady Mary Murray. The telephone number at their house, Yatscombe, was *Boars Hill 1*.[154] On call nearby at the rambling vicarage, Heath Barrows, was socialist philosopher Edgar Frederick Carritt (Lindsay's former tutor), his wife Winifred and their numerous children. Gravelled paths bordered by trim box hedges gave way to a croquet lawn, orchard, grass tennis court, paddock and a modest copse.[155] Though Edgar (unlike Winifred) wasn't a Communist, he gave lectures on Dialectical Materialism throughout the late 1930s; his classes heaved with undergraduates and copies of *Labour Monthly* were sold in the quad.[156] At Scar Top, set in grounds of two and a half acres, lived the Indologist and writer Edward (E. J.) Thompson, his wife Theo and their sons Frank and Edward (E. P.). During the by-election, Theo could be seen circling round Oxford with a sign proclaiming 'Save Czechoslovakia!' pasted to the family car, until she was stopped by a policeman.[157] When Gandhi visited Oxford in 1931, he was driven up the hill to the Thompsons, where Lindsay (who regarded Gandhi as a saint) hosted an informal discussion on Indian independence. (The philosopher Dorothy Emmet, formerly Lindsay's tutee, had picked Gandhi up at Oxford Station in her old open-top Baby Austin.)[158] The Poet Laureate Robert Bridges, whose daughter Margaret had married the Platonist philosopher

H.W.B. Joseph, was at Chilswell House. Margaret's sister, the poet Elizabeth Daryush, lived at Stockwell. The fertile imaginations of these Boars Hill romantics and Idealists and their associates had helped to form the League of Nations, the Oxford Committee for Famine Relief (Oxfam) and the Society for the Protection of Science and Learning (a council founded by William Beveridge to aid scholars escaping the Nazi regime).

Men like Murray and Lindsay had been vital allies in the fight for women's education too. Lindsay's mother, Anna Dunlop, who in the 1880s had helped found the Scottish Council for Women's Trades, had been one of the first women to study at the University of Edinburgh. She won the top prize in Moral Philosophy and Experimental Physics. When Emily Penrose retired as Somerville's Principal in 1923, Gilbert Murray and Sandie Lindsay sat beside her at the celebratory formal dinner. The pair remained supporters of the college: Murray was friend and mentor to the new Principal, Helen Darbishire, and to historian Isobel Henderson. Lindsay married Somerville's poetic and intense Erica Violet Storr, though she proved ill-suited to the role of Master's wife: when the Balliol Eight rowing team came to the Master's Lodging for a celebration party, she trapped them in a corner and read to them from Charles Montagu Doughty's *Travels in Arabia Deserta*.[159]

Lindsay once joked, 'I am a conservative, a liberal and a socialist'[160] – a self-description forged on the battlegrounds of Ypres, the pottery towns where he gave tutorial classes to miners, and in Glasgow, where as a child he was woken by the hammering of the Clyde shipyards. But while this outlook spoke to many in interwar Britain – a hatred of competition, belief in national community, the unity of an established Church, an active State and a national education system[161] – to the younger dons and undergraduates it looked out of date. Down the hill, in the maze of Oxford's little streets, student digs and smoky pubs, Lindsay's self-description made no sense. 'By nature a lotus eater, a reactionary and a believer in the aristocracy, he has deluded himself and his friends into regarding him as an idealist, a radical and a collectivist,' reported the undergraduate magazine *Isis*.[162]

The word 'teenager' had not been invented, but teenagers had been, and they were to be seen all over Oxford, doing recognisably teenage things.[163] Duke Ellington records spun in undergraduates' rooms, Bessie Smith blues wafted out from college windows and most colleges had a jazz band. Dixieland group The Bandits played to smoking reds.[164] Maurice Bowra hosted an exclusive dining club in Wadham, at which he wined and dined the crème of (almost exclusively male) teenage talent. At his table, entertaining use of language was everything. Gossip was high art. Comments that were malicious without being funny were ignored, as were jokes that merely shocked without illuminating. But cruel jokes that were clever were admissible. 'The Master of Balliol has been ill, but unfortunately is getting better.'[165]

Lindsay would not send Balliol men to Bowra for tuition. When Gilbert Murray led a campaign to prevent undergraduates from owning cars, the back seats of which were surely a natural site for fornication, it was Bowra who defeated him.[166] For a new generation of undergraduates and younger dons, being fenced in by rules, however paternalistically conceived, was quite out of the question, as were the lingering imperialist dimensions of Lindsay's internationalism. The teenagers were looking for a world view with an emphasis on freedom and individuality, and which was less buttoned up.

The Agamemnon Class

As Isobel Henderson stuffed envelopes alongside Mary and Iris, she strategised about their education. The Mods translation exercises chosen by Mildred Hartley had little in them to excite a budding Classicist. Caesar or Cicero were rarely chosen, Mildred instead preferring passages that would test her tutees' wits. Lewis Carroll was a special favourite; the passage in which the Cheshire Cat disappears, leaving only his grin, proved almost impossible to render in Greek. 'The point about this Cheshire smile, or "grin" as Carroll calls it, a tougher word than "smile", is that there is no Greek word for the noun of it; it has to be a participle of the verb, an adjectival participle attached to a noun; so you will at once appreciate the difficulty of dealing with a smile which remains after the cat has vanished,' complained one tutee, Prue Smith.[167] So it was that Iris and Mary first felt the power and magnetism – the pure thrill – of scholarship, outside their college walls, when Isobel Henderson dispatched them together to Corpus Christi College. They were to attend Eduard Fraenkel's *Agamemnon* classes.

Professor Eduard Fraenkel's learning was unmatched by any classicist living and his almost religious devotion to his work was legendary across Europe.[168] Yet, like the rest of his generation of Jewish scholars, he had been forced from his university post in 1933 when the Nazis passed the Law for the Restoration of the Professional Civil Service.[169] Martin Heidegger, in his capacity as rector, presided over the dismissal of Fraenkel from his Chair at Freiburg University.[170] With the help of the Society for the Protection of Science and Learning, Freiburg's loss was Oxford's gain. Regius Professor of Greek, E. R. Dodds, testified: 'I know of no-one better worth saving from the point of view of scholarship.'[171]

Mary and Iris would have entered the ancient cloister of Corpus Christi with some trepidation as Isobel Henderson's words echoed in their ears – 'great privilege', 'distinguished', 'serious'. 'One is always wrong not to like things', she would tell her students by way of encouraging them to overcome any timidity.[172] Iris and Mary were also sent with a warning: Fraenkel will 'probably paw you about a bit, but never mind'.[173] As they straightened their scholars' gowns and pushed open the tiny sixteenth-century door to the visibly ancient room (low ceiling, long Tudor windows, a large table in the centre) they joined a changing cast of twenty scholars (dons and undergraduates) working their way, line by line, through Aeschylus' drama. The class having begun while they were still schoolgirls, Mary and Iris entered at line 83 ('The matter is where now it is; it will be fulfilled to its destined end', laments the chorus, waiting for news of the far-off war in Troy).[174] For two hours, between 5 p.m. and 7 p.m. each week, the class crept forward through the translation, with Fraenkel presiding at the head of the table.[175] The format – the German trad- ition of the *Seminar* – was new to Oxford, hitherto accustomed to lectures and tutorials (an undergraduate or two and a college tutor).[176] A strict con- dition of participation was that no session should ever be missed.[177]

Mary was thrilled by the 'sense of being part of a great timeless effort'. Fraenkel's undertaking was to discover what Aeschylus had meant and written, words from a pen that had made its mark over twenty-four centuries ago. The vast temporal and cultural distance between past and present was spanned only by the continuous human activity of preserving, copying, protecting and reproducing papyrus, parchment and paper. Fraenkel studied the surface of different copies, sifting out idiosyncrasies and corruptions introduced by repeated transcription, peeling back layers of time. The work required know- ledge of a network of tiny facts: how were works produced, how were they copied, what were the habits and idiosyncrasies of the men who made them? And then there were facts that had left a trace only in the text: a mistake in transcription might reveal the hand of 'a weary monk' who was 'writing at the end of his day'. Once he had removed the layers of accumulated error and accident, Fraenkel would transform the clear, clean text into sound; Mary was dazzled by the recognition that the verse was written to be spoken.[178]

Fraenkel's status as a refugee inflected his treatment of fellow exile Cassandra, a Trojan priestess held captive by Agamemnon: 'The wretchedness of her situation is increased by the alien environment, and it is a contributory factor that it can be assumed at least for a time that she does not understand the language,' he would write.[179] Ruth von Velson, Eduard's wife (who had given up her academic career in classical philology when she married), was the only one of the family who could speak English when the couple and their five children arrived in England in 1934.[180] The German Jewish Aid Committee, fearing anti-German feeling among the British public, advised German refugees like Ruth and Eduard Fraenkel: 'Spend your spare time immediately in learning the English language and its correct pronunciation. Refrain from speaking German in the streets and in public conveyances and in public places such as restaurants. Talk halting English rather than fluent German – and *do not talk in a loud voice*. Do not read German newspapers in public.'[181]

For the undergraduates, some still in their teens, the enormity of the world stage on which their futures were to be played out gave weight and pathos to the story of a warrior's return. Iris would later capture this in her poem 'Agamemnon Class, 1939'.

> Did we expect the war? What did we fear?
> First love's incinerating crippling flame,
> Or that it would appear
> In public that we could not name
> The Aorist of some familiar verb.

The older dons, many too young to fight in the first war and too old to fight in the one that was coming, did their best to help their young classmates with translation. Aeschylus' chorus regret their old age: 'But we, insolvent [i.e. unable to serve as soldiers] with our aged frames, were left out of the supporting expedition that then was sent, and remain behind, moving a childlike strength upon staffs.'[182] All they can do is bear witness, while at Troy all 'the youth of Greece' fall, the logic of generation disrupted.[183]

> Between line eighty three and line a thousand
> It seemed to us our innocence
> Was lost, our youth laid waste,
> In that pellucid unforgiving air,

The aftermath experienced before,
Focused by dread into a lurid flicker,
A most uncanny composite of sun and rain.[184]

Iris was 'pawed about' by Fraenkel (she claimed not to have minded), but not Mary who was busy falling in love with quiet and beautiful Nick Crosbie. Nick's friend Kenneth Kirk meanwhile mooned over Mary, and Noel Martin came only so he could gaze at Iris.[185] For Frank Thompson, Iris, the girl in the green dress, was his 'dream-girl' – 'a poetic Irish Communist who's doing Honour Mods', he wrote to his parents up on Boars Hill; 'I worship her.'[186] The future military historian Michael Foot, Frank's Winchester schoolfriend, was in love with Léonie Marsh, but would later recall that 'practically everyone who was up with Iris fell for her'.[187] Iris entreated Frank to join the Communist Party. 'Come to tea in a couple of days and convert me,' he half propositioned.[188] She did and she did.

A Revolution in Philosophy: Freddie Ayer Declares War on Metaphysics & Ethics

Generations of Greats students, passing through Oxford, had been taught speculative metaphysics – philosophers' attempts to construct theories about the nature of reality by reason alone – alongside their diet of (lots and lots and lots of) Plato and Aristotle. An undergraduate from the class of 1900, once he had recovered from the shock of seeing unchaperoned, unhatted women, would have felt at home alongside Elizabeth Anscombe as she attended lectures on the Ancients in her first year of Greats – Plato's *Republic*; Aristotle's *Ethics*; Aristotle's *De Anima*; Plato's *Theory of Ideas*. He would, however, have been quite at sea in H. A. Prichard's lectures on 'The Idea of Moral Obligation' or W. D. Ross's on 'Moral Philosophy'. The first third of the twentieth century had seen a dramatic shift in philosophical orthodoxy, reflected in the lecture schedules set out in the Oxford University *Gazette*. As Elizabeth took her seat the power struggle was reaching a climax.

At the beginning of the century, the Idealist metaphysicians had the stage – or at least the lectern – at Oxford: Green, Bradley, Bosanquet, Muirhead, Collingwood, Mure. The inspiration for these men was the

German philosopher G.W.F. Hegel, who in their view offered a true metaphysical vision of reality as a unified whole, with a rational or 'ideal' order. This order, they urged, is constituted in and by consciousness, and interconnects all subjects and all things – knower and known folded into one all-embracing Absolute. The task of philosophy is to come to know the Absolute. This was to be achieved, however partially and inadequately, by self-transcendence; through this, the structure of the whole (to which the self-transcending philosopher belonged) would be revealed. Human knowledge, the Idealists argued, is not exhausted by the mere sensory apprehension of separate and individual things such as tables and mountains, but instead progresses towards a unifying vision: the recognition of the Absolute. Poetry, art, religion and historical understanding are crucial to this task; scientific, empirical methods of observation and measurement can play only a small role. The ultimate aim of philosophical enquiry, the Idealists proclaimed from their podiums in the early 1900s, is to bring life into harmony with the world. Philosophy contributes to how things *ought to be*, to making actual the Ideal.[189]

Just before the First World War, the Idealists had come under attack from the earthbound Realists. Inspired by the Cambridge philosophers Bertrand Russell and George (G. E.) Moore, and working from the latter's 1903 manifesto 'The Refutation of Idealism',[190] the Realists insisted that, contra the Idealists, the knower is distinct from the known. There is no interconnection between mind and world, no all-embracing Absolute. The task for philosophy is not so very different from the task of science: it is to discover and describe a wholly independent reality. Knowledge would be built up, fragment by fragment, piece by discrete piece. Observation would replace speculation; and a realistic spirit would replace a romantic one.

At their lecterns, through the 1920s and 1930s, the Oxford philosophers Harold (H. A.) Prichard (a short slight figure, with wispy white hair, a thick black moustache, and a high reedy voice) and David (W. D.) Ross (a few years younger, bald-headed and bare-faced, with a Scottish accent) expounded an 'Intuitionist' ethics that sat within this Realist framework. Humans possess a faculty of moral intuition, they explained, which is akin to ordinary vision but especially attuned to reality's moral features. It is through this faculty, rather than by self-transcendence, that moral reality could be apprehended. For an undergraduate of the 1900s, this idea – that moral knowledge could be understood somewhat on the model of the observational knowledge of the scientist – would have been shocking.

The original Realist G. E. Moore had set the Bloomsbury group's hearts racing by including the property of 'goodness' among the world's furniture. When he dismantled the Absolute, he preserved the autonomy and purity of the Good by insisting on a fundamental cleavage in reality: natural fact and non-natural value. Goodness exists, he insisted, even though it is not a 'natural property' and cannot be reduced to, or even understood in terms of, anything that falls within the province of psychology or the natural sciences.[191] Still, reality is populated with manifold valuable things that we recognise as such through the experiences they give us – the pleasures of human intercourse, personal affection and love, the appreciation of what is beautiful in art and nature. Each person's duty, Moore claimed, lay in increasing the amount of value in the world, by creating objects that give rise to these experiences.

Though Oxford's Prichard and Ross were Realists like Moore, they rejected his account of the connection between duty and value. It has been a pervasive tendency among moral philosophers, Prichard explained from the lectern, to answer the question 'Why should I do my duty?' with 'Because it is good'. The next step had then been to show that doing your duty is good either because it benefits you to do your duty (it's good for you) or because dutiful acts are themselves good. But, says Prichard, if the reason to do your duty is that it will benefit you, then morality is reduced to self-interest. And though it may be true that dutiful acts are good, they are good because they are the discharge of duty, and not (as Moore mistakenly thought) the other way around. Attempts by moral philosophers to make out the idea of a 'good action' independently of duty, by appealing to notions that Aristotle stressed, like 'virtue' and 'character', just muddy the water, Prichard argued. Motive is simply irrelevant to the question of whether what I do is right.

Prichard's famous paper, 'Does Moral Philosophy Rest on a Mistake?', presented a parallel between moral philosophers' search for a theory about duty, and Descartes' famous attempt to prove to himself that he had knowledge of the external world. We sometimes feel the tug of sceptical doubt (What do I really know?) and we sometimes wonder whether we are foolish in unquestioningly carrying out our somewhat irksome duties (Why should I do my duty?). But in both cases, Prichard argued, the search for a theory that can provide reassurance is misguided. When duties conflict and I am genuinely unsure about what I ought to do – ought I to return the library book or keep my promise to help a friend? – a theory or a proof will not help me. 'The only remedy lies,' Prichard ends his 1912 paper by saying, 'in actual[ly] getting into a situation which occasions the obligation . . . and then letting our moral capacities of thinking do their work.'[192] I must rely, that is, on moral intuition.

Prichard and Ross's Moral Intuitionism left their students despairing. 'Prichard and Ross seemed to live in a world of moral certainties which had ceased to be ours,' complained the philosopher Dorothy Emmet, who had arrived at Lady Margaret Hall, and sat (chaperoned) in their lectures just after the first war. 'They were quite sure what kinds of acts were right and wrong.' But she was unconvinced, both by their confidence that their 'moral capacities' would always deliver a verdict on what was right, and by the sharp division that they made between the right and the good. 'I wanted a background to ethics in which what was right bore some relation to what was good. This meant a reference to the kinds of human relations and the kinds of ways of life we believed were good'.[193] Later, she would provide this depth and background in her books. When Iris took her seat in the lecture hall to listen to David Ross, her reaction echoed Dorothy's: 'shallow stupid milk & water "ethics"', she complained in a letter to an Oxford friend.[194]

The final phase in the power struggle at Oxford came as Elizabeth was overseeing her mock trial at Sydenham. Much to the surprise of Ross and Prichard, it was an attack on them as much as on their opponents.

In 1933, at a public philosophy meeting, an unknown youth with slick black hair and a brightly coloured shirt stood up in a sea of grey-haired dons. The 'older men were dumbfounded and scandalized' when there came from his mouth a declaration of war. 'You are all', he proclaimed, facing an 'early extinction'. The processes by which Realist and Idealist were to be wiped from the earth had been set, inexorably, in motion, he explained. 'The armies of Cambridge and Vienna are already upon you!'[195] That young man was Freddie (A. J.) Ayer, a twenty-six-year-old research fellow at Christ Church. His old tutor, Michael Foster, thought him unfit to teach the young,[196] but Wadham's warden Maurice Bowra, at whose table Freddie had been schooled, considered him a 'young genius'.[197]

While the Realists were arguing with the Idealists in Oxford and Cambridge, a circle of intellectuals had been gathering in the cafés of Vienna to discuss the future of philosophy in the wake of the collapse of the Austro-Hungarian Empire.[198] Their figurehead, Moritz Schlick, occupied the Chair of Natural Philosophy at Vienna University, a post that had been created for the polymath Ernst Mach, whose empiricism, Schlick now believed, could salvage democracy and humanism. Revolutions in geometry in the nineteenth century had shattered Enlightenment philosopher Immanuel Kant's idea that Euclidean space is the form of all possible experience, and with it his idea of a kind of *a priori* knowledge that is not derived or acquired from experience. Mach stepped in with an alternative: there is no need to posit anything that sensory experience does not confirm or predict. Politically, Mach's rejection of the *a priori* was an anti-authoritarian lesson that could be applied as effectively to social theory and economics as to psychology. Mach's 'psycho-physics' would, he hoped, pave the way to attributing sensation to matter, and explain mental phenomena continuously with the physical world. Oxford would wait until 1935 for its Institute of Experimental Psychology (founded after one Anna Watts donated £10,000 for the purpose), but in the 1870s Mach was developing concepts that would make its experiments possible.[199]

Mary would have run past Mach's bust in the summer of 1938, white marble atop pink granite, when she took a shortcut through the Rathauspark on her way (almost late) to see Smetana's *The Bartered Bride* ('it put me off opera for a long while').[200] By then, Moritz Schlick was dead (murdered by a former student) and almost all the living Vienna Circle's members had lost their academic positions, or had, with foresight, given them up and emigrated. Later, we will run into one of them, Friedrich Waismann, in the lecture halls of Oxford and Cambridge.

Though Freddie Ayer made the declaration of war, it had been Britain's first female professor of philosophy, Susan Stebbing, who had originally invited the 'armies of Vienna' to join forces with the Cambridge Realists. Stebbing had met Schlick in England in 1930 and at once saw ways of bringing logical positivism (the Viennese turn towards science, measurement and observation) into a conversation she had been having with G. E. Moore, her friend and former mentor, about the need for clarity. She recognised the potential of 'analysis' to reveal the hidden structure of language and the world. She thought that analysis might be applied to facts (as well as sentences) to uncover the fundamental building-blocks of our everyday experience. And she saw a purpose outside the philosophy lecture rooms. If the general population could be schooled to ask 'What does this mean?' when confronted with a piece of political propaganda, advertising or journalism, and shown how to answer it by breaking sentences and arguments down into their component parts, this would lead to a better-informed and more politically savvy public. Meanwhile, G. E. Moore, following his 'The Refutation of Idealism', had continued his assault on the esoteric, and had been alarming undergraduates, speakers and colleagues alike with his repeated question, 'What ON EARTH do you mean by that?'[201] Initially targeted at Idealists (whose claims about 'the Absolute' were certainly obscure) his repeated use of the question, accompanied by the banging of tables and tearing up of papers, had helped (along with Stebbing's less iconoclastic efforts) to bring about a methodological turn at Cambridge. Under Moore's unsettling and persistent challenge, and Stebbing's careful advocacy, by the late 1920s Cambridge philosophers were no longer asking 'What is Good?' but 'What does "good" mean?'

Stebbing saw in the work of the Vienna logicians a method for answering such questions. In 1933 she delivered a lecture 'Logical Positivism and Analysis' at the British Academy, in which she showed how the methods of logical analysis of the Vienna Circle, with its emphasis on observation, could be a tool in the quest for clarity. She helped found *Analysis*, a journal devoted to 'analytic' philosophy, in which Schlick and his circle of associates published. In 1936, the Slovakian-born American philosopher of science, Ernest Nagel, penned an 'appraisal of analytic philosophy in Europe', based on a year's study, in which he described to his American readers the methodological and doctrinal connections that already existed between 'the philosophy professed at Cambridge, Vienna, Prague, Warsaw, and Lwów'.[202] 'An extraordinary amount of energy has been expended by Miss

Stebbing,' Nagel remarked.[203] This was noted by her colleagues too: 'I always wished that she would write a book, or at least a paper, free from the pressure of other duties or any promise to have it done by a certain time,' lamented one. 'But no – there was always something, if not a committee meeting then a taxi for Ireland, and with a suitcase in her hand and a hat a trifle insecure upon her head she would be gone.'[204]

Much of Stebbing's energy went into creating a community of scholars, but she also worked to explain the new logical methods to a general public. Her *A Modern Introduction to Logic* (1930) was the first textbook in modern logic – the technical methods that the Logical Positivists used to analyse propositions. 'Logic, in the most usual and widest sense of the word, is concerned with reflective thinking,'[205] she begins. To think logically is simply to think clearly and to purpose. But, 'recently has it been recognized that there is a science of pure logic that is concerned with nothing but form'. This technical, narrow, sense of 'logic', she explained, concerns the general and abstract structure of reasoning. Consider the argument: 'If all politicians are inconsistent and Baldwin is a politician then Baldwin is inconsistent.' The premises and conclusion may be true or false or irrelevant or scandalous, but these qualities are of no interest to the modern logician, for he is interested only in the argument's form. 'The ideal of the logician is complete generality [and] he attains this ideal by making his assertions completely formal' through the use of his new logical gadgets of 'constants' and 'variables'. He swaps 'Baldwin' for 'b', 'inconsistent' for 'β', and 'politicians' for 'α' to obtain: 'If all α are β and b is an α, then b is a β.'[206] Next 'all', 'if then' and 'and' can be exchanged for symbols too: $\forall$, $\rightarrow$, &. The logician does not need to look at the world, nor at the behaviour of Baldwin and his fellow politicians, to apprehend the logical validity of the string of symbols: $((\forall x)(\alpha x \rightarrow \beta x)$ & $\alpha b) \rightarrow \beta b$.

As the by-election was fought in Oxford, Stebbing published *Thinking to Some Purpose*, which aimed to communicate the power and importance of logical thinking (in the widest sense of the word) to a country on the brink of war, and to inoculate readers against the dangers of manipulation. Propaganda, for instance, often relied on forms of 'potted thinking', which, though easily digested, lacks the vitamins essential to mental nourishment.[207] In phrases like 'lily-livered pacifist', 'bloated capitalist', 'milk-sop Christians', the 'epithet has been tied to the noun it qualifies in a way that makes it psychologically impossible to think, for instance, of a Christian apart from a milk-sop'. What is needed to break the hold of these clichéd, 'potted', forms of thought is 'a reconsideration of the facts'.[208]

When Moore's Chair at Cambridge became vacant in 1939, Susan Stebbing applied. 'Of course everyone thinks you are the right person to succeed Moore,' Gilbert Ryle, a friend and a Student (senior member) of Christ Church, told her, 'except that you are a woman.'[209] It went to Ludwig Wittgenstein.

It was Gilbert Ryle who, in 1933, sent his young tutee, Freddie Ayer, first to Cambridge (where he met Stebbing and Wittgenstein) and then to spend a few months in Vienna. Ayer's new wife Renée Orde-Lees accompanied him. A highly cultivated (but expelled) convent girl with smart bobbed hair, house boots and a Persian cat on a lead, she was 'as unlike Oxford women as he was unlike Oxford men'.[210] It was assumed that men should walk women home at night (the curfew for men's colleges was accordingly later than for the women's) but Renée transported Freddie by motorbike, her husband reading and writing in the sidecar.[211]

While Renée toured the cinemas, dance halls and museums of Vienna, Freddie attended the meetings of the Vienna Circle. At the time the exegesis of Wittgenstein's *Tractatus Logico-Philosophicus*[212] was their central concern. 'Everything that can be thought at all can be thought clearly. Everything that can be said can be said clearly', writes Wittgenstein; 'Whereof one cannot speak, thereof one must be silent.'[213] 'Wittgenstein is treated here as a second Pythagoras', Freddie Ayer wrote to Gilbert Ryle, 'and Waismann is the high priest of the cult.'[214] Ayer couldn't understand much of what was said – his German was too poor to process the flow of words – but after a short time he was convinced he knew all there was to know. 'On the whole I have got very little out of them all,' he wrote. 'I think that with your help, I have already got from Wittgenstein all that he has to give us and that is the correct attitude towards philosophy, the appreciation of what is and what is not a genuine philosophical problem.'[215]

The two ideas that Ayer had extracted from Ryle and from the half-understood conversations in Vienna were that of logical analysis and empiricism: everyday propositions could be formalised and clarified using the new symbolism, and then tested one by one by appeal to experience. Any proposition that did not yield to this analysis and method of testing failed to express a thought. In his enthusiasm for the new logical methods, Ayer proposed that the analysis should proceed until a description in terms of 'sense-contents' had been reached: 'the sentence, "I am now sitting in front of a table" can, in principle, be translated into a sentence which does not mention tables, but only sense-contents', he would explain.[216] Modern logic thus led Ayer to hold a linguistic version of an ancient view, known as *phenomenalism*: to say something about tables is really to say something about sense experiences. An analysis of 'I am now sitting in front of a table' does not commit the wary philosopher to the existence of tables; 'tables are logical constructions out of sense-contents'.[217]

Returning to England, Ayer locked himself in a room above a tobacconist's in Foubert Place in Soho, and set to work hunched over a typewriter. He saw a quite different use from Stebbing for the Cambridge–Vienna synthesis. He would harness its destructive power to 'wage a campaign' against his buttoned-up tutors, the old Victorians.[218] No more would the esoteric organicism of the Idealists be used to limit individuality by their insistence that each person must subsume themselves within the whole! Finally, the young could break free of the demands of obligation and duty imposed by the Realists! He transformed the dense and subtle text of the *Tractatus* into a manifesto against speculative metaphysical theories (of the Idealist and Realist variety alike).

The first to fall under the hammers of Ayer's typewriter were the Idealists. What possible observations could verify propositions like 'the Absolute enters into, but is itself incapable of, evolution and progress'?[219] None at all! The proposition is meaningless and those who utter it are speaking nothing but nonsense. Into the dustbin went centuries of metaphysical speculation about the nature of the universe. Next the Realists' claim that moral statements, said to be known by intuition, were meaningful. What possible observation could verify 'One ought to help one's neighbours'?

What remained, in Ayer's vision of philosophy, was a *technique*. Philosophers analyse propositions and scientists verify them. Gone was Stebbing's and Moore's vision of modern logic as a source of metaphysical insight. Gone too was Stebbing's conviction that a general public educated in linguistic analysis would be better able to resist propaganda, and better able to understand the world around them. Ayer repurposed the methods of analysis in a way that made the everyday world alien and inscrutable. The new logic, with its repertoire of logical gadgets, could be used to construct unfamiliar models of the world, the structure of which would be discovered through the manipulation and movement of a calculus. New symbols, not to be found among the keys of Ayer's typewriter, moving according to the laws of logic: $\exists x[(Kx \,\&\, \forall y(Ky \to y=x))] \,\&\, Bx.$[220] Whatever is inexpressible in the system is declared 'Nonsense!' Whatever cannot be verified by observation, 'Nonsense!'

In the end only the poets escaped Ayer's massacre. Ayer is merciful on the grounds that poets, unlike the metaphysicians, make no claims to truth or knowledge.[221] They speak nonsense self-consciously.

Ayer's Criterion of Verification made 'a violent impact upon ethics', Iris would later write.[222] By mixing the methods of the Vienna circle with the British empiricist tradition, Ayer had created a deadly potion: Mary described it as 'pure weedkiller'.[223] In the eighteenth century David Hume had used the empiricist method of refusing to deduce statements of value from statements of fact to critique the repressive Christian morality of the Calvinistic Church of Scotland.[224] His was a targeted attack on dogma and humbug; and a refusal to accept that how things *ought to be* can be derived from how things *are*; Ayer's was an indiscriminate attack on the very idea of moral philosophy.[225]

Though Idealists and Realists disagreed on the structure of reality, they never doubted that moral judgements like 'Friendship is good' or 'Stealing is wrong' made sense. They never doubted that human beings are gifted with the capacity to discover moral truth, and that such discovery is of profound importance to human life. They agreed that there was more to reality than could be measured and observed by the natural scientists. Now Ayer declared that since talk of right and wrong, good and bad, justice and virtue cannot be translated into the language of the empirical sciences, this talk is nonsense. There is nothing deep, transcendent, or valuable to be discovered. There is no such thing as the painstaking and lifelong task of contemplating our purpose and duties, to which philosophy is dedicated, and of seeking to live in accord with those discoveries. Moore's 'non-natural properties' and Ross and Prichard's 'intuitions' were as bunk as the Idealists' Absolute. Ayer's version of 'Moral Subjectivism' – the philosophical view that morality is not objective – held that so-called moral 'judgements' are merely expressions of personal preference, little more than cries of emotion, like cheering or booing. The work of moral philosophy must thus be strictly circumscribed if philosophers are not to fall into the trap of talking nonsense or embarrassing their readers with emotional outbursts. 'A strictly philosophical treatise on ethics', Freddie Ayer prescribed – locked in his room, stamping out the words with two index fingers[226] – 'should therefore make no ethical pronouncements.'[227] The transcendent and mysterious world that inspires doubt and despair, poetry and art, was annihilated with a final badly typed flourish.

Ayer's *Language, Truth and Logic* was a nine-shilling bombshell. 'What comes next?', asked a friend. 'There's no next', replied Freddie, 'Philosophy has come to an end. Finished.' [228]

Despite its popularity with the public, serious discussion at Oxford of Ayer's destructive manifesto was first confined to a small, all-male huddle of his contemporaries which formed in the summer of 1936 and met in Isaiah Berlin's All Souls rooms. They called themselves the Brethren: A. J. Ayer, J. L. Austin, Isaiah Berlin, Stuart Hampshire, Tony Woozley, Donald MacNabb and Donald MacKinnon. Their meetings were intense, noisy and relentless, their debates akin to 'hunting with a pack of hounds'.[229] They were delighted to consign to the dustbin any works that failed to meet their standards of precision and positivistic rigour. 'Nonsense' was used as a deadly weapon. It was not long before the Brethren began to appear with new topics on the lecture lists. Between 1936 and 1939 'Phenomenalism', 'Problems in the Theory of Knowledge', 'Propositions and Events', 'Statements and Induction' appeared for the first time, alongside Prichard's 'The Idea of Moral Obligation' and Collingwood's 'Nature and Mind'.

Only one of the Brethren, Donald MacKinnon, was troubled. A young man of towering physique, MacKinnon attracted animal epithets. Bearheaded; Lion-pawed; Owl-eyed. He spoke with a Scottish growl. Those who attended his lectures on 'The Possibility of Metaphysics' in the winter of 1939, MacKinnon pacing like a creature caged, learnt how unsettled he was by his friend's mission to annihilate philosophy. Donald was deeply religious and saw that Freddie Ayer's attempt to kill off metaphysics placed in peril the very soul of the human animal. '*The elimination of metaphysics is before all else an assault on man in the interests of a method.*'[230] It prepares man for his 'subordination' to the process of empirical science.[231] On the cusp of a fully mechanised world war, MacKinnon feared the ethical and religious implications of that subordination.

As the trickle of Jewish-German refugees appearing on the pavements of Oxford became a steady stream, Ayer's battle-cry began to be heard in the junior common rooms and the classrooms.[232] Mary and Iris arrived at Somerville's gates, to find themselves among 'a whole generation of undergraduates . . . excited to find that all they needed to do if they wanted to refute some inconvenient doctrine was to say loudly and firmly "I simply don't understand that" or "But what could that possibly mean?".'[233] The kind of curiosity and bewilderment that had led Mary, Iris and Elizabeth to philosophy had been decreed a sign of embarrassing naivety. 'I don't understand that' was no longer the beginning of a philosophical conversation but the end of one. The Idealists' and Realists' mysterious certainty that many of life's most important questions fall outside the remit of the empirical sciences was viewed as an outdated dogmatism. Thousands of years of human endeavour to contemplate the significance of human life and ethics was a long episode of meaningless chatter. That this declaration had been made at a moment in world history when serious thinking about ethical life was so evidently needed, made it all the more distressing to the old men whom Ayer had declared extinct.

The Realist Prichard (aged sixty-eight) and Platonist H.W.B. Joseph (seventy-two) were overheard in Blackwell's bookshop complaining that Ayer's book had ever found a publisher.[234] The Humean H. H. Price (thirty-eight), who was more sympathetic than most, agreed that Ayer was 'a young man in a hurry'.[235] For Gilbert Murray (seventy), Ayer lacked reverence.[236] Father Martin D'Arcy (forty-eight), celebrity priest and philosopher of love, called Ayer the 'most dangerous man in Oxford'[237] and wrote a damning review in which he thanked Mr Ayer 'for showing us how modern philosophers can fiddle and play tricks while the world burns'.[238] After finishing the review, he threw his copy on the fire.[239] Hegelian G. R. G. Mure (forty-three) raged that in Ayer's hands the British empiricist tradition was 'reduced from naiveté to absurdity'.[240] A young Peter (P. F.) Strawson, who came up in 1937, read the book in 'one absorbed sitting' in St Peter's Hall garden, but when one of Sandie Lindsay's undergraduates brought it to a tutorial, the older man dropped it out of the window.[241]

A Last Word from the Idealists

As Mary and Iris stuffed envelopes with Isobel Henderson for the Lindsay campaign, unaware that the philosophical tide was turning around them, the ailing Idealist Waynflete Professor Robin (R. G.) Collingwood (Isobel's former tutor) was aboard the motor vessel *Alcinous*, somewhere in the

Indian Ocean, en route to Java. He had recently suffered a stroke and hoped that the trip on the Dutch cargo ship would prove restorative to his health. In an outdoor study, rigged up for him by the captain, he was penning *An Essay on Metaphysics*.[242]

'The importance of Mr. Ayer's work . . . lies in the fact that he has not only made the mistake, he has also refuted it', he wrote, with a smile. 'The error here takes an exacerbated form, committing public suicide like the legendary scorpion in a ring of fire.' It is Ayer's claim that '[a]ny proposition which cannot be verified by appeal to observed facts is a pseudo-proposition'; and from this Ayer draws the conclusion that since metaphysical propositions are 'pseudo-propositions', they are therefore nonsense.[243] But, writes Collingwood, metaphysics is not expressed in what Ayer calls 'propositions' – fully analysed statements that can be individually verified. Metaphysics is an attempt to understand the transcendent background to human life, against which individual propositions may be verified by observation and scientific investigation.

'I write these words sitting on the deck of a ship'; his pen moves across the page. 'I lift my eyes and see a piece of string – a line, I must call it at sea – stretched more or less horizontally above me. I find myself thinking "that is a clothes-line".' But this single proposition, 'that is a clothes-line', cannot be verified by observation. A minute examination of the string, a scientific investigation of its parts, cannot reveal its truth, because 'that is a clothes-line' means, in part: 'it was put there to hang washing on'.[244] And this at once situates the object against a vast, rationally structured background of human life and history – a background that contains clothes and baths and soap, hygiene and standards of taste, ideas about cleanliness and smell and beauty, and reasons and motives and desires. This transcendent background, the reality that surrounds us, is the subject matter of metaphysics, and without it Ayer's favoured propositions are left, like the clothes-line, hanging in the air. Collingwood saw in Ayer's suicide note a death sentence for logical positivism and Realism alike.

Before setting sail, on the eve of the by-election, Collingwood had written a brief note to his old friend Lindsay – both men had been tutees of Boars Hill socialist philosopher Edgar Frederick Carritt. Lindsay himself had tried a modest defence on the part of the Idealists in his 1924 Presidential Address to the Aristotelian Society, 'What Does the Mind Construct?' Our world, he says, is filled with *entia rationis*: artefacts like maps and models and pictures, arrangements of symbols on paper, successions of sounds in spoken language. We are creatures who make things to serve our purposes of knowing, and those creations are 'as much part of the physical world as the things they represent'.[245] A Realism that insists that the knower is distinct from the known, and that reality and mind have no common structure, cannot be correct.

'My dear Lindsay', Collingwood wrote, 'I am leaving for the East tomorrow but I cannot go without sending you my deepest good wishes for your success in your candidature. I do not think that the country has ever in all its history passed through a graver crisis than that in which it is now involved.'[246]

CHAPTER 2

Learning in Wartime

OXFORD

SEPTEMBER 1939–JUNE 1942

The War Begins & the Young Men Leave – Miss Philippa Bosanquet Arrives
at Somerville – Pacifism & Elizabeth Writes Her First Pamphlet – The Four
Friends Meet – An Old Man: H. H. Price on Hume – A Refugee:
Heinz Cassirer on Kant – A Woman: Mary Glover on Plato –
A Conscientious Objector: Donald MacKinnon & the Metaphysical
Animal – Our Four Unfashionable Philosophers All Get Firsts

The War Begins & the Young Men Leave

On 1 September 1939, Iris Murdoch was lying in a field on a Gloucestershire farm. She was a guest of the Brüderhof, a pacifist Christian community that had been expelled from Nazi Germany. It was the last stop of her summer tour with the Magpie Players, a troupe of Oxford undergraduates travelling around the south of England performing ballads and comic pieces to raise money for the Oxford University Refugee Appeal Fund.[1] That morning, just before sunrise, the first Luftwaffe bomb had descended though low-lying cloud on to Warsaw. Neville Chamberlain had thought Czechoslovakia a 'far-off country whose name, in his view, most English people probably could not spell'; but, observed Mary, they could certainly spell 'Poland'.[2] The declaration of war turned 70,000 Germans and Austrians living in Britain, including the Brüderhof, into 'enemy aliens'. Internment tribunals would impose further classification: (A) To be interned; (B) To be restricted but not interned; (C) To be neither restricted nor interned.[3] The Magpies abandoned their costumes and scenery and headed back to Oxford. Skirting over the Berkshire Downs, in the back seat of a yellow sportscar, '[g]rey-blue clouds & streaks of green & pink sky wreathed the horizon', Iris found it 'intensely exhilarating'.[4]

Iris arrived back at Oxford tanned, invigorated and pleased to have raised much-needed funds for the city's increasing numbers of European refugees. Mary, by contrast, returned dusty and deflated, and doubtful that she had achieved anything useful. Working as a volunteer in some forgotten division of the Labour Party, she had spent her summer tasked with trying to work out what Fifth Columnists were intending to do. Rather than conducting clandestine operations and meetings with the suspects themselves in the pubs of Westminster (as Iris might have), she treated the task like a large-scale history project and had spent the summer in a dark corner of the British Museum Library under a heap of old copies of The Times.[5]

*

Almost 1,000 fewer men were in residence that Michaelmas Term in 1939.[6] Conscription applied first to men aged twenty and twenty-one. The Anscombe twins and Mary's brother Hugh were among those conscripted, along with the young men for whom Freddie Ayer's destructive empiricism and aggressive incomprehension were a model of philosophical sophistication. The Oxford Joint Recruiting Board (in the Clarendon Building on Broad Street) invited all other undergraduate and resident postgraduates under twenty-five to volunteer. Of some 3,000 men who were able, 2,362 came forward.[7] Perhaps some did so thinking that it might improve their employment prospects after the war – such was the calculation of the schoolmaster in Philip Larkin's precocious novel *Jill*. But most had fathers and grandfathers who had served in the First World War, and they saw it as their duty to hang up their gowns. Knowing that Neville Chamberlain's promise of peace was an empty one, many had joined a volunteer corps the previous winter, Frank Thompson and Michael Foot among them. Michael's father, Brigadier Richard Foot, had sent for him in that pre-war limbo. He didn't like what he was reading in the papers: another war was coming, hadn't Michael better join the show?[8]

Before the boys left, Iris set about gathering up the 'literary remains of all her friends': with a combination of jest and juvenile ambition, she declared that she was 'going to make lots of money with a slim anthology when war ends'. Enthusiasm for this project was mixed. Noel Eldridge (whom Iris had met through her student journalism) told his mother, 'I've refused to give her anything yet, as I'm holding out for a cash payment!', while nevertheless commending the sanity of 'the Murdoch'.[9] Michael Foot, in a flourish of bohemian youth, made Iris his literary executor.[10]

Frank Thompson, a talented linguist, was recruited to Phantom, a secret regiment set up to gather and share intelligence between allied forces. They were more like cat burglars than soldiers and would be treated as such by both sides.[11] Allied forces viewed them with suspicion, operating as they did backstage in the theatre of war and outside ordinary chains of command. If captured by the enemy, they were almost certain to be executed. Frank left Oxford in love with Iris, his 'green-haired Sibyl': 'I attach importance to this epithet. With this I feel I have trapped your personality. A good green, mind you – none of your ghoulish pre-Raphaelite stuff. Hair that flows naturally in dreamy shamrock tresses. That is your ego materialised in hair.'[12] Before he had left they had visited Boars Hill together, walking up through the field footpaths, over stiles and around horses and cows.[13] He wrote her a sonnet, 'To Irushka at the Coming of War'.

If you should hear my name among those killed
Say you have lost a friend, half man, half boy
Who, if the years had spared him, might have built within
Courage, strength and harmony.
Uncouth and garrulous, with tangled mind
Seething with warm ideas of truth and light,
His help was worthless. Yet had fate been kind,
He might have learned to steel himself and fight.
He thought he loved you. By what right could he
Claim such high praise, who only felt his frame
Riddled with burning lead, and failed to see
His own false pride behind the barrel's flame?
Say you have lost a friend, and then forget.
Stronger and truer ones are with you yet.[14]

Once he had left, he remained for Iris as 'half man, half boy'. From Oxford, she wrote to her 'Frank, darling' ('brave & beloved', 'wild & gentle chevalier') of a faded and dreamlike city.[15] Together, on paper, they wove a fantasy, fixing themselves in the romantic idealism of 1939 and casting themselves as archetypal lovers in a shape-shifting epic Greek, Arthurian, Shakespearean tragedy.

Nick Crosbie joined the Navy. 'I have drifted a long way from Oxford and Oxford life,' he wrote to Mary from HMS *St Vincent*, the Royal Naval training camp on the south coast. 'It is amazing how the human organism will adapt itself . . . Still more amazing is the way we have got used to turning night into day.'[16]

Male students arriving at Oxford were permitted to defer their call-up in order to complete shortened courses. The 'Eighteens' and 'Nineteens' arrived, unpacked their suitcases and donned their gowns, but were to leave after just one or two years. This created the uncanny impression for Iris and Mary, on a four-year course, that they themselves were prematurely old. 'Oxford is not exactly a front line city – but in its slow and pensive way it is changing, in tune with a changing world. The students are all younger – rushing, if they are men, through incomplete and inadequate one-year courses', Iris explained in the Badminton School magazine: 'the University is a strange interlude between school and the war'.[17] C. S. Lewis (another former tutee of Boars Hill's E. F. Carritt), addressed the fears and doubts of enrolling students from the pulpit: 'If men had postponed the search for knowledge and beauty until they were secure, the search would never have begun. We are mistaken when we compare war with "normal life"', he told them. Humans 'propound mathematical theorems in beleaguered cities, conduct metaphysical arguments in condemned cells, make jokes on scaffolds, discuss the last new poem while advancing to the walls of Quebec, and comb their hair at Thermopylae. This is not *panache*; it is our nature.'[18]

While some women undergraduates did join up, it was not encouraged. Mary was shocked to hear from Iris that a fellow Somervillian was 'throwing up the sponge, ie leaving Oxford to serve Her Country'. Iris thought it 'sheer lunacy'.[19] They were told 'quite early in the war that women might well make themselves more useful by finishing their courses than by enlisting at once'.[20] Helen Darbishire, Somerville's Principal, wanting her students to be useful straight away, invited tutors and undergraduates to meet in her room to knit squares that would be sewn together into warm blankets for soldiers far from home. She was exasperated by the shapeless emanations that fell from the needles of her friend Vera Farnell: Vera was an excellent dean but she 'couldn't knit for toffee'.[21] Soon Helen confiscated Vera's needles and assigned her the task of reading aloud from Henry James to keep up the knitters' spirits.[22]

While in the women's colleges the stodgy, the middling and the wild of Somerville dining room remained differentiated by colour and cut (beige, navy, red, fur and silk), Iris complained that 'every month batches of men fade away into khaki'.[23] 'I continue my work in a faded, disintegrating, warminded, uneasy, evacuee-haunted Oxford that likes me not', she wrote to David Hicks, an Oxford friend, three years her senior and now with the British Council in Egypt. 'Everyone is younger & far more hysterical.'[24] Even the boys with whom they had first come up seemed not to age in memory: 'It's harder still to think of you as an independent three dimensional entity developing parallel to myself in time.'[25] Their existence began to seem fantastic. 'I always imagine you with a thousand miles of sky behind you – that individual in the room at Merton doesn't seem to be you at all', she told Paddy O'Regan, an admirer who had joined the Air Force.[26] She buoyed comrades up with newsy humour. Sometimes she spoke to their fears directly. 'That was a sad letter – I'm very sorry you feel so low'; 'it's a hellish feeling'; 'you can hardly avoid this sort of unhappiness in this bloody sort of world'; 'The gods go with you & send you brighter days.'[27]

Miss Philippa Bosanquet Arrives at Somerville

Into this uncanny scene stepped Miss Philippa Bosanquet. It was now her turn to stand, hesitant, before the Somerville College gates. Gloved and belted, she and her elegant tailoring and fine manners gave off an aura of unapproachability. Her face was a little foxy.[28] Throughout her life people would often take her to be aloof, but in fact she suffered the double disability of prosopagnosia (an inability to recognise faces) and deafness in one ear.[29] She was adept at placing herself to favour her 'good' side.

Hardly believing it herself ('It was remarkable really'), Miss Bosanquet was to study the Greekless degree of Philosophy, Politics and Economics, or 'Modern Greats' as it had come to be called.[30] It had been introduced in 1920, and while some had argued that the degree would be 'a soft option for the weaker man',[31] many recognised that the 'weaker man' was often a woman. PPE was a natural choice for a girl like Philippa, who lacked Greek ('I didn't know the Greek alphabet, not even the first letters')[32] and wanted to do 'something theoretical'.[33] The degree would provide 'the intellectual discipline of Philosophy' combined with training in history and economics that would prepare its students for 'business, the Civil Service, or public life'.[34] In 1936, Helen Darbishire and principals from the other women's colleges had written to the editor of *The Times* to object to the exclusion of women from the consular and diplomatic services. Their PPE students were among the 'ablest' of any at the university and their interests carried them naturally into international affairs. The state needed 'the best brains of the nation', without limitation 'on whatever ground'.[35]

Philippa had been raised in a social milieu many layers higher than Mary, Iris or Elizabeth. She was the granddaughter of US President Grover Cleveland; her mother Esther was the first (and to date only) presidential baby to be born in the White House. In Switzerland in the summer of 1915, a year after Esther's New York 'debut' and a minor scandal of a rumoured then denied engagement, Esther had met Captain Bosanquet of the Coldstream Guards.[36] The pair married in Westminster Abbey and settled in Kirkleatham Old Hall, a sixteen-bedroom mansion set in fifteen acres of Yorkshire countryside.[37] There, Philippa and her sister Marion ran with the Zetland Hunt.[38] As young as eight, she rode out on her own in all weather, something that troubled her in later life ('No-one seems to have thought to ask "Does this child know how to ride?" . . . . What <u>did</u> Mummy think

about all day?').[39] When she contracted abdominal tuberculosis around the age of eight, the cure involved her sleeping on a balcony for a year, right through the North Yorkshire winter.[40] Unbeknownst to her at the time, the tuberculosis left her infertile.[41] Philippa and Marion looked to their nanny for the attention that children need to flourish. ('Something about this total lack of care left me . . . fearful for ever'.)[42]

Philippa had her own word to conjure up the peculiar irrationality of the life her upbringing had prepared her for – 'dementing'.[43] Among its dementing prohibitions were appearing on the ground floor in nightclothes, wearing pearls before midday and drinking dark beverages – sherry excepted.[44] Oloroso, Fino, Manzanilla, Amontillado. She knew that '[i]f you're called "Lady Mary" somebody, you've got to be terribly grand, much grander than being called "Lady Murray"'. ('I hated it, this sort of knowledge: I can't help it, I know this.')[45]

While Philippa could navigate upper-class mores by instinct, she was perhaps less well prepared to speak on the topics of politics, philosophy or economics. The speech of young upper-class women between the wars was carefully prescribed and monitored, with the expression of opinions on, say, the League of Nations, the Treaty of Versailles and Divine Foreknowledge very much beyond the pale. Debutantes were expected to 'keep up the conversation' with eligible young men but to do so without 'acquiring the reputation for being intelligent' – a reputation disastrous to marriage prospects. The Duchess of Westminster advised: 'two good subjects if you are stuck for conversation are ghosts and the royal family'.[46] Any whiff of bookishness might prove fatal. Spectacles were a complete disaster. Apart from a brief spell at St George's School, Ascot, Philippa was taught by governesses who, unlike Elizabeth's mother's male tutors, left her ignorant of whether the Romans came before or after the Greeks.[47] 'I had no education,' Philippa would later insist.[48]

As she grew older Philippa felt increasingly sure that the norms that had structured her early life had not been akin to those of a benevolent gardener, creating a nurturing and protective walled nursery, but something rather damaging and certainly not conducive to flourishing. Her upbringing had not left obvious injury – aside, that is, from the partial deafness caused by a botched operation on the kitchen table and long-term health problems that were a legacy of tuberculosis – but it had taught her unusual self-reliance, and left her 'pathologically discreet'. To Iris, she was 'morally tough', yet 'subtle' – a 'sphinx'.[49] Throughout her life Philippa would return again and again to the idea of happiness, a question mark over her early years at Kirkleatham. Was happiness a feeling, or was it the name we give to a life lived well? Could a person feel happy though their life was not a happy one? Could things happen to a person that would put the possibility of happiness for ever beyond their grasp? She was still asking these questions in her eighties.[50]

When Philippa won a place at Somerville, Esther, the White House baby, needed consoling: 'Never mind, dear: she doesn't *look* clever!'[51] It is likely that this kind of depreciation, which must have formed a backdrop to Philippa's childhood, had an effect on her self-conception. A constant refrain in later interviews is 'I'm not terribly clever; quite intuitive, but not very clever.'[52] She would live in expectation of being 'sent away from Somerville for incompetence in philosophy'.[53]

At nineteen, she thought of herself in full revolt against her upbringing. Though not a member of the Communist Party, she was 'very left wing', and had picked the college after hearing that Lady Margaret Hall (for Rich Girls) was 'socially OK and that Somerville wasn't'. 'So I said "Somerville, please, for me".'[54] After a correspondence course, she had a stint in Oxford, where she stayed in digs and received private coaching.[55] At the same time as Classics tutor Mildred Hartley was cajoling Iris and Mary through Mods, she 'struggled, against all odds' to teach Miss Bosanquet 'enough Latin to get through the First Public Examination for P.P.E'.[56] A girl who by her own account 'couldn't do mathematics',[57] Philippa would race to complete, after two terms, prelims in logic and mathematics in preparation for final papers in 'Statistical Methods' and 'Principles of Economics'. In politics, she would grapple with 'Political History 1871–1914' and 'Political Institutions'. For PPE students, philosophy began in the seventeenth century, with Descartes.[58]

As Philippa stood on the Woodstock Road that October 1939, her gas mask on her hip, a nagging feeling in her stomach that her offer of a place had been an error, and a scattering of indistinguishable faces on the college lawns before her, she might have been expected to feel rather hopeless. But she did not. She was fearlessly determined to become educated, to make up for a childhood of 'dementing' conversations about the royal family. Deep happiness seemed at last in her sights. While Somerville, like the rest of Oxford, transformed around her she perhaps felt, for the first time, that she was precisely where she belonged.

Oxford was unmistakably at war. The cloistered quads of colleges no longer offered scholars refuge from ordinary life: their gardens teemed with men in uniform; hospital huts and water-storage tanks were planted on the lawns; one could soon 'Dig for Victory' in previously manicured flower beds. In the *Oxford Magazine*, once unimaginable notices could be read. Blood was to be donated at the New Bodleian Library – 'it does not matter if the donors have had malaria'.[59] 'Spotters' were trained to give warning of a daylight bombing raid. Work should not be discontinued for sirens, but lectures and other engagements involving movement from one building to another should not be started until after the warning period ceased.[60] Spaces previously reserved for learned endeavour were repurposed into instruments of war. Tweedy academics poring over the Bodleian's treasures and manuscripts were replaced by glossy Whitehall civil servants generating legal letters and Cabinet briefings and Red Cross volunteers sorting books for the Prisoners' Library.[61] The Foreign Office's 'intelligence department' moved into (brain-powered) Balliol while the Ministry of Transport dined on hare soup in Merton. From St John's (the wealthiest college), the Ministry of Food regulated food prices.[62]

The women's colleges did not escape disruption. St Hugh's was converted into a hospital and brick huts were erected as ward blocks on top of Miss

Rogers's beautiful lawn. Part of Somerville was taken over to provide wards for the Radcliffe Infirmary[63] and for a time there were fears that Somerville's 150 undergraduates would be transferred to New College to form a 'Mixed Party'. Helen Darbishire eventually found a less troubling solution to the incoming hospital beds: Mary, along with thirty others whose rooms were in West, was ejected to make space for nurses, and replanted in the much grander, more bucolic, Lady Margaret Hall.[64] Passing Philippa at the Somerville entrance: patients, beds and medical supplies in; armchairs, library books and undergraduates out.

Lady Margaret Hall's enormous college gardens run down to the west bank of the Cherwell. On two occasions when Mary stayed out past curfew, rather than climbing back in over the wall, she crossed High Bridge to the river's east side, slid into the murky water and paddled in: 'just to be different'.[65] In the summer, she swam in the river each morning before breakfast. Dripping across the lawn on her way back for a soft-boiled egg, she may have spotted Elisabeth Blochmann, former Professor of Social and Theoretical Pedagogy at the Academy of Education at Halle an der Saale, fighting gallantly with the college bees.[66] An expert in women's education, and former lover of Martin Heidegger, Blochmann (whose name was listed in

Hitler's 'Black Book'), had arrived in Oxford around the same time as Eduard Fraenkel and had taken on the college hives as a contribution to the war effort. ('The endeavour was disastrous; bees and keeper hated each other equally and it was Miss Deneke [the tutor in German] in a gas mask and veil who had to come to the rescue when the stinging was intolerable.')[67]

Iris meanwhile, together with Jean Coutts and two other girls, was moved to 43 Park Town[68] – a corner house with a large copper beech just a few hundred yards upstream from Lady Margaret Hall. The group were happy to escape the college dining hall, at least in the evenings, though they still congregated at Somerville for lunch, to chew on whatever the beleaguered cooks could conjure up. The meagreness and inventiveness increased as the war progressed in proportion to the strictness of rationing. Butter, sugar, bacon, ham, cheese, jam, syrup, tea and margarine were all to go on coupon.[69] Electric light too was in short supply. At the outbreak of war, it was decreed that the whole island of Britain was to be wiped out from the sky at night. College windows were covered with blackout fabric stretched on frames. Cars and buses were rendered invisible, headlights switched off. A 20 mph speed limit was in place, but motorists had to intuit their speed as their speedometers were invisible in the dark.[70] The driver had little chance of spotting a pedestrian who had strayed off the pavement. Occasionally a luminous synthetic flower might appear in the blackness, attached to a collar or a coat or a dog; these, along with glow-in-the-dark armbands, walking sticks and fascinators crept into wartime apparel. The *Daily Telegraph* suggested that its readers carry a white Pekingese. And the blackout posed other dangers.[71] 'What could be done to protect young men not only from the threat of bombs but the solicitations of prostitutes in the darkness?' the Master of Pembroke College asked the University Council in 1939.[72] Perhaps for him the full moon, dilated on the swampy rivulets of Oxford, gave some reassurance – then vision could briefly replace the touch and sound that otherwise guided wayward undergraduates home, nipping in and out through unlit doors and over invisible walls.

Pacifism & Elizabeth Writes Her First Pamphlet

After his brief cameo during the by-election as leader of the youth, the war had seen Sandie Lindsay return to a more natural role, as chairman of the

Oxford Joint Recruiting Board. Undergraduates who had once canvassed for him as reds and pinks now stood before him as proto-servicemen.[73]

For a sizeable minority of Oxford's undergraduates and dons, the question of whether to fight was more fraught than we might imagine, knowing now what we do of Hitler's regime. It was not just Quakers who saw pacifism as a fundamental tenet of Christianity; many in the Church of England did so too. Mary's brother Hugh had been arguing with his friends for at least a year prior to joining up.[74] Richard Hare, standing in the middle of the back row below, struggled to decide.

Richard had come up to study Mods and Greats at the same time as Elizabeth.[75] Many of his friends, Anglicans like him, were pacifists. He gave himself twenty-four hours to grapple with the dilemma, hoping moral intuition, in which the Realists Ross and Prichard placed so much confidence, might reveal where his duty lay; but in the end the decision felt more like a guess: he would fight.[76]

Peter Geach, Elizabeth's fiancé, would have been called up to display his conscience before the Recruiting Committee. He and Elizabeth were both members of Pax, a lay Catholic peace movement (though not a pacifist one) formed in 1936. The pair attended seminars and talks at Blackfriars on St Giles' (the home of a community of black-habited Dominican friars that had arrived in Oxford some seven centuries earlier). There they heard theologians discuss the Catholic conditions for a just war, as set out in the writings of St Thomas Aquinas.[77] Elizabeth was also taking tutorials on

Aquinas with the prodigiously intense Victor White, the assistant editor of the Dominicans' in-house journal.

According to Aquinas, for a war to be just, seven conditions must be met. Four concern the circumstances under which it is just to fight *a war*; three ask whether it is just to fight *a particular war*. Once war was declared, Elizabeth adopted the 'judicial air' that had carried her through the mock trial at Sydenham. Together with Norman Daniel (a History undergraduate at St John's; later a scholar of Islam), she set to work producing a short pamphlet examining the justice of the war. Elizabeth wrote the first half. They had it printed and sold for sixpence in bookshops in Oxford and London.

Even a casual reader would have been struck by the insurrectionist tone of Elizabeth's first sentence: 'In these days the authorities claim the right to control not only the policy of the nation but also the actions of every individual within it; and their claim has the support of a large section of the people of the country, and of a peculiar force of emotion.'

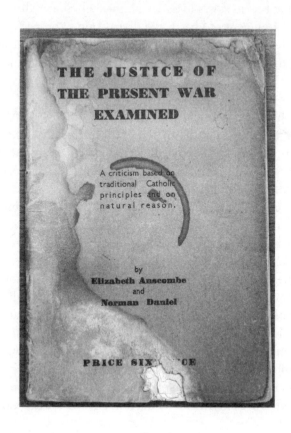

THE JUSTICE OF
THE PRESENT WAR
EXAMINED

A criticism based on traditional Catholic principles and on natural reason.

by
Elizabeth Anscombe
and
Norman Daniel

PRICE SIXPENCE

Elizabeth warns her reader: emotions must not 'blind men to their duty of considering carefully, before they act, the justice of the things they propose to do'.[78]

For Catholics, following Aquinas, a particular war is just only if: the intentions of the government are just; the means to be taken are moral; the outcome is likely to be on balance good rather than evil. But, she urged, none of these conditions are met by the war Chamberlain had declared. The government's intentions are not just because they are 'unlimited': 'They have not said: "When justice is done on points A, B and C, then we will stop fighting"' but have 'talked about "sweeping away everything that Hitlerism stands for" and about "building a new order in Europe".'[79] On means, she noted that the government had not given a promise that German civilians would not be bombed, starved or subjected to wicked reprisals. Rather, they had promised that they wouldn't be unless the Germans tried such things against British civilians. On the outcome, she said she had no confidence that the good would outweigh the evil. She predicted the 'death of men, the curtailment of liberty, the destruction of property, the diminution of culture, the obscuring of judgement by passion and interest, the neglect of truth and charity'.[80] As she was preparing the pamphlet Elizabeth's father, Allen Wells Anscombe, died, suddenly and unexpectedly at just fifty-four.[81]

The pamphlet's life was short but notorious. In May 1940, only a few months after it appeared in bookshops, it attracted the attention of the Roman Catholic Archbishop of Birmingham, Thomas Leighton Williams. He wrote to the prior of Blackfriars: they 'had no right to call it "Catholic" without getting an *imprimatur*'. The pair were forced to withdraw all the unsold copies – they thought the demand 'wrong and unreasonable',[82] but the authority of the Catholic archbishop was a matter of fact.

Peter Geach perhaps gave a version of Elizabeth's argument to Lindsay's Recruiting Committee, when called upon to explain his objection to joining up. But he may also have refused to fight for King and Country on the rather surprising ground that he did not recognise the English monarch, George VI, as king. In 1937, in the midst of the constitutional crisis caused by Edward VIII's abdication (in order to marry the American divorcee Wallis Simpson), 'pink-cheeked' Peter committed high treason by declaring a new king.[83] Not the recognised heir, Edward's brother Albert (King George VI), but the former Crown Prince Rupprecht of Bavaria. To a small crowd of 'Jacobite rebels' at Martyrs memorial, just outside Balliol College, Peter declared that the sixty-seven-year-old German was England's rightful king and the direct descendant of the beheaded King Charles I. 'We hope for the restoration of a true monarchy with the same power which the Stuarts had before 1688', Peter told a journalist, who couldn't quite believe that the protest was not an elaborate prank. During the five-month gap between Edward's abdication and the coronation of a new king, Peter claimed to be coordinating an armed rebellion from his rooms in Trinity College. The *Daily Boston Globe* printed his warning: 'I'm afraid there will have to be some violence – though a lot can be done by propaganda. If the King cannot be restored except by bloodshed, blood must be shed.'[84]

Whatever his case before the Recruiting Committee, Peter would spend his war years as a lumberjack in timber production, one of the industries hardest hit by the sudden absence of men. His unit of 'conchies' worked alongside prisoners of war, displaced persons and, later, 'lumberjills'. Peter picked up Italian from the prisoners, reading Dante in the original. He learnt Polish, his mother's tongue, from Casimir Lewy, later to be G. E. Moore's literary executor.[85]

The Four Friends Meet

Surrounded by underaged boys, over-aged men and growing numbers of refugee scholars, life at Oxford remained structured by the rhythm of Michaelmas, Hilary, Trinity (the three Oxford terms), and by the changing seasons of the year. January 1940, as Mary and Iris entered their final term of Mods, was the coldest since 1895. The Thames froze for eight miles and ice-storms raged in the provinces, snapping telegraph poles and wires. Branches fell; birds were unable to fly for the weight of ice on their wings.[86] Port Meadow, the ancient expanse of common ground a mile north-west of Somerville, flooded and froze, and the whole of Oxford took to the ice – the River Isis now crossed by skaters rather than swimmers. Mary, more at home in the water than on it, broke her ankle and badly sprained her right wrist. She scrawled an only passably legible note to Eduard Fraenkel excusing herself from the *Agamemnon* class.[87] 'Slushy snow and Oxford fog' were her enemies as she spent that term singing Greek declensions in her 'miserably cold' room and 'stumping around with [her] leg in plaster'.[88]

The weather had 'not relaxed in the least' when, in March, she and Iris cycled down Parks Road to the Divinity School, clutching hot-water bottles, to take their exams. At this rare and beautiful site for examinations, Mary looked up at the vaulted ceiling, the hot-water bottle on her lap now stone cold, searching for inspiration.[89]

To Mildred Hartley's credit both passed. Seconds. Onward to Greats.

'[B]y the time I was doing philosophy,' remembered Mary decades later, 'the men had all gone to the war except a few, and there were as many women as men in the classes that I went to. And a lot of them were rather harmless.' More than a quarter of senior university members were absent by the time the war entered its second year. In Mary's words: the men that remained were all 'conscientious objectors or cripples or ordinands'.[90] The young revolutionary Freddie Ayer had joined his former tutor Gilbert Ryle at Sandown Park training ground in Surrey. In November 1940, J. L. Austin departed for training at the military intelligence school in Matlock, Derbyshire.[91] Soon, 'Woozley', 'Hampshire', 'Ayer' and 'Austin' were present only as names in the *Oxford Magazine*. The Brethren, along with their conversation-killing 'I don't understand!', vanished from the classrooms, and while 'Modern Logic' remained on the lecture schedule, taught by refugee scholar Friedrich Waismann, all other traces of Ayer's weedkiller – from 'Phenomenalism' to 'Statements and Induction' – vanished with them.

With the younger dons called up, the older dons, whom it had been Ayer's mission to reduce to silence, found themselves able to speak again. A smattering of articles appeared in learned journals making the case for a return to 'the classical tradition in philosophy'. According to this tradition, 'philosophy is, or at least should be, concerned with the whole conduct of human life', wrote fifty-one-year-old political philosopher Cyril Joad, before criticising those whose 'preoccupation [. . .] is the philosophical analysis of the meaning of sentences'.[92] 'Clarity is not enough', became the unofficial slogan of the fightback. Dorothy Emmet, Sandie Lindsay's former student, began work on a book on the nature of metaphysical thinking.[93] Society needed a '*Weltanschauung*, a unified outlook on the world': we must not 'allow our zeal for "tightening up language" to run away with us', argued the Humean H. H. Price.[94] Recovering their lecture notes from earlier in the decade the Realists and Idealists were free again to speculate from the podium – among them, William Adair Pickard-Cambridge, Edgar Carritt and Leslie Walker, all in their sixties. The emeritus Chair of Philosophy at Reading, and Merton College alumnus, William George de Burgh (born in 1866) was called out of retirement to lecture. Throughout the war,

Father Martin D'Arcy, who had called Ayer the 'most dangerous man in Oxford' and had consigned *Language, Truth and Logic* to the flames, lectured continuously on Aristotle's ethics.

Mary's talk of 'classes' reflects the fact that the German seminar now sat alongside the tutorial and lecture. Close behind Eduard Fraenkel, scholars from all over Europe had found their way on to the pavements of north Oxford and into the lecture listings of the *Oxford Gazette*. 'From the languages being spoken around one', it is as if one were 'inhabiting a bit of old Vienna or some Central European university town', remarked the historian A. L. Rowse.[95] It was sometimes said that you had to speak German to get by in north Oxford.[96] In reality, the community of refugee scholars was highly disparate; they spoke a variety of languages, and were from different cosmopolitan centres, of diverse political persuasions and religions. Some refugees were practising Jews, but most were secular and several were Christian converts.[97] Many were among the greatest names in European scholarship. While pre-war Oxford had been an academic backwater[98] it was now awash with Europe's academic giants, 'elderly German Jews with faun-eyes & Central European scholars with long hair & longer sentences', as Iris observed.[99] Mrs Loisel Palm, a refugee from the Sudetenland, soon opened a *Delikatessen* in the Covered Market to cater for their dietary habits: a discerning array of sausages, as well as her own Sauerkraut.[100]

Flicking through their copies of the *Gazette* at the beginning of Trinity Term 1940, Mary and Iris could have taken a tour of German universities as they were before Hitler, without leaving the half-mile square between New College and Corpus Christi. On Saturday, at 10 a.m., Frankfurt's Fritz Heinemann (another whose name was in Hitler's 'Black Book') lectured on 'Philosophy and Science'.[101] On Monday, would they join Mr F. Waismann (formerly of the Vienna Circle) for the 'Philosophy of Mathematics' or Heidelberg's Raymond Klibansky (also in the 'Black Book') for informal instruction on 'Medieval Philosophy'? On Wednesdays and Fridays, Hamburg's Heinz Cassirer was offering a seminar at noon on 'General Problems in Moral Philosophy'. Thursdays saw Berlin's Kurt Koffka convening a class on the Gestalt psychology he had developed with Max Wertheimer and Wolfgang Köhler. On Fridays, something brand new to Oxford: another Berliner, Richard Walzer, on 'Platonism in Islamic Ethics'.

Mary and Iris met Elizabeth during that first term of Greats, Trinity 1940, over a Somerville wartime lunch. Elizabeth was dining with her friend (and

Iris's flatmate) Jean Coutts, who had just become president of the Jowett Society, Oxford's student philosophy club.[102] Mary was struck by Elizabeth's quiet, beautiful voice as the four fledgling philosophers discussed Plato's Forms – strange and unworldly-seeming objects, changeless and eternal, outside space and time, and quite separate from the world of refugees and rationing and air-raid sirens. Mary found herself in sympathy with Plato. Perhaps she was captivated by the elegant solution to her Protagorean bath-time puzzle that these strange objects offered. If there is a realm of Forms, then an individual does not have to construct the material world out of fragments of private sense data. Rather, our souls reach out to something objective and communal that explains patterns of similarity and difference, such as the form of *Whiteness*. Likewise, there must be *Goodness* itself, so Mary thought, and *Man* behind the many particular examples of goodness and men, binding them together and giving them their essential nature. But Elizabeth pressed her: what sort of 'behindness' is that? What does it mean to say Goodness exists and is there?[103] When lunch ended they all went to Jean's room and spent the afternoon burrowing on.[104] 'This woman's worth cultivating,' thought Mary as she listened to Elizabeth.[105]

The conversation, now begun, continued in the evenings in their lodgings or college rooms, sometimes over a haphazard assembly of bread, oranges and sardines.[106] Occasionally, they might have found themselves together in queues at one of the wartime British restaurants in town, or at the Lyons' tea room or the Taj Mahal. Such queues were long and 'sometimes led to quite hard feelings'.[107] Better luck was had by those who got up early and cycled to the cake factory in Summertown; 'celestial cake' was more than appropriate fare for any student of Plato, weary of sardines. Elizabeth sometimes took matters into her own hands; Mary was once alarmed to see her take two eggs at lunch instead of her allowance of one.[108]

Philippa and Mary also became friends that term, when Philippa, along with two other 'handsome and lively people', was added to her classes.[109] Gradually, each of the trio emerged as their own person. One was Daphne Vandepeer, like Philippa there to study PPE. The second was Classics undergraduate Ruth Collingwood, the daughter of philosopher R. G. Collingwood (it was she who had been the History tutor Isobel Henderson's bridesmaid). He had returned from Jakarta and was delivering lectures on 'Nature and Mind' on Tuesdays and Thursdays at Schools. Mary judged Philippa, who was 'the tallest and most handsome', to be 'the most rewarding' of the three,[110] and she determined to collect her as a friend. They began to see each other regularly.[111] Philippa was a little afraid of Mary, fearing that her scholarly friend would discover, and be appalled by, her ignorance. In return, Mary felt rather in awe of her: 'Philippa seemed to me a little formidable – her standards, I felt, would be very high, could I hope to meet them?'[112] When Mary visited Philippa's home one holiday the aura at the Old Hall in Kirkleatham stunned her. In Philippa's world, 'Girls simply did not go to college'.[113] But in Mary's family girls simply did. Mary's godmother, Bessie Callender, had been among the first set of girls to take a degree at Durham University in 1894. Her mother's sister, Aunt Maud, had studied English at Lady Margaret Hall, while her father's sister, Aunt Jane, had read History at Girton in Cambridge.[114] And while Mary's progressive childhood had been filled with intergenerational friendships, and bonds of affection that took no account of age or hierarchy, Philippa had been among the legion of upper-class children presented to their parents at tea-time, washed and brushed, and for an hour at most. It was within the limits of this ritualised setting that parental feeling was formulaically expressed. Philippa's first philosophical thought as a child was 'when a grown-up used the words "If I were you", and I wondered how we should notice the difference if she *were* me!'[115]

Like all great love stories, there are competing tales about how Iris and Philippa's friendship began. In one of Iris's versions, the pair met almost as soon as Philippa arrived, so that by the time Iris was sitting her Mods exams next to Mary, in the freezing Divinity Hall, her reality was already being reassembled by the presence of the tough and subtle Miss Bosanquet. Iris remembered 'the joy at which I found her, so brilliant, so beautiful. We talked about philosophy, and everything.'[116] Philippa told a different beginning. Her first memory of Iris was as a candidate for president of the Somerville Junior Common Room Committee. She nominated an alternative candidate: despite being 'very left wing', she found Communists a nuisance and feared that Iris would call meetings unnecessarily. Iris did not win – it seems her charm was not completely unassailable.[117] In a third story, they did not meet until the very end of their time at Oxford – in circumstances we will hear about later. A mix of the three seems most likely: they saw each other among mutual friends and across dining tables in the normal sort of way; but the meeting that really mattered came later and cast its light backwards to infuse what had gone before with a special kind of significance.

The beginning of Philippa, Mary, Iris and Elizabeth's philosophical friendship coincided with the end of the so-called Phoney War and the start of a disturbing and destabilising thirty months, during which the immediate anxieties at home (caused by loved ones away fighting, food scarcity, bombing raids and evacuations) were compounded by the ever-present, but unimaginable, prospect of invasion and defeat. On 10 May 1940, German troops invaded Belgium and began an apparently unstoppable and bloody advance west and south. By the end of Trinity Term, the fighting in western Europe was over: Belgium, the Netherlands, Luxembourg and France had all surrendered to the Nazis. The *Manchester Guardian* reported the evacuation of 340,000 British troops from Dunkirk as a miracle, but with the German armies now less than thirty miles from the south coast of England, the British public were told to prepare for an invasion.

British policy, and British attitudes, towards 'enemy aliens' abruptly changed. Neighbours with foreign accents and those who were slack about the blackout became suspected Fifth Columnists. At the start of the war, Fritz Heinemann, Lorenzo Minio-Paluello, Friedrich Waismann, Heinz Cassirer and Richard Walzer had all been classified (C), 'To be neither restricted nor interned'. But now they were all arrested.[118] The government ordered church bells to be quietened: they were to be rung only to signal an invasion. Civilians looked up to the clouds, expecting to see German paratroopers, disguised as milkmen or nuns, floating down to earth.

In September, the sky over England's southern coast filled instead with planes, and the Luftwaffe bombing campaign began. In Oxford, evacuees from London and Birmingham filled the pavements. The Platonist H.W.B. Joseph sat on the city's evacuation committee and recorded in his diary the challenges of finding homes for the arrivals from London; in the first month of the Blitz, Oxford's population increased by up to 15,000.[119] Children and teachers from nineteen London schools arrived.[120] 'Official' evacuees (estimated at 7,500) were joined by the 'self-evacuated'.[121] A disused cinema became a temporary billet, and colleges functioned as camps. University College's Second Quad was 'festooned with babies' nappies' and its seventeenth-century hall 'resound[ed] to the screeching of hungry children'.[122] Cockney patter mixed with the halting English of the German refugees. 'The town is full of evacuees, civil servants and friendly aliens', Iris reported back for the Badminton School magazine.[123] To her friend Paddy O'Regan, whom she had succeeded as treasurer of Oxford's Irish Club, she was less prosaic. 'East London & East Europe jostle for Lebensraum on the pavements of the High & Corn. A thousand people sleep & live in unimaginable conditions in the Majestic Cinema.' Brick surface shelters sprang up all over the city. 'Things are moving here in a confused sort of way.'[124]

The Blitz would leave Oxford untouched. 'Hitler is keeping Oxford for himself,' warned Helen Darbishire. 'He wants it to look as it always has when he comes for his honorary degree.'[125]

An Old Man: H. H. Price on Hume

Mary found Elizabeth patient and generous when she came to Somerville for lunch, but to some her single-mindedness was testing. Another Mary, Mary Wilson (whom we will meet properly later), would be quite absorbed reading Hume or Kant in the library, but she was happy to put their problems out of her mind when she got together with friends to play games, chat or listen to music. But when she tried to socialise with Elizabeth, there was no escape. 'What are you *really worried about?*' Elizabeth would press her. Mary Wilson struggled to fake a worry of her own, too intimidated to confess that the problem of causation didn't keep her awake at night.[126] Elizabeth, however, lived the problems of philosophy, she felt gripped by them and she probed her friends relentlessly. Her regular trips to Blackfriars gave those problems personal and religious urgency.

While still studying Mods Elizabeth had begun attending H. H. Price's lectures on the great Scottish Enlightenment philosopher David Hume. President of the Society for Psychical Research, H. H. Price was a slightly unworldly man who resembled an owl. He avoided the boisterous taverns of Oxford, preferring to stay at home with his sister, often retiring early with cocoa, at that time considered a somewhat feminine drink, which he erroneously thought to be a sedative.[127] Price was the antithesis of a 'young man in a hurry' – the description he had applied to Ayer. He had seen action in the First World War and was now too old to be threatened with conscription again.

Elizabeth read Price's *Hume's Theory of the External World* from first sentence to last,[128] and the Hume she encountered in its pages was barely recognisable as the proto-analyst portrayed by Ayer, bent on attacking metaphysics and diminishing philosophy.[129] Price's Hume was fascinated by the richness of our ideas when compared to what is given in experience, and his genius (for Price) lay in his attempt to span the gap with a theory about the workings of the human mind. '[O]f all the people I heard at Oxford, [Price] was the one who excited my respect; the one I found worth listening to', said Elizabeth.[130] In Trinity Term 1940, Mary and Iris joined Elizabeth in New College to hear H. H. Price lecturing on 'Some Points in Hume's Theory of Knowledge'.

Price began with a question: Why do we believe in the continued, independent existence of objects? 'The asking of such difficult questions', he informed the undergraduates gravely, 'might very well be the main business of a philosopher.'[131] He prepared them for Hume's heroic but torturous answer with a homely example of his own. 'I see a black cat in one corner of the room. I turn to read *The Times* for half a minute; then I look up again and see a black cat in the opposite corner of the room, while the first corner is empty.' My experience of the cat is broken or fragmentary. I see the cat at one moment (a); then I see it later somewhere else (d). In the interim, at times (b) and (c), I have been reading the newspaper. But does it occur to me that the cat disappeared while I was reading my newspaper and then reappeared in the other corner of the room just as I looked up? No! So, what explains my belief that a continuously existing cat walked continuously across the room while I was reading my newspaper?[132] He steadied his students for Hume's astonishing proposal. Well, I have watched black cats walk across rooms (and roads and gardens) before. In those cases, my experience of the cat did not form a broken or fragmentary series (a . . . d), but a continuous one (a, b, c, d). When our experience is fragmentary, Hume says that our imagination fills in the missing parts of the series with memories of previous continuous ones. And it is by filling in the gaps with memories of past experiences that we come to believe in the continued existence of things we are not sensing.

H. H. Price believed that Hume's story could be scaled up. The same mechanism that explains our belief in the unobserved cat could explain our belief in events far away in space and time. When a porter delivers a letter, I do not observe the transit of the letter, nor the man coming up the stairs outside the door, said Price (dispensing with his own examples and drawing straight from Hume's *Treatise of Human Nature*). But 'previous experience tells me that letters can only pass one from place to another when they pass through intermediate places, and when there are "posts and ferries" to convey them'.[133]

Finally, Price tackled the master head on. David Hume had queried the imagination's capacity to build so vast an edifice as the External World just by yoking together variegated fragmentary impressions.[134] But Price (whose imagination was vast) turned Hume's scepticism on its head. We can know that there is a transcendent reality, a world beyond our immediate experience *because of* the gappy, fragmented nature of our experiences, Price explains. Without interruptions, gaps and obstacles – newspapers, naps, closed doors, closed eyes – we would not have an idea of a world existing unobserved at all. We do not need (as Hume feared) to pass (*per impossibile*) through the veil of experience in order to have knowledge of a reality beyond. Rather, our gappy experience shows us that there is more than meets the eye, the world itself provides all we need to patch up the veil. The only 'behindness' that enters into the matter is the ordinary literal behindness: the cat behind the newspaper, the postman behind the door.[135]

Elizabeth found Price's lectures 'absolutely about the stuff'. But had Mary or Iris glanced over at her, they would not have seen pleasure or agreement in her countenance. She sat through Price's lectures tearing at her scholar's gown.[136] Afterwards she would head to Oxford's Cadena café, where she sat, her dark hair scraped back, eyes determinedly focused on the coffee cup and cigarette packet on the table in front of her. In her head, like a mantra: 'But what do I really see? How can I say that I see here anything more than a yellow expanse?'[137] And the back of things?[138] (The back of the cigarette packet on the table, the cat behind the sofa, the porter behind the door, all unobservable.) Or (head in her hands, staring through her fingers like a grid), do I see the whole packet in seeing its surface? Elizabeth's power of focus, her ability to screen out whatever mess, noise or demand surrounded her, would become legendary. The world beyond the confines of her gaze hardly impinged on her consciousness at all, as waitresses swept past and impatient customers cleared their throats waiting for this odd girl in trousers to vacate her table.

What gripped the young Elizabeth were not Price's (or Hume's) answers, but the questions he asked and the curious manner with which he approached them. Price did not try to banish mystery and speculation but addressed it head-on. At some point in the early 1950s, he would take his curiosity to an extreme, volunteering to take mescaline in the hope of seeing pure sense data for himself. Dr John Smythies, of the Society for Psychical Research, administered four tenths of a gram, and at twilight Price had a visual hallucination.[139] He saw a large pile of holly-like leaves on the counterpane of his bed, each leaf and the whole pile markedly three-dimensional and solid. 'If one believed the world was created by a wholly good Supreme Being who loves everything, this is how it *ought* to look,' he reflected. 'Perhaps that is the way the world *is*,' though in our everyday state of consciousness we cannot see it so.[140]

Mary and Iris, alongside Elizabeth in the lecture, would have been thinking their own thoughts. Mary was perhaps reminded of the pieces of peeling plaster in her Downe House bathwater. Like Price, she believed in sense data: 'appearances are part of the world; they do actually appear. I've seen them,' she mused quietly to herself.[141] Mary did not require mescaline. Iris, sitting beside her, did not much take to Hume. But she was struck by the quantity of feline life in Price's phenomenal world. 'I am making (in the way of academic business) the acquaintance of Professor Price of your college,' she wrote to Frank Thompson. 'He is, as I expect you know, a felinist like yourself. His lectures & his books abound with cats – cats that are observed in one corner of the room, then cross the room unobserved in the other corner, cats that stand behind the sofa with their tails sticking out, cats that are positively known to like milk – & other cats whose partiality to milk is mere induction. Cats in general . . .'[142] She would have been delighted to know of Price's belief that 'cats are notoriously sensitive to super-natural influences, and so are horses'.[143]

When Iris wrote to Mary in the summer of 1940 her indifference to Hume was evident. No, she doesn't have Price's book on Hume, she tells Mary, 'but whistle for what you require'. With wartime paper shortages, books were scarce – one student often standing by while another scrambled to finish an essay before handing over the precious item. Iris had been reading in cellars and air-raid shelters. She was staying with her parents at 9 Waller Avenue, Blackpool, where they were evacuated after their home in Chiswick was damaged by a bomb that landed feet away. Iris thanks Mary, 'Honey m'love', for sending her 'Paton'[144] – this is probably H. J. Paton's 1936 *Kant's Metaphysic of Experience*. Nevertheless, she explained to Mary, she didn't know if she'd get round to reading it. She is busy selling the *Daily Worker* on Blackpool pier.[145]

A Refugee: Heinz Cassirer on Kant

When Richard Walzer, Fritz Heinemann, Friedrich Waismann, Lorenzo Minio-Paluello and Heinz Cassirer, along with many more of Europe's finest scholars, were arrested and interned, their wives and children were left fearful and desperate. Iris was troubled: 'It drives me frantic to think of these men & women, who've done far more for humanity than I shall ever do, suffering mental misery. Those in the Forces do at least know more or less what's happening, & most of them feel they're defending something they love – but to be imprisoned, physically & mentally at a time like this – that, especially for people who've been fighting fascism all their lives.'[146] Lady Edith Ross (wife of Realist philosopher David Ross) sat on the female-run Oxford Refugee Committee, which was instrumental in assisting refugee families with school fees and employment references.[147] The Rosses were harbouring the Minio-Paluellos when Lorenzo (who lectured on Aristotle and Medieval Philosophy) was bundled into a lorry by the police in front of his distraught wife, Magda. When Heinz Cassirer was arrested, Classics tutor Mildred Hartley and another Somervillian took turns sleeping at the Cassirers' home, at 19 Carlton Road, ready to take their eight-year-old daughter Irene to live in Somerville College should soldiers return for Eva, his wife. One night, when Eva momentarily switched on a light to comfort Irene without having first checked that the blackout blinds were pulled down, an anonymous neighbour called the police to tell them a German woman was signalling to the enemy. A visit from the chief constable only increased the anxiety.[149]

Mildred's stint as watchdog reflects ties of affection and friendship that had been established between the Cassirer family and Somerville over the previous twelve months. Lotte Labowsky, Heinz's friend from Hamburg and a fellow refugee, was Somerville's librarian. A classicist, Lotte, along with her mother and sisters, had fled Germany and arrived penniless in Oxford before the war. Her mother took in other refugees as lodgers and their Summertown home became a hub of German culture and conversation. Somerville Principal Helen Darbishire's fundraising efforts enabled the college to offer Dr Labowsky an honorary research grant and guest membership of Somerville Senior Common Room, which entitled her to free meals.[150] She joined fellow refugees Margarete Bieber, Käthe Bosse, Elise Baumgartel and Leonie Zuntz as Somerville's guests.[151] It was this friendship and welcome that convinced Heinz Cassirer that he too would find there a place of refuge and sympathy.[152] Mildred Hartley became a frequent visitor to the Cassirers', taking her place in the sitting room amid the austere German furniture to read passages from A. P. Herbert's very Oxford comedy-crime series *Misleading Cases*.[153]

Mildred slept at Carlton Road for a whole five months. While initial support for the government's policy of interning enemy aliens was high, mixed in with anti-Semitism and xenophobia, public attitudes shifted after a passenger ship transporting Italian and German refugees to Canada was sunk by a German U-boat in July 1940. More than 800 people drowned.[154] By September 1940, as the new academic year and the Blitz began, many of Europe's finest minds had been released from internment. Only then did Mildred return to her own bed.

So it was that refugee scholar Heinz Cassirer, home from a prison camp on the Isle of Man, taught Kant to Mary, Philippa and Iris in Hilary Term 1941.[155] '[W]e toured a lot of major problems,' recalled Mary, but at least they got a notion of 'how everything hung together'.[156] If Mary's Paton remained unread on Iris's floor, and both were still without a copy of Price, they may have found the tour rather disorienting. We can fill them in.

David Hume's empiricist philosophy found its way across the English Channel, by 'post and ferries', and onward into the hands of Immanuel Kant in Königsberg. The words of the Scot were like an alarm clock, Immanuel said, they interrupted his dogmatic slumber.[157] Hume's sceptical claim, the one H. H. Price would explain to Elizabeth nearly 200 years later, was that our experience of the external world is made up of fragmentary impressions woven together by the imagination. On this view, causality is not part of the world, but a matter of custom, of what has previously been found to follow what. This kept Immanuel awake. He could not accept the Scottish philosopher's proposal that causality is only a matter of what in the past has been found to follow what. He found this idea intolerable; causation is not 'a bastard of the imagination', he complained.[158] He set himself the task of restoring causation to its proper place: not a figment of our imagination but, thanks to the operation of human understanding, a concept that is justified and objective.[159]

His solution was elegant. Causation is not an imaginary ribbon that conjoins one experience to another; rather, human experience comes already structured by the concept of causality. Our understanding applies the concept of causation to sensations to form the world as we know it. We cannot step outside our experience to know what the world is like independent of this interplay between concepts and sensations; the world that we experience is, for creatures like us, all we can know. It makes no sense to ask about what things are like beyond our experience. This is one of the lessons of his first Critique: the *Critique of Pure Reason*.

Kant's second Critique, the *Critique of Practical Reason*, points to one possible exception to this limitation: morality. At the heart of morality, says Kant, is a moral law that he calls the *categorical imperative*. This law tells us: 'Act only on that maxim through which you can at the same time will that it should become a universal law.'[160] It is a distant echo of Christianity's Golden Rule: 'Do unto others as you would have them do unto you.' The profound mystery, Kant thinks, is that we sometimes recognise that we ought to do something irrespective of our desires. When we see that we *ought* to do something we thereby judge that we *can* do it. This reveals to us our freedom, our place outside the pattern of cause and effect that governs our sensations and desires. If we recognise the authority of the moral law over us, Kant thinks, it will stir within us a deep feeling of respect (*Achtung*) – and recognising this we gain an insight into our own peculiar nature. We are finite beings and, like letters, cats and billiard balls, we belong to the world of causation. The movement of our bodies, like the movements of billiard balls, is determined by the laws of causation. And yet, we belong too to the world of freedom; we can choose freely, our will is unconstrained.

It was 'something of a bumpy ride', Mary recalled.[161] To Iris, it was 'a complete mystery'.[162] Nevertheless, a small fragment of thought belonging to Kant's third Critique seems to have caught Iris's attention. She copied out in longhand on a flyleaf of her copy of Cassirer's 1938 *A Commentary on Kant's Critique of Judgment*: 'A feeling for the Sublime in Nature cannot well be thought without combining therewith a mental disposition which is akin to the Moral.' In the *Critique of Judgment*, she sees, Kant links *Achtung* with the feeling of the wonder that is elicited by the great expanse of the starry heavens.

Cassirer conducted his tutorials in his Carlton Road sitting room, scene of Mildred Hartley's readings from *Misleading Cases*. Once the class ended and the majesty of Kant's transcendental idealism was put to one side, Irene would sometimes appear through the door. As an only child, expected to have academic interests, Irene didn't relate easily to other children. She saw the young women her father tutored as friends.[163] Heinz Cassirer was dazzled by Philippa and thought her the most philosophically gifted person among the younger generation. She lodged for a time with the family when a recurrence of her childhood tuberculosis made college life difficult.[164] She gave Irene a copy of *Animal Farm* when it was published in 1945. Later Iris recommended Badminton as a suitable school for her (she duly went).[165] 'Take Crit. of Prac. Reason seriously' will be one of the items on Iris's to-do list in 1947.[166]

A Woman: Mary Glover on Plato

As Elizabeth began preparing for her Greats exams (to be taken in Trinity Term 1941), it was Miss Glover, St Hugh's philosophy tutor and another of Sandie Lindsay's former tutees,[167] to whom she turned. For most of the 1930s Mary Glover was a lone 'Miss' in the male-dominated pages of the *Oxford Gazette*. An intense and brilliant teacher, Miss Glover was a beautiful former Somervillian with a First in Mods and Greats. She laughed easily and had the 'gift of originality'. 'You never knew what she was going to say next,' her niece recalled.[168] A skilled gardener – a classic hallmark of a St Hugh's fellow – and a lover of the outdoors, she would arrange picnics for her undergraduates on the Berkshire Downs 'as a cure for any kind of overwork or worry'.[169]

Miss Glover's guidance is visible in Elizabeth's neglect of all those parts of the syllabus that didn't interest her. She encouraged tutees to attend lectures that strictly speaking were not relevant to the passing of exams

and to be guided by interest rather than syllabus (a lesson which she supplemented with a recipe for exam success: do your best question second).[170] It was Mary Glover who permitted Elizabeth to receive philosophy tuition from the Dominican Victor White at Blackfriars – an otherwise unheard-of arrangement (this 'special' assignment would not interfere with her ordinary work, White assured Miss Glover).[171] When Elizabeth herself became a don, she carried Mary Glover's lessons into her own teaching – her tutees became used to fascinating and challenging tutorials on topics that bore no relation to any of the finals papers they were due to sit. In one comical episode in the 1960s, Miss Anscombe tried to make it up to a girl by sending her to her husband, Peter Geach, for additional tuition; the overwrought undergraduate was too terrified to report that he too instructed her in texts that would form no part of the examination.[172]

The year after Elizabeth had arrived at St Hugh's, Mary Glover's paper 'Obligation and Value' appeared in the prestigious journal *Ethics*.[173] In it, Glover attempted, modestly but forthrightly, to make the case for moral philosophy of the kind that H. A. Prichard had labelled 'a mistake' and Freddie Ayer had declared extinct. Glover's paper begins: 'Under pressure of experience of the concrete world, new concepts are being formed.' A similar rejuvenation, she argues, is needed in morals. '[I]t has been common to suppose that either the category of obligation or the category of the good interpreted as the object of desire is the final irreducible notion in terms of which we must understand the moral life.' But, she adds, these are the wrong terms. Instead, we should look to reconnect with the moral language of Plato and Aristotle, to speak not of duty and desire, but of moral character and motive.[174]

In her paper, Mary Glover looked to reinstate the background of human life that H. A. Prichard had removed, by rethinking the nature and identity of human action. Human actions, she says, are 'discriminated by motive as well as by intention'.[175] Here she drew on work by the Platonist H.W.B. Joseph, his attention now occupied with finding beds for evacuees.

'A man who was fond of oysters might eat a plateful put before him for the sake of their flavour; a man who loathed them might do so to avoid hurting his host's feelings; a man who loathed or was indifferent to them might do so to prevent his neighbour, whom he knew to be fond of them and he disliked, from having two portions,' Joseph had written. 'I think these are three different acts, one morally good or else kindly, one morally bad or spiteful, one indifferent.'[176]

'Different acts, having different motives, may work themselves out into the same movements of bodies,' says Joseph, but the movements of bodies 'are not the acts'.[177] Joseph used the term 'bits of living' to designate human acts. Movements of bodies are physical events, subject to the forces that govern the physical world and amenable to mechanistic causal explanation. 'A completely physical interpretation of what we call the actions of men or other animals would hold that the conscious states of desire ... are irrelevant; an adequate account of the changes that occur in any process carried out by animal muscles could be given without reference to them.' A psycho-physical psychologist, of a Machian bent, might even find a place in a physical explanation for 'conscious states of desire, aversion, fear, pleasure, pain, and all thinking and imagining'.[178] But bits of living, Joseph says – the innocent, fraternal or spiteful eating of oysters – will elude the scientist's scrutiny. They belong to a different pattern of explanation, one that speaks of intention and purpose, motive and character. Bits of living are not independent links in a causal chain (as the movements of bodies are) but have their identity as parts within a whole. The unity, harmony and beauty of that whole constitutes goodness in human life. What animates the ethical rather than physical life is consciousness of a whole 'all-embracing form of life', and it is this idea, rather than blind obedience to an aggregate of rules or principles, that lies at the heart of our judgements of particular acts.[179]

Elizabeth perhaps repeated Miss Glover's words to Iris, Mary and Philippa in the Somerville dining hall: 'morality has a transcendent reference.' Something 'more is involved than our own purposes, however exalted', namely, 'an objective standard that may be progressively discovered by us, but which is not our creation'.[180] The name for the spirit or attitude that will make such progress possible is 'reverence' or 'love'. Love can motivate us in a way that involves desire but not self-interest. 'In a sense very difficult to express and especially difficult to express without metaphor, we are aware of transcendent values, truth, beauty, and goodness; we are aware that our lives can somehow incarnate something of these values and that therein lies this chief glory.' How close this distant transcendent good is to Plato's Goodness. 'The metaphysics of all this is very difficult', Miss Glover warned, and 'it is the supreme importance of Plato that he realized that there must be such a metaphysic.'[181] Iris would not have been impressed – she hadn't yet learnt to love Plato. But later, when asked by a journalist about her and her friends' interests during the war, she told him: they were all interested in 'the reality that surrounds man – transcendent or whatever.'[182]

Throughout Elizabeth's time at St Hugh's, Mary Glover had kept a close eye on her most unconventional of undergraduates as Elizabeth roved around Oxford in search of whatever ideas caught her interest. Tutors sent reports back to Mary Glover that ranged from 'really more than a little lazy'[183] to 'real power of mind';[184] these Mary Glover filed, one after the other, in a slim cardboard wallet. Miss Anscombe's 'chief obstacle is her reluctance to give the necessary attention to philosophers who repel her', complained the retired 73-year old William George de Burgh.[185] Donald MacKinnon, who tutored on Plato, noted her 'very quick and definite mind' and predicted 'first class work'.[186] Isobel Henderson, who taught her Ancient History, did not. 'She really knows very little, & is unable to use even her set books with any freedom', she despaired. 'I enjoy teaching her, but I can't say it has been a great success.'[187] As for Mary Glover herself, she thought Elizabeth's essays on Aristotle 'somewhat slight', but she was inclined to be sympathetic: 'Miss Anscombe loves system' she observed, '& the N. E. is not systematically written'.[188]

In the run-up to exams Elizabeth made an effort to make good. 'She has begun too late', lamented Isobel Henderson. The evening before her final exam on Political Theory Elizabeth appeared in Mary Scrutton's rooms and explained 'thoughtfully in her beautiful quiet voice' that she had just started looking at the books for it. 'Some of the stuff is actually quite interesting,' she confided. 'But there's one thing here that I don't understand. As far as I can see, this man', she said, holding up Hobbes's *Leviathan*, 'is just saying that you mustn't revolt unless you can. Can that be what he means?' Mary reassured her it was a common complaint but was rather astonished at her friend's lack of preparation.[189]

Elizabeth's refusal to attend to anything that didn't interest her left her examiners with no option but to hold an oral examination (or viva). Elizabeth was awarded a First at the insistence of her philosophy examiners, despite spectacularly failing the Roman History paper. Famously, when asked in her viva: 'Miss Anscombe, is there *any fact at all* about the history of Rome which you would like to comment on?' the learned Catholic replied: 'No,' with a 'mournful shake of the head'.[190]

For many of the men in this story, a First led to a college post; in Ayer's case, despite Michael Foster's objection that he was unfit to teach the young, he was offered a fellowship even before he had finished his degree. But the women's colleges, being fewer, smaller and poorer, could not easily accommodate all their first-class undergraduates. So instead, Elizabeth began graduate work on Aristotle and Aquinas, the subject of her 'special' study at Blackfriars, but now under the supervision of Wittgenstein's high priest Friedrich Waismann. Her dissertation was provisionally entitled 'An enquiry into certain problems of numerical identity and difference, and, (subordinate to these) of extension and space, with an examination of the solutions proposed to them by the Aristotelian philosophical tradition, in the light of logical and epistemological method'.[191] She was awarded a Gilchrist Studentship Grant, open to those who 'have made proper provision to fund a degree or higher education course but find themselves facing unexpected financial difficulties which may prevent completion of it'. It is probable that the unexpected and early death of her father in 1939, compounded financial difficulties felt more generally as a result of the war.

On Boxing Day 1941, a dreary Friday, Elizabeth married Peter Geach in the neoclassical Brompton Oratory in west London.[192] Her brothers had instructed her to break off the engagement on the grounds that Peter was 'absurd', but she ignored their warnings.[193] Though now Mrs Geach, Elizabeth would always be known as – and would insist on being known as – Miss Anscombe. Elizabeth's marriage certificate protected her from a new conscription act, passed that month. The National Service Act (No. 2) applied to unmarried women between the ages of twenty and thirty. Voluntary recruitment of women had not been sufficient to satisfy the War Office's insatiable needs, and the government was forced to invite the inevitable 'public stir' and recruit by compulsion. Agnes Hardie, Labour MP for Glasgow Springburn, was not alone in feeling that the war was a 'man's job': 'I am as good a feminist as anyone,' she argued, but 'I say they have no right to conscript women.'[194] Need overwhelmed qualms.

Wife to Peter Geach was not, however, a position of obvious safety. While Peter objected to joining the British Army, he was determined to fight for Poland. His initial efforts to join the Polish Army had failed, and at the time when Elizabeth became his wife, Peter was making efforts to become a Polish citizen.[195] Isobel Henderson warned Elizabeth that 'she would find herself a Russian after the war' if Peter was successful. This 'chilled her somewhat,' Isobel relayed to Mary, 'although she had professed total indifference to nationality.'[196]

A Conscientious Objector: Donald MacKinnon & the Metaphysical Animal

By the time Mary, Iris and Philippa began their final two terms as undergraduates, the US, under President Franklin D. Roosevelt, had entered the war, provoked by the Japanese attack on Pearl Harbor. Clothes rationing was in force and the fade to khaki, or at least to drudge, had swept along all three tables of the Somerville dining hall. In Boots the make-up shelves were bare, lipstick and rouge almost impossible to get. With youthful dons and adult male undergraduates 'as rare as butterflies in March',[197] invitations for cinnamon toast were also in short supply. Still, when Mary unexpectedly found a new nylon nailbrush in stock at the chemist (extortionate at *nine* shillings), she treated herself to the last one, '[c]arried away by the splendour of the occasion'.[198]

Each week, Mary, Iris and Philippa in turn crossed the Woodstock and Banbury roads and headed under the neo-gothic arches of Keble (now giving sanctuary to MI5 secretarial staff).[199] Just as Elizabeth had before them, they were sent there for tutorials with the conscientious objector Donald MacKinnon – one of the few young men still to be found.

A devout high-church Anglican, MacKinnon had formed his pacifist commitments during the Spanish Civil War and consolidated them in the summer of 1938, partly in discussion with members of Pax, the group to which Elizabeth belonged. But as the conflict with Hitler developed, MacKinnon began to have doubts about his position. Was bearing witness to the life of Christ really compatible with conscientious objection in the face of Hitler's aggression and purpose? He was weighed down with guilt that he was not suffering while others were. 'I am drawn . . . into the place where my fellows are suffering, & sometimes I think I cannot hold out much longer,' he had written to a friend in July 1940.[200] When he finally tried to sign up, he was turned down on medical grounds – asthma.[201] His wife, Lois Dryer, whom he had married in 1939, was distressed by his wavering pacifism; hers was an absolute or 'simple' pacifism which excludes all war.[202] She had been the prize student at Edinburgh in 1936–7, when Donald was lecturer, but in Oxford she found herself snubbed and excluded by the epithet Donald's students used for her: 'the wife'.[203] As she tried to find her feet, she was teaching written English to Heinz Cassirer and Friedrich Waismann. 'Fundamentally, she thinks I have raked,' MacKinnon told his friend.[204] He was sleeping in his college rooms.[205]

Just a few years older than his tutees, Donald MacKinnon had beaten to his Keble post a promising young philosopher (Herbert) Paul Grice, who would go on to do foundational work in the philosophy of language. H. H. Price wrote a joint reference for the candidates. Grice was 'in his own way distinctly the better'. MacKinnon possessed 'less steadiness and common-sense' and was likely 'to strike some of his pupils as rather an odd character'. However, MacKinnon would possibly 'go further in the long run'. What was more, his direction of interest was 'most unusual' and even sufficed to make him 'remarkable': devoted to the ideals and methods of logical analysis, as well versed in symbolic logic as any non-mathematician could be, but keenly interested too in religious problems. 'I cannot think of any philosopher in this country – or indeed abroad – at the present time who has precisely this combination of abilities and interests,' Price concluded.[206] (Price had read an essay by Elizabeth on causality, written during the vacation of 1939, and 'considered it good',[207] but he could not have known that she already shared MacKinnon's 'most unusual' interests.) This was not an easy cocktail to reckon with. 'He's perpetually on the brink of a nervous break-down,' observed Iris.[208]

To be sent to him was 'an enormous stroke of luck', reflected Mary, 'without which I may well have drifted away from academic philosophy altogether'.[209] While Sandie Lindsay had tossed *Language, Truth and Logic* out of the window, Donald MacKinnon, himself a onetime member of the Brethren, thrust it urgently into his tutees' hands. Though he rejected Freddie Ayer's 'very slick' assurance that 'you needn't worry because none of it means anything', he wanted his tutees to see the lie in it for themselves.[210] In temperament MacKinnon was the opposite of Ayer (by now training with the Welsh Guards, sleeping in barracks).[211] He worried about it all and thought 'there was a lot of sense in everything'. He was always looking for the angle from which the sense in things could be seen. 'He made a lot of Kant, and also Idealists like Bradley who other people were not reading, and Wittgenstein, he was into Wittgenstein already you see, which other people were not,' Mary recalled. 'So we got ahead with our philosophy, and enjoyed ourselves.'[212] To the increasing distress of Lois, Iris worshipped him. Iris wrote to 'Brave & Beloved' Frank Thompson in January 1942: 'He inspires a pure devotion.'[213] He is a 'jewel'. Philippa went perhaps the furthest of the three:

'No one has influenced me more . . . He *created* me.'[214] Let us follow her as she crosses the quad under the eyes of the MI5 secretaries to see how.

Donald MacKinnon's Keble room is approached down a dark passage. White-walled and utterly bare, save for two battered armchairs and, in the centre of the room, a table piled high with masses of paper and books by Kant.[215] Notes for lectures are scribbled on the backs of envelopes.[216] Philippa places herself in the slightly less broken down of the two chairs.[217] Dressed in a boiler suit (he was proud of his fire-watching), MacKinnon lies on the floor. (Iris would occasionally replicate his 'supine' tutorials a decade later, when herself a tutor at St Anne's.)[218] As Philippa (like Elizabeth, Mary, and Iris) turns out from her satchel her earliest handwritten essays in philosophy, MacKinnon lays out a background against which she can see and understand *Language, Truth and Logic*.

Logical positivism, MacKinnon begins, presents itself as a thesis about logic and meaning, but it contains an implicit and dangerous 'doctrine of man'.[219] While the Vienna Circle's careful logical empiricism was meant to be democratic, to place knowledge beyond the clutches of authoritarian myth or prejudiced superstition, Ayer's manifesto extracts from that source a vision of humans as 'efficient calculating machines'.[220] Ayer makes human rationality a matter of the manipulation of symbols, rather than the exercise of capacities that, when used wisely, bring genuine comprehension. Under threat from the newly weaponised 'I don't understand', MacKinnon explains, the human animal is 'subordinated to science' and forced to renounce not just his morality but his connatural curiosity, his very essence. 'I will not deny that more and more I have found myself compelled to adopt some such conception of a norm of manhood as the basis of ethical judgement,' MacKinnon had told an audience of theologians in January 1941. This would be, he recognised, a task of 'appalling difficulty'.[221]

Now on two feet, he sketches for Philippa his vision of philosophy. The philosopher must learn to think historically, Donald MacKinnon tells her – his own undergraduate brush with R. G. Collingwood's philosophy of history fresh in his mind.[222] Our enquiries are not isolated from history nor from ourselves. Historical causes point human intellectual attention in a particular direction;[223] each philosopher must ask herself how far her historical situation and condition determine her undertaking and the principles that inform her procedure.[224] Philosophy, he continues, is an expression and an index of human dignity. A human being is an animal, and its nature – its essence – is expressed in its curiosity and imagination. Human animals speak and ask questions about goodness and beauty, meaning and truth. Even the young of the species do it. Children are naturally inquisitive: 'How would we know if you were me?' thought Philippa. 'Are baths and ceilings no more than constellations of appearances?' wondered Mary. 'Why?' asked Elizabeth. Deprive human animals of the capacity and opportunity to ask metaphysical questions, as totalitarianism does, urges MacKinnon, and what is left? Cynicism, scepticism, fear. Mere beastliness. (His bearlike head turns towards Philippa as he pauses to let this thought germinate.)

Humans are *metaphysical animals*, he ventures, still unsure himself what this means.[225] Metaphysical animals need to speak about the transcendent, about the human spirit and the infinite. But Ayer had declared such speech to be nonsense. How to break free? Perhaps, by using concepts analogically, he suggests, drawing on the work of Catholic theologians. Thomas Aquinas claimed it is possible for humans to speak of, and comprehend, God's attributes through analogy. We know what it is for a human to be good, or to create, or to be wise. We speak of God's goodness, of His creation, of His wisdom by analogy, by transposing concepts that have their use in the finite human realm to the infinite.[226] 'Can we take up this structure?' he asks, flinging himself into the other armchair.

But now the Kantian in him gives pause. When human beings hazard speech about God, freedom and immortality, they attempt to leap, with human words, across an unbridgeable chasm. The most we can hope is that our words can somehow catch the sense of our world.[227] We know that by 'freedom' we mean something more than 'the difference between spontaneous and forced action'; yet our words cannot quite 'catch' what we know.[228] But we must not throw up our hands. The analogical use of a word is a creative act, an appeal to another to see a submerged connection, to take up a hint, to accept a new use of language. Freddie Ayer had mercifully spared the poets from his bonfire on the grounds that they make no claim to truth. But MacKinnon wanted to turn the metaphysician into a poet, the poet's language of paradox, parable and metaphor allowing us to 'catch the sense of a world' that cannot be directly comprehended.[229] (And now surely Miss Bosanquet is gripped – she hangs on to the armchair, destabilised). 'It is impossible to distil the essence of moral philosophy',[230] says MacKinnon, the hour-long tutorial now winding up. 'There is a delicate overlap between contributing to the debate of the practically involved and setting out the logical order of the categories of the moral universe.'[231]

Miss Bosanquet rises, slightly dazed, to her feet, she and her tutor both exhausted and perplexed but somewhat elated. She makes her way out across the quad, back past the MI5 secretaries. Donald, meanwhile, enters the Lamb and Flag through the passageway that connects it directly to Keble. The 'Lamb' is *Agnus Dei* of the Book of Revelation. The barman knows him: double whisky for MacKinnon.[232]

Our Four Unfashionable Philosophers All Get Firsts

Philippa's PPE was a three-year course, compared to Iris and Mary's four, meaning that in spring 1942, the three friends approached their finals together, their peculiar education received from old men, refugees, women and conscientious objectors almost complete. In that final term, Philippa and Mary both became quite seriously ill. Mary was later diagnosed with irritable bowel syndrome, a condition that would debilitate her throughout her life whenever she suffered stress.[233] Letters of reassurance from Donald MacKinnon and Isobel Henderson appeared in her pigeonhole ('sorry to hear that you have been seedy'; 'I shall give you as much time as you feel you can stand'; 'ideas are more important than knowledge – & you've always had ideas!').[234] Meanwhile Philippa was bedbound. The childhood abdominal tuberculosis that had prevented her from living in college now recurred with especial violence. She was corseted in plaster of Paris and was staying in 2 Bradmore Road with friend and fellow Somervillian Anne Cobbe.[235] Anne's mother arranged for MacKinnon and her economics tutor, Thomas Balogh, to give her lessons at her bedside.

Donald MacKinnon suggested to Iris that Philippa might appreciate a friendly visit.[236] Philippa found herself face-to-face with the 'nuisance Communist'. Iris was standing in front of her bed, holding a bunch of tremulous wild flowers. 'Above all there was magic about Iris', Philippa recalled.[237] Iris remembers the joy with which she found her, her lifelong best friend – this is the third story of their beginning. Iris will appear with flowers many times throughout this book. Her first philosophical question, aged six: '*The snowdrop hangs its head. Why?*' 'Why indeed!' she reflected as an adult. 'A thought-provoking question, a good introduction to a world which is full of mysteries.'[238]

*

Women's examination results were published in a separate list until 1952.[239] 'I'll get a second of some sort with luck (my philosophy tutor [MacKinnon] expects me to get a first but he suffers from delusions anyway). And thereafter? God knows,' Iris had written to a friend.[240] But Iris and Mary's names both appeared in the same division: Class I. Philippa also got a First. The June weather had helped – no hot-water bottles now. Unlike Iris, however, Mary had suffered an agonising three-hour viva in the Ashmolean before her mark could be confirmed. She blamed Elizabeth: 'these Greats examiners had lately been having a lot of trouble in grading previous undergraduates whose work was good in one part of the course and resoundingly awful in another.' After Elizabeth's 'specially bad case of this' the previous year, Mary suspected the authorities had tightened the rules.[241] Her Roman History paper proved a sticking point. In the event, the oral examination went off well enough to satisfy the examiners of a First – 'alpha plus benzedrine', observed Isobel Henderson gleefully.[242] Her achievement was 'magnificent', said Donald MacKinnon, especially considering her illness.[243] The results arrived on a postcard in the Scrutton household.[244] To thank them for their help, Mary gave Donald a book token[245] and, to Isobel, a finely bound copy of Alexander Pope's mock-heroic *The Dunciad* – quite the thing for Isobel whose love of witty allusion and understatement chimed with hers.[246] 'You & Mary have provided such wonderful instances of Mind triumphing over Matter,' wrote Iris to Philippa. 'Now there is nothing for you to worry about, & you can lie in a dreamy coma and rest that back. And don't read Virginia Woolf.'[247]

Isobel thought Iris and Mary a pair of 'live wires' and 'two of the least dull people' she knew.[248] She wanted to celebrate their Firsts in real style with a dinner party. 'I propose to carry you off with Iris, J. B. Trend and A. L. Rowse to Bablock Hythe' (a small hamlet 8 miles along the river).[249]

> Thee at the ferry Oxford riders blithe,
> Returning home on summer-nights, have met
> Crossing the stripling Thames at Bab-lock-hithe,
> Trailing in the cool stream thy fingers wet,
> As the punt's rope chops round.[250]

As the evening wore on, the distinguished sages offered their contemporary opinions. The new graduates listened attentively. The bracelets stacked high on Isobel's evening gloves shivered. Mary fought the urge to yawn.[251]

Afterwards, trailing home to Somerville down a cool moonlit St Giles', Mary turned to Iris. 'So finally,' she asked, 'what about it? Did we learn something new this evening?' 'Oh yes, I think so,' said Iris, contemplating the enormous moon. 'I do think so ... *Trend is a good man and Rowse is a bad man.*' Both fell about laughing at that exact but 'grotesquely unfashionable' judgement. Hadn't they read *Language, Truth and Logic* and learnt that such judgements were nonsense? 'Hurray for Trend and Boo for Rowse!', Iris should have said. The rare passers-by on St Giles' looked round in alarm and the cats ran away, as the nascent rebels made their first academic stand. 'Iris, however, never minded being unfashionable,' Mary recalled.[252] And with the Reverend Canon Tom Scrutton's imperative before her ('REFUSE TO ACCEPT OUTWORN PRESUPPOSITIONS'), neither did she.

CHAPTER 3

Disorder and Hardship

CAMBRIDGE & LONDON

JUNE 1942–AUGUST 1945

Mary & Iris Move to London – Elizabeth Returns to Aristotle &
Human Nature – Iris & Philippa in Wartime London – Elizabeth's
Plan Stalls – Love & War at Seaforth – Mary Finds Herself Among
'Strange Tribes' – Miss Anscombe Meets Professor Wittgenstein –
Philippa & Iris Wait for News – Elizabeth's New Plan –
The End of the War & Three Friends Return to Oxford

Mary & Iris Move to London

Only ten days after sitting her finals, Iris was busy packing her bag. Mary may have watched, cross-legged, as bits of youthful paraphernalia and mementos of their lives together were hastily stowed away; Lindsay's campaign leaflet, a sewing kit, Heinz Cassirer's book on Kant. They were preparing to enter the war effort. Mary had raised a sceptical eyebrow when Iris, with some dramatics, declared that the civil service wouldn't want her, not 'with a political record like mine'. She was wrong and they received their call-up letters on consecutive days: Iris to the Treasury and Mary to the Ministry of Production. Mary's post caused some confusion ('Ministry of what?'),[1] but the stage was now set for a go at adult life. Iris was ready for a new, more sophisticated part to play, and she boarded the train to London without a backward glance. She had no intention of becoming a philosophy don. 'I always wanted to be a novelist,' she said later, 'though I thought I wanted to be an archaeologist and art historian.'[2] She was already at work on her first novel. Mary was more hesitant and waited for the city to disappear from view before turning to her book. She had hopes of returning for graduate studies after she had done 'something publicly useful'.[3]

The London Iris and Mary arrived in was no longer the London of their girlhood, but a strange and disquieting, disorienting place. Emerging from Marylebone Station on to Harewood Avenue, through the station's bomb-damaged exit, they were greeted by an abundance of butterflies. So many of the city's birds had been driven away by the Blitz, joining the one million child evacuees in the surrounding countryside, that the capital now suffered plagues of caterpillars through the silent springs, followed by butterfly-filled summers.[4] The city was attempting to rearrange itself after those eight months when night-time bombing raids destroyed more than a million buildings, killed 43,000 people and threw animal life into disorder.

During the bombing, the government tried to keep the public out of the London Underground, citing disruption to transport and public safety, but they also harboured darker fears: what might be the result of allowing Londoners to indulge the primitive, animal instinct to burrow when afraid? In Dover, frightened townsfolk dug a warren into the cliffs like rabbits. Were Londoners to be permitted – encouraged even – to behave as if they were moles or ostriches? In Whitehall, there were whispers of 'deep-shelter mentality', a neurosis that would reduce housewives, grocers and factory workers to a herd of 'timorous troglodytes' living by candle-light in the tunnels that criss-cross the city. So great was this fear that many government-built air-raid shelters were surface structures, even though they offered less protection than their subterranean counterparts.[5] By the time Iris and Mary arrived, the city was host to half a million homeless.

The war had reshaped the lives of other animals too. At least 400,000 dogs and cats had been killed during the first two weeks of the war, following the advice of a government pamphlet, 'Air Raid Precautions for Animals'.[6] *In memoriam* notices for beloved companions appeared in the papers: 'Happy Memories of Iola, sweet faithful friend'.[7] From London Zoo,

Elephants have started harrowing the ground at Whipsnade which has been judged suitable for agricultural purposes. Whilst it may be a fairly common sight in the East to see an elephant thus employed, this is believed to be the first time these animals have been thus used in this country. Special harness has been made for the three Whipsnade elephants selected for this job. Above : Dixie, who is thirty-six years old, starting off on the first shift.

NEWS from the ZOOS

the pythons, Komodo dragons and elephants, along with the dangerous predators (tigers, lions and crocodiles) were evacuated to Whipsnade animal park, thirty miles north-west of London. They were followed by several zoo keepers and their families, and Whipsnade village found itself with enough young girls to form a pack of Brownies.[8] Special harnesses were made for the elephants, who could now be seen harrowing the fields and helping to 'dig for victory'.[9]

In the end, London Zoo had suffered only one direct, but non-fatal, hit. A monkey and a crane took a short holiday in Regent's Park but returned to captivity when they became hungry. The zebras made the most daring escape; a pair were caught heading north along Kentish Town Road.[10]

Mary and Iris were heading south. A pair of metaphysical animals on their way to Westminster.

Elizabeth Returns to Aristotle & Human Nature

The money Elizabeth received towards her postgraduate studies at Oxford from the Gilchrist Studentship grant was meagre, even when supplemented with a little paid teaching. But as Mary, Iris and Philippa had been taking their exams, she received welcome news about her application for a Sarah Smithson Studentship at Cambridge. Myra Curtis, Principal of Newnham College, wrote to Barbara Gwyer of St Hugh's:

24th June 1942
Dear Miss Gwyer,

I am glad to write and tell you that my Committee has decided to award the Sarah Smithson Studentship to Miss Anscombe. It also agreed to her continuing her teaching work in Oxford and to her reading for the Oxford D. Phil. I am not quite clear as to her position with regard to National Service, and I should be very glad to know whether she has obtained deferment or whether it will be necessary for me to make an application on her behalf to be allowed to continue her work as a University Student.[11]

Barbara Gwyer replied. Miss Anscombe 'has never been threatened with anything in the nature of a call-up', she writes:

had anything of the sort occurred I should have described her during the year 1941–42 as in the penultimate year of a University course which she began in October 1941; or alternatively, if this had not sufficed, as worthy of deferment owing to first class ability and the intention of obtaining if possible a University post in the future.[12]

Barbara Gwyer (who thought of herself as the last of the amateur principals)[13] recommended to Miss Curtis the policy she herself had adopted: 'let sleeping dogs lie'.[14]

Pregnant with her first child, Elizabeth Anscombe arrived in Cambridge just in time for the city's 'mock blitz': students role-playing casualties, sacks of straw labelled 'CORPSE', fake ambulances and a fake bomb.[15]

Like Oxford, Cambridge was dull with khaki and emptied of young men. Unlike Oxford, it had experienced bombs. The bulk had fallen in 1941, but in the summer of 1942 a single low-flying plane dropped explosives 100 yards either side of Trinity College in a full-moon raid.

In order to continue preparing for her D.Phil., Elizabeth remained an undergraduate of Oxford University, and continued with her tutoring at Somerville. She would graft her Greek-dominated Classics education – Plato and Aristotle, the background to her thought – on to the more modern, ahistorical methods of Cambridge analysis. So while Peter was in the open air, amid forests, she began a period of split living, moving back and forth between the libraries and tutorial rooms of Oxford and Cambridge. The old 'Varsity Line' (most of which was closed in 1968 as part of the Beeching Cuts) connected the two universities in a journey of under two hours. It had become a strategic route for freight during the war as it allowed cargo to be moved around the south of England without going via London. This reduced the number of passenger trains that could run.[16] The service stopped at Bletchley, and Elizabeth would have been squashed into a packed compartment with uniformed men and women. 'Is Your Journey Really Necessary?' asked posters at every station. Train windows were not exempt from the blackout and, unlike domestic blackout curtains, the sticky covering could not be removed during the day. Even had she squinted through the diamond-shaped slit she would not have seen the names of the stations she passed: *Bicester – Verney Junction – Bletchley – Bedford – Sandy*. The post-Dunkirk directive that had seen church bells silenced and Richard Walzer, Fritz Heinemann, Friedrich Waismann, Lorenzo Minio-Paluello and Heinz Cassirer interned, had also decreed: 'No person shall display or cause or permit to be displayed any sign which furnishes any indication of the name of, or the situation or the direction of, or the distance to any place.' Information boards were removed from platforms and announcements on trains were stopped. Even orientating a fellow passenger could see you arrested.[17]

When Elizabeth arrived in Cambridge, Professor Ludwig Wittgenstein was in London, not far from where Mary and Iris would spend a large part of the coming year. He only ever remained at Cambridge for a short time before he found the atmosphere intolerable and declared work impossible. Gilbert Ryle (Freddie Ayer's erstwhile tutor) introduced Wittgenstein to his brother John, a doctor at Guy's Hospital. 'I feel I will die slowly if I stay in Cambridge,' he told John dramatically. 'I would rather take a chance of dying quickly.'[18] So it was that Wittgenstein had spent the Blitz as a hospital porter and then, once his identity as one of the most important living philosophers became known, as a researcher on a team studying wound shock.[19]

Wittgenstein's absences gave essential respite to members of the Cambridge philosophy department, dons, spouses and undergraduates alike, whose classrooms, clubs, living rooms and sleep were thrown into chaos when he was around. He so dominated the Cambridge Moral Sciences Club, the philosophy department's regular colloquium, that the following convention was introduced: certain meetings would be 'starred' and would appear in the programme as such*; Wittgenstein was not permitted to attend starred meetings.[20] He called regularly on an exhausted Bertrand Russell at midnight, staying for hours and pacing his rooms like a caged tiger.[21] Dorothy Ely had once banned him from visiting her husband, G. E. Moore, for more than sixty minutes at a time for fear that the exhaustion would kill him.[22]

Elizabeth lodged in various rooms across Cambridge. An early address was 58 Bateman Street, a four-storey Victorian terraced town house and the home of Margaret Masterman and her family: husband (and fellow philosopher) Richard Braithwaite and their two young children, Lewis and Catherine.[23] Philosopher, linguist, novelist and religious contemplative, Masterman was a friend of Dorothy Emmet (the philosopher who had once transported Gandhi in her baby Austin). Later Margaret and Dorothy would found the Epiphany Philosophers: a group of Anglican intellectuals interested in finding a place for religious belief within a scientific world view.[24]

Friedrich Waismann (now Elizabeth's doctoral supervisor) had lodged at 58 Bateman Street along with his wife Hermine and their infant son Thomas when they first arrived in England in 1937 as refugees, penniless and guilt-ridden, having left behind their parents, siblings and other family members.[25] In his suitcase, Friedrich carried a draft manuscript of his magnum opus, *Logik, Sprache, Philosophie* – an introduction to, and defence of, Wittgenstein's *Tractatus*, written by Friedrich when he was a member of the Vienna Circle. But by the time he and his manuscript arrived in Cambridge, Wittgenstein had rejected the work around which Friedrich had built his intellectual life and turned fiercely against his old 'high priest'. In Lent Term 1938, Wittgenstein had warned his students not to attend Waismann's lectures.[26] And when Friedrich published a short paper based on the conversations he and Moritz Schlick had shared with Wittgenstein in Vienna before the rise of Hitler, Wittgenstein accused him of plagiarism.[27] In Michaelmas Term 1939, a devastated Friedrich, along with Hermine and Thomas, fled to Oxford, just in time for him to appear briefly in the *Oxford Gazette* lecture listings ('Philosophy of Mathematics') before being arrested and interned as an enemy alien.[28]

In the early 1930s, 58 Bateman Street had been home to Alice Ambrose, a brilliant American mathematician and philosopher, and Wittgenstein's first and last PhD student.[29] Small, dark-haired and with round, black-rimmed glasses, she conformed to Esther Bosanquet's nightmare image of a University-Educated Woman. Alice's relationship with her supervisor was fatally damaged when Wittgenstein tried to stop her publishing her paper 'Finitism in Mathematics' in the journal *Mind*. When he couldn't persuade her to withdraw it, he tried to convince G. E. Moore, who was the editor, to reject it. Alice had courage enough to tell Wittgenstein where to go. 'It is doubtful whether what I write at the end of further discussion with you will be satisfactory to you,' she wrote to him, '– unless you dictate the material. This latter I refuse to be partner to. If you want to write an article, that is your affair; but there is no point in giving a quotation from you with my name to it.'[30] She told him that he was an 'egoist' and ought not to use his 'power over people to extract worship'.[31]

With Wittgenstein away, Elizabeth's first exposure to his post-*Tractatus* philosophy may well have come from Margaret Masterman. Along with Alice Ambrose, Margaret had been part of a small cluster of six undergraduates who, between 1933 and 1935, produced an 'official' record of his new thinking. Their work began at 9.30 a.m. in the tower in Trinity College's Whewell's Court, with no interruption except for a morning coffee. On 'alternate days when the cream was new and heavy we had *Kaffee mit Schlag* in the Viennese manner'. Dictation occupied up to four hours a day, four days a week. On days when he also lectured, the group were with Wittgenstein for up to seven hours. They were exhausted. Alice and Margaret would go for 'lunch' as late as 4 p.m., often in Lyons' tea rooms on Petty Cury, just a stone's throw from Trinity. If they needed more distance between themselves and Whewell's Court they would go instead to Bateman Street, a thirty-minute walk from the tower. There they could try to carve out a moment's relaxation – something that was impossible in Wittgenstein's company – but also compare notes. Margaret recorded hers in a large yellow notebook. After two years of exhausting work, Wittgenstein declared the task over.[32] Three notebooks existed: yellow, brown, blue. But once again he refused to let them be published. Instead, limited copies of these notes began to circulate, sometimes with his permission, sometimes without, and the rumour mill continued to turn.

Elizabeth's dissertation had by now the more digestible title 'The Identity of Bodies', a topic that had its roots in the classical philosophy she had absorbed at Oxford and Blackfriars. She had begun to focus her attention on the identity of living things, or, as she put it, 'organised bodies'. In her dissertation outline she now 'listed "men" with such objects as "cats" and "turnips"'.[33] (Like Price and Iris's Frank, Elizabeth was a felinist.) 'I want to examine the traditional definition of a man as a rational animal,' she would explain at the end of the year, in an application to extend her Sarah Smithson funding.[34] Her central question was to be 'What is a man?'[35] – her question, of course, not limited to males. The early modern philosopher René Descartes had argued that a human individual is made up of two distinct substances, a mind and a body. Meditating in his dressing gown by the fire in Leiden one winter – around 1629 – Descartes had declared: 'I am not that set of limbs called the human body.'[36] That assemblage changes over time. None of the physical matter that emerged from his mother Jeanne Brochard's labour in 1596 was part of the human body that Descartes now peeked at beneath his dressing gown. As Elizabeth Anscombe would later say, any particular human being is 'materially in a state of flux'.[37] So, Descartes reasoned, *I* am not *this body*. But if he is not his body, what is he?

Descartes concluded that '"I am", "I exist", whenever I utter it or conceive it in my mind, is necessarily true.'[38] The only thing that he could be sure of was that he was a conscious being; all else could be doubted. I am a thing that thinks: that is my essential nature. Not an animal, not a man. '*I* am a conscious being; that is, a being who doubts, asserts, denies, understands a few things, is ignorant of many, is willing or unwilling; and that has also imagination and sense.'[39] Descartes calls each of these varied kinds of events, states and processes a *cogitatio*. Even a toothache is a *cogitatio*, so long as 'toothache' is understood as something one can have without any teeth, Elizabeth later notes.[40]

Elizabeth's plan was to begin not from Descartes but much further back, from Aristotle. A human individual, Aristotle had argued, is a kind of organised body.[41] Not mind plus matter, but matter organised according to a form. Humans are not the only kind of organised body – cats and turnips are organised bodies too. Indeed, every living kind is matter conforming to an organising principle – an organism. Aristotle calls the organising principle a soul – so according to his philosophy, turnips have souls just as much as cats and humans. The vital operations of vegetative life – for example turnip life – include nutrition and reproduction, and these operations form the pattern, the organising principle, in the life of a plant. Individual turnips, on the whole, conform to a pattern that is characteristic of turniphood. The turnip begins as a seed, grows into a root, flowers. Unlike heaps of sand, lumps of rock and oceans, the identity of organised bodies, like turnips, is connected to the organising principle for individuals of that kind.

On Aristotle's picture, the concept *life* applies to an individual living thing in two ways.[42] A turnip, a cat and a human can all be said to *be alive* at a particular time and then, at a later time, to be dead. But a turnip also lives in the mode proper to a turnip, a cat proper to a cat and a human proper to a human. This second use of the concept *life* does not pick out a state of an individual cat (alive as opposed to dead), but a pattern (form) that characterises cathood, and in which any individual cat will participate. We can call this pattern the *essence* of cat.[43] Of course, the life pattern of a human is much more complex and varied than that of a turnip or a cat – if an individual turnip differs from its brethren, it will not be because of the turnip's own particular tastes or preferences, much less its free will or personality. Nevertheless, there is a pattern of birth, childhood, adolescence, adulthood and old age there to be found in human life, as well as characteristic ways of going on.

As she was shuttling back and forth on the Varsity Line, her first child growing inside her, Elizabeth gestated this very unfashionable, indeed idiosyncratic, idea. '[A]re introspection and extraspection qualitatively different activities?' Elizabeth wondered, scanning the overcrowded carriage of the Varsity Line train for a seat to squeeze into (underneath her baggy coat, no one has noticed her shape). Descartes looked inward and found toothless toothaches. Now, in the blacked-out gloom of the compartment, she tried an outward glance. She will take an 'objective approach', but not one that is 'merely "external"' – 'there is an objective approach to oneself as a perceived object'. Instead, she will ask: 'What sort of objects do I perceive when I perceive human beings?' Her intensity of focus had begun to shift from Gold Flake cigarette packets and their surfaces on to the living beings, 'intelligent objects', that smoke them. Leaning against the rubber margins of the carriage door, she saw men in boiler suits, cigarettes between thumb and forefinger, inhaling. She makes a mental note. 'We recognise life when we see the vital operations being performed.' The train shunts suddenly into a siding to give way to a priority train, one carrying goods or troops. Women with children on their knees hold them tighter, whisper reassurances. 'I certainly perceive organised bodies that can use language.' At Bletchley, the conductor checks her ticket – 'we recognise rational life when we see the operations of reason being performed: e.g. when we hear men talking'. More passengers pour on. 'Even if what they say is silly and inconsequent, it is a rational operation to <u>say</u> anything.'[44]

*

In June 1943, Elizabeth gave birth. Elizabeth and Peter named their first daughter Barbara, after the logical syllogism and the patron saint of artillerymen, military engineers and others who work with explosives.

Iris & Philippa in Wartime London

Mary's wartime post was in the Raw Materials Section of the new Ministry of Production, a name that did little to answer the 'What?' that hovered over her call-up letter. (In fact, when the letter had been written, the department did not yet exist.) It shared its Whitehall building with the Cabinet Office, and Mary's desk ought to have offered her pleasant views of the ducks and squirrels in St James's Park. Instead, an ornamental parapet ('a strange aesthetic quirk') blocked the window and the view, forcing her and her fellow inhabitants to live by electric rather than natural light.[45] Her boss, Betty Ackroyd (later Dame Elizabeth Ackroyd), had read PPE at St Hugh's and was brilliantly quick and tough; she struck fear into 'men of the type who were accustomed to waffling on committees'.[46] But she was not a natural delegator. Once Mary had finished an initial report on 'the History of the Combined Resources Board' ('Piles of paper were put in front of me and I beavered away at them for about a month'), she found herself with nothing to do.[47] Her boss 'operated like a whirlwind – rushing in early, constantly engaged on the telephone, dialling telephone numbers at twice the usual speed, often with a pencil, then rushing out to a meeting' – but Mary remained in the dark about how to allocate raw materials ('zinc, rubber, steel and so forth'). She found it impossible to catch Betty's attention for long enough to find out what she ought to be doing. Nor was she missed when she indulged in long lunch breaks, joining choir practices and touring local bomb-damaged churches:[48] St Anne's, All Souls, Christ Church, St James's, Westminster Abbey, St Clement Danes. She had stopped attending church services when she went to Oxford, offering a feeble answer when her father, Reverend Scrutton, asked her 'Why?' And though she still occasionally tried to pray, Mary had always felt herself something of a failure in that department: 'I just had a sort of, sense of an empty room, you see, and I did try from time to time, but it didn't get very far.' Still, she believed in 'something greater'[49] and felt at home sitting in a pew in Westminster Abbey and eating her fish-paste sandwiches, looking down at the rubble and up to the sky through the crumpled architecture.

Iris's Treasury job, meanwhile, involved reading, drafting, sorting, filing and researching legal letters. She wrote to Philippa:

> Life is all rather dreamlike – I live in a fantastic world, ringing with telephone voices, & peopled by strange fictional personalities such as the lords commissioners of His Majesty's Treasury ... (Oxford has nothing on the Treasury as far as tradition goes.) I can't believe that it's <u>me</u> writing these peremptory letters & telling people over the phone where they get off.[50]

She launched herself into the role, though admitting to Philippa, 'all I do at present feels like play acting'.[51] At work she met Peggy Stebbing, a fellow assistant principal, and was delighted to discover she was the niece of the philosopher Susan Stebbing.[52] During the week she lunched and dined (as satisfyingly as rationing would allow) with a different person every day,[53] and then stayed out late in the city after work, rushing about a blacked-out Soho in search of friends, romance and excitement.[54] For Iris 'entering a pub was a delightful adventure'. Though publicans were by now somewhat used to seeing young unchaperoned women in their establishments, she still 'profoundly felt that a woman in a pub was an odd bird'.[55]

Mary and Iris saw Oxford friends too, many of whom had found wartime postings in London. Iris kept close to two men who loved her while maintaining on paper her epic romance with her 'Brave & Beloved' Frank Thompson. The first, Michael Foot, was in London working for the intelligence services. Léonie Marsh (the Somervillian and red-lipsticked Communist) with whom he had been in love, had married, sending him into a state of despair. Iris felt 'terribly sorry' for Michael, 'a lost soul', but also thought him 'damn silly'. She couldn't 'do anything except look sympathetic and tell him in no very decided tones not to be such a fool,' she told Frank.[56] In gratitude for Iris's attentiveness, Michael sent her juvenile poems, bought her a box of expensive Turkish cigarettes and made her the sole beneficiary of his will.[57] They also – and this she did not put in a letter to Frank – began a semi-romance, more serious on Michael's side than on Iris's, spending evenings together in his Rochester Row flat (furnished by his maiden aunts and located above an Italian café, smells of cooking drifting up through the floorboards).[58] They made the most of whatever pockets of culture and entertainment remained.[59]

At the beginning of the war the National Gallery's priceless works had been secretly evacuated to Snowdonia in Wales, where they lived in a cave known as the Cathedral, accessed through a honeycomb of disused slate mines.[60] The absence of the paintings was keenly felt; a letter to *The Times* in January 1942 pleaded with the gallery: 'because London's face is scarred and bruised these days, we need more than ever to see beautiful things . . . [P]icture lovers are denied their Rembrandts just at a time when such beauty is most potent for good.'[61] In response, each month the gallery brought one picture up from the mines, escorted it under armed guard 250 miles by train and put it on display. Rembrandt's *Portrait of Margaretha de Geer* and Titian's *Noli Me Tangere* were the first two escapees.[62]

Michael and Iris often visited the current picture; Michael would remember seeing Holbein's *Duchess of Milan* ('she had the good fortune not to be married to Henry VIII') exhibited in November 1943.[63] He was one of 23,845 who stood before it that month.[64] Guards were on standby, ready to rush the picture back to its underground Cathedral if a bombing raid began.[65]

The second of Iris's loves was her bear-headed tutor Donald MacKinnon, for whom (she told Frank) she would 'walk through fire'. To the increasing vexation of Lois, Donald's wife, Iris and Donald were mutually infatuated by the time she took her finals: 'I think I'll always be a bit in love with Donald, in a Mary Magdalen–Christ sort of way,' she told her friend David Hicks.[66] In the autumn of 1943, Lois would ask Donald to break contact; he, recognising too the danger that his relationship with Iris posed to his marriage and, through that, to his faith, did so. But not before sitting at his desk at Keble College and writing to Philippa to ask her to take care of Iris.[67] Philippa and Donald would exchange letters with each other for many years; at some point, she burnt a suitcase of them.[68]

After leaving Oxford, Mary had moved home to her parents' in Kingston. She commuted overground into Waterloo daily. Squashed and standing throughout the thirty-minute journeys, she read Samuel Richardson's enormous novel *Clarissa*.[69] At first, Iris stayed with family friends on Barrowgate

Road in Chiswick, travelling on the District Line, reading Homer aloud and matching the rhythm of the verse to that of the train.[70] But she wanted to be at the centre of the action, and immediately began looking for a flat of her own. She considered 'a single room in Gerrard Place – with a wonderful view of the Blitz and practically no plumbing'.[71] But though a flat at the centre of London's bohemian pub life would have been convenient for Iris's literary aspirations – struggling poets, authors and refugee intellectuals frequented its bars alongside prostitutes, draft dodgers and black-marketeers – something better came up. Iris discovered a flat so perfect she must have wondered whether she had brought it into being through the sheer force of her imagination.

5 Seaforth Place, Buckingham Gate, SW1, is an attic above empty stables formerly used for brewers' horses. It is down a dark alley, just off busy Victoria Street, 300 yards from Whitehall. Nevertheless, on her short walk to work, Iris would pass eleven bomb sites. Today, Seaforth Place is surrounded by high-rise offices, glass, concrete and chrome. In 1942, it was surrounded by shattered buildings and warehouses. In neither period does a domestic space have any business being there. The entrance to the flat is hidden, and it would never cross your mind that someone might be living down this dark little alleyway. Climbing the open stairs you pass a windowless cupboard halfway up: this is the bathroom. There is a bath but the ceiling is low so you must crawl, rather than step, into it.[72] You emerge up through the floor into the centre of a large open roof-space, seventy feet long. Only the bottom two feet of the walls are vertical, after which they slope sharply inward along various intersecting and surprising planes. The floor is bare wooden boards through which you can see the old stables below. In place of external walls, and extending across part of the ceiling, there is glass ('some six square miles of window to guard in Blitz and blackout', Iris observed).[73] In place of internal walls, an open space to serve for bedroom, living quarters and kitchen. In place of neighbours, the District Line. On her morning commute from Chiswick, Iris would have been packing up her Homer and standing to alight as she passed beneath her soon-to-be home.

When Iris took the lease the flat was empty. She spent the first few weeks on all fours scrubbing the floor or on tiptoe painting every surface white or seated sewing miles of blackout curtains.[74] She installed a 'kitchen' by adding an ancient gas stove alongside the improvised wash-stand and

pitcher that served as a sink. The luxury of the bath weighed against the inconvenience of having no water, hot or cold, in the 'kitchen'. She hung blue curtains to create a living room and built bookshelves either side of a chimneybreast, now fitted with a gas fire. This fire served as a toaster, and upturned orange boxes as chairs. The bookshelves she filled with poetry ('various moderns, Wilfred Owen (a magnificent poet) – and Pindar') and Russian literature.[75] During the day Seaforth had the light of an artist's studio; once dusk fell and the blackout curtains went up it felt more like a Victorian garret. To Iris it was a flat of 'utterly irresistible personality' and 'indescribable charm'.[76] To Mary, who would sometimes wander over for a sandwich, it looked like a stage set for a school production of something by Dostoevsky.[77] She couldn't shake the feeling that the Underground Man might appear through the floor as the District Line rattled the windows. Ever practical, Mary lent Iris a Scrutton armchair, which was manoeuvred awkwardly up the winding stairs. Iris conjured up a second, crowned with her turquoise cushion. The pair were installed, in imitation of Edwardian domesticity, around the gas fire.

Iris shared the flat with a noisy rat and some mice who, she complained to Frank, were eating her letters. 'I am very angry about this, chiefly because your letters are rather precious documents, but also because I am not on very good terms with the mice, & the fact that I have been careless enough to leave valuables around where they could get at them can be chalked up as a point to them.' Nevertheless, she forgave them on account of their 'nice long tails'.[78] The papery mouse meals arrived regularly from the sweltering dry heat of Cairo, then from Tripoli, and from everywhere in between as the front of the North African campaign traversed the 1,250 miles east and west across the intervening desert. Frank praised Beatrice Webb's memoir *My Apprenticeship*: 'I found it wholly delightful to follow the thoughts, perplexities and sorrows of a highly intelligent woman.' He told Iris that the desert's 'most depressing feature, – worse than flies, heat or sandstorm, – is the predominant masculinity of its inhabitants'.[79] But he was downplaying the conditions: when the sandstorms came, men were relieved that the killing had stopped; but after three days they would be praying that killing recommence so the sandstorm might stop. It was so hot an egg would fry on the armour of a tank. And the flies were in biblical quantities, so bloated from the blood of corpses that they stank of rotting flesh.[80] There was not enough water to wash, let alone to bathe – one cup per day per man.[81]

But still letters got through. Despite the paper shortage, each week 3 million air letters, 4½ million items of surface mail and postcards, and half a million airgraphs passed through the Army postal services and countless unobserved intermediary places.[82] At a time when resources, manpower and economy were orientated almost solely towards the objectives of war, a postal service, comprising men and women, machine and vehicle, convention and law, all cooperating, made it possible for a girl in bombed-out London to share her thoughts with a lovelorn boy in the Western Desert simply by putting a small square of wartime paper into a slot in a red box on the corner of Tothill Street and Storey's Gate.

Frank received regular reports of Iris's diurnal and nocturnal life. By day, she produced, filed, moved, copied and shredded papers, 'dry as dust', as a cog in the giant machinery of government. She developed 'a liking for machine-like efficiency, a desire to regiment humanity into cast iron categories'.[83] Her colleagues were 'pleasant men and women', intelligent '(and some of them very beautiful)', smiling and discreet,[84] often Oxford or Cambridge graduates. After work, they would share a glass of beer or a whisky in the pubs round Westminster before they disappeared to their suburban homes or bedsitters with landlady gatekeepers. Then Iris entered her night-time world. She would head north, away from the river and up through St James's Park and Leicester Square to Soho.

Iris was in search of 'Ultimate Human Beings' and 'knowledge & experience & freedom'. She was experimenting with a literary persona, *Iris Murdoch, writer*. The freedom she found in that night-time world was that of 'a complete lack of any sense of responsibility' within '[a] strange society – composed of restless incomplete ambitious people who live in a chaotic and random way, never caring about the next five minutes, drunk every night without exception from 6 o'clock onwards, homeless & unfamilied, living in pubs & copulating upon the floors of other people's flats'.[85] They were unreliable and rudderless, living outside the usual framework where concern for the future and the past imposes itself on the present. They could not be regimented. Free to do as they wished, they lived in fragments, acting on every passing thought or desire; nothing mattered. In this society the only thing that was serious was poetry, and all were orientated towards their deity, T. S. Eliot.[86]

Among Iris's nocturnal friends were many refugees and migrants who, like her, were living double lives, working for the British government's war machine during the day and indulging their alter egos by night. She drank with Mulk Raj Anand, struggling novelist, Bloomsbury intellectual and propagandist for the Indian independence movement – by day, a scriptwriter for the BBC. She escaped the unwelcome sexual attentions of Hungarian refugee writer Arthur Koestler – by day, a propagandist for the Ministry of Information. She fell for Tambi – Meary James Thurairajah Tambimuttu – the Sri Lankan poet with beautiful hair.[87] She danced with Dylan Thomas at the Gargoyle, a private members' club on Dean Street, the interior of which was designed by Augustus John, Edwin Lutyens and Henri Matisse and included a fountain on the dance floor.[88]

Seaforth was also living a double life. Despite Mary's poetic remonstrations, Iris's faith in Communism remained unshaken. A Party cell borrowed the attic for meetings. They sat on the floor and scribbled encoded notes on the lower part of Iris's newly whitewashed walls. At work Iris copied Treasury papers and hid them in a tree in Kensington Gardens.[89]

Letters also went back and forth between London and Oxford, Pip and Iris. Philippa wrote her replies in bed, under her dark-red bedspread, 'board across knee, and teapot to hand'.[90] She had stayed in Oxford after receiving her First in PPE. Her claims not to have been very bright were surely implausible given this result, achieved by a girl who had arrived at Oxford with almost no schooling and who had sat her finals following months confined to bed in plaster and agony. Thanks to her training in economics (by now she could do maths), she was employed as one of a staff of sixteen at the Nuffield Social Reconstruction Survey, a research group established to gather data and provide analysis on population and industry distribution during and after the war. Her specialism was the furniture industry.[91] Here we meet Sandie Lindsay again. Not as political candidate, Boars Hill Idealist, Master of Balliol, or examiner of consciences, but as the driving force behind the Survey, which he helped to establish at the start of 1941.

Philippa's office was at 17 Banbury Road, just a three-minute walk from the gates of Somerville. She took a room nearby, in the house of the economist David Worswick, and enjoyed furnishing it. She made pink silk cushions to go with her bedspread, recreating the colours of the sweet peas she and her mother had grown together at the Old Hall at Kirkleatham and which she loved. In a junk shop she found some 'rough and heavenly' Italian pottery 'which came off a ship they seized on its way to Norway with exports'. The decor was completed with 'a lamp shade – grey with a bit of red on it.' Alongside her work, there was teaching for the Workers' Educational Association, evenings with Donald MacKinnon and regular trips to the Cassirers' home to 'entertain Eva' and listen to Heinz. 'The Cassirers are being a bore at the moment,' she confessed in a letter to her mother, 'and complaining of neglect. He's written a book on Kant, and is really just grouchy because of that.' She went riding with her meat purveyor: 'By the look of him he should have good strong horses.'[92]

Her role at the Nuffield saw her working closely with Thomas Balogh and Nicky Kaldor, a pair of Hungarian émigré economists who were employed at the (also new) National Institute of Economic and Social Research. Tommy, fifteen years her senior and Sandie Lindsay's Balliol colleague and friend (Tommy had a framed photo of Sandie on his mantelpiece),[93] had tutored Philippa through her finals, and like Donald MacKinnon had visited her when she was in bed. Then, at some point in 1942, he had joined her in it, and the pair became an item. 'Balogh put women under a spell', recalled David Worswick; Tommy loaned him some furniture and used it as an excuse to visit his home, and Philippa, freely.[94] The relationship brought Philippa into Tommy's group of friends and a world of 'crazy' parties. The morning after one especially wild night, perhaps feeling a little the worse for wear, she typed a letter to her mother. 'We started at Balliol, and then went on like a pack of locusts to the

George where an enormous meal was eaten, mostly by Nicky who eats for six and looks as if he always has.' Then back to Philippa's room for coffee and to 'sew Nicky into his waistcoat again as . . . the buttons hadn't stood the strain', before heading out.[95]

In the summer of 1943, the survey was wound up and Philippa's time rampaging around Oxford came to an end. A new posting came through: she was to go to London to the Royal Institute for International Affairs, also known as Chatham House.

When Philippa stepped off the train, in August 1943, she would have exited Marylebone onto Melcombe Place – the bomb damage to Mary and Iris's Harewood Avenue entrance had proved fatal. By then, her relationship with Tommy was officially, but not unofficially, over. They had ended it one evening, after a drunken post-party row, at 'precisely 12.56 British Summer Time'.[96] But Tommy spent part of every week in London and the pair remained 'on off'.[97]

At first Philippa lived once again with fellow Somervillian Anne Cobbe in a grand flat on nearby Weymouth Street. Anne had taken a First in mathematics and was now working at the Admiralty.[98] The flat came with help; an older couple lived in, preparing meals and doing the housework for their young mistresses. They also provided a slightly chaffing routine of set dinner times and curfews. From the beginning (and much to the disapproval of Anne's mother, Lady Cobbe),[99] Philippa spent a good deal of time with Iris, toasting crumpets on the Seaforth gas fire, nestled in the Scrutton armchair and eating picnic dinners whenever the mood took them. Tommy and Nicky occasionally took them out for dinner to L'Étoile on Charlotte Street.[100]

Philippa found her new job as 'baby' research assistant[101] a 'joy' – 'I couldn't have invented a better for myself.'[102] She would have attended Chatham House's regular lecture series, designed to give employees access to the latest social and economic studies on post-war reconstruction. That year, Margaret Mead, the American anthropologist, came to speak on food habits. She had turned her ethnographical gaze on to the lives of Allied soldiers and civilians. Philippa would have listened to Mead's detailed description of the 'dietary patterns' she had found among the populations she had studied. She explained how environmental change, scientific knowledge and symbolism could all disrupt or alter patterns of eating and living.[103]

Bertha Bracey, head of both the Friends Committee for Refugees and Aliens and the Central Department for Interned Refugees, also came to speak about pattern, disruption and deprivation. Bracey had been a driving force behind the *Kindertransport*, which carried more than 10,000 Jewish children out of Germany, and her rescue work continued throughout the conflict.[104] Philippa would have heard her warning: as soon as fighting stopped 30 million displaced people would start to move across the globe. In the confusion of a war-torn landscape these journeys would appear chaotic, unprincipled, formless. But each was the path of an individual drawn by a strong and irresistible homing instinct. The inevitability of these journeys must be recognised and planned for, urged Bracey; however, the task would be supremely difficult. 'The picture is one vast kaleidoscope whose movements are still in process, so that the pattern formed at one point of time is quite different from that formed at any other.'[105] Some things were known. Two million Spanish Republicans had crossed into France at the close of the Spanish Civil War: tens of thousands had gone on to North Africa or Mexico, but hundreds of thousands were still in France when it fell to Germany. From the island of Mauritius, 1,500 detained refugees would move north-west towards Europe before scattering to Austria, Czechoslovakia and Poland. Sweden sheltered 4 million refugees from central Europe, Switzerland more than 62,000. As for the uncountable number of Jews deported from Germany, Austria, Czechoslovakia, Poland, Russia, the Ukraine, Belgium, Bulgaria, the Netherlands, France, Norway, Romania, the Baltic States: how many survived she did not know. Bracey spoke of the 'Nazi policy of extermination', but the real meaning of Hitler's Holocaust was not yet understood.[106] In June 1942, the *Daily Telegraph* had reported that in occupied Europe the Nazis were murdering 1,000 Polish Jews a day in gas chambers. Astonishingly, this made only page six, and was not picked up by other papers.[107]

As well as work and Seaforth, Philippa continued to make regular weekend trips to Oxford: catching the train ('Is your journey *really* necessary?'); staying with the Cassirers' at 19 Carlton Road; spending evenings with Donald MacKinnon. One Sunday she stayed with him too long and arrived back in London just before 1 a.m., missing the last underground train. 'However,' she reassured her mother, 'on my long trek across London I met a taxi which only had 7 American soldiers in it so they sat me on their knees to St James. (thank heaven.)'.[108] Little did the soldiers know that the foxy-faced hitchhiker perched on their laps was the granddaughter of a president. Taxi headlights off, careering through the dark.

While Philippa was, by all accounts, happy, her flatmate Anne was struggling to cope. In 1940 her beloved brother Bill (Alexander William Locke), a schoolfriend of Michael and Frank, had been reported missing presumed dead. By the time Anne took her finals any faint hope that he had been taken prisoner was gone. Her wartime work, for which she used statistical analysis of past naval battles to inform future tactics, left her drained and distressed.[109] Not long after Philippa's arrival, Anne suffered a mental collapse and returned to her family home. This left Philippa in need of a place to live.

At first, Philippa looked for a place of her own and took a lease on a two-room flat on Charlotte Street in Bloomsbury. But Chatham House, the Institute's headquarters, was only a mile north of Seaforth, across St James's Park, and Iris proposed Philippa move in with her. Otherwise, Iris reasoned, they'd just be spending half their time at Charlotte Street and half at Seaforth and wasting a good deal of rent money. So Philippa's pink silk cushions joined Iris's turquoise one on Mary's chair, her red-and-grey lampshade balanced over the light fitting. Crumpets could now be served on Italian pottery. There would be a Bosanquet at Seaforth for the next fifty years: Philippa's sister Marion took the lease when Iris and Philippa moved out at the end of the war.

Philippa was under her dark-red bedspread at Seaforth just in time for winter: blackout curtains were pulled from the windows after lights-out to double as extra blankets, overcoats as pyjamas, hot-water bottles a necessity. They warmed up each morning with tea and sticky buns in Lyons' tea rooms across the street.[110] Lyons' too was living a double life: while it served up treats in its cafés, its factories were given over to the manufacture of bombs. One in every seven dropped on German civilians was produced by the baker and confectioner.[111]

Philippa had never looked after herself before and tended just to put things down, as if an invisible servant would spirit them away. Iris kept things orderly and her seriousness about learning was both unexpected and a delight to Philippa, who felt herself still at a disadvantage owing to her lack of schooling. Iris would return from work and immediately pick up a book.[112] At her suggestion, Philippa read Beckett, Dickens and Proust. A bank holiday visit to Kirkleatham did not intimidate Iris, who astonished Esther Bosanquet by making her own sandwiches.[113] Later, Philippa recalled (seemingly with some delight) her mother's shock when Iris 'committed the awful sin of pushing her empty plate away and putting her head down on the table. Now you just don't <u>do</u> things like that, do you!!!!'[114]

At home in their mousey attic, Iris and Philippa had three pairs of shoes between them, in the end dwindling to two. In a reprise of Mary and Iris's conversation on the Cherwell, they compared lists of men who had proposed to them. Philippa went first: her list was respectable but short. Iris's, once started, seemed like it would never end: 'It would be quicker', Philippa said crossly to Iris, if she listed 'the ones who hadn't asked her rather than those who had'.[115] They threw a party – bring your own bottle – perhaps for Philippa's twenty-third birthday that October. Characters mixed from their three personae: bluestocking, bohemian and Miss Murdoch and Miss Bosanquet of the Treasury and Chatham House. Turkish cigarettes were passed around as Balogh and Kaldor danced with PPE Somervillian Vera Hoar (another of Donald MacKinnon's tutees).[116] Jane Degras, Mark Benny, Stevie Smith and Tambimuttu made their way, with bottles of beer and spirits, through the dark from Soho.[117]

Elizabeth's Plan Stalls

In Cambridge, Elizabeth took out her typewriter and wrote a rough scheme of the work she'd been doing and proposed to do in the hope of renewing her Sarah Smithson funding for another year. A crawling and teething Barbara weaved in and out of her legs. By April 1944, the pair were living at 19 Fitzwilliam Street, opposite the house occupied 100 years earlier by Charles Darwin on his return from his voyage on the *Beagle*.[118] Elizabeth was preparing to take up the task of 'appalling difficulty' which had daunted and fascinated her tutor Donald MacKinnon.[119] 'Examine the definition "animal rationals" [sic],' she typed (Barbara perhaps needing attention just as her mother's finger landed on 's' not 'e').[120]

Elizabeth's idea had been finessed over a year of hard study. She proposed to follow Aristotle and to learn about humans using the same sorts of methods we have for learning about turnips and cats. 'The use of language is that in virtue of which we say that a man has a rational part.' She would consider the logical character of statements that express the operation of sensitive faculties, statements like 'I see red' or 'I see a red postbox'. 'Follow up this line,' she typed decisively.[121]

Her central question would not be Descartes' 'What am I?' but one that looked outward: what is *that*?: 'What sort of objects do I perceive when I perceive human beings?', she would ask.[122] Descartes' introspective glance took him away from his body and into his consciousness – imaginings, fears, thoughts, itches, toothaches, all of which he supposed might occur without the extended body (headaches without heads; itches without places to scratch; toothless toothaches). Elizabeth's extraspective glance took her in a different direction towards observations about the nature of the human animal.

'*Man has 32 teeth*.'[123] This sentence is more unusual than it first seems. It is not an empirical statement that can be verified by counting teeth in the mouths of humans (in the darkness of the shuddering carriage, a gappy smile reveals the hopelessness of such a method). Thanks to the efforts of dentists and the temptation of sweets, human animals have on average far fewer. Still, 32 is a complete set of teeth and anyone with fewer is missing some. This is because 'man has 32 teeth' is about the species *human animal*: it is how many teeth a human *ought* to have. It would be true that man has 32 teeth, even if each and every one of us had missing molars.

Later, Elizabeth would argue that just as it is the norm or ideal for man to have a complete set of teeth, a 'complete set of virtues' is a norm for man, looked at 'from the point of view of the activity of thought and choice in regard to the various departments of life – powers and faculties and use of things needed'.[124] But just as many of us lack a full set of teeth, few possess a full set of virtues – we may be patient but not courageous; diligent but lack kindness. To be deficient in this way is to be missing something, even if many others are deficient too. For now, Elizabeth registered a worry about her new 'extraspective' method. She typed it urgently: 'Is there work here for a philosopher or only for an experimental psychologist?'[125]

In April, as she was preparing her 'rough scheme', Elizabeth discovered that her brother John had been killed in the defence of Jessami, India, in the first of six gruelling battles for which his regiment was later awarded honours.[126] Elizabeth's mother, not long since widowed, was overwhelmed with grief. Taken in initially by John's twin, Tom, Gertrude was eventually hospitalised in St Andrew's Hospital for Mental Diseases in Northampton.

The hospital was well known for its experimental treatments, which included pre-frontal lobotomies, the effect of which on a patient's intellect and personality provides ample evidence of the deep connections between matter and mind. In the year that Gertrude was admitted, thirty-five such operations were carried out.[127] She spent the remainder of her life in the institution. A Beguildy parish history, written in 1961, records that 'although she lived more than ten years in a home, it was only in the days of her childhood that she lived, the days of her Father's lifetime, at Beguildy Vicarage'.[128] Thus, aged twenty-six, Elizabeth joined her husband Peter as a de facto orphan, having buried her father and lost her mother.

It fell to the analytic philosopher John Wisdom, of Trinity College, to review and reject Elizabeth's application, for which she submitted her 'rough scheme' and a draft of her dissertation. 'Mrs. Geach's dissertation seems to me hardly to reach fellowship standard, by which I mean that it would not be quite good enough for a fellowship even if there were no other candidates,' he began. Wisdom was impressed by discussion of the peculiar role of quotation: Elizabeth's insistence that when we say '"Grass" is the subject in "Grass is green"' we are neither talking about grass nor about the word 'grass' reminded him of some remarks made by Professor Wittgenstein in his lectures on grammar. But the point was ruined by Miss Anscombe's 'eccentric use of the word "word"'. It 'isn't merely that the exposition is confusing, the writer is confused'. And when she came to the topic of identity, instead of turning to the British Empiricists with whom Wisdom was familiar, she looked to Aristotle and Aquinas, of whom Wisdom admitted himself 'ignorant'. He had to ask G. E. Moore for help reading the lengthy passages of Greek and Latin that Elizabeth had not troubled to translate. Her 'real effort' and her 'learning in Aristotle and Aquinas' cannot make good the 'obscurity, disconnectedness, dogmatism, inadequate knowledge of opposing views and downright muddles'.[129]

A positive reference from Waismann was not enough to undo the damage. Friedrich commended her 'great concentration and singleness of mind', her 'considerable faculty of insight into the structure of thought as it manifests itself in language' and her 'lively philosophical imagination'.[130] But he was distracted. In April 1943, his wife Hermine had died by suicide, leaving him to care for their son, Thomas, then just seven. She had not been able to cope with the guilt of finding safety in Britain while her family remained behind; her sister was among those murdered in the

Holocaust. Donald MacKinnon, who had become Waismann's friend at Oxford, recalled her funeral, 'on a bitterly cold April morning', as 'undoubtedly the most harrowing I have ever attended'.[131] Nine years later, Thomas followed his mother and ended his own life, aged sixteen.

Elizabeth's failure to secure an extension to her Sarah Smithson funding left her in a state of poverty that would last for another six years. With Peter still away in the forest, and wartime rationing that left everyone hungry, it is difficult to know how she kept Barbara in food and herself in cigarettes as the war progressed.

In October 1944 Ludwig Wittgenstein returned to Cambridge.

Love & War at Seaforth

As the war entered its final phase Seaforth was deep into a love drama that would resonate through Iris and Philippa's friendship for many years, as well as providing Iris with the archetype of a tangled erotic muddle for her novels. (Iris had by now abandoned one novel and finished a second, the latter rejected by T. S. Eliot at Faber & Faber, with no encouragement to resubmit.)[132] Tommy 'is very bored with me & he & his friends have dropped me', Philippa had told her mother, some time after she arrived in London. She missed the group but thought it 'a good thing'.[133] However, when Tommy dropped Philippa (or perhaps slightly before) he took up with Iris. Iris fell in obsessive love or lust with him in much the way that characters do in her novels. For a short while, she managed to divide her attention between Tommy and Michael Foot, but the older man would not tolerate a rival and Iris ended things with Michael in January 1944, having strung him along for several months. When Iris described her own behaviour to David Hicks, looking back from November 1945, the word she used was 'nauseating'. 'It's a quadrilateral tale that would make rather a good psychological novel', she added.[134]

Michael sank into a despair matched only by his earlier episode, three years before, over Léonie.[135] He later comforted himself with the notion that the Official Secrets Act was to blame for his failure to capture Iris's heart.

Iris and Tommy's behaviour left Philippa miserable and she now found herself often abandoned while Iris raced around town with her ex-lover and her old set of friends. One evening in April, alone in Seaforth, she heard a knock on the door below.[136] Opening it, she saw a desperate and desperately dashing young man, pacing about in the alley. It was Michael. The pair had not met before (Iris tended to keep her friends separate), but after Philippa told him that Iris was out, he accepted her invitation up to the attic for a drink and a sympathetic ear. Philippa was a natural protector, as Donald MacKinnon had recognised. Michael thought Seaforth 'gaunt',[137] and Philippa with her regal presence and elegant clothes, must have looked especially beautiful in such a setting, as they talked of hunting, horses and the trappings of their upper-class childhoods. Michael had known Anne Cobbe's brother Bill. The misery that Iris found vaguely foolish, Philippa found charming and they took to each other instantly. Soon he warned her that he might disappear at any moment, to be parachuted behind enemy lines.[138] What girl could resist a heroic, handsome and heartbroken intelligence officer, ready to risk all if duty called? Michael once again transferred his affections to a woman who was willing to look after him.

Philippa's blossoming romance with Michael put further strain on her damaged friendship with Iris, as did Iris's increasingly selfish behaviour. Her epic list of proposals perhaps looked less innocent to Philippa in the face of Michael's misery. Meanwhile, Seaforth supplied its own challenges. Iris's blue curtain provided the attic's only interior wall, so Iris and Philippa had to negotiate continuously whose lover was to spend the night there. When Iris was at Tommy's in Chelsea, Philippa would send for Michael. When Philippa stayed at Michael's, over Tommy might come.[139] When the two friends were alone in the flat together, they wept constantly. Iris saw how morally tough Philippa was – there was something of the Kantian in her. (Iris's principles were not exactly of the kind that one would or could will to become universal law.) 'Michael hated me for deceiving him & then for seeming indifferent. Pip hated me for making Michael suffer. I hated Michael because he spoilt my celestial relation with Thomas,' Iris recalled. For this, she later hated herself, but at the time she was so 'insanely in love & utterly devoid of willpower' and could not muster genuine remorse or pity, which might have saved her in Philippa's eyes. 'I saw my relation to her gradually being destroyed, by my own fault, yet I did nothing to save it. She behaved wonderfully throughout.' There was nothing to do but weep, write letters and talk to the mice.[140]

Mary Finds Herself Among 'Strange Tribes'

While Iris and Philippa played out their semi-adult tragedy in London, Mary was back at her girlhood school in Berkshire, Downe House. She had become increasingly anxious in her job at the Ministry of Production, having nothing to do while those around her were rushed off their feet. Iris, in her position, might have demanded a job or invented one for herself, but Mary waited and watched. 'I ought to have seen', she reflected later, 'that things actually were wrong and taken firm steps to get them changed.' However, '[t]he world is divided at any time into those who can see that it is possible to do this and those who can't. At that time I was one of the can'ts.'[141] The stress led to a repeat of the illness that had almost scuppered her First. As she grew older, she would develop a habit of removing herself promptly from any situation likely to induce anxiety, along with a pragmatic aversion to extremes of emotion, behaviour or temperament. She adopted 'neurotic' as her most scathing pejorative, one that she would reach for perhaps a little too readily, where a more just vision might have delivered 'overwrought', 'disorganised' or even 'passionate'. Olive Willis, headmistress at Downe, was 'not neurotic . . . conspicuously sane, lively, effective' – the highest praise.[142]

Mary would teach Classics to future Marys – something 'useful' at last.[143] Some things at Downe had changed little since her schooldays. Looking from the hilltop classroom window across the lawn and down to the fields and copses below she may have fancied herself an overgrown schoolgirl. But Mary could not have missed the constant reminders that, though her own life had looped back, the world around her had evolved. In nearby Newbury, Elliott's Joinery Company, just along from Woolworths, was making aircraft parts rather than furniture. The stables at the racecourse, requisitioned early in the war, housed prisoners of war instead of horses. The singular and magical Maria Nickel – rumoured in Mary's schooldays to be a Polish princess[144] – had not only dug a long tunnel under the main house (to serve as an air-raid shelter), but had sprayed all the buildings green (with a view to camouflaging the school in its bucolic setting). Three hundred pine trees from the grounds had gone to the Admiralty, an event the origins of which perhaps lay in a report generated within Betty Ackroyd's Raw Materials Section. And there was another, sadder gap. In the weeks before Mary's arrival, Lillian Heather, Olive Willis's partner for thirty-six years, died after a long illness through which Olive had nursed her. She was buried in the school's parkland, in a plot Olive was later to share.[145]

Mary recovered her health and balance at Downe. She taught Plato. Talk in the staffroom was agreeable and undemanding, even if the wartime coffee was unpleasant. But while as a child Mary had no ambitions to move beyond Downe's confines, she now knew a little of the world outside and was soon feeling the isolation. Wartime petrol rationing ruled out weekend trips, and as Michael was courting Philippa in London, Mary was wondering how she might move on.

Something cropped up during her fourth term '[b]y some channel that I can't now remember', she later recalled. She drifted into teaching Classics at Bedford School – a 'welcome change'.[146] She and a younger woman, Peggy Torrance (a History graduate from St Hilda's who had arrived straight from Oxford),[147] were the only women in the school, which catered mostly for the sons of ambitious captains and majors, men who expected their sons to be caned, bullied and whacked into shape. If she had hopes of pairing up there, they were soon dashed. Peggy and Mary stood together agog in the Senior Common Room at mid-morning break and surveyed their colleagues. In place of the relaxed chatter and bad coffee of the Downe staffroom, they were confronted with a room that 'offered no refreshment whatever and very little talk. Some of the masters just stood, staring into space,' and '[a]nybody who did talk did it apologetically in a low voice, rather as though they were at a funeral'.[148] In later years, when asked why so many women were put off pursuing careers in philosophy, Mary would reply: 'Don't ask what is wrong with the women, look at what is wrong with the men.'[149] One imagines she may have formed this policy in that moment, as she and Peggy exchanged the silent thought: 'These people must be crazy.' Mary studied this strange 'tribe' with an ethologist's eye, hypothesising a range of underlying motives for their silence ranging from shyness to fear to sexism. She compared her field notes with Peggy. Their fifteen-minute break was just long enough to scamper down the school's long drive to the milk bar across the street, devour a jam tart and share a joke about the 'customs of the tribe' among which they had found themselves.[150]

Elizabeth Anscombe Meets Ludwig Wittgenstein

When Elizabeth met Wittgenstein, she was twenty-five. He was fifty-five and had only seven years to live. The chaos and disorder that he caused in the lives of those around him, combined with Elizabeth's isolation and poverty, would have made an outside observer fear for her. But she was ready for Wittgenstein, and he for her. She had two things that he needed in an interlocutor and philosophical friend. First, she was deeply perplexed. Part of his cycle of disgust at his teaching, and at those he taught, was his sense that those studying philosophy at Cambridge University were not genuinely puzzled.[151] But Elizabeth really was. She had spent her teens worrying over divine foreknowledge and a faulty proof that every event must have a cause. She had aroused censure over the conditions for a Just War. She had sat as MacKinnon paced and growled in his room. She had spent hours staring at packets of cigarettes in the cafés of Oxford. She had stayed up late at night with Mary trying to figure out what Plato could have meant by the 'behindness'. Eyeing uniformed soldiers on the train, she had thought of cats and turnips.

And this was the second thing: she had a religious faith that made her serious. For Elizabeth, the problem of the identity of bodies was neither a technical nor a scientific puzzle: it was a matter of her immortal soul. The problem of knowledge of the external world was the problem of faith and hope. The problem of counterfactual conditionals was the problem of theodicy. The problem of causation was the problem of God as first cause. When the analyst Bertrand Russell once asked Wittgenstein: 'What are you thinking about, logic or your sins?' he had replied: 'Both.' This was true also of Elizabeth. These two aspects of Elizabeth – her genuine philosophical puzzlement and her faith – may also explain how she was able to sustain her philosophical independence and her sanity while so many others who found themselves drawn into Wittgenstein's orbit did not.

Peter visited over Christmas and, as 1945 began, Elizabeth was pregnant again. This was to be the year that she, like Margaret Masterman and Alice Ambrose before her, climbed the staircase to Whewell's Court for Wittgenstein's disorientating, foggy, electrifying classes. That winter, it would already have been dark by 5 p.m. as she made her way along All Saints Passage. Wittgenstein would not have minded the gloom; he thought best in the dark.

Room K5 is at the top of a neo-gothic tower and in the daytime has views across Trinity College. Wittgenstein used strips of black card to reproportion the windows to conform with his modernist architectural taste. In the centre of the room stood a small stove. Apart from that, the room contained a deckchair, a trestle table, an armchair and virtually nothing else. 'No pictures, no curtains and almost no books', recalled an under-graduate.[152] Visitors would pick up a light-green canvas deckchair from the stack outside the room, entering to find Wittgenstein also in a deckchair, 'bent forward, with his elbows resting on his knees and his hands pressed against each other with fingers outstretched, almost as if he were praying'.[153] At precisely 5 p.m. Wittgenstein's body would unfold and he would begin his lecture. He spoke without notes. Though scheduled to finish at 7 p.m., there was no way of knowing how long a lecture might go on. Like Fraen-kel's *Agamemnon* classes, the experience inspired one undergraduate, Ivor (I. A.) Richards to poetry.

Few could long withstand your haggard beauty,
Disdainful lips, wide eyes bright-lit with scorn,
Furrowed brow, square smile, sorrow-born
World-abandoning devotion to your duty.

Such the torment felt, the spell-bound listeners
Watched and waited for the words to come,
Held and bit their breath while you were dumb,
Anguished, helpless, for the hidden prisoners.[154]

A few years earlier Elizabeth had been in H. H. Price's lecture in Oxford tearing at her gown in frustration. In the Cadena café, '*What do I really see?*'. As she sat in Wittgenstein's tower, she saw him parodying that struggle, but the parody was not mockery. 'I am sitting with a philosopher in the garden,' Wittgenstein begins. The philosopher 'says again and again: "I know that's a tree", pointing to a tree that is near us. Someone else arrives and hears this, and I tell him: "This fellow isn't insane. We are only doing philosophy".'[155] For Wittgenstein, the philosopher's struggle, which seems insanity to an onlooker, begins when the things that we take for granted, that form the background of our everyday lives, suddenly become strange or uncanny (cigarette packets evanesce, cats disappear, '*I know that's a tree,*' someone says repeatedly). Wittgenstein had come to realise that these were moments of profound importance for philosophers. The temptation is always to step back from this seeming loss of sanity, to cover over the withdrawal of certainty with arguments and theories. Instead, Wittgenstein insisted, the philosopher must attempt to understand the source of this mysterious and distinctive loss of balance, rather than seeking to explain it away. By sticking with these moments of perplexity, by looking at them and turning them around, the philosopher can begin to recognise that the strangeness of these moments arises when bits of language are lifted out of daily life. The philosopher's job, recognising this strangeness, is to search out the patterns of life into which those bits of language fit, the goings-on from where they have been lifted, and to replant them in their proper soil.

Wittgenstein's lectures continued through the winter and into the spring and Elizabeth would have attended every week. Wittgenstein (like Fraenkel) despised 'tourists'.[156] While his presence left others exhausted and in need of vitamins,[157] Elizabeth began to see in his method a way out of the difficulties she was grappling with in her dissertation. She stared boldly at him, unfeigned perplexity and seriousness etched on her face. In addition to her talent for this new sort of thinking, she worked uncommonly hard, harder than her peers. A roomful of undergraduates focusing on their own anxieties (the fear of being picked) rather than on the philosophical problem made Wittgenstein nauseous and enraged. To be able to look up and see Elizabeth, thinking as hard and furiously as he was, was an anti-emetic. As for her, Wittgenstein's approach to philosophy and philosophical questions was opening up new ways of approaching the old metaphysical problems of her dissertation. A new way of making an extraspective glance. She was soon, as she later put it, in a 'state of besotted reverence' for him.[158]

Wittgenstein: Suppose that for some people counting were learnt first as a sort of poetry, and then later used as a way of measuring fields. You see someone pacing in a field. What makes you say he is measuring and not doing poetry?

Student 1: You find out if he is counting?

Wittgenstein: You don't know his language.

Student 2: You see if his pace is a constant unit?

Wittgenstein: That might be a dance.

Wasfi Hijab: You study their lives.

Wittgenstein: Yes, you need the context of a lot of other things they do. Take any such phenomenon as comparing colours, measuring time, comparing lengths, playing games. These are specific. "I'll show you things we humans do."[159]

Each week, Wittgenstein exhibited fragmentary scenes from human life and from lives that are like ours but uncanny or changed. Things we humans do are: give orders, measure, draw, report an event, speculate, form hypotheses, make up stories, play-act, sing, guess riddles, tell jokes, translate, ask, thank, curse, greet, pray.[160] Each activity has its place among the overlapping patterns that make up the human form of life. Elizabeth began to see a new way to describe the soul of a human. Not an efficient calculating machine, but a social, creative, curious, spiritual animal.

Philippa & Iris Wait for News

Fifty miles south in London, fog was enveloping Seaforth. '[T]he fog even in this room is so thick that I can but dimly discern Iris across the other side,' wrote Philippa to her mother, as the pair of friends continued their uneasy cohabitation.[161] Summer 1944 was the season in which the war came to Seaforth. On 6 June, D-Day, Allied troops landed on the beaches of Normandy and prepared to push the German armies back south and east. In retaliation, the Germans began their 'flying-bomb' campaign. *Vergeltungswaffen* (vengeance weapons) were launched from France, each with just enough fuel to carry it low over the water and into the sky above London before the engine cut out. Then followed fourteen seconds of silence as the bomb fell to earth. Londoners were once again forced back into their burrows.

Iris took the precaution of sending part of the novel she was writing to a friend in Oxford for safekeeping,[162] but she and Pip stayed above ground and crawled into the Seaforth bath when the air-raid siren went. One morning they were woken at 7 o'clock, a few minutes before their alarm clocks sounded, when 'the windows & window frames were blown in'.[163] Iris had not heard from Frank for many months and over the summer she became increasingly anxious. Throughout July, Philippa spent many hours in the National Gallery getting acquainted with Goya's *Don Andrés del Peral*,[164] the 'Picture of the Month'. Then, a few days after *Don Andrés* was returned to its Cathedral cave (replaced by Bellini's *The Virgin and Child*) Michael simply vanished. Now Philippa and Iris were both waiting for news.

After Michael's disappearance, Donald wrote to Philippa every day. On 27 September he telephoned her at work with news, not of Michael but of Frank. A Missing Believed Killed notice had appeared that morning in *The Times*.

Iris's 'Brave & Beloved' Frank Thompson had been captured, tortured and murdered four days after D-Day and three days before the first *Vergeltungswaffen* drove Iris and Philippa to shelter in the bathtub.[165] He had volunteered to be parachuted into occupied Serbia from where he and his unit walked into German-allied Bulgaria to liaise with members of the Bulgarian resistance. The mission was suicidal. Frank had been in the country for less than four weeks when he was shot.[166] Uncannily, he stayed alive on paper for 103 days after his death. To relieve officers of pressure to write to family and loved ones, forces policy was to send officially generated fortnightly telegrams home. The messages followed a formula, rotating between a statement of health, acknowledgement of receipt of letters, and a greeting. His parents received and replied to these over the summer and into the autumn, though the un-Franklike quality of the messages began to trouble them. However, the pretence was bolstered by deliveries to Scar Top of food hampers from high-end department store Stuttafords that Frank had prearranged. On 16 September his mother, Theo, wrote to thank him for the crystallised fruit and tinned tongue. In preparation for his return, she cleaned his room and reconditioned his piano. She received the Missing Believed Killed telegram five days after the tinned tongue.[167]

Philippa went home from work to break the news. She found Iris in the kitchen.[168]

The nights drew in. After the liberation of Paris at the end of August, French literature started to filter across the Channel and into Seaforth.[169] *Pierrot Mon Ami* by Raymond Queneau was an early arrival.[170] Finally, in October, the news Philippa had been waiting for appeared. '[A] letter has come through from Michael via the Red Cross in Nantes,' she wrote to her mother. 'It seems so unbelievable to link the two worlds like that, and so wonderful a letter saying that all was well with him.' Michael, she now knew, was a prisoner of war in Brittany: '[h]e said nothing of how things were in the camp except that he had two books – a New Testament and Antony & Cleopatra – and was just starting 10 days' solitary confinement, one doesn't know why'.[171]

On receipt of Michael's letter, Philippa decided she ought to track down Michael's father, to whom she had not yet been introduced. She did this with some trepidation, 'knowing a priori that he would not have heard of my existence'. It took her '21 telephone calls' to get hold of his address. She sent a letter, and when she arrived at work the following morning she was astonished to find Brigadier Richard Foot waiting for her in the common room of Chatham House: 'we fell on each other's necks with tears of joy'; he kept repeating: 'Oh but I'm so glad he had someone he wanted to write to.'[172]

News of Michael had reached his parents a fortnight before his letter to Philippa, carried by a fellow prisoner who had managed to escape. Between them they had enough fragments to piece together a narrative ('We fitted the jigsaw together gradually'). Michael had parachuted into occupied Europe and, like Frank, been taken prisoner almost immediately. He had made two failed attempts to escape, and it was the second of these that had landed him in solitary confinement. His fellow escapee had managed to evade capture and it was he who had brought news to the brigadier. He was able to give a 'very detailed report . . . on just how they lived, what they ate for each meal and how the guards treated them'. Philippa was reassured to learn that Michael's father was 'moving heaven and earth every way to get more news and trying too to arrange an exchange'.[173]

Behind the scenes, the brigadier had secured an interview with Andrew Hodges, of the American Red Cross. Hodges had recently handled a successful prisoner exchange, and Richard Foot begged him to do the same for his son. Hodges finally agreed to do what he could to help a desperate father after what began as a stiff interview turned personal and sentimental. The brigadier shared a pumpkin-pie recipe that had belonged to his mother; Hodges spoke of his childhood in rural Alabama.[174] After careful negotiations Hodges arranged that German and Allied prisoners would be exchanged, one for one, rank for rank. Now all there was to do was wait with renewed hope. 'It makes things look very different.'[175]

Michael, who did not know of his father's efforts, made one final, almost fatal, attempt at escape. He climbed the perimeter fence, half drowned in a swamp and eventually got clear by following the North Star through the night. Things went to plan until he was taken for an intruder by a French farmer who almost killed him. He was stabbed through the forehead with a pitchfork and kicked in the head, breaking his neck, before being recaptured. When the prisoner exchange took place Michael was in a coma, weighed six stone, and was not expected to live. Red Cross film footage shows him being carried, near lifeless, into a waiting ambulance. Miraculously, in hospital in France, he regained consciousness.[176]

So it was that in February 1945, after three months in a military hospital, Michael Foot reappeared in London. Philippa packed up her cushions, pottery and lampshade and moved to Rochester Row where she could nurse him, relieved to leave Seaforth behind.[177]

Elizabeth's New Plan

In April 1945, Elizabeth pulled out her typewriter once again to put together a third application for funding at Newnham: 'I should like to apply as a candidate for a research Fellowship at Newnham College, if there is one for which I am eligible.'[178] In a covering note Elizabeth explained why she had still not submitted her D.Phil.: 'in the past seven months I have been forced to submit all my thought and ways of thinking to a far more radical revision than I had expected (and this is still going on) with the result that I have not yet applied for the degree.'[179] It had been seven months since she began attending Wittgenstein's lectures. 'I was too much

<u>Starting-points for a discussion of the concept of the soul</u>

1.   Someone might answer an enquiry by saying: "the soul is the thinking part; the seat of the intelligence and the will" - and perhaps "of the passions." Such a statement raises many problems - part? seat? the performer of certain operations? - but what operations and how are these observed? - the subject of certain properties? - but we ask the same about them.

2.   Plato's thought of the soul and the forms, the intelligence and the intelligible, as the same kind of entity. Try to discover the drive behind this: what would make one wish to say it? The concept of the immaterial - how is this arrived at? Immaterial <u>substance</u> (thing, object, entity, what you will) - our notion of substances is a notion of bodes: is there any sense in an idea of immaterial objects - <u>or</u> what is the mistake, what is the temptation to make it?

3.   In Aristotle, the empirical and the Platonic lines of thought are in conflict. Aristotle's soul vegetable, animal, rational - "soul" = "life". The idea of life that of a pattern of behaviour? - is there any significance in the dispute between e.g. " vitalists" and "mechanists"? Examine Aristotle's "the soul is the form of the body."

4.   Examine the post Carterian <u>introspective</u> method of examining the problems - ideas of "self", "consciousness", observable"mental events" and so on.

5.   Think about Wittgenstein's psychology:- the destructive commentary both on the "introspective" line of thought, <u>and</u> - if I have understood rightly - the "substantial" concept, as "pneumatic". Psychological statements - e.g. "He is thinking", "he is full of joy", "he knows botany" - though there are radical differences between these samples, - yet none of them asserts a bodily movement, or bodily state. But they hang together with statements about bodily movements and states - the latter being evidence: but is this as smoke is evidence of fire? We can find fire itself.

As for conclusions, I do not know <u>at all.</u>

dissatisfied with my dissertation to submit it for the Oxford degree and set about rewriting it', she continues in her note. Wittgenstein's judgement on reading her efforts: 'bought for a farthing'.[180]

She proposed to do more work on 'The Concept of the Soul', and though the one-page outline is much more tentative than the three-page 'Rough Scheme' that accompanied her previous application, it shows that she has not abandoned Aristotle, nor moved away from the metaphysical problems that engaged her.

Of her five points of investigation, only the fifth mentions Wittgenstein explicitly. The first four explore Platonic, Aristotelian and Cartesian conceptions of the soul, and there Wittgenstein's fingerprints show up in only one or two places: she will enquire into Plato's description of 'the soul and the forms, the intelligence and the intelligible, as the same kind of entity', but as well as seeking to understand what Plato meant by this, she will 'try to discover the drive behind this' and will ask, 'is there any sense in an idea of immaterial objects – or what is the mistake, what the temptation to make it?' The emphasis on diagnosis, and on locating the source of a temptation, comes perhaps from Wittgenstein. In (1) she raises an eyebrow to Descartes in Wittgensteinian mood. The intellect is the 'seat' of the intelligence. The seat? Then, again, she had been asking Mary for years, '*behindness?*'

But, as for the remainder, her work is still distinctively metaphysical and historical. Before meeting Wittgenstein, she had already switched her attention from the surfaces of objects to 'the logical character of statements expressing the operation of sensitive faculties'.[181] Now she was on her way to replacing 'logical character' with Wittgenstein's notion of 'grammar'. With this switch, she would break open the Aristotelian picture that had already formed the core of her metaphysics.

It is a mark of Elizabeth's move from Oxford to Cambridge, geographically but also intellectually, that this time she received references from Wittgenstein and Bertrand Russell. Russell reports that 'Mrs. Geach's knowledge of scholastic philosophy [. . .] is exceptional among those who have acquired modern logic' (an echo of the reference H. H. Price had written about her tutor Donald MacKinnon). But he worries that she does not 'pay sufficient attention to physics' nor 'consider the bearing of quantum theory on her problem'. Nevertheless he 'shall be glad if she is awarded a research fellowship' and thinks 'that her work will justify the award'.[182] Wittgenstein writes that he has 'been able to form a definite impression of Mrs. Geach's philosophical abilities'. She is, he says, 'undoubtedly, the most talented female student I have had since 1930, when I began to lecture; and among my male students only 8, or 10 have either equalled or surpassed her'. Her essays, he continues, 'show a good soil for growing philosophical thoughts' but 'are still very immature'. This ought not to weigh against her, he recommends. 'It is the unavoidable consequence of her having been, on coming to Cambridge, subjected to new philosophical influences which she has not had the time to digest.'[183] In person, Wittgenstein told Elizabeth her writing was 'not house-trained', which she glossed as 'shit on the floor'.[184] But, though not yet trained, he thought her worthy of training, and he recommended her 'most warmly' for the fellowship.

Once again, Elizabeth's application was turned down. It is possible that the final line of her proposal irked the committee: 'As for conclusions, I do not know <u>at all</u>.'

A few days after Elizabeth received her rejection letter, there was a knock at Newnham Principal Myra Curtis's door. There behind it was Professor Wittgenstein dressed up in a tie (most unusual).[185] He argued Elizabeth's case, but Miss Curtis was not intimidated by academic men, no matter how egotistical or used to extracting worship. Before taking her seat behind the Principal's desk, she had enjoyed a sparkling career in the Ministry of Food, the Ministry of Pensions and the Post Office, rising through the ranks as an expert administrator.[186] Procedure must be followed. The college did, however, award Elizabeth a £50 research grant.[187] Her period of hardship was to continue. When she gave birth to her second child, John, in October, Wittgenstein paid for her stay in a maternity hospital.[188]

The End of the War & Two Friends Return to Oxford

On 8 May 1945, victory was declared in Europe. After six years of darkness, the end of the war was the end of the blackout, and people celebrated up and down the country with light, as varied and plentiful as possible. Streets were illuminated with torches; Buckingham Palace and the BBC's Broadcasting House were floodlit; bonfires were started wherever there was something to burn; Big Ben's clockface shone again; the windows of pubs and homes lit up.[189] Philippa and Michael wandered, dazed and dazzled, through the crowds around Pall Mall and St James's, flames everywhere.[190] Mary too was in London, in Trafalgar Square. She had always wondered at reports of people 'dancing in the streets' – how did sensible people do such a thing? '[I]t turns out to be quite easy. Dance music was being broadcast when I came to Trafalgar Square with some friends, and everyone just drifted into concentric circles that went round in alternate directions.'[191] By 2 a.m., as Mary drifted round and round the lions that guard Nelson's column, Iris (who had stopped off to thank God in Westminster Cathedral), was dancing in nearby Piccadilly.[192]

Mary was the first of the four to find her way back to Oxford. It took a little friendly shove from Jean Rowntree, the teacher who had unadvisedly suggested she go to Vienna in the summer of 1938. Having spent the first year of the war arranging homes for child evacuees from London, Jean took a wartime post in the BBC talks department as a producer.[193] She invited Mary to speak on the radio. Jean's educational series *What's the Point of . . . ?* took to the airwaves of the Home Service in April 1945 and was broadcast each Monday at 7.40 p.m. Its first question: What's the point of Astronomy? After that Philosophy, Poetry, Ceremonial, History and Music took their turns to defend their art. In each episode, an expert explained to the British public the importance of their subject to human life and post-war society. The seventh episode was to be 'What's the Point of the "Dead Languages"?'

The format broke with the previous six episodes in having two guests: Mary Scrutton and the Boars Hill classicist, Gilbert Murray. Perhaps there was a worry that a defence of dead languages by a man approaching his eightieth birthday would be a little absurd. Mary was there to represent youth. Fraenkel's *Agamemnon* class would have been in her mind as she settled down to write her defence. It was in those classes she had first felt herself to be 'part of a timeless sequence of scholars' and had understood the enormous task of bridging the gap between present and past with only the written word as guide. She had started to see the ways in which a monk's uncomfortable chair, or a scribe's inky fingers, might introduce errors into the text, and why if the words were to come alive with meaning the men who wrote them would have to cease being mere names – Stephanus, Bentley, Porson, Housman – and become living historical individuals.[194] No doubt she spoke in these terms in her broadcast. Gilbert Murray was impressed enough that when Somerville's Isobel Henderson, his former tutee, suggested Mary to him as a secretary, he was happy to offer her the post when a vacancy arose.[195] So Mary waved farewell to her strange tribe in Bedford and returned to Oxford.

*

The next to return was Philippa. Soon after VE Day she was released from Chatham House. She and Michael married and they moved to 8 New College Lane, in Oxford's town centre.[196] Michael still had a degree to finish and Philippa was to begin graduate work alongside a teaching post at Somerville. Iris had hoped to fill the role but was gracious in defeat: 'she deserves it anyway, as she is much better at philosophy than I am, & will be a real Susan Stebbing'.[197] Philippa's referees were Sandie Lindsay, Donald MacKinnon and Heinz Cassirer: her work is of the 'most unusual ability,' wrote the first;[198] 'I unhesitatingly rank Miss Bosanquet as one of the ablest pupils I have had,' wrote the second;[199] 'I have never met a young person with even comparable ability,' wrote the third.[200] The Foots' new home had been empty since 1943, when its previous occupant, H.W.B. Joseph, died. His last lecture, in the New College garden, was a tremendous onslaught against A. J. Ayer and the new 'analytic' philosophy. It was said that he died in a state of intellectual despair.[201]

Iris would be the last to leave London. The affair with Tommy ended badly, a reluctant marriage proposal during a pregnancy scare adding to the hurt and pain.[202] In January 1944 she had written to David Hicks, expressing a wish to escape into 'Europe & do some thoroughly menial & absorbing job . . . [t]hen come back to England at the age of 29 or so . . . to play the experienced woman round what's left of Bloomsbury'.[203] But she was still in London at the beginning of June 1945 when fifty paintings returned to the National Gallery:

> The Van Eyck man & pregnant wife. Bellini & Mantegna Agonies. Titian Noli me Tangere. Ruben's Bacchus & Ariadne. El Greco Agony, Rembrandt portraits of self & of an old lady. His small Woman Bathing (lovely!) A delicious Claude fading into blue blue blue – blue lake, mountains, sky. Incredible distances to breathe. Two Vermeers, so blue & lemon, honey stuff, girls at the Virginals. And then oh more Bellini & Rubens, & then the Ruisdaels the Hobbemas, & chaps like Cuyp that one had forgotten about. I still feel delirious with the first shock. It felt really like peace. And all the people wandering round looked dazed.[204]

That month she applied to the United Nations Relief and Rehabilitation Administration (UNRRA), in hope of being posted in France, but was instead given a desk job in London.[205] Her main consolation was in the French literature that was now accumulating on the shelves at Seaforth.[206] In early August she sat in Westminster Cathedral; on her lap, a copy of *La soif*, a play in three acts by the French Christian philosopher Gabriel Marcel, from which she copied notes into a journal. The writer must not 'degrade mysteries into problems', she jotted.[207] A 'problem', Marcel told her, can be publicly formulated, using concepts that are 'objective', and its solution can be discovered by anyone.[208] But a 'mystery' belongs to a realm of human experience that cannot be formulated publicly using objective categories, and its solution must be personal and individual. Among the mysteries of being are our experience of our own bodies, the nature of sensation, and love, hope and faith.

As Iris reflected on mystery, the 'problem' of the continuing war in southeast Asia was about to be 'solved'. Despite his physical frailty, Michael had resumed his work quickly after his return to London, and before he and Philippa left for Oxford, he completed a calculation of the expected casualty rate of a conventional land invasion of the Japanese mainland. He returned a 'butcher's bill of about a million and a half'.[209]

On 6 and 9 August, the Allies dropped atomic bombs on the Japanese cities of Hiroshima and Nagasaki. 'When we talk about the hydrogen bomb', Donald MacKinnon reflected on the radio, 'we are talking about something we have chosen to develop and to use. We are talking about choices we have actually made; we are not talking about events in which we have become involved . . . [W]e are referring to human actions.'[210] In two flashes of blinding light, so bright they turned human beings into shadows, the bill of 1.5 million soldiers was paid by 200,000 civilians. The exchange was not like for like but it ended the war. Japan surrendered six days later.

CHAPTER 4

Park Town

OXFORD, BRUSSELS, GRAZ, CAMBRIDGE & CHISWICK
SEPTEMBER 1945–AUGUST 1947

The Men Return to Oxford & Mary Visits Boars Hill – Philippa
Determines to Show that Ayer is Wrong – Iris Meets Jean-Paul Sartre –
Philippa, Iris & the Refugee Relief Effort – Elizabeth & Philippa Begin a
Philosophical Conversation – Iris's Communist Past Catches Up With Her –
Lieutenant Colonel Austin Takes the Revolution Forward – Elizabeth Brings
Wittgenstein to Oxford – Mary & Iris Prepare to Re-enter Philosophy

The Men Return to Oxford & Mary Visits Boars Hill

Each morning Mary descended from her bedsitter on the top floor of 55 Park Town and mounted her bicycle. She peddled past Iris's second-year lodgings, Number 43, memories of tinned sardines and grainy newspaper photographs of troops lined up on the beaches at Dunkirk drifting through her mind.

Mary had to keep her wits about her as she joined the swarm of cyclists clattering through the streets and along the pavements of Oxford. As undergraduates, she and Iris had found themselves ageing while the men grew younger – an illusion created by conscription. Now the illusion reversed direction. The undergraduates stepping off the trains, army-issue boots swapped for lace-up Oxfords, were mature adults. Many, like Michael Foot, had left Oxford as young boys, just out of school. After a six-year hiatus during which they had become officers, war heroes, prisoners, invalids and military strategists, they now picked up their books where they had left them. There was something a little absurd about these bearded undergraduates, many of them husbands and fathers, crammed into packed lecture halls alongside those for whom the university was, as it had been for them a lifetime ago, their first taste of freedom after school. The older undergraduates were exotic. They had had a 'proper' war.

Oxford colleges were 'crowded to suffocation' with nearly 2,500 more undergraduates than before the war, a 40 per cent increase made up almost entirely of men.[1] The Cherwell teemed with rowers and punters, but now American accents could be heard among their shouts and calls. Servicemen, awaiting repatriation, were permitted to register for a term or two.[2] Once again women were vastly outnumbered in the Senior Common Rooms of the men's colleges, anxieties that female dons, along with refugees, had 'invaded the field'[3] could be tidied away along with the water tanks and the air-raid shelters. Civil servants packed up their Whitehall files. College treasures and manuscripts were retrieved. Flower beds were replanted. Temporary hospitals and blood-donation wards morphed back into familiar dormitories and libraries. Signposts and place names went back up. In the women's colleges, blackout curtains were turned into scholars' gowns.[4] The structures within which civilian life could be resumed were put back in place.

The great influx of scholars helped to mask the absences left by war. The Roll of Honour in 1945 was shorter than 1918's, but behind the clatter of bicycles the gaps were there and plenty – at least 1,800 of them. Mary's Nick Crosbie did not return; he had been killed on his first encounter with the enemy. On 17 January 1941, he was on board HMS *Goshawk* when she was sunk by a torpedo. Noel Eldridge, Iris's friend, was killed in action in Italy, in September 1944. As Richard Hare returned to finish his degree, Frank Thompson, Bill Cobbe and John Anscombe did not. None of the five undergraduates who had shared a New College staircase with Michael Foot had survived.[5] But, despite the terrible losses and the post-war hardship, the mood in Britain was optimistic.

In the July 1945 general election the British people voted out the Conservative Winston Churchill and voted in Labour's Clement Attlee on a manifesto of radical social change. Those anxious to be getting on looked forward to a new era of public works: the Beveridge Report, the Butler Education Act and the National Health Service were all becoming a reality and clever young men – and women – would be needed to research, implement and manage new state machinery. Rationing continued, but queues for cigarettes, cakes and sherry now buzzed with talk of gripping lectures by returning academics.[6] Lines formed outside libraries as undergraduates and dons competed for seats and books.[7]

'It is psychologically impossible that we should just begin again where we left off six years ago,' the Humean H. H. Price began his 1945 address to the Aristotelian Society. 'And even if we could, I do not think we should wish to.'[8] Yet to begin where they had left off was precisely what many of Elizabeth, Iris, Mary and Philippa's male peers intended. Now back in Oxford, the young men dusted off their 1936 copies of *Language, Truth and Logic*.

Freddie Ayer had spent the war in perpetual motion, being sent from Sandown to London to New York to Ghana to Algiers, and returning to Oxford from Paris where he had witnessed the liberation from a brothel café. 'Intellectually brilliant but, we think, possibly more suited to office work than for leading men in the field', reads a note on his military file.[9]

He was down to deliver lectures on 'Perception' in Hilary Term. Cycling along Parks Road, Mary might have spotted him entering Wadham College gate, alongside Maurice Bowra. Warden of Wadham, Bowra had found Freddie a post as tutorial fellow, his former protégé enlivening the Senior Common Room and securing the reputation of his dining club. Having spent time in France, Ayer had made himself an authority on existentialist philosophy. Bowra would have approved of the twist Ayer gave to its nihilism. Sartre was right that life has no transcendent purpose but wrong to despair, explained Ayer. There is no tragedy. Hedonistic utilitarianism, life for pleasure's sake, follows.[10] He lived by his philosophy. His wartime activities had occasioned many opportunities for romance,[11] and he soon dedicated himself to affairs with beautiful women, many of whom were other men's wives. He was as likely to be found on the dance floor of Soho's Gargoyle as at High Table.[12]

Another morning, cycling along, someone else Mary recognised: Susan Stebbing's friend and mentor (and Ayer's old tutor) Gilbert Ryle. He had shed his military uniform (again, Intelligence Services) and was arriving at St John's College for a meeting with philosopher John Mabbott (now also safely married, and not to a student). The pair were about to implement a great non-military expansionist campaign and its instrument was to be a new graduate degree, the B.Phil. When the Idealist philosopher R. G. Collingwood had died in 1943, Gilbert Ryle was appointed Waynflete Professor of Metaphysics in his place. For many, this event, which followed quickly after the death of H.W.B. Joseph, marked the final victory of Oxford's 'revolution in philosophy', the triumph of analytic empiricism and linguistic method over the metaphysical excesses of pre-war Idealism and Realism. An unspoken consensus began to develop, sustained in the journal *Mind* (now edited by Ryle himself) about 'who was and who was not a "negligible back-number"'.[13] Discussion papers on Urmson, Woozley, Austin, Ayer, Ryle, Ewing, Carnap and Strawson filled its pages; but no one 'would have felt it worthwhile even to *disagree* with, say, Joseph or Collingwood.'[14] Some time around the late 1940s, J. L. Austin would feign faint recollection of the previous Waynflete Professor of Metaphysics – 'Some kind of historian wasn't he?'[15]

In Trinity Term, J. L. Austin, back from the Intelligence Services, would lecture on 'Problems in Philosophy'. Somervillian Jean Coutts, now his wife, had taken a First despite being injured in a Blitz bombing a few months before her finals. Elizabeth had been persistent in her opposition to Jean marrying her tutor. 'I hear you're getting married to that awful man,' she had said when she spotted her engagement ring.[16] Mary also had doubts: 'Are you sure you want to?'[17] Austin would not hear of Jean working,[18] and she and their two toddlers were now stowed away in a house on Frilford Heath, eight miles south of Oxford, along with a Goblin vacuum cleaner, bought for her by her husband.[19] (Jean emerged again to become a fellow of St Hilda's only after her husband had died, by which time she had rather lost confidence. A short, clear paper on 'Pleasure and Happiness' begins: 'in trying to sort the subject out a little . . . I fear I may rather have generated confusion than diminished it'.[20])

In 1945, the extinction of metaphysics had been declared but not yet chronicled, the publications proclaiming its defeat still to be written. Over the coming two decades, the story of an Austrian movement embedded in a Cambridge tradition by refugee scholars and women logicians, whose target was propaganda and confusion, would become that of an Oxford revolution against metaphysics, masterminded by Ryle, ignited by Ayer, coordinated by Austin (supporting cast: Paul Grice, H.L.A. Hart, Stuart Hampshire, Isaiah Berlin) and carried brightly into the future by their intellectual sons and by their sons' sons.[21] Susan Stebbing, who had died in 1943, would soon be written out of the story, along with Margaret Mac-Donald (the post-war editor of Stebbing's *Analysis*) who passed away just as the first official history *The Revolution in Philosophy* (1956), edited by Gilbert Ryle, went to print. Neither of these women gets a mention – an inexcusable omission by Ryle, who knew Stebbing and MacDonald, and their work, well. The 'revolution in philosophy' had been won bloodlessly, by a combination of mortality and studied neglect.

But despite the victory cries, the Idealist and Realist metaphysicians were not entirely extinct, and some were making plans. Swerving to avoid a group of ancient undergraduates, Mary may have glimpsed Sandie Lindsay outside Balliol, chatting with his former pupil, Mary Glover. In 1942, as Elizabeth boarded the Varsity Line, Mary Glover had been too old to be conscripted, but enlisted as a volunteer. Swapping academic dress for industrial overalls, she moved to Birmingham to work in a factory. The experience had been transformative. She had resigned her lectureship in May 1945 and was now at work on a book about the effects of mechanised factory work on the mind and spirit. Her co-author John Winnington was a fellow machine operative who had 'worked his way up in various firms from the lowest-paid jobs to the managerial grade'.[22] 'Fantasy is the constant compensation for the rebuffs and failures that are so common in factory life,' they would observe. 'But if [a man] takes refuge in fantasy', though he may 'evade defeat and challenge' he will also 'lose the sense of fact'.[23] However, if this flight to fantasy can be kept in check, machines offer 'the possibility of a good life for the labourer'. This will come if the 'bits of living' that comprise his machine-work do not dominate his life, but rather form one part of it. The worker will need 'good leisure', time that is not mere recovery from fatigue but involves purpose and the enlargement of human life: 'one could attend an art school, explore the Cotswolds on a bicycle, enjoy a circle of friends', suggested Glover.[24] If fantasy could be resisted, the transcendent values she had described to Elizabeth, 'truth, beauty, and goodness', could, she argued, find a home.

Sandie Lindsay was 'like a boy in elation and happiness' at Clement Attlee's victory; it was 'the dawn of a new era . . . I knew this would happen!'[25] Lindsay was preparing for yet another role, and was perhaps sharing his half-formed plan with Mary Glover: if he were to establish a new experimental university in Staffordshire, designed to nurture and cultivate working men and women, would she join him?[26] She was keen. In her mind, there was no surer sign that educators were going wrong than when ordinary people thought education remote from real life. She had begun penning these ideas in a series of journalistic pieces in the *Spectator*. 'These questions depend on another', she explained, 'what sort of creature are we trying to train? What is he capable of?' 'Man is at least a spiritual animal.' In human life, eating and drinking are transformed into fellowship; sex into love; the herd into society. And inquisitiveness 'has carried the human mind into the heart of the atom and along the flaming ramparts of the universe beyond the Milky Way'![27]

Had Mary Scrutton's bicycle swept past Balliol only five minutes earlier she would perhaps have seen a welcome and familiar sight: her former tutor Donald MacKinnon, now a fellow at Lindsay's Balliol, heading westwards down Broad Street towards the offices of the Clarendon Press. In his briefcase was a copy of H.W.B. Joseph's 1932 lectures on 'Internal and External Relations and the Philosophy of Analysis'. MacKinnon was using Joseph's lectures in preparing his own and was in no doubt as to their lasting value; he was on a mission to get them published. But he had got wind of a 'rumpus' among the press's ranks about what – and who – was worth publishing.[28] The war years had put a practical stop to the production everywhere of all 'serious books',[29] and now explosive undergraduate numbers meant that more books were needed than ever and at a time when paper was still in limited supply – 'to publish the remains of old and long departed persons like Joseph' was not a priority.[30] What's more, Joseph was, in the end, a metaphysician.

Along the Abingdon Road, Mary's bike turned right over the Hinksey Stream and she began the steep climb up to Boars Hill, her surroundings more pastoral with every (effortful) turn of the pedals. At Yatscombe, breathless from the ascent, Mary dismounted and walked up a flight of stairs and into another world.

In Gilbert Murray's study, with views over treetops to Oxford's distant spires below, Mary could at last immerse herself in books, papers and Murray's dazzling mind. It was his translations of the Greek plays that she had studied and dramatised as a schoolgirl at Downe House. 'The scholar's special duty', he had written, 'is to turn the written signs in which old poetry or philosophy is now enshrined back into living thought and feeling. *He must so understand as to relive.*'[31] His translations did this so successfully that at the end of a 1918 performance of Euripides' *The Trojan Women* the audience cried out: 'Author! Author!' Murray stood up to tell them apologetically: 'The author is not here, he has been dead for many centuries, but I am sure he will be gratified by your reception of his great tragedy.'[32] Words and symbols, Murray saw, do not carry their meaning with them like luggage, but come alive in the context of a society, at a place and time. To bring a 'written sign' to life one must acknowledge the reality of the past and imagine and relive the culture in which it was spoken. And now here was Mary turning the pages of letters to Gilbert Murray from Bernard Shaw, Bertrand Russell, Marie Curie, Ralph Vaughan Williams.

Mary often accompanied Murray on his daily walks round Boars Hill, past the Carritts' and the Thompsons' houses, each now mourning a lost son. Back at Yatscombe, Mary and the Murrays had fizzy ginger pop and nut cutlets for lunch, fare for teetotal vegetarian Idealists.

Philippa Determines to Show that Ayer is Wrong

As an old woman, almost ninety, Philippa Foot would recall: 'it was significant that news of the concentration camps hit us just when I came back to Oxford in 1945. This news was shattering in a fashion that no one now can easily understand. We had thought that something like this could not happen.'[33] Photographers, journalists and film crew had entered Bergen-Belsen along with liberating British troops. They sent back images around which the concept of human nature would have to reshape itself. 'Nothing is going to be the same again,'[34] Philippa said to Donald MacKinnon.

'What is *that*?' Elizabeth was asking in her dissertation. What is the form of life, the shape of the soul, of a human being? Here were pictures of humans: well-fed SS girls, hair nicely set; starved men and women lifted into trucks; children playing beside trenches filled with naked bodies; skeletal blank-faced survivors who looked like corpses. The 'Belsen cruelties were inflicted by people who saw what they did', observed Mary Glover; but there 'is little ground for self-congratulation if we prefer the cruelties we cannot see'. Nagasaki has shown us 'that there is no degree of cruelty from which we shall shrink if it seems to assist in the achievement of national purpose'.[35] 'Nothing comparable to the horrors of the first half of the twentieth century occurred in the lifetime of Plato,' reflected the Idealist G. R. G. Mure. 'He did not find his faith in the Good poisoned at the roots by revelations of evil so abysmal and so ubiquitous that he must wonder whether, if the human race should succeed in extinguishing itself, much would be lost worth the keeping.'[36] Janet Vaughan, the new Principal at Somerville, had greeted the intake that year with a first-hand report of the conditions in newly liberated Bergen-Belsen.[37] 'She described the unspeakable and revolting conditions, sights, smells and sounds.' Prue Smith, a new scholar who had arrived at the hall expecting a pep talk, felt certain many years later 'that not one of us who were there has forgotten that talk, and the news it carried about the depths to which the latent savagery of mankind may sink'.[38] Confronted by the terrible knowledge of what was possible for human animals, of the uses to which they might put technology and industry, and deprived of the reassuring divisions between sanity and madness, human and beast, Philippa quietly resolved to become a moral philosopher.[39]

Freddie Ayer's pre-war assault on metaphysics and ethics had left moral philosophy speechless in the face of this new reality. Expression of personal disapproval or subjective emotion fell grossly short of what was needed, and Philippa was repulsed by the thought that, if morality was subjective in the way Ayer insisted, 'there is no way ... one could imagine oneself saying to a Nazi, "But we are *right*, and you are *wrong*", with there being any substance to the statement'.[40] In the newspapers, journalists reached for heavy, thick, dark words: evil, wicked, hell, abyss, depravity, degradation. But such a language could not get a grip on the value-free world that Ayer had left for philosophers to inhabit. Philippa formed the question that would drive her for the rest of her life: could there be a secular philosophy that could use this language of morals, and speak of objective moral truth? She was convinced that Ayer's moral subjectivism must rest on a mistake; her task was to find it.

Philippa, like Mary, put down roots in Park Town. She and Michael decamped from H.W.B. Joseph's former home and purchased Number 16, a five-storey house in yellowing limestone on the grander of Park Town's two crescents. Built in the 1850s as a habitat for married dons, Park Town had begun to acquire a risqué reputation when Oxford's celibacy requirement (which prevented dons from marrying) remained in place rather longer than expected. While they waited for permission to wed,

'celibate' dons had moved in their mistresses. The crescent remained vaguely scandalous as mistresses turned into grey-haired spinsters with odd habits and unusual manners. Michael nurtured suspicions about the 'elderly maiden lady' in the house next door. Philippa's family expressed concern. Even the bank manager warned against the purchase.[41]

North Oxford (being unfashionable and therefore cheaper) had become the home for many of the refugees who had arrived in the city before the war. Although some moved on once the fighting stopped, for many Park Town and its environs was now a permanent home.[42] The Russian poet and chemist Lydia Pasternak, who had fled Munich in 1935, lived in Number 20 with her father, the painter Leonid Pasternak. The Berliner biochemist Hugh Blaschko (whose name was in Hitler's 'Black Book') was at Number 24. Lotte Labowsky (the Classics scholar and Somerville librarian) and her mother (rumoured to have 'translated Dante in her youth')[43] were a mile north of Park Town, in Summertown. The Summertown circle had at one time included the German artist Emilie Cosman, the Cassirers and Richard Walzer. Many of these pioneers would remain on the Gazette's lecture lists through the 1940s and 1950s: Richard Walzer, Friedrich Waismann, Fritz Heinemann, Georg Katkov, Lorenzo Minio-Paluello, Jovan Plamenatz. Memories of their night-time arrests, their neighbours' hostility, their imprisonment, were woven into their lives among the English.

Cycling home from Boars Hill (an exhilarating freewheel down Foxcombe Road), Mary's bicycle would have rattled past the homes of the German-born Renaissance scholar Nicolai Rubinstein, the Viennese art historian Otto Pächt, the Austrian musicologist Egon Wellesz and the German archaeologist Paul Jacobsthal (another 'Black Book' entry). Karl Popper might be seen emerging from Parker's bookshop on a day-trip from London.[44]

Mary's decor in her small upper-storey bedsitter (noisy plumbing, inadequate heating) ran to a 'very encouraging' bedspread made out of a 'pre-Mao flag displaying a big purple dragon with bulging black-and-white eyes on a sulphur-yellow ground'.[45] From her sash window, she had a bird's-eye view over the communal gardens and across Park Town, as Philippa and Michael moved into Number 16. A procession of heavy sideboards, oversized vases, alarming-looking fur coats and an eighteenth-century mahogany wine box were carried up five steps and through the columned doorway. Michael's female relations were responsible for many of these unfashionable items: Aunt Lindsey had just died, and Grandmother Dolly visited her cottage and picked items to send to him and his new wife.[46] Philippa's lampshade and silk cushions contributed a splash of modern colour.

Now that they were neighbours, Philippa and Mary began to see a great deal of each other, Mary finding Philippa as rewarding as ever. The war had provided concrete pictures around which each woman's moral philosophy would later take shape. We cannot throw up our hands and claim to find the actions of an Eichmann unintelligible, Mary thought; we must be 'willing to grasp imaginatively how [wickedness] works in the human heart, and particularly in our own hearts'.[47] Wickedness is not like aggression, 'whose intrusion into human life needs a special explanation'; rather it is 'a general kind of failure to live as we are capable of living'.[48] Evil is something we must understand from the inside, as fellow humans, with many shared instincts, desires and goals, and with an imaginative recognition of the ways in which a human life can fail. Philippa, in turn, confronted human action at the other end of the spectrum. She read the story of a pair of farm boys from the Sudetenland who had refused to join the SS and wrote to their parents on the eve of their execution: 'Both of us would rather die than stain our consciences with such deeds of horror. I know what the SS has to do.'[49] Any account of human action, Philippa would later say, must make sense of these Sudetenland farm boys and their choice. An account that cannot recognise their goodness, truth and reason must be mistaken.[50]

The Foots let out the upper rooms as flats to a pair of Smiths: Honor and Prudence. It would be a few years yet before Philippa Foot would begin to publish papers on the importance to ethics of virtue, or character, but perhaps the names of her lodgers were a daily reminder that there is a richer vocabulary than Ayer's 'hooray!' and 'boo!', one that connected back to ancient philosophy's concern with virtue and motive, to pick out ways of acting well.

It is likely that Philippa complained to Mary about her teaching workload – that first post-war year she was overburdened with undergraduates and a look of exhaustion clouded her face at the end of each day.[51] Her determination to treat each undergraduate seriously, as an intelligent adult, made her a patient and encouraging tutor, but the effort required to meet each undergraduate face-on, as a particular individual with particular needs and wants, took its toll. Sometimes, she confided, it was so bad that she lay on the floor in her college room between tutorials.[52] Still, despite the exhaustion she made time to attend their old tutor Donald MacKinnon's lectures on Kant's *Critique of Pure Reason*.[53] Mary would have taken an interest in Somerville gossip, the more surprising the better, and enjoyed tales of Philippa's tutees, an echo of themselves six long years ago. Philippa would have shared news of appointments. There were to be two new research fellows at Somerville from October, and, wonderfully, one would be Elizabeth Anscombe. Philippa and Mary would have heard of Elizabeth's closeness to Wittgenstein – Mary had visited Elizabeth in Cambridge.[54] They had heard rumours of his secret, explosive new work. Both women would have looked forward to picking up with their most brilliant and unconventional friend. Mary was beginning to dream of returning to philosophy herself.

Iris Meets Jean-Paul Sartre

Iris, meanwhile, far away from her friends, was about to encounter those who found themselves unable to complete their journeys home. After months behind a desk in London, her wish to be sent abroad by UNRRA was finally granted. She left England on 1 September 1945, by train and boat, arriving in Brussels 'just in time for the *Fête de la Libération*!'[55]

Once in Brussels, Iris waited for details of her posting to come through. Jaded by her affair with Tommy and the mess with Philippa, but determined to make a clean start, she went out again into the world in search of 'Ultimate Human Beings'. She aligned her rhythm and pace to her new habitat: gilded statuettes and high roofs and towers and churches – 'and also (not less amazing to my innocent uncontinental eye) the thousand & one cafés & the insane tramway system. Just being here & breathing the air & walking on the cobbles & reading the advertisements & hearing the soft twitter of French & the harsher music of Flemish fills me with a crazy joy.'[56] By mid-September, she sensed 'a sort of loosening of the knots, a sense of being myself again, & an interior eloquence which I always have when I'm really well!'.[57] It was, she said later, 'a time of sheer frenzy' – of 'wanting new things – & being to that extent different'.[58] She sought out a highbrow bookshop and chatted with the assistant, enjoying the sound of her voice speaking French. ('The intellectuals of Brussels are insanely francophil[e] (naturally) & that suits me very well').[59] She made a whirlwind tour of Antwerp, by tram and on foot, traipsing after a brass band, seeing the cathedral by moonlight and ordering a cognac in a bar. She hung a copy of Brueghel's *Fall of Icarus* in her office. She heard Charles Trenet sing.

She began to use the endearment *chéri*. She would invent herself anew: adventurer, author, *flâneuse*. And soon: Existentialist.

On 25 October, a few weeks before her posting arrived, Iris joined a crowd at Salle Giroux, an avant-garde art gallery on Boulevard du Régent, not far from Parc de Bruxelles, to hear France's great 'pop star' novelist–philosopher Jean-Paul Sartre.[60] Sartre arrived in a newly liberated Belgium excusing himself – he had not prepared anything. But once introduced by writer Charles Bernard, he proceeded, for a full two hours, to hold the overheated room enthralled.[61]

When Sartre delivered the same lecture four days later in Paris, at Club Maintenant, too many attended. 'Heat, fainting spells, police', reported *Combat*, the once clandestine newspaper of the French resistance. In Brussels, Iris did not faint. She was there, a pale blue cloth notebook in hand (price 78 francs),[62] as Sartre set out an existentialist revolutionary manifesto. His words may have recalled to her an undergraduate lecture by refugee philosopher Fritz Heinemann, who had coined the word '*Existenz-philosophie*' to capture a current of Western thought a decade before Sartre took his place in that tradition. But, hearing it spoken of again, translated from Heinemann's stuttering English in a half-empty lecture room in New College to a packed gallery in post-war Belgium, in the language of *la Résistance*, it must have seemed brand new.

'Man first of all exists, encounters himself, surges up in the world – and defines himself afterwards,' Sartre announced.[63] For man, '*existence* comes before *essence*.' With this slogan Sartre meant to create a form of secularism that went beyond the 'philosophic atheism of the eighteenth century'. He wanted to remove not just God but the very idea of human nature. Man is not 'a kind of moss or fungus or a cauliflower',[64] Sartre urged the audience. Not a turnip, certainly. 'Only existentialism', he told them, humiliated after over four years of Nazi occupation, 'is compatible with the dignity of man.'[65] Sartre promised to make each of them, defeated as they were, a monarch – or demigod – declaring: 'if God does not exist there is at least one being whose existence comes before its essence, a being which exists before it can be defined by any conception of it. That being is man.'[66]

It is not hard to imagine how 'ruthlessly gorgeously lucid'[67] Sartre's talk might have seemed to Iris. Her faith in the Communist Party had provided an orientation throughout her twenties. But Tommy Balogh had worn away at her certainty while they were together, making it his mission to 'talk her out of it'.[68] Sartre held out the promise that she could reinvent an authentic self, could start again. It is 'the first principle of existentialism', Sartre told his rapt audience, that 'Man is nothing else but that which he makes of himself.'[69] The world into which we are born is value-less. There is nothing I am or that I am destined to become. My humanity places no limits or form on my existence. Each individual creates value through his choices and actions, through his own will.

It may have struck Iris that Sartre was offering a version of Kant's categorical imperative, but radically altered from the one she, Philippa and Mary had encountered in Heinz Cassirer's front room in Summertown. Sartre had transformed morality for a newly liberated Europe by cutting it free from human nature and a transcendent reality. The norm of man is not, as Elizabeth thought, to be found in the form of life of the species. Rather than seeking to align ourselves to some external measure of goodness and value, each of us, individually, is the source of an image of the human as we believe it should be. When each individual chooses for himself, Sartre explained, 'he chooses for all men.' In choosing he 'creates himself as he wills to be', and so endorses 'an image of man such as he believes he ought to be'.[70] We must therefore always ask ourselves: would I through my choices legislate for all mankind?

With no external standard from reality, nature or God against which to evaluate our creations, responsibility becomes ours and ours alone. For Sartre this depth of responsibility elicits pure anguish. Given this, we must not act unquestioningly, performing our life as if we had some predestined essence; to do so is *mauvaise foi*, bad faith. If there is any kind of objective value at all, Sartre urges, it is authenticity. (Fresh memories of collaboration and resistance perhaps rippled through the audience.) Peering through his thick round glasses, Sartre struck home with one more blasphemous flourish. 'Dostoevsky once wrote: "If God did not exist, everything would be permitted"; and that, for existentialism, is the starting point.'[71] These words would reverberate through Iris's life – if God does not exist, how can the Good?

As Sartre neared the end of his lecture, Iris must have heard the cry of a lone heckler. The Jesuit philosopher Roger Troisfontaines had turned up at Salle Giroux to make his protest: '*Une philosophie née au café! Milieu frelaté!*' he shouted from the floor, an echo of fellow Jesuit Martin D'Arcy's reaction to *Language, Truth and Logic*. Born in a café, cut off from tradition and scholarship, here was a debased philosophy to corrupt the youth.[72]

*

If any woman could realise Sartre's picture of self-defining 'man', Iris might have fancied her chances. She was exuberantly bright, ambitious, serious and with an Oxford First; perhaps she already knew that gazing out from under her fringe was someone with the power to seduce almost anyone.[73] After the lecture she pushed to the front so she could hear Sartre and his circle's plans. The next day, she turned up at a select *séance* with a copy of the first volume of *Les chemins de la liberté* in hand. Sartre inscribed it 'à Miss Iris Murdoch en sincère hommage'.[74] In the days that followed, she sat in cafés, a *Sartriste*, cigarette in hand, filling the pages of her expensive cloth notebook. On the first leaf, she carefully copied out a quote from Simone de Beauvoir's essay 'Pyrrhus et Cinéas'; then follow nine pages of notes on Sartre's lecture; then detailed remarks on some wider-flung parts of Sartre's philosophy; the remainder of the notebook is occupied with *L'être et le néant*. On the last leaf: *FIN*. 'It's the <u>real</u> <u>thing</u>', she later wrote to her Oxford friend, David Hicks; 'so exciting, & so sobering, to meet at last – after turning away in despair from the shallow stupid milk & water "ethics" of English moralists',[75] 'just what English philosophy needs to have injected into its veins, to expel the loathsome humours of Ross & Pritchard [sic]'.[76]

Iris's UNRRA papers came through in December: she was to be Communications Officer in Innsbruck in the French quarter of Allied-occupied Austria. She left for Innsbruck before Christmas, with a clear image of her future self and the first steps towards it already taken. The copy of *Pierrot Mon Ami* by Raymond Queneau that had arrived in Seaforth in the final months of the war held the key to one part of that future: Iris hoped to become its English translator, and the bookseller Ernest Collet of *Horizon*

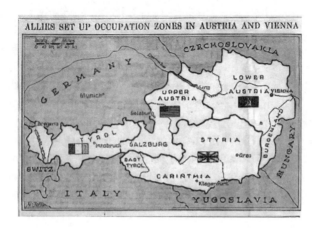

was angling for the rights on her behalf.[77] The other part lay with David Hicks. Like everyone else, David had been a little in love with Iris in 1938, describing her as a 'fairy-tale princess'.[78] In the excitement of post-war euphoria, he proposed to her during a week of leave in London. 'It was a tornado. Ten days that positively shook the world.'[79] She planned their future together on paper. 'Europe, & long talks in cafés & dancing together & getting drunk together, & long evenings at home too, writing things, & criticizing each others' [sic] things, & quarrelling, & having crazy friends & crazy new ideas, & reading books & seeing pictures, & new cities, & making love, & a little later having splendid children & bringing them up beautifully.'[80]

By the time Iris (now picturing her future self as Mrs Hicks) reached Innsbruck, almost all British troops had returned home. Even those who had had to wait for the atom bombs for their liberation were back among loved ones, attempting to recover their health and wits. But the situation elsewhere in Europe was quite other – as Bertha Bracey had warned in her Chatham House lecture, Europe was now teeming with 'displaced persons', uprooted, traumatised and hungry, the background of their lives obliterated. A kaleidoscope pattern that would not resolve. In the early days of the Allied occupation of Austria, there were an estimated 700,000 displaced persons and refugees in the country and all in need of food, clothing, accommodation, fuel and medical treatment. Many were stateless. There were thousands of unaccompanied children.[81]

Iris was to live in the requisitioned Mariabrunn Hotel and commute by *téléphérique*, a mountain railway down through the snowfields. At its steepest section, the incline reached a 48-degree gradient. Climbing back up for lunch, her body slanted heavenwards. A great thaw had left behind green mountains and 'an admirable river'.[82] Living in the French Zone entitled Iris to US Army rations and gave her access to luxuries like grapefruit and condensed milk, echoes from her pre-war childhood. This struck her as 'immoral'. Cigarettes were international currency and a thriving black market saw Red Cross parcels exchanged for anything from motor cars to women, though more often for blankets or medicine for children.[83] Some of those parcels arrived from the Oxford Committee for Famine Relief, collected and packaged by the newly founded organisation dreamt up on Boars Hill and physically realised in a small shop on Broad Street.

Philippa, Iris & the Refugee Relief Effort

Passing the Oxford and District Co-operative Society on George Street – a large ornate red-brick building, its construction date '1908' displayed on the central gable of the facade – Philippa had paused one day. An advertisement in the window asking for volunteers to sort clothes had caught her eye. In she went.

The Oxford Committee for Famine Relief had been founded in 1942, during the darkest days of the war, in response to mass starvation in Greece caused by the Allied blockade, an unintended consequence of an effort to force Germany's surrender. Some 410,000 had died of hunger in a single fortnight. Gilbert Murray had been a founding member, and Lady Mary Murray made an initial donation of £500. As the committee expanded their work across a war-ravaged Europe, 'Oxfam' sought the human scale in a still unfolding tragedy: Women's Skirts, Men's Hats, Children's Trousers. Philippa was immediately drawn to the 'daring' and 'dashing' response of this small bank of volunteers[84] – a little bit of human creativity and cooperation that allowed items of clothing to find their way from one individual in surplus to another in need. Something warm, soft or clean

No clothes are too old

(if reasonably clean and free from moth and infection)' for war-victims dreading another Continental winter. Repairs can be left to D.P.s sadly needing work. Scraps of cloth, wool, leather, etc., and mending materials also are welcome.

Lord Pakenham wires: "IMPORTANCE OF YOUR WORK IN CAUSE OF INTERNATIONAL PEACE AND GOODWILL CANNOT BE EXAGGERATED." "Oxford Relief" is entrusted to Friends' Relief Service, and now goes mainly to Austria, Poland and British Zone of Germany through British Red Cross and C.O.B.S.R.A.

Headington residents can give at the Methodist School-room, Quarry High Street, from 6 to 8 p.m., Sept. 24th and 25th. Other readers please respond as below (after hearing "Week's Good Cause" Appeal on B.B.C. Home Service, 8.25 p.m., Sunday, Sept. 21st):—

CLOTHING and FOOTWEAR as above;
BOOKS and MAGAZINES (any language);
FOOD, SOAP and CHOCOLATE;
MONEY FOR FOOD AND MEDICAL SUPPLIES (economically and without spending dollars or reducing British rations);
VOLUNTARY HELP, occasionally;
PREMISES, or VAN for mobile office.

Oxford Committee for
FAMINE RELIEF
(Reg. War Charities Act, 1940)
42, HYTHE BRIDGE STREET
to Sept. 29th approx.
From Oct. 6th
7, NEW INN HALL STREET
(opposite Newspaper House)
weekdays 10-1 and 2-5, Sat. 10-1
Collections by arrangement.

to remind a stranger that they still belonged to the human community, to pull them, knit them, back in; something previously loved and treasured that could speak to a history and a future. Philippa sorted donated clothes into piles: Michael's aunt's fur coat went into 'Women's Shabby Unmended'. Items unsuitable or saleable – a pair of false teeth, a live donkey, and a diamond ring among them – were sent to the brand-new Oxford Committee for Famine Relief Gift Shop and Collecting Centre at 17 Broad Street, where they were sold to raise money. Each week a Quaker van came by to collect the packages of clothes to bring to Europe. In Innsbruck, women not long ago in concentration camps or fleeing across borders, might soon be wearing cardigans from Cornmarket's Marks & Spencer and skirts made by dons' wives from *Vogue* patterns.

Jean Rowntree (Mary's former teacher), writing of her work with fellow Quaker Doreen Warriner, spoke of her realisation that the great need of displaced people is not just warm clothes but 'the human background of

life'. 'The women wanted to knit, the men wanted to play chess.'[85] These habitual activities – creating, playing, sharing, making – provided a connection to a past that made it possible for those living in camps to imagine a future in which ordinary human life would be resumed in a place called home. To Philippa, quietly folding clothes in Broad Street, perhaps something in the pattern of a human life was becoming visible.

UNRRA's aim was to repatriate displaced people (so-called DPs), but thousands were 'non-repatriable' because to send them 'home' would be a death sentence. One incident particularly affected Iris. A Yugoslav driver, fearful at having crashed an UNRRA truck, made a foolish dash for Italy with a loaded pistol. He was intercepted at the frontier. Iris, the only French-speaker in the office, was called to interpret and bring him back to Innsbruck. He was about her age and he cried all the way. She shared his fear and his certainty that he would be sent back to Yugoslavia to be murdered by Josip Broz Tito's men. The scene made her sick: 'how <u>irrevocably</u> broken so many lives have been by this war. Nothing nothing nothing ahead for these people.' Perhaps she felt ashamed when she remembered 'Irushka' walking lightly through Kensington Gardens to make a letter drop, untroubled by the far-reaching consequences of her action on lives in

Eastern Europe. She was miserable and got drunk on Slivovitz 'with some of the worst HQ offenders'.[86]

In February 1946, David Hicks ended their engagement as quickly as it had begun, and with it the future Iris was imagining. She received a letter: the thought of marrying her, he wrote, terrified him. No longer a fairy-tale princess but a real flesh-and-blood woman. 'Brain, will and womb, you are formidable,' he said.[87] He had fallen in love with another girl, one he wasn't afraid of. His letter crossed with hers in the post: 'My dearest, I miss you constantly, with a sort of physical pain. I love you, and I'm conscious of you all the time. I long for next year, and for the trials and the high winds of our life together! In expectation of that, I greet you joyously!' she had written.[88] Her attempt to be Sartrean man, as woman, had failed.[89] She later recorded a fear, perhaps linked to her family's identity as Protestant Irish exiles, 'that I would get nowhere, would hang around and ultimately become a DP myself'.[90]

Iris's mood began to lift in late March; she visited Vienna ('Lots of music & a fair amount of life, tho' one still has to climb over mountains of débris in the streets') on her way to UNRRA's headquarters at Klagenfurt. Once there she lodged at a nearby farmhouse, 'violets & gentians & anemones rioting up to the door'.[91] She recorded feeling an exquisite stillness, within and without.[92] By late April, she was in the British Zone, at a camp with a makeshift outpost of Graz University. Under the administration of Margaret Jaboor, a teacher from northern England who would later direct the World Council of Churches services to refugees,[93] accommodation in the camp was arranged by field of study, not by nationality.[94] 'I *love* this camp', Iris wrote to Raymond Queneau, whose novel she was now translating. 'As I cross the "quad" at evening to check on the accommodation in Barrack V I meet the two Jančars, just back from the university. They are studying medicine.' Barrack III housed students in the Philosophy Faculty; outside, '[u]nder the trees is Pardanjač, one of the *philosophes* . . . deep in a book'. Evenings often featured some kind of cultural exchange. A student orchestra was formed, with instruments donated by the YMCA. There was a camp newspaper, and a volunteer fire-service which sometimes donned fancy dress. One night, Taras Grigorievich Shevchenko's poetry was read in its original Ukrainian and then in Slovene translation. 'Kamnetsky lounges on the horizon, a problem child, but remember he was in a concentration camp.'[95] Iris, like many arriving from other camps, found in Studentenlager Hochsteingasse 'the promised land'.[96] 'There is so much *life* here – quite mysterious to me still, like fishes in a dark aquarium, but very moving and obscurely significant,' she told Raymond.[97]

It was at Hochsteingasse that Iris determined to have a try at returning to philosophy, despite reservations. ('It's hopeless, but I have to do it – after that I won't bother about the academic life', 'I don't feel at all confident in myself at the moment'.)[98] In April 1945 she had written to a friend of how '[t]he usual caucus race goes on in my mind about what to do after the war: university, WEA, British Council, BBC, journalism, League of Nations, (or whatever) Allied Control Commission – anything, anywhere, heaven only knows'.[99] Now her mind had settled; she had a plan. She prepared three applications: for a scholarship at the women-only Vassar College in New York; for a post at the University of Sheffield; and, following Elizabeth, for a Sarah Smithson Studentship. She submitted her applications on UNRRA headed notepaper.

'Dear Madam', her letter to the Principal of Newnham began. Since coming down her interests have 'shifted in the direction of ethics', she explains. As taught to her at Oxford, she found the subject formalist and lifeless, and unable to speak to the moral problems distressing her contemporaries; though in her final year she had become convinced that ethics could be done seriously (she was thinking of Donald MacKinnon in his Keble room). She admits that her thinking has not been disciplined since that time, but she has read: Dostoevsky's *The Possessed*, the Christian existentialist Gabriel Marcel and 'a number of books by that strange genius Jean Paul Sartre'. She mentions Sandie Lindsay's appeal to Kierkegaard in his own account of the 'duties of the democratic citizen'.[100] What attracts her to these thinkers, she says, is their attempt to treat ethical questions 'not insulated in an academic void, but from the point of view of the whole man'.

'Any given attitude to ethics must be based, explicitly or implicitly, on some definite theory of the nature of the self and of communication between selves,' she continued,[101] thinking of Martin Buber's *I and Thou*. Buber, an Austrian–Jewish philosopher who had fled Vienna for Israel just before the war, distinguishes two ways in which humans relate to their world. The first, which he calls *I-It*, involves an attitude of detachment; *I* classify or treat a person or thing as an object, an *It*, to be used, measured or manipulated. The second, *I-Thou*, exists between living things – people, animals, nature – when they meet or encounter each other as the beings that they are. This relation he calls 'dialogical'; both parties retain their uniqueness as selves and their relation together has a special wholeness, of the sort that belongs to real friendship. 'I notice in you & your letters a certain lack of interest in or curiosity about <u>me</u>. I suspect that you are more concerned about my effect on you than about me myself', Iris had complained to David Hicks.[102] 'All real living is meeting',[103] Buber writes.

In her application, Iris observes that much of 'what often passes as ethics is unsatisfactory because based on too naive a psychology'. She promises to speak of living man 'with blood in his veins, and a complicated psychology (and partly conscious of it) and with definite social and emotional problems to face – the man who goes to the cinema, makes love, and fights for or against Hitler'.[104] And, of course, under this description she means to capture women too.

Iris's letters of reference were written by Donald MacKinnon and Mildred Hartley. Donald's is somewhat vague – he had kept his promise to his wife Lois, and no longer shared an intimate friendship with his devoted student. 'As far as I can gather Miss Murdoch wants to research into the problem of moral responsibility' as treated by the 'so-called <u>existentialist</u> school'. She has, he writes, remembering their intense tutorials, an 'abiding interest in the more abstract logical and metaphysical branches of philosophy' and is 'well qualified to pursue this line of study.' She 'has really exceptional ability' but 'she is badly in need of time to sort out, criticize and order her ideas'.[105] Mildred Hartley, who had spent the final years of the war working for the Foreign Office Intelligence,[106] was brief and to the point. She commended Iris's 'immense energy & determination, great intellectual curiosity & staying power'. Her verdict: 'She is not, in my opinion, so striking as Miss Anscombe', but a 'good investment' nonetheless.[107] (Later, before sealing the envelope, Mildred went back in with her pen and added a qualifying 'quite' before the 'so').

Elizabeth & Philippa Begin a Philosophical Conversation

The striking Miss Anscombe took up her Mary Somerville Research Fellowship in October 1946, and was soon making her presence known in Oxford. Her husband, Peter, remained at 19 Fitzwilliam Street, Cambridge, with Barbara (now three) and John (who had just turned one). Elizabeth took rooms in Oxford. She was often to be seen with Philippa, walking slowly up the Woodstock Road towards Somerville. The two women would be bent towards each other deep in conversation: Plato, Aristotle, Aquinas, Descartes, Kant, Wittgenstein. Though at Cambridge women were still not permitted to graduate, Oxford had recently appointed its first female professor, ophthalmologist Ida Mann, a married woman to boot. For Philippa and Elizabeth, already with university posts, the possibility of a future in which they could become Professors Foot and Anscombe now existed.

The pair would have been eye-catching. Philippa: tall, tailored, poised. The Oxford men knew what to make of such a woman, even a clever one. She would have reminded them of their sisters, fiancées, wives. Elizabeth: shapeless, trousered, long hair untied, smoking. Occasionally carrying a toddler or baby. Peter Geach, her 'conchie' husband nowhere to be seen. She would have reminded them of no one.[108]

Sometime in 1946, Elizabeth began learning German. Wittgenstein was glad: 'if you learn German, then I can give you my book to read'.[109] On days when Philippa's teaching commitments allowed, they could be found after lunch in the Somerville Senior Common Room, seated on the stools at the end of the room, one either side of the fireplace. Wittgenstein's philosophy, Philippa would later tell her students, 'really needs to be done live, with two people, one trying to articulate what one naturally wants to say, the other trying to get deep into their head and diagnose what is going wrong'.[110] If Lotte Labowsky or Isobel Henderson had dropped in for a coffee, they would have seen a live performance of a philosophical investigation. Elizabeth deep in Philippa's head; Philippa brave and resistant but animated and

having fun. Recalling those days many years later, Philippa wrote: 'Every week I was defeated and I thought of myself like a character in a child's comic where a steamroller has gone over them and you're just a silhouette on the ground – but you're there in the next episode. Elizabeth liked this very, very much and we had become great friends.'[111]

In those early days, Elizabeth was still experimenting with Wittgenstein's philosophy of psychology. She had been writing reams on Descartes' argument, 'I am thinking, therefore I exist',[112] asking, 'What sort of argument is it? Is it supposed to prove the existence of some object, & if so what is that object? Isn't it incommunicable? Should it lead one to solipsism?'[113] She found that her discussions in Cambridge were beginning to illuminate the problem at the heart of her thesis in a new way. What is the difference between perceiving myself doing something and seeing someone else do it? What is the difference between understanding what someone says and saying it myself?[114]

She could give Philippa an illustration. Descartes' proof, she explained, is one I can only do for myself. 'I am thinking therefore I exist. Now – you do it!' This is of crucial importance. 'I have pain' and 'Elizabeth has pain' are radically different statements, even though the same fact, Elizabeth's headache, makes both true. You say: 'Elizabeth has pain' when you recognise a particular person by her bodily characteristics (her trousers, face, gait) and notice her behaviour – she is wincing or rubbing her brow. But 'I have pain' is not like this: it is more like moaning. I don't recognise anyone; I don't look for behaviour; saying: 'I have pain' *is* pain behaviour. Her German was perhaps now good enough to read to Philippa from Wittgenstein's notes: 'Here is one possibility: words are connected with the primitive, the natural, expressions of the sensation and used in their place. A child has hurt himself and he cries; and then adults talk to him and teach him exclamations and, later, sentences. They teach the child new pain-behaviour.'[115]

Elizabeth explained it to Philippa. The words 'Cogito, ergo sum' cannot be an argument for the existence of a self, any more than moaning or scratching one's head can be. Elizabeth was still groping towards the significance of this in 1946, but she was already convinced that, somehow, it held the key to 'shewing that the conception of the metaphysical subject of consciousness is both barren and fallacious' and to reclaiming Aristotle's idea that human individuals are like cat and turnip individuals.[116]

Wittgenstein's point about 'pain' opened up a new perspective on our psychological concepts, Elizabeth saw. In time, she and Philippa, Iris and Mary would all use this idea to overturn the naive psychology Iris had complained of in her application letter. Emotions like pride and fear and grief and joy and love are not simple inner experiences, but each is connected with patterns of speech and action, patterns that are part of the deep fabric of human lives; of our lives together. '"Grief" describes a pattern which recurs, with different variations, in the weave of our life', Wittgenstein had written (in the German notes Elizabeth was beginning to read). 'If a man's bodily expression of sorrow and of joy alternated, say with the ticking of a clock, here we should not have the characteristic formation of the pattern of sorrow or of the pattern of joy'.[117] Grieving takes its course over time. To make sense of human grief is to see our lives as interconnected; our pasts and futures and hopes entwined. It is against this background that we can recognise 'occasions for grief' – a gap at the table, a locked door, a joke untold; an 'occasion for grief' is 'interwoven with 1000 other patterns';[118] all the everyday patterns of human life.

At some point in those conversations, Philippa and Elizabeth began to read Aquinas' *Summa Theologica* together – Philippa initially relying on the scant Latin taught to her by Mildred Hartley in 1939. Unlike Iris and Mary, who were agnostic, Philippa was a 'card-carrying atheist'.[119] 'You ask why I am an atheist,' she would write to Elizabeth several years later. 'I don't know that I can give any very specific reasons: it's rather that I feel I'd need very good reasons <u>not</u> to be, and that I don't see any.'[120] But despite this, Philippa was soon ready to declare that Aquinas was 'one of the best sources we have for moral philosophy' and 'as useful to the atheist as to the Catholic or other Christian believer'.[121] It was reading Aquinas on the virtues, she later said, 'that first made me suspicious of contemporary theories about the relation between "fact" and "value"'.[122]

If the conversation spilt back to Number 16, Philippa and Elizabeth could be spotted moving north up St Giles' towards Park Town, where Mary would join them, sunk into the Foots' divan sofa. They make a strange trio: aristocrat, vagabond, scholar.

Iris's Communist Past Catches Up With Her

On 11 October 1946, a letter arrived at 16 Park Town. Return sender: Iris Murdoch, 4 Eastbourne Road, Chiswick. Michael Foot perhaps blanched a little as he saw it on the mat. Iris, then, was not in Innsbruck, nor Cambridge, nor Sheffield, nor New York.

Iris's parents' semi-detached house in a west London suburb was a long way from literary life, the pubs of wartime Soho and the cafés of post-liberation Brussels and Paris. In one journal entry, penned perhaps as she looked out from her old bedroom window at trimmed hedges and tended lawns, Iris notes Kant's assertion that English taste in gardens verges towards the grotesque.[123] The suitcase that she had packed for New York, complete with an unpublished novel, was back under her childhood bed. Perhaps for the first time in her life, her father, Hughes, was annoyed with her.[124]

Hughes's anger, such as it was, was a little unfair. It had not been her fault. Iris had written her letter of resignation from UNRRA, which was anyway folding operations, and had withdrawn her application for the Sarah Smithson Studentship at Cambridge, only after she was offered a more exciting opportunity: a Durant Drake Fellowship at Vassar College, New York.

During the war, in their last year of Greats, Iris had described to Mary her new life plan: 'the whole set up is complicated but it includes

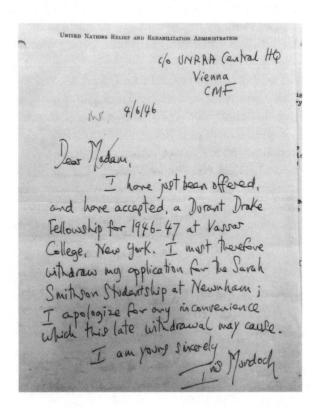

Ambitions to know the human race, to write a novel, & to go to America!'[125] By 1946 she had made good progress on items one and two; New York would make a full set. But her visa application was denied. In 1942, she had told a sceptical Mary that the Civil Service wouldn't want her: not 'with a political record like mine'.[126] She had been wrong then, and America's refusal now took her by surprise. When she had completed the visa application she had been honest. She affirmed: 'Yes, I am or have been a member of the Communist Party.' Oxford did everything it could to 'persuade the authorities to relent': Sandie Lindsay 'took the matter up in Washington'.[127] But to no avail. Without an income she had no choice but to return home.

Iris's depression was severe. Her translation of Queneau's novel had run aground and would soon be rejected by the publisher. David Hicks had sent her a photo of his new fiancée.[128] Taking a pen to a photo of herself, she glossed it grimly: Nadir.[129] She must have written to Donald MacKinnon in despair; breaking loyalty to his wife Lois he stepped back into her life. In October 1946 he organised for her to visit Malling Abbey in Kent. The Abbess was said to be 'good with difficult cases'.[130] Iris found some comfort in the high Anglicanism practised by Benedictine nuns: incense, singing, Latin vespers.

The letter that dropped on the Foots' doormat suggests that Iris had been reliving her past through the lens of existentialist philosophy, with its emphasis on authenticity, anguish and radical responsibility. She wrote to Philippa:

Dear,
I expect you have heard tell of my recent misadventures. Our
efforts in London to get the Yanks to relent have drawn a
blank – & altogether I conclude I've had the USA. Never
mind –
    Look, Pippa – it does occur to me that you & M. may have been
worrying about me – in general, I mean. I should be sorry if that
were so. One doesn't – as I know you realize – get over an histoire
like that of 1944 very quickly. When one has behaved as I then
behaved to two people one loves the hurt and the sense of guilt go
very deep. In a way it's only since I came home from Austria that
I've realised those events <u>fully</u> as things that I did, as apart from
things that I suffered. You understand. I have lived through them

again, seeing my own responsibility. This has not been pleasant, but was necessary. Forgive me for intruding this into your happiness with M. I am truly glad that you & M. have found this happiness together. It seems perhaps a foolish useless gesture after so long to say – I'm sorry I caused you both to suffer – but I do say it, most humbly, and believe me I do <u>feel</u> it. I have been very deep in the pit over this affair, but I think that that time has passed now. You are <u>not</u> to worry about me, either of you, for there is no cause any more.

Pippa, you know without my telling you that my love for you remains as deep & as tender as ever – and always will remain, it is so deep in me & so much a part of me. I cannot imagine that anyone will ever take your place. I think of you very often. My dear heart, I love you –

Yes, all goes well with me now. I am working very peacefully & begin even to understand one or two things. (eg about Kant, who I now realize was a complete mystery to me at Ox.!) I'll let you have news of my movements when I have any movements.

Be tolerant to this perhaps tiresome letter.

My love & blessings on you both –

I[131]

Pip sat down to pen a reply. She still cared for Iris, loved her, wished for a future in which the past could be overcome. She told Iris that there was no opposition between her love for her husband and that for her friend. That even when Iris was hateful in Michael's eyes she still loved her. 'Hang on,' said Pip. '[B]e patient & don't let go your hold,' replied Iris; 'it is a long way back & I have still far to go & many knots to untie'. This way of moving forward, by untangling the past, is far from the one preached by the existentialist Sartre. We must put down roots, wrote Pip slowly: like plants, we must wait for regrowth. Iris replied with a wish: 'what is good may grow, & what is bad may die'. '[T]hat this precious central thing in my life, my friendship with you, does remain gives me such courage & calm of mind.'[132] She looked back on the frenzy of Brussels: 'I did feel sure of <u>wanting</u> new things – & being to that extent different. But there was no joy at all.'[133]

One weekend in November, timidly, gently, the pair were reunited. Iris caught the train from Chiswick to Oxford – the District Line to Ealing

Broadway, then overground, changing once at Slough. She saw Pippa, talked with Michael, vowed to be patient, distant, calm. They spoke, carefully, of philosophy. Philippa, her head still full of Elizabeth, told Iris about the *cogito*. Iris must have taken an envious pleasure in Philippa's new closeness to Elizabeth. They joked: 'a man who comes up to me in a dream & says cogito ergo sum. (To which I reply, "oh, no you don't, pal!")'.[134]

Lieutenant Colonel Austin Takes the Revolution Forward

It was Elizabeth's habit during Michaelmas Term 1946 to exit Somerville each Friday afternoon and make the short, one-mile walk to Magdalen. She would arrive at J. L. Austin's rooms for a graduate class just after 5 p.m. 'Things', it said in the lecture listings in the *Gazette*. If there was one class to set ration queues buzzing, this was it.

In November 1940, J. L. Austin had left Oxford for military training at Matlock.[135] He ended the war as Lieutenant Colonel Austin, responsible 'more than anyone' for the 'life-saving' accuracy of the intelligence behind D-Day.[136] He had been one of only a handful of people outside Bletchley who had access to 'Ultra' intelligence (information obtained through breaking German encryption).[137] Back at Oxford, he had masterminded a new phase of attack in the war on metaphysics begun by fellow Brethren-member Freddie Ayer. Like Ayer, who was one year his senior, Austin 'disliked and distrusted' so-called metaphysical ambitions. He accepted what 'Wittgenstein had written in the *Tractatus*: "Everything that can be said can be said clearly"'. But, like H. H. Price (for whom Ayer was 'a young man in a hurry'), Austin was suspicious of the 'staggering rapidity' with which Ayer delivered his results.[138] He believed that the problems of philosophy could be solved without metaphysical angst or positivist flamboyance by a small corporation of young men.[139] As such, though he rejected the dogmas of Ayer's logical postivism, he admired 'the workshop, no-nonsense atmosphere of the Vienna Circle' and he initiated his equivalent in post-war Oxford.

His invitation-only Saturday-morning no-nonsense workshops took place in a mishmash of rooms in the men's colleges. Some were held in the 'shabbily comfortable, leathery, Victorian common-room in the front quad of Balliol' and others in a 'smaller and older room in Trinity'. Austin's favourite was a 'rather splendid modern room in St John's, with a big central table and highly executive chairs, looking like the board-room of a prosperous and soberly go-ahead commercial company'.[140] Asked, many years later, whether being a woman had ever caused her difficulties, Philippa gave this as her example. 'He [Austin] had something that got called Austin's Kindergarten. On Saturday morning he would just informally ask everyone his own age, or younger, hence the Kindergarten, round to a discussion of philosophy. Everyone was asked who had any teaching post in Oxford but the women were not asked. That was a place where work was being done.'[141]

During the war, Lieutenant Colonel Austin's team of men had collated, sifted and interpreted intelligence to generate a formidably detailed description of possible landing sites for the British troops. The philosopher Austin now applied this strategy, a piecemeal approach to a mass of conflicting data, to the English language. The method, which would later be known as 'Ordinary Language Philosophy', was as follows. First a team of philosophers selects 'an area of discourse in which it is interested, often one germane to some great philosophical issue'.[142] A prime territory for J. L. Austin was discourse involving visual reports: 'I see a cat', 'I see a rainbow', 'The stick looks bent', 'John and Tom are identical' and so forth. Austin believed that metaphysical excess in philosophy of perception arose because there was no clear map of this area of our language.

Once a terrain had been selected, the next phase was to gather intelligence. Here, collaboration would be essential because the task was enormous: all the words and phrases that belong to that area must be collected, 'first by thinking of and listing all the words ... that one can – not just the most discussed words or those that at first sight seem most important – then by looking up synonyms and synonyms of synonyms in dictionaries, by reading the non-philosophical literature of the field'.[143]

With the first set of data gathered, the team now produced meta-data. They did this by making up '"stories" in which the legitimate words and phrases occur' and in particular 'stories in which it is clear that one can appropriately use one dictionary "synonym" but not another'. For example, 'slip', 'accident', 'mistake', 'inadvertence', may be dictionary synonyms, but (writes Austin), by 'imagining cases with vividness and fullness we should be able to decide in which precise terms to describe, say, Miss Plimsoll's action in writing, so carefully, "DAIRY" on her fine new book: we should be able to distinguish between sheer, mere, pure and simple mistake or inadvertence'.[144] Complex narratives could be constructed to illuminate subtle features of linguistic use. 'Linguistic phenomenology', an ear for the language, was central to this part of the work, as was linguistic knowledge, encoded in idiom and poetry.

Finally, with all the linguistic data in, the team would proceed to analysis and modelling: they would 'attempt to give some account of the meaning of the terms and their interrelationships that will explain the data'.[145] The work would be boring and the results often disappointing, but gradually the ground would be mapped.[146]

Though Elizabeth, like Philippa, was excluded from the boardroom on grounds of sex, J. L. Austin could not stop her from attending his graduate classes. In 'Things' he applied his method to talk about perception. The intelligence his team delivered revealed some crucial results. First, the linguistic data revealed that the notion of 'perceiving indirectly' occurs when we see things with mirrors or periscopes ('I saw him *indirectly* in the mirror'), but not when we are looking straight at a bath or cigarette packet.[147] Thus the linguistic data did not support the sense-data theorists' claim that we see cigarette boxes and cats 'indirectly' via surfaces and sensory impressions. Second, linguistic data collected on the use of the words 'indistinguishable' and 'the same' uncovered significant divergences in meaning. The sense-data theorist assumed that the experience of hallucinating a cat and the experience of perceiving a cat must be experiences that have a common nature. Such experiences must be, in some sense, 'the same' because the two are 'indistinguishable'. But, Austin pointed out, sometimes 'the same' means something quite different from 'indistinguishable'. For example, 'John and Tom are the same man' means something quite different from 'John and Tom are indistinguishable men'.[148] Again, the sense-data theory is at odds with the linguistic data.

To Peter Strawson, it was 'exhilarating to see these huge and imposing edifices of thought just crumbling away'.[149] From Plato onwards, philosophers had been attempting to build a bridge from appearance to reality; all these efforts were dispensed of with a single linguistic observation, wittily delivered. Like logical positivism, the method seemed democratising. Mary Wilson, now a final-year Classics undergraduate at Lady Margaret Hall, found Austin's method thrilling. After the war, 'we were sick of propaganda',[150] she recalled, and Austin's philosophy seemed the antidote. But the Scottish philosopher Clement Mundle (like H. H. Price, a future president of the Society for Psychical Research) was not alone in suspecting that what Austin's team were really describing was how English was spoken by men who got a First in Classical Greats at Oxford.[151] Those whose ears were attuned to German or Czech – or indeed to Scottish English – were likely to lack the linguistic phenomenology the method required, and by which a catalogue of legitimate and illegitimate uses of words was to be produced.

Elizabeth saw 'Things' very differently to Mary Wilson. No longer the young, cardiganed undergraduate photographed in the St Hugh's College garden, Elizabeth was now a formidable intellectual presence who, since getting her First, had taken two toddlers, a difficult husband, and Ludwig Wittgenstein in hand. She disrupted the class and 'frequently intervened to pour scorn on what was being said'.[152] One Friday evening, Mary Wilson had found Elizabeth's rudeness 'notable', even by her usual standards. Not wanting to find herself an unwitting ally, as soon as Austin dismissed them, Mary tried 'to evade her . . . by scuttling very fast out of the Magdalen back gates'. Elizabeth followed, catching up with her in Longwall as she was struggling with her bicycle lock. Snared. 'To think that Wittgenstein fathered that bastard,' Elizabeth hissed.[153] Mary Wilson was shocked.

It would, in time, become part of the official history of the Oxford Revolution, that J. L. Austin developed his 'Ordinary Language Philosophy' quite independently of Wittgenstein, but Elizabeth had good reason for speaking of Austin as fathered by Wittgenstein. Though Austin cultivated a studied casual disdain for Wittgenstein (calling him 'Witters', and letting it be known that he was 'repelled' by the 'personal atmosphere' that surrounded him),[154] Austin had in fact studied the 'blue book' notes.[155] In February 1940, just a few months before he left Oxford for his army training, Austin had presented a paper, 'The Meaning of a Word', to the Cambridge Moral Sciences Club.[156] In it he 'discussed the view that the meaning of a word is the object which corresponds to this word'. Austin did not mention Wittgenstein by name in that talk, but the audience would have been in no doubt that Austin was drawing ideas out of the 'blue book', the first sentence of which is: 'What is the meaning of a word?' Austin's talk takes up so many of Wittgenstein's ideas – that we must attend to the particular, that we can be misled by language, that we should look at how a word is used and how it is explained – that the talk was almost a homage to the Austrian.

J. L. Austin may have started from the 'blue book', but when Elizabeth attended the 'Things' class she discovered a philosopher, seated soberly at the head of the table in his leather chair, who could hardly have been more different to the one who paced and prowled in Whewell Court's tower. Austin seemed to have taken Wittgenstein's idea that to understand human language you must understand human life, and turned it into something utterly dead. 'I thought that he would agree with much of what had gone on in the Things class,' Mary Wilson (foolishly) remarked to Elizabeth one day. 'After all, had he not spoken himself of bringing back words from their metaphysical to their everyday use?' Elizabeth 'turned white with rage'.[157]

Austin's way of 'bringing words back from their metaphysical to their everyday use' was to appeal to rules of linguistic use, and to intuitions about which words sound right in specific situations. Just as Freddie Ayer had used the Criterion of Verification to reduce the Idealist and Realist metaphysicians to silence, J. L. Austin used the Criterion of the Dictionary to limit philosophers to the language of the plain man and the omnibus. But for Wittgenstein, a dictionary was a tool that could be used to settle the definition of a word only after almost everything about language and life was already understood. The place to look for the rules of a language is not in a list of definitions, words understood in terms of other words, but in the human practices in which sound, action, nature, instinct and culture weave together to create living patterns of significance and sense.

It began snowing on 22 January 1947 and continued for fifty-four days; it was to be the coldest winter since the end of the Napoleonic wars. Pipes froze. The heating in Mary Scrutton's bedsitter broke. Once again Oxford swapped shoes for skates, and took to the ice. Mary was 'getting back into the philosophical scene', picking up old conversations with Elizabeth on Plato's forms, and new ones with Philippa on ethics. Iris and Philippa were tentatively nurturing their relationship. Letters were exchanged and occasional visits made. Outside, everything was muffled. 'Intense cold. Degrees of reality. (Degrees of frost!),' wrote Iris in her journal.[158] She had been reading H. H. Price's preface to *Matter, Mind and Meaning*, the posthumous work of psychical researcher Whately Carrington. As after the First World War, many turned to mediums in the hope of filling the gaps left by the dead with their spirits. Price wrote in his capacity as former president of the Society for Psychical Research, and expert on paranormal phenomena, but for him there were deep connections between the philosophy of perception and parapsychology. All that is real are sense data, appearances, which cluster together to form what we call individual things, argued Whately. We might not be inclined to call a ghost or apparition a 'full-blooded "Thing"', but these complex systems of appearances form their own unities and are as much part of reality as bedspreads and bicycles. Price hoped that seeing reality as a matter of degree would be the key to understanding the world of seances, poltergeists and the paranormal. Elizabeth too was dipping into parapsychology, reading Joseph Banks Rhine's recently published experiments in psychokinesis. His subjects were instructed to 'will' dice to fall a certain way. Elizabeth was unimpressed. It was a mistake to say that '[t]he soul can or cannot move matter outside <u>as well as</u> inside its own body – for I can't move my hand by willing it to move <u>any more</u> than I can move a match-box in that way.'[159]

Around this time, Elizabeth began experimenting with a new approach to expressing Aristotle's idea: 'I have tried to get at what he means by calling the body the organ of the soul as the eye is of sight.' The organ of sight is the eye; it is the eye's function to see. The organ of the soul is the body; it is the body's function to . . . [160] She was moving, tentatively, towards an idea: '[T]he "soul" as "life", i.e. "having a soul" as "exercising vital functions"'.[161]

Mary was called home to look after her mother. Lesley had fallen on the ice, breaking a bone, just as Mary herself had during the last big freeze. She politely resigned from her post as Gilbert Murray's secretary and headed down Boars Hill for the last time, this time taking the bus out of deference to the icy road and her proneness to accident.

Elizabeth Brings Wittgenstein to Oxford

For years, Oxford's dons had been desperate for Wittgenstein to come. They had read his *Tractatus Logico-Philosophicus* but his new work was unpublished, and the snippets that reached them from Cambridge were sufficiently interesting that they wanted to know more. Few had been able to lay hands on the 'blue book', as J. L. Austin had. Before the war, every Oxford philosophical society had sent letters to *Professor Wittgenstein, Trinity College, Cambridge*: carefully worded then increasingly sycophantic, begging him to come. He often said he would, but as the anticipated date approached the unlucky secretary or Chair would receive a telegram: he had a cold, an appointment, a crisis.[162] With friends he was more candid: 'I'm sure you'll think me a beast for changing my mind again about attending that bl ... congress. But the truth is, I'm glad I have changed my mind. It was an awful thought to go and sit there among logical positivists and the like.'[163] Now, just six months after she had been appointed at Somerville, it was Elizabeth who finally brought him. She had not managed to persuade Wittgenstein to give a paper, but he had agreed to attend the Jowett Society (the undergraduate philosophy club) and to respond to a paper by the society's president, Oscar Wood.

Oscar had begun his degree in 1942 and now, nearly five years later, was on the verge of completing his four-year course. Like Elizabeth's husband Peter, Oscar had been a conscientious objector and he was viewed with suspicion, bordering on disgust, by some of the fellows. When he was appointed to a lectureship at Worcester College in 1952, the Dean threatened to resign. The parents of many of the undergraduates, he urged, 'would certainly not have selected a College where they knew their sons on coming out of the Fighting Services would be guided in their approach to a consideration of the principles of conduct by a Conscientious Objector'. For the college 'officially and knowingly to appoint as a Lecturer in Philosophy a gentleman holding Mr Wood's unusual opinions comes near to being an insult to the living and the dead'.[164] This glimpse of the feelings at large about 'conchies' may explain why Peter Geach, despite his First from Balliol, was still without a proper post.

Elizabeth brought Wittgenstein to the meeting in Magdalen College.[165] At the front of a packed room, Oscar Wood was seated at a little semicircular table. Wittgenstein took the chair at the other end and Elizabeth sat on the floor at his feet. She did so because there were no remaining chairs, but the symbolism of this arrangement raised eyebrows and contributed to the myths that were developing around her relationship with Wittgenstein. Mary was struck that her friend had lost her judicial air and 'became quite small and submissive'.[166] There were lit candles at either end of the table, so as Oscar rose to his feet it looked as if he might begin a seance or a Mass. Elizabeth surely eyed the front row warily: enemies from the 'Things' class. Mary Wilson, present as usual, noticed that '[p]ractically every philosopher [she'd] ever seen was there'.[167] Lined up in the front rows were J. L. Austin, Gilbert Ryle, J. O. Urmson, Isaiah Berlin and H. A. Prichard. Philippa was there too, and Mary Wilson noticed her 'good' clothes, conspicuously not home-made. Mrs Foot wore stockings while others, prohibited by the expense, showed bare legs spattered with bicycle mud. Mary Scrutton, 'unlovely mauve legs' on display, had returned with the fair weather.[168] Further back was Richard Hare, a painfully thin bespectacled figure. He was Mary's age, but with his receding hair and gaunt face he looked much older – if she had spotted him, she might not have recognised him as the young boy she had last seen in Fraenkel's *Agamemnon* class,[169] caught in the same sunbeam as Nick Crosbie and Frank Thompson.

Oscar read a brief, carefully constructed paper on whether Descartes' '*Cogito, ergo sum*' was a valid argument. When he stopped speaking, Witt-genstein began to respond. His voice was so quiet that the audience had to hold their breath to hear. Mary Scrutton, whose natural inclination against the neurotic predisposed her to be unimpressed by this small, electrical sage, was surprised to find herself drawn in: 'For about five min-utes what he said seemed incredibly important and illuminating.' She was grateful for the patient explanations Elizabeth had given in Philippa's front room: 'language has to be rooted in the complexities of real life, not imposed on it from outside as a calculus derived from axioms', Elizabeth had explained. 'I am thinking' must be brought back into the context of human life, where its use can be described and its meaning and significance can be seen. Mary scolded herself for not having brought a notebook, her leaky pen idle in her pocket; but no sooner could this regret surface than things began to break down. Wittgenstein started to interrupt himself; 'No, no, that isn't it – What should one say? You see, the real difficulty here – Oh no, no, it is terrible . . .'.[170] 'Say what you *want* to say. Be *crude* and then we shall get on',[171] he demanded of Oscar Wood, who replied – much to Wittgenstein's frustration – with a morose but lucid exposition of key points of his paper. Mary was struck by the contrast between Oscar's objective calmness and the tremendous violence and fear that animated Wittgenstein's rejection of solipsism; his animal sense of the cold lonely endless isolation of a thinking ego, cut off not just from others but from the flesh and blood of a living creature; his desperation to 'replant us in our proper soil as social beings'.[172] If Iris had been there she might have drawn on the writings of Gabriel Marcel. For Oscar, solipsism was a problem; for Wittgenstein it was a mystery.

As the meeting became disordered, Philippa found herself in a moment of profound clarity. She felt something change in her: later she would say 'those five minutes, I am sure they have had more influence on my philosophy, therefore on my life, than anything else that anyone has ever said to me'. She stored away a lesson: when you find yourself saying 'something absolutely crazy – the thing to do is not to try and drive the thought out but to stick with it, to give it its day, its week, its month, its year if need be, in court'.[173] This was the exact opposite of Freddie Ayer's approach, which had left a generation of male undergraduates too terrified to speak in case their stuttering sounds were declared 'Nonsense!' She perhaps caught Elizabeth's eye as they shared that silent thought.

'If a man looked up at the sky and said "I think it's going to rain, therefore I am" I should not understand him,' continued Wittgenstein, making an attempt to remind his audience of the tenuous ties of recognition, intelligibility and sanity that bind us together in language and life. But for the aged Realist H. A. Prichard, fidgeting in the front row, this was too much.[174] His friend, H.W.B. Joseph, had spent his last years tormented by intellectual despair as he desperately tracked and exposed the absurdities in Ayer's position, only to find himself ignored by him and the other analysts.[175] Prichard, by contrast, had determined to waste no effort on the young men who were intent on wasting no time on him. He had pulled up a drawbridge and concerned himself with his own continuous efforts to worry things out.[176] But here was more than he could endure. The landmark paper which had made his name in 1912, 'Does moral philosophy rest on a mistake?', had detected an important overlap in Descartes' struggle for certainty and our tendency towards practical perplexity about duty. *What do I really know? Why should I do what is right?* Prichard had argued that no philosophical theory can help us with these questions. Still, the struggle itself must be taken seriously – to send it up as a piece of raving lunacy does not remove our questions nor the temptation to ask them. It only serves to undermine the great, if faltering, efforts of those metaphysical animals that have been gripped by them. He rose to his feet and, to everyone's horror, headed towards the door. His parting shot: 'What Descartes was interested in was far more important than any problem you have addressed this evening.'[177] The 'you' was directed to Wittgenstein, but was aimed as much at the Brethren in the front row.[178] These would be the last words many in that room would hear him speak: six months later he was dead.

As bewilderment and embarrassment descended, the audience began to interject and a young man towards the back made several unwelcome comments that seemed to irritate Wittgenstein enormously. Oscar, rather heroically to Mary's mind, attempted to steer Wittgenstein back to his central argument about the role of knowledge in the *cogito*, but to no avail. Richard Hare, meanwhile, was beginning to fret. It was his first time at the Jowett and he was there with one aim: to make a comment. He had no particular interest in the *cogito*, nor even in Wittgenstein, but it was a condition of membership of the Jowett Society that one make a comment at a meeting while an undergraduate. This was Hare's last chance – he would be taking his Greats examinations in a few weeks. If he failed this evening, he would not be permitted to attend future meetings as a don. Sensing that things were unravelling he shouted out: 'I must make an observation!' before saying the most innocent thing he could think of – so innocent that no one afterwards could remember what it was he had said. Wittgenstein thought the observation had come from the young man seated behind him, whose earlier remarks had been so irritating: 'it was the last straw. And Wittgenstein then turned upon <u>him</u>, who hadn't made the observation, and tore him in pieces.'[179]

'It was a terrible business,' Mary Wilson recorded in her diary that evening.[180]

Mary & Iris Prepare to Re-enter Philosophy

Though Mary had spent a year pedalling up and down Boars Hill, she had not really been going anywhere. Now she had resigned. Like Iris, she thought she would like to give philosophy a go, and she went to visit their Somerville Ancient History tutor Isobel Henderson – it was Isobel who had recommended Mary as a secretary to Gilbert Murray at the end of the war and now Mary hoped she could help her along again.

Mary's best option if she wished for a career in philosophy, Isobel explained, was the new B.Phil., the course designed by John Mabbott and Gilbert Ryle to create an army of analysts to be stationed in philosophy departments across Britain. The B.Phil. recruits met each evening before dinner in specially designed classes in various men's colleges – Austin's 'Things' class was one such offering. To the untrained eye, these small discussion groups seemed modelled on the German seminar, but John Mabbott insisted otherwise: 'they were as unlike German seminars as it is possible to imagine', he explained; unlike their 'instructional' Teutonic counterparts, these classes were 'genuinely exploratory'.[181] The aim was not to learn how the great philosophers of the past had grappled with the mystery of human life and its place within the cosmos, but to master the new and powerful linguistic technique and to understand how it could be universally applied to transform mysteries into solvable problems. A typical week might see the B.Phil. students with Exeter's William Kneale on Tuesday, to study 'Development of Logic'; Wednesday in Magdalen with Waismann and Ryle on 'The Logical Force of Expressions'; and ending the week in Balliol for 'Legal and Moral Responsibility' with J. L. Austin and H.L.A. Hart.

If the undergraduate classes before the war had been full of 'clever young men who liked winning arguments' (the aggressive 'I don't understand' a crucial weapon), graduate classes were now led by such men and full of others who were being specifically trained in modern methods and hothoused for jobs in a profession that would reward cleverness, quickness and aggression. Even Ryle himself grew concerned that the B.Phil. was training not philosophers but philistines.[182] Some of his recruits delighted in terrorising younger, or less confident, tutors. Herbert Hart, just appointed to New College and not yet up to speed on the new linguistic method, would turn pale when Geoffrey Warnock interrupted his class to inform him: 'But Mr. Austin said exactly the opposite in his lectures.'[183]

As nothing would more surely have extinguished Mary's nascent philosophical dreams than such a setting, Isobel suggested she try for the D.Phil. instead. Here Mary could spend three years ranging widely over a single problem. There would be no requirement for her to be modern and quick; instead, she could settle down to contemplate the sort of 'large-scale metaphysics' that she and Philippa were now beginning to discuss. As Donald MacKinnon had taught them, A. J. Ayer's philosophy contained an implicit and dangerous 'doctrine of man';[184] to overcome the subjectivist ethics it spawned, an alternative picture would be needed. Mary would be neither modern nor perhaps employable at the end of her course – metaphysical enquiries were viewed with 'suspicion, disapproval or sometimes outright ridicule'[185] – but she would be shielded from the orthodoxy of the B.Phil.

In her quest for 'large-scale metaphysics', Mary was drawn to Plato, as she had been when she first met Elizabeth in the Somerville dining hall. For many of the philosophers who surrounded her, brought up on a diet of (what she called) 'extreme empiricism', there is just one reality, the value-less world of empirical sensible facts.[186] But Plato, like H. H. Price, spoke of degrees of reality. In the *Republic* (the first philosophy book in the Downe library that had really fascinated Mary) he tells the allegory of the cave, a story of prisoners who ascend from the unreal shadow-world of the cave towards something *more real*.[187] Out of darkness into light, towards Knowledge, Goodness and Beauty. She had learnt from Donald MacKinnon that allegory needn't be fairy tale, that paradox and poetry can help us to 'catch the sense of a world' that defies direct comprehension. But what did Plato mean when he said that the world of forms was *more real* than the world of things? 'What kind of behindness is it?' as Elizabeth had asked.

Mary's dissertation would begin from a distinction between existence and reality. It makes 'perfectly good sense to say that a great deal exists that is not real,' she writes in an early essay. We say: '"He's just an actor, his whole life is unreal", "your real intention", "the whole thing was as unreal as a nightmare".' (When Mary protested about Marcel waves in women's hair to Lesley, 'I don't believe in them,' she knew they existed, but she thought they weren't real.) The Idealists, she points out, recognised this distinction. Experience shows that something exists, F. H. Bradley had written in 1893, but it is 'a mere superstition to suppose that an appeal to experience can prove reality'.[188] The Realist G. E. Moore had been wrong, Mary wrote, to 'treat [this] dichotomy' as 'an embarrassing slip'.[189] What is real must have 'a particular kind of importance and regularity', she writes. Perhaps, tucked underneath her bedspread, Mary had been reading Dorothy Emmet, now a professor at Manchester University. There is a connection between reality and importance, wrote Emmet in the journal *Philosophy* (Mary's favourite) in November 1946.[190] Not 'importance' in terms of passing interests, purposes and concerns, but in terms of what *really matters*.[191] We have a responsibility to protect these things. But first we need to learn to recognise them.

Mary planned to explore these ideas in the work of the third-century neo-Platonist philosopher Plotinus, who himself had lived at a time of political and social collapse. In her thesis outline, Mary observes that 'when a good society ceases' practical life becomes difficult. Without a good society, 'the sequence of events becomes entirely irregular' and when an individual acts 'the traditional result does not necessarily follow'.[192] When the relation between means and ends breaks down, the questions of how to be a good person, and how to do one's duty, become pressing. I want to help my friend by sending her a food parcel, but if the postal service is run by crooks and gangsters, all I can do is deliver the parcel to the post office and hope for the best. A judge who does her duty in a corrupt society will find no connection between doing what is right and doing good. 'In such situations the coincidence of varying moral motives, on which optimistic systems rely, vanishes.'[193]

She would work with the Regius Professor of Greek, E. R. Dodds. Like H. H. Price, Dodds served on the council of the Society for Psychical Research and would later become its president. He had once performed an exorcism. Recalling the topics he was interested in that year, Dodds listed: 'dream, trance, magic, and the mysterious forces denoted by such words as *menos, ate,* and *daemon*'.[194]

Dorothy Emmet's 1945 *The Nature of Metaphysical Thinking* shared a shelf with Buber on Iris's bookcase at Chiswick.[195] 'Degrees of reality. Consider the word "importance"', Iris had written in her diary some months earlier She too had been slowly figuring out what was important. She was not creating herself anew, but putting down roots in what was familiar: philosophy. 'I just don't see how any intellectual institution could ever dream of employing me', she had written to Pip in the winter. 'Not having anyone to talk to about the stuff, or indeed about anything else that matters, is sometimes a sheer agony. I lose all sense of my reality as a thinker. Some days I just can't imagine what I'm about, or what I am at all.'[196] Still, by early summer 1947 she had gathered herself and typed up a second proposal for the Sarah Smithson Studentship. It was tighter, more focused. She had been working at home, back under Donald MacKinnon's supervision, writing for him essays on 'topics on the borderline of the philosophy of logic, metaphysics and the theory of language'.[197]

Iris's application shows marks of MacKinnon's influence, most clearly in a deepened engagement with Gabriel Marcel, whose work *Être et avoir* was now appearing regularly in her journal. Donald gave her a copy which she inscribed on New Year's Day, 1947. Her plan was to take up Marcel's distinction between problem and mystery, alongside Martin Buber's identification of two realms, *I-It* and *I-Thou*. She would use these distinctions to show why 'Sartre is wrong to make the free act alone the crucial feature of his ontology.'[198] When I treat things and people in an objective manner, Buber writes, I relate to them as an *It*. And when I explain things from this point of view, I do so using concepts that can be publicly formulated and expressed to anyone. For example, my explanation of why a dropped cup has broken, using concepts about surfaces and fragility, can be communicated to any speaker. But when I relate to another as a *Thou*, much is often unsayable and difficult to express. This is not 'an obscure mystical conception, but a normal experience which most people will recognize if they consider their own lives', Iris observed in her application. She was perhaps thinking of her own life – of quadrilateral entanglements, love letters and broken promises.[199] Sartre supposes that we each encounter an empty world, in which as a lone individual we create value through our freely chosen actions. But he is wrong. The world is already teeming with value. Friends, lovers, animals, trees. All living *Thous*. Still, Marcel and Buber 'err' in a certain 'vagueness', a 'failure to define their terms', she continues. Buber calls the *I-Thou* relation dialogical, but he does not consider that many dialogues between *I* and *Thou* use language and symbol. Iris planned to find a logical framework that can capture such uses of language.[200] She was sure that logical positivism, with its 'logical gadgets'[201] of operators and variables, could not. As she had written in her journal that February: 'No verification in Thou world'.[202]

MacKinnon again wrote her reference, and this time his personal involvement is clear. Her experience of life in the last few years had been 'bitter'.[203] But this year she is more mature. She is 'on the threshold of creative work of a high order'. Her second application to Newnham was successful. Lois MacKinnon was, once again, distressed as she watched as '[t]he same situation repeated itself',[204] and Donald and Iris fell back into their pattern of infatuation and hysterics. Donald was perhaps as relieved as Lois by an offer of a Chair at Aberdeen (Regius Professor of Moral Philosophy) that would see husband and wife leave Oxford before Iris arrived.

During the summer of 1947, Mary and Iris celebrated their re-entry into philosophy with a holiday in France. They had arrived together at Somerville and the pair would now step synchronously into graduate studies. They travelled with Mary's friend Tom Greeves, later to become a celebrated draughtsman of fantastical architecture – not of futuristic skyscrapers but of mid-Victorian buildings, dilapidated and overgrown. The three tripped round Tours on hired bikes, taking in the chateaux of the Loire with their pepper-pot pinnacles – and then Paris, with knapsacks loaded with provisions from England: Ryvita, tins of sardines, soup powder, soap and a small stove on which to make tea. This haul was needed to make the £50 that each traveller could take out of the United Kingdom last as long as possible. Mary and Iris tended to lunch together, parsimoniously, on whatever contents of the knapsack were left – the idea of running out of money made Mary jumpy so she stuck with the more seasoned Iris. Tom, more the gourmand, went off in search of local delights. Their budgeting worked and they could manage to stay a week in the Collège Franco-Britannique on the Left Bank's Boulevard Jourdan. Iris took her friends to meet Queneau. He wrote Iris a poem on a metro ticket: 'Tom's tempo may be slo', while Mary's varys, mais tu passes Iris ma chère comme vu éclair.'[205] At a fair in Montmartre, Iris volunteered for a go on its new marvel – the Rotor, a spinning drum whose increasing speed, by centrifugal force, caused those standing against its walls to be held fast while the floor dropped away. But here was the curiosity. Pleasure-seekers were allowed on for free, while spectators in a little gallery above paid to watch the hair-raising spectacle.[206] Mary forfeited a small portion of her £50 to watch Iris spin.

CHAPTER 5

A Joint 'No!'

OXFORD & CAMBRIDGE
OCTOBER 1947–JULY 1948

The Quartet Unite Against Ayer & Hare – Iris & Elizabeth
Talk About the Reality of the Past – Philippa Reconnects Facts & Values –
Elizabeth Starts to Think About Human Action – Aristotle Comes to Life

The Quartet Unite Against Ayer & Hare

When she was in her nineties Mary Midgley told us a story about the past. It was the story you are reading now. Her version started in October 1947, when she, then Mary Scrutton, returned from Paris, and once again stepped with Iris into philosophy. Mary, no longer an overgrown schoolgirl, but at twenty-nine an impressive scholar, was about to begin work on her thesis on Plotinus. Iris, now the 'experienced woman' she had dreamt of being, knew more about the new French and European existentialist philosophy than almost anyone in England. She would be living in Cambridge, in the Pightle (a house for graduates owned by Newnham College), but she was to be seen emerging from Philippa's Oxford home, 16 Park Town, as often as from the Pightle's powder-blue tiled arch. Philippa's position had been converted into a lectureship.[1] Elizabeth was a research fellow at Somerville College and living in Oxford. Her husband Peter, along with Barbara and John, remained in Cambridge at 19 Fitzwilliam Street.[2] Iris sometimes played postman and delivered Barbara and John to a waiting parent at one end or the other of the Varsity Line.[3] 'Thus', Mary wrote, 'for a time the sweeping view from my attic window included them all and I soon began to see them a good deal.'[4] She could still picture them; 'the four of us sitting in Philippa's front room and doing our collective best to answer the orthodoxies of the day, which we all saw as disastrous'.[5]

By the end of 1947, the miniature moonlight rebellion that Mary and Iris had made after their Bablock Hythe graduation dinner with Isobel Henderson had grown into a philosophical mission. 'Trend is a good man and Rowse is a bad man', the young Iris had unfashionably declared, taking a stand against Ayer's assault on objective moral judgement. Now, with the war behind them there was urgency to the task of finding a way back to moral truth, objective value, and an ethics that connected to what *really matters*. Iris's plan that year was ambitious: 'Revise moral philo. Demolish Ross. Take Crit. of Prac. Reason seriously. The limits of the linguistic method. i.e. discover real extent of the present crisis in philosophy.'[6] Elizabeth, in her report to the Mary Somerville Fellowship Committee, proposed to 'work out my doubts about what is called analytical philosophy'.[7] Philippa wanted to show that 'it can't just be a matter of booing and hooraying: when we say there was something absolutely wicked about the Holocaust, this is not just a personal decision, decision not to do such things, or an expression of disapproval. There is something objective here.'[8] Mary's aim in philosophy was to 'make sense of the relation between older and newer ways of dealing with the subject'.[9] At the end of that academic year, at home in the Pightle, Iris recorded in her journal: 'Back from Oxford. A world of women. I reflected, talking with Mary, Pip & Elizabeth, how much I love them.'[10]

In her nineties, Mary thought their story still important. As she saw it, the orthodoxies that she and her friends had done their collective best to answer still persisted. '[D]espite a lot of surface activity,' she wrote at the beginning of the millennium, 'the colourful, fantastic screen of up-to-date ideas inside which we live ... has not actually changed much.'[11] In her version of the story (Mary never lost her flair for drama) she cast Richard Hare as the anti-hero. 'As with many philosophical schools,' she told us, 'the starting-point was a joint "No!".'[12]

In February 1942, as Mary and Iris had been preparing for their final exams, Richard Hare was nearly 7,000 miles away and preparing for the defence of Singapore against an invading Japanese army. Along with Nick Crosbie, Kenneth Kirk, Frank Thompson and Noel Martin, the war had cut short his time in Fraenkel's Corpus Christi seminar, the fate of the captive Cassandra interrupted. A week-long battle ended with unconditional surrender. Along with 80,000 British, Indian and Australian troops, 2nd Lieutenant Hare himself became a prisoner of war; 'I prefer to pass over our sufferings,' he said when asked of what followed.[13] Richard Hare was among those to be liberated by the atom bomb, without which, he would later write, 'we should probably not have survived'.[14]

In late 1945, Richard had been among those ancient undergraduates who were back to finish their degrees before getting on. He was still suffering from the after-effects of torture and starvation, along with monthly bouts of malaria (sweating, shivering, headaches, vomiting). Sandie Lindsay, his old Balliol Master, sourced pamaquine for him, a new and 'scarcely obtainable' malaria medication.[15] Richard had only just managed to get to the Jowett Society meeting to which Elizabeth had brought Wittgenstein; it was the first he had been strong enough to attend – had it not been for the necessity of asking a question he might well have stayed at home, with his new wife Catherine, and rested. He was tutored through his final year by Donald MacKinnon. Hare couldn't understand anything that his tutor said, but he was grateful to him for making him read the right books.[16] Hare and MacKinnon were two devout Christians who had made opposite decisions in September 1939. We do not know the psychological effect on the older man when he confronted this weakened malarial student. Richard Hare's attitude towards pacifism had hardened since those days: 'rather like living on the immoral earnings of women', he would write.[17]

Like Philippa and Mary, Richard had been turned into a moral philosopher by his experience. 'Up to the War, if there hadn't been a war, I might have gone back to the classics and become a classical scholar. The War raised so many moral problems and philosophical problems that after that I couldn't be anything but a philosopher,' he said.[18] His moral philosophy, which he developed over the coming decade, formed itself around his own wartime experiences, and in particular around two totemic and horrifying scenes.

The first took place in February 1942, at the moment when Lieutenant Hare's unit surrendered. They had taken only two Japanese prisoners during the entire Malayan campaign, and after the surrender the pair were freed. 'When they were released [. . .] they did what they thought they ought to do: they at once went to their units, saluted their commanding officers, and then committed hara kiri'[19] in order 'to expunge the disgrace of being taken prisoner.'[20] For Richard Hare, this became the moment that made him 'stop believing in a universal objective moral standard known by intuition without reasoning, such as is posited by Sir David Ross'.[21]

The second scene occurred in the latter part of his captivity, after the long and terrible march up the River Kwai to work on the Thailand–Burma railway. Each morning, the camp commander ordered the prisoners out to work on the railway. All were starving and some were terribly sick with malaria, cholera and dysentery. Richard told the story of the camp interpreter (who may well have been himself), who tried as far as he could to persuade the commander not to send out the sickest prisoners, for whom the exertion would be fatal. But the commander seemed unmoved by the fact that the men would die. The commander's attitude and actions were for Hare further evidence that Ross and Prichard must be wrong. While Hare was certain that men ought not to be sent to their deaths, the commander 'had an equally clear intuition, in all respects as indubitable', that he 'ought to magnify their emperor and their country'.[22] If moral intuition was attuned to an objective moral reality, then such a stark and insurmountable clash of intuition ought not to be possible, Hare thought. Intuitions and emotions cannot, then, be ways of perceiving an independent moral reality; they are merely the upshot of one's particular upbringing.

When, as a young philosopher at Lady Margaret Hall, Dorothy Emmet found the 'world of moral certainties' described by her Realist lecturers unrealistic, her response was to seek a connection between morality and what is important in human life. But for Hare, thousands of miles from home and confronted with conditions and a set of values he could barely recognise, the existence of different moral certainties seemed fatal to the idea of universal, objective moral standards. 'What must be understood about a prisoner-of-war community is that it is a society which has to be formed, and constantly reformed, out of nothing', Hare recalled. There was no background, no shared understanding of what mattered, on which he could depend. In 'this very strange, constantly disintegrating situation . . . one can never know from day to day whether personal survival – which seems in any case rather unlikely – is rendered more likely by cooperation with one's fellow-prisoners or by looking out for oneself'.[23] As Mary had learnt from Plotinus, an individual forced to act outside a 'good society' cannot rely on like effect to follow like cause, and so must choose without expectation or hope that acting from a good motive – friendship, duty, benevolence, honour – will result in him doing good. Hare, like Plotinus, retreated inward. He fixed in his mind his own set of moral principles, and attempted to bind his future self to them come what may.

In the run-up to his finals (Hare would graduate with a First in June 1947), Lindsay offered him a fellowship at Balliol.[24] It is likely that Richard Hare was appointed as replacement to the outgoing MacKinnon. Richard began meditating on those two scenes. He had not been convinced by Ayer's *Language, Truth and Logic* before the war, but his loss of faith in objective moral reality now led him to accept its basic picture of a value-free world.[25] What he could not accept, however, was Ayer's claim that moral language is nothing more than the expression of emotion, and that his disagreement with the Japanese commander was a simple clash of feelings. He wanted to show that even though there was no value in the world, moral disagreement could be approached rationally and, where both parties were intellectually honest and open, reason could prevail. Back in Balliol, Richard Hare had formed the ambition 'to find a way of answering moral questions rationally'.[26]

In order to bring the language of morals back into the realm of reasons, Hare began by reclassifying it. This was to be the third time in the twentieth century that philosophers made use of G. E. Moore's suggestion that moral philosophers should study the word 'good' and not goodness or the Good, in order to find a place for ethical concepts in an increasingly alien world. For Realists Ross and Prichard, moral statements were subject to objective standards of correctness – standards which they understood as residing in an independent moral reality. For Ayer they were expressions of emotion, communicating subjective feelings. For Hare, they would be prescriptions or imperatives, employed to recommend or oppose courses of action. A moral judgement, Hare argued, is akin to an order: 'Do it!' or 'Don't do it!'

Unlike expressions of emotion, imperatives can stand in rational relation to each other – this was the prize Hare was after. The order 'Leave now!' is contradicted by the order 'Don't leave now!' And the order 'Make an omelette!' implies the order 'Break some eggs!'[27] Imperatives have their own system, he saw, and he began work on charting this peculiar logic. As Mary and Iris returned to philosophy, he was ready to begin presenting his findings in papers, lectures and classes: 'Imperative Sentences' (Jowett Society, Hilary 1948), 'Moral Objectivity' (Westcott House, Cambridge, Michaelmas 1948), 'Some Logical Problems in Ethics' (lectures, Michaelmas 1948), 'Good' (graduate class, Trinity 1949 and Philosophical Society, Hilary 1950), 'Practical Reason' (entered for the T. H. Green Moral Philosophy prize 1950). Soon his theory, which he called 'Moral Prescriptivism', was the talk of the Junior Common Rooms.[28]

Hare had attempted to show that there could be a rational basis for moral disagreement, even after Ayer's ethical weedkiller had stripped reality bare of value. It was this that elicited the joint 'No!' from Philippa, Mary, Iris and Elizabeth. Philippa Foot certainly couldn't stomach this repackaged version of Ayer's subjectivism. She wanted to be able to say to the Nazis: 'But we are right, and you are wrong.' She wanted the idea of an objective moral reality against which actions could be judged *wrong* or *bad* and not just *inconsistent* or *irrational*. Hare had settled for consistency: if a man held an internally consistent set of moral principles, and acted in accord with them, there could be no ground for complaint.[29] Moral criticism would proceed, not by saying: 'You are mistaken about what really matters for human life', but by saying: 'Your chosen moral principles are internally inconsistent' or 'Your actions are not in line with your principles'. Once consistency is established, 'I can only leave him to choose; for it is after all his choice,' Hare said of the Japanese commander.[30]

Later, Iris would describe 'this piece of our philosophical history' – from Ayer to Hare – as 'the elimination of metaphysics from ethics'. While Idealists and Realists had aimed at discovering objective moral truth, whether by self-transcendence or intuition, in Ayer's and Hare's worlds, we confront 'a stripped and empty scene' in which morality is 'not pictured . . . as being attached to any real natural or metaphysical structure. It is pictured without any transcendent background.'[31]

Thus, for the older Mary reflecting on the past, the way to tell the story of herself and her friends was to begin with them knitting together the great cleavage in reality that Ayer celebrated and Hare accepted – bringing fact and value back together. From this, she said, 'a lot of metaphysics would follow'. On to the knitting needles would go Philippa's notes on Aquinas (one of 'the best sources that we have for moral philosophy'); fragments of Wittgenstein's latest writings turned out of Elizabeth's pockets (forms of human life); Mary's inky notes on Plotinus (reality not existence); Iris's heavily annotated copies of Gabriel Marcel's *Être et avoir* (problems and mysteries). Memories of wartime lessons: Ross and Prichard's moral intuition; Collingwood's clothes-line and Lindsay's *entia rationis*; Price's un-observed cats; Cassirer's lessons on Kant's *Achtung*; Joseph's 'bits of living' and Miss Glover's talk of love's capacity to reveal the Good; Plato, Aristotle and Donald MacKinnon's analogical concepts and this insight: *we are metaphysical animals*.

Iris & Elizabeth Talk About the Reality of the Past

For Elizabeth and Iris, the 'world of women' anchored by Philippa and Mary in leafy Park Town was only half of intellectual life. The other half was 'unsettled, impatient, restless' Cambridge, from which women were not yet permitted to graduate, and where it seemed to Iris as if only one word was on the lips of every graduate student: 'Wittgenstein, Wittgenstein, and Wittgenstein'.[32] Wittgenstein had resigned from his Chair in August 1947, as Iris was spinning on the Rotor in Paris. He was taking his final term (Michaelmas 1947) as a sabbatical. His absence made it easier for the post-graduates to settle into arguments about the meaning of his philosophy, safe from his glare. He was hiding out in remote Rosroe, Connemara, on the west coast of Ireland, where he frightened the neighbouring family; they considered him mad and forbade him from crossing their land. He had run out of his preferred American pulp crime magazines and was reading Dorothy L. Sayers – her detective stories, starring the fictional Somerville graduate Harriet Vane, depressed him.[33]

Iris had arrived in Cambridge in early October 1947. Out of her suitcase had come at least two copies of *L'être et le néant*, Albert Camus's *La peste* and some French literature of the avant-garde. That month she travelled twice to London to give talks on Sartre in the bomb-damaged St Anne's church in Soho.[34] Her journals from the previous year brim with reflections on Marcel, Kant, Bradley, Sartre, Hegel, Buber, Heidegger, Plato, Ayer, Russell, Kierkegaard and the Thomist philosopher Pierre Rousselot. She was ready to do serious work; Philippa sent her a scholar's gown.[35]

As soon as she had unpacked, she headed out to track down Elizabeth. 'No second rate philosophy is any good,' Elizabeth told her gravely. 'One must start from scratch – & it takes a very long time to reach scratch.'[36] 'Any talk with E. even on generalities' is 'enlivening & stimulating', Iris wrote to Pip.[37] Over the next year her friend's name, 'E.', appears in her journal nearly 150 times.

Iris had heard about Elizabeth's new way of doing philosophy from Philippa, but her first direct encounter with it came a few days after her arrival in Cambridge. On a dark Thursday evening, Elizabeth presented her paper, 'The Reality of the Past', to the Cambridge Moral Sciences Club, the department's long-standing discussion group (of which she had been Secretary 1945–6). It was almost a year to the day since the club had witnessed the famous incident when Wittgenstein had threatened Karl Popper with a poker.[38] Elizabeth was nervous. This was to be a very early attempt to use what she had learnt from Wittgenstein and she began with an apology: 'Everywhere in this paper I have imitated Dr Wittgenstein's ideas and methods of discussion. The best that I have written is a weak copy of some features of the original, and its value depends only on my capacity to understand and use Dr Wittgenstein's work.'[39] When she began to speak, however, those present would have recognised how far Elizabeth had come from the stuttering, abandoned remarks available in the tower in Whewell's Court. She was presenting not fragments but sustained philosophical argument.

She began with a puzzle that is first stated by the pre-Socratic mystic Parmenides: '"It is the same thing that can be thought and can be,"' so "what is not and cannot be" cannot be thought. But the past is not and cannot be; therefore it cannot be thought, and it is a delusion that we have such a concept.'[40] This fragment of Parmenides does not express a form of 'Cartesian doubt', Elizabeth told her Cambridge audience – Parmenides is not worried that it might not be possible to *know* about the past. No, he is raising a more fundamental puzzle: how is it even possible to *talk* or *think about* the past? His question is about meaning and intelligibility: 'Is not our apparent concept of the past impossible?' he asks.

Parmenides' paradoxical puzzle, Elizabeth told her audience, results from a particular picture of the way that thought and language connect to the world, a picture that is so natural that we may not even notice it at work. The picture is as follows. The name 'Iris' names Iris by, as it were, pointing to her. A thought or sentence that employs the name 'Iris' is about Iris because the name points to Iris; the thought or sentence is meaningful and capable of being true because of this primitive connection between name and named. 'When I think of my acquaintance A, and think that he is in Birmingham, it is he, A, the very man himself, and Birmingham, that very place, that I mean', explains Elizabeth. The problem about the past emerges, she continues, when we try to understand our talk about it by applying this model of language. We find that we cannot do it. 'The name or thought of something past seems to point to its object in just the same way as the name or thought of any other actual thing; yet how can it, since its object does not exist?'[41] So we find ourselves forced, with Parmenides, to the absurd conclusion that it is an illusion to suppose that we can think about the past.

Elizabeth had seen that Parmenides' worry was one that should trouble phenomenalists like Freddie Ayer, who wanted to analyse statements about material objects – tables, bathtubs, cats and turnips – in terms of statements about sensory experiences. The phenomenalist tries to deal with statements about unobserved objects using counter-factual analysis: 'There is a table in the next room' means: 'If one were to go into the next room one would see . . .' and so on. But, Elizabeth explained, when it comes to a statement about the past – 'There <u>was</u> a table in the room' – the problem is not how anyone could have got into a position to have made observations of things at past times. It is rather that the concept of the past already appears unanalysed on both sides of the phenomenalist's analysis! 'There <u>was</u> a table in the room' = 'If someone <u>had been</u> in the room <u>at that time</u>, they <u>would have</u> seen . . .'. But this is no help at all with Parmenides' paradox.

The phenomenalists, Elizabeth went on, 'proceed as if we had a prepared empty time scheme and the only work to be done were the analysis of what is to be put into the various places of the scheme'. It is as if 'I have a set of pictures in a row: those on my left represent the past, and those on my right represent the future,' said Elizabeth, 'and the row moves constantly to the left.' In this image each of us is a static point, events passing us by, and fixing themselves as they do so. 'To speak of something past' would then be to 'point our thought' at 'something *there*', but out of reach. But, as Parmenides asked, *how* can we 'point our thought' at events and objects that have passed us by and which no longer exist?[42]

The portrayal of past and future events as a set of pictures on a prepared timeline, Elizabeth goes on, is also connected to a particular way of understanding the idea that the future, but not the past, can change. The idea that the past cannot change but the future can change, 'could be represented by the fact that once a picture has passed me it cannot be removed from the row, whereas a picture on the right-hand side can be removed'. And 'by the fact that the pictures become set as they pass me so that they cannot be altered whereas the pictures to the right are in a fluid state or are as yet mere blanks'.[43] But this leads to more philosophical problems. Why can't the past be altered? Is it merely an empirical impossibility, as when a set of photographs is placed in a sealed box, stored in an archive or printed on a special material that fixes the images? Or is the unchangeability of the past somehow written into the nature of reality? Can't we imagine a change in the past, as if one of the cards that has passed us by suddenly alters?

Elizabeth was now ready to try out Wittgenstein's method, to show how it might be used to dissolve this knot of puzzles and paradoxes. Points of confusion, Wittgenstein had taught her, indicate places where we are 'in the dark' about how our concepts work.[44] These are the places where philosophers find themselves tempted to go beyond the limits of our meaningful talk – to say crazy things like 'It is not possible to think about the past!' or

'Isn't it conceivable that the past could change even though it never actually does?' (or: 'Do I know that this is a tree?', 'Do I really see this cigarette packet?') She had learnt from Wittgenstein that it is at these edges of sense, where we pass from intelligibility to unintelligibility, sanity to madness, and where our everyday confidence that we understand what we mean falls away, that the philosopher should get to work. Iris, in the audience, was attending fiercely to Elizabeth's words and now she reached for her notebook.

'The past is real', 'the past cannot change', Elizabeth told her audience, are remarks that belong to daily human language-using life. They are parts of a practice that we can set out to describe. She was asking her audience to join her in taking an extraspective glance. To help them, she presented a tiny fragment of our practice: 'Let us imagine that someone is taught (1) to say "red" when a red light is switched on before him, "yellow" for a yellow light, and so on; and (2) next to say "red", "yellow", etc., when lights of the appropriate colours *have* been switched on but are now off.'[45] We might imagine her playing this game with Barbara and John – the four-year-old Barbara quickly catching on to the rule, John, just two, on the cusp of grasping the first part.

Elizabeth wanted to show how this tiny fragment, a game for children, could be handled and enriched in ways that would begin to unlock the structure of our concept of the past, as the image of pictures passing by a stationary observer could not. When asked: 'What happened?', the child must answer: 'The yellow light was on, and went off', or 'The red light was off and went on', and so on, in accord with how she has been taught to go on. The adult will say 'yes' if the child's report matches the one she herself would give and will correct her if not. Later, when the child can answer the question 'What happened?' in the course of everyday conversation, other kinds of mistake may occur. For example, the child might say: 'I went to the park tomorrow.' The adult might reply: 'No. You can't say that.'

In these little scenes part of the structure of the concept of the past can already be seen. Statements about the past are corrected or revised or confirmed by other witnesses. ('That's not what happened. I saw . . .') The adult uses the expression 'You can't say . . .' to teach the child the rules of the game, to teach her what it is to speak of the past.

Elizabeth's fragment is a dialogue between child and adult who are witnesses to the events they are speaking about. In an enrichment of the language game, Elizabeth explains, we go on to teach a child to speak of a past neither she nor we have witnessed. 'Belief in recorded history', she would later write, 'is on the whole a belief *that there has been* a chain of tradition of reports and records going back to contemporary knowledge; it is not a belief in the historical facts by an inference that passes through the links of such a chain.'[46] The 'historical past' is preserved jointly as witness testimony is recorded, repeated and passed down. To believe that Aeschylus wrote *Agamemnon* is to trust in continuous human endeavour that has preserved for us the testimony of those who bore witness. This is something that Mary had cottoned on to early in Fraenkel's class, then in Gilbert Murray's study atop Boars Hill, and now as a D.Phil. student. She was giving it metaphysical roots in Plotinus' distinction between existence and reality. The scholar chases down the past through continuous layers of human effort, of copying and reproducing, of retelling and reimagining.

In her talk on the reality of the past, Elizabeth swapped a picture of a solitary and stationary observer for a community of humans, each of whom is a witness to a tiny part of human life. She transformed the lonely individual into someone who is alive at a particular historical moment, with one perspective among many, living in a human society that weaves together the common past by answering various forms of this question: 'What happened?' 'What did you do?' 'What did you see?' Each contributes a thread to that tapestry, one thread in a pattern that transcends each individual and that is beyond what any one of us can know. We, together, keep the historic past alive by recording and preserving testimony through the generations. What becomes our shared past is contingent on that activity.

That the past is real, that it does not change, Elizabeth was telling her audience, is shown in these practices, in how we go on in the present. We share memories, give witness reports, hold each other accountable, write history books. In our own lives, our past actions shape the way we confront our futures: we plan revenge, make penance or reparation. These practices reveal the reality of the human concept of the past.

Back home at the Pightle after Elizabeth's paper, Iris took out her journal and scribbled seven pages of notes. 'Relate E's stuff to my own vague generalizings about the linguistic method & appeal to [ordinary] language,' she wrote. 'E. is not "appealing to ord. lang." Is <u>describing facts</u> about how we learn use of words (hence concepts.) What <u>is</u> this method? What are its implications for moral propns [sic]? Its relation to psychology?'[47]

The following week in London, Iris met the French Christian

philosopher, Gabriel Marcel, whose words she had inscribed in her journal in Westminster Cathedral a few days before the atom bomb: '*Not to degrade mysteries into problems*'. Twenty years her senior, and grieving over the recent death of his wife Jacqueline Boegner, Marcel was now at work on the Gifford Lectures he would deliver the following year: his topic, 'The Mystery of Being'.[48] He had been in Cambridge the week of Elizabeth's talk,[49] but whether he attended is not known. Gabriel and Elizabeth perhaps met only in Iris's thought and on the pages of her journal.

Marcel considers a 'cinematographic' conception of time, whereby the past is thought of as a fixed series of discrete events (like the row of pictures that Elizabeth uses to illustrate the idea of the past as something there and unchanging).[50] This is the picture of time that operates in the *I-It* world, writes Marcel (borrowing Martin Buber's way of speaking). But when it comes to living individuals, the *I-Thou* world, the cinematographic conception of time is inadequate. In the world of human beings, the past remains alive in the present and the future. 'Past is <u>all</u> "open to be recreated" – my own & others', Iris summarises.[51] The interweaving of past, present and future in the *I-Thou* world is seen most vividly in the case of promises: 'Reln of lang. to past & future. Promises.'[52] A promise is an act of faith, or 'creative loyalty';[53] 'faith' because although a promise orientates us, together, towards a shared future, neither of us can know what kind of people we will be when that future comes.[54] Iris perhaps remembered her broken engagement with David Hicks, when for a brief time the words 'We will . . .' had shaped her future as one of 'long talks in cafés & dancing together & getting drunk together & long evenings at home too . . .'. A remembered past future that never was.

Iris and Gabriel walked in St James's Park and looked at the ducks,[55] then made their way to Soho where he gave a talk (probably in St Anne's church). Iris somehow forgot to mention it to Pip ('I feel most sick about this', '<u>Very, very sorry</u> about this idiotic failure to think').[56] Philippa, like Iris, was more knowledgeable than most in Britain about French existentialist thought, and had continued the reading she had begun during her last days in Seaforth. Over the summer she had read Martin Buber and André Gide,[57] and at her recommendation Iris had read the metaphysician Louis Lavelle. His Platonic tendencies are 'nuts to Elizabeth', Iris reported back.[58]

When in Cambridge, Iris spent much of her time at Trinity, half a mile from the Pightle and across Clare Bridge on the other side of the River

Cam. She was 'almost living there', in the rooms of Wasfi Hijab and Kanti Shah, two of those postgraduates for whom the word 'Wittgenstein' was a refrain.[59] I am 'cooking meals for Shah and Hijab', she told Pip in a letter, 'who think this is a good way of saving money! (They hope I will learn quickly!)'.[60] The previous year, Wasfi and Elizabeth had attended tutorials together with Wittgenstein on the philosophy of religion.[61] The trio could have been seen circling, dizzily, round the Trinity lawns discussing the nature of religious belief. 'A man would fight for his life not to be dragged into the fire', Wittgenstein had said. 'No induction. Terror. That is, as it were, part of the substance of the belief.'[62] Wasfi's faith and intellectual foundations had been shaken by the encounter.[63] By the time Iris was cooking him meals in Trinity College his homeland was engulfed by civil war – no longer a Palestinian Arab, his home town of Nablus had been temporarily absorbed by Jordan.[64] Kanti Shah, a south Indian Jain, had been another of Wittgenstein's favourites. He had spent the previous year, along with Allan Jackson and Peter Geach, taking meticulous notes in Wittgenstein's lectures on philosophical psychology.[65] Georg Kreisel, a mathematician and refugee from Austria, made up the Wittgenstein-obsessed band. Elizabeth, Peter and fellow Catholic Yorick Smythies added voice. The mix of religions – Muslim, Jain, Jewish and Catholic – created only culinary challenges, but no less serious for that. Muslim Wasfi ate meat, but Kanti was a vegetarian and 'this poses many moral problems', Iris explained to Philippa more than half-seriously, 'such as should I mix the meat fat with the vegetable fat, or keep them scrupulously separate? Such things are much more important than philosophy.'[66]

Iris was a newcomer to the set, and unlike the others had not been exposed first-hand to Wittgenstein's philosophy. She met him just once before he left Cambridge, after she persuaded Elizabeth to act as emissary. Iris presented herself in his stage-set of a study in late October 1947. 'His extraordinary directness of approach and the absence of any sort of paraphernalia were the things that unnerved people,' she would later tell a journalist. 'I mean, with most people, you meet them in a framework, and there are certain conventions about how you talk to them, and so on. There isn't a naked confrontation of personalities. But Wittgenstein always imposed this confrontation on all his relationships.'[67] She made a record in her journal of their brief and surreal conversation, conducted sitting on deckchairs. Wittgenstein (who was irritated by the constant stream of travellers knocking on his door in search of answers) complained: 'It's as if I have an apple tree in my garden & everyone is carting away the apples & sending them all over the world. And you ask: may I have an apple from your tree?' Iris quick as anything had replied: 'Yes; but I'm never sure when I'm given an apple whether it really <u>is</u> from your tree.' 'True,' he answered. 'I should say tho', they are not good apples.' Then he proffered a gnomic summary of the pointlessness of the introduction: 'What's the use of having one philosophical discussion? It's like having one piano lesson.'[68]

Philippa Reconnects Facts & Values

By 1948, Philippa, Iris, Mary and Elizabeth had enjoyed, on and off, almost ten years of joint piano practice in philosophy. Philippa's weekly encounters with Elizabeth had been doing her good. She would never shake off her imposter syndrome (despite, as her three referees had written in 1945, her extraordinary ability), but for now she was confident enough that at least she had a talent for sniffing out a problem. Whenever she read a philosophical paper, or heard an argument, she would know if there was something wrong by a feeling of bodily discomfort that she had now come to recognise.[69] Hare's 'moral prescriptivism' gave her just that feeling, and she was about to make a start on a response.

One afternoon that year the four women met in Lyons' tea rooms, 3 Cornmarket Street, Oxford.[70] On the inside, one Lyons' tea room is the same as any other: white tablecloths, artificial flowers, ashtrays, aproned 'Nippy'

waitresses (so-called because of the way they nipped around the tea shops). This one would have reminded Philippa and Iris of tea and sticky buns in their Seaforth days. Ever since the government had lifted the wartime ban on ice cream, the company had been developing a method for producing it without dairy products (which were still in short supply as milk remained on ration). Chemist Margaret Roberts, a recent Somerville graduate, was at work in the ice-cream division: many years later, she would be Prime Minister Thatcher.[71]

Philippa explained her idea over the clatter of the busy café, the Nippy serving up a pot of hot tea for Mary and Philippa, black coffee for Iris and Elizabeth.

'It would not be an exaggeration', Philippa perhaps began, 'to say that the whole of moral philosophy, as it is now widely taught, rests on a contrast between statements of fact and evaluations.' (This would be how she began her 1958 talk, 'Moral Beliefs', that grew out of this conversation.)[72] For Freddie Ayer, evaluations are expressions of emotions (Boo! Hooray!); for Richard Hare they are prescriptions (Don't do it! Do it!) But if we accept this contrast on which contemporary moral philosophy rests, it means that two people may give opposite evaluations in the face of the same facts without either making a mistake. And this, as Philippa had seen, prevents us from saying to a Nazi: 'But you were wrong, and we were right'.

By 1948, though she was not yet able to defeat the moral subjectivist, Philippa was starting to see that the contrast from which that philosophy began was deeply unrealistic. So much of our language, she pointed out, is both evaluative and descriptive. 'Take the word "rude",' she said. To call someone 'rude' is to express disapproval: if I say: 'Putting your head on the table is rude' I mean that it ought not to be done (perhaps a quick glance at Iris). So, calling something 'rude' is clearly an evaluation. 'But', she continues, 'the meaning of "rude" *is* connected with the factual statement on which it is based. I cannot just call walking up to a front door slowly or sitting on a pile of hay, "rude".'[73] If I try, what I say won't make sense. For the evaluation to make sense I would need to make a connection between the facts and the evaluation by pointing to some conditions of offence that we all recognise. When, in the Old Hall at Kirkleatham, Iris had pushed her plate aside and put her head on Esther Bosanquet's dining table, the older woman had been offended. Though there may be cases where we disagree about what is and isn't offensive, occasions for offence – like occasions for grief – belong to a pattern in the weave of life; a dinner guest is grateful (even for bad spaghetti), remains attentive (despite uninteresting conversation), stays approximately upright (though exhausted). Philippa's point is a simple and elegant extension of Wittgenstein's: our evaluative language does not peel off the world, leaving behind a stripped-out, valueless scene that we might call 'reality' or 'nature'. Rather, an evaluative description makes sense only when it is located in a pattern of human life.[74]

Philippa's way of starting to bring back together values and facts caught everyone's interest and an animated discussion developed.[75] We do not know precisely what was said, but we might imagine the Nippy overhearing as the tallest woman leans forward, pushing up her round spectacles on her nose: 'The meaning of "offensive" is not found solely in the dictionary but in human life: to give its meaning would be to describe not just the rules of etiquette and offence, but the social life of human animals, how hierarchy is achieved and sustained, how relationships are built and sundered.' Mary too is weaving in lessons from Wittgenstein: 'Language has to be rooted in the complexities of real life, not imposed on it from outside as a calculus derived from axioms.' Next, a surprisingly beautiful voice from the chain-smoking woman in trousers: 'Suppose I said "Eating a cracker is rude!" How puzzling! But if I fill out the background and you see a genuflecting atheist about to receive the host, you can see straight off why it's offensive. The ethical dimension of the judgement comes into view when the background makes a connection to something that is of serious importance in a human life; namely a relation to the divine.'

And now we can rest our imagination, because we do know how the conversation ended. Iris, who had been thinking about how the evaluative meaning of rudeness might differ from individual to individual depending on their past experiences, interjected: 'For instance, Elizabeth, I should imagine that some people might sometimes describe you as "rude"?'[76] Elizabeth's 'ruthless authenticity' was one of the things about her that Iris had so admired and valued since she had returned to philosophy,[77] but many at Oxford would have agreed with Mary Wilson that her directness went beyond acceptable bounds. Her rudeness was 'so proverbial' that Mary Scrutton assumed she took some pride in it. But, to everyone's shock, 'Elizabeth froze and was wholly silent for a long time, removing herself to an arctic distance.' Iris perhaps shared imploring looks with Mary and Pip, but no one knew quite what had happened or how the situation might be mended. After some time, Elizabeth stood up and made a short speech at Iris. She 'regarded any such suggestion as an intolerable and extraordinary insult'. Pushing back her chair 'she marched out in dignified silence', leaving behind three stunned faces and half a cup of cold coffee.[78]

Elizabeth Starts to Think About Human Action

Mary, remembering their conversations about Hare from that time, told us: 'From this joint "No!" a lot of metaphysical consequences would follow.' Knitting together the language of facts and values means knitting back together matter and mind, in order to understand how the physical movements of human bodies can be called 'good' or 'bad', or how good or bad motive can make a difference to the facts about what happened. While Philippa went to work on moral language, Elizabeth was digging deeper into human action. Her first book, Intention, was several years off, but it was already foreshadowed in the paper she addressed to Oxford's Socratic Club in February 1948. 'The metaphysics of all this is very difficult',[79] as Mary Glover had said.

It was Elia Estelle Aldwinckle, a one-time tobacco farmer from South Africa, who had invited Elizabeth to speak. Stella had come to Oxford in 1929 to study theology, following a revelation and conversion at the age of twenty-one. After a brief spell teaching Divinity at St Christopher College (a school in Blackheath, London) she had returned to Oxford University in 1941 as Chaplain for Women Students. The Socratic Club, which she had founded, was conceived of as an evangelical tool to reach those who were interested in 'untidy questions' but were not yet Christians.[80] Her position as chaplain rendered her unstoppable, recalled Iris. She 'entered the colleges of Oxford boldly, not always welcome, but as of right, taking her role among us for granted'. She did not appear as a 'converter' but taught by what she was – 'by her presence, her faith and her concern'.[81]

Stella and Iris became friends, but Mary was not convinced. She found Stella exasperatingly smug, and it had not helped the latter's cause when she woke Mary at 11 o'clock on the night before her finals Logic paper by knocking loudly on her door. 'Would you like to come and argue at the Socratic Club?' Stella had asked, smiling sweetly. 'Dilly dilly duckling, come and be killed,' thought Mary. She could later recall Stella's 'martyred and forgiving smile' at even 'the politest refusals to give in to her unreasonable demands'.[82]

Elizabeth was friends with Stella through Iris,[83] but would not have been expecting an easy time at the Socratic Club. Stella insisted that the meetings were 'quite civil': 'we wanted to get to the truth of things, and to follow the argument in good faith and good temper wherever it went'.[84] However, the club's president, C. S. Lewis, a don twenty years Elizabeth's senior, had a reputation for enjoying fierce debate: he would 'talk for victory', it was said.[85] 'Atheists and Agnostics, All Welcome!' declared a poster pinned to the noticeboard in the St Hilda's Junior Common Room that evening.

C. S. Lewis had heeded his own plea to continue 'learning in wartime' and had just published a book, *Miracles*; Elizabeth was there to discuss it – in front of its author. She had picked out chapter three. 'I want to discuss your argument that what you call "naturalism" is self-refuting because it is inconsistent with a belief in the validity of reason', she began, addressing the president directly. 'With this argument you propose to destroy "naturalism".'[86] In that chapter, Lewis had argued that 'naturalists' cannot account for thought's rational character. Thought, he had argued, is governed by rational relations. Conclusions follow logically from premises. Yet the naturalist insists that all relations are ultimately causal. Human behaviour and thought follow causally, not rationally, from other physical events. Lewis claimed that this position is self-defeating. The naturalist thinks he has rational grounds for his belief in naturalism. But if naturalism is true, then his belief has no rational grounds at all. It is just a physical event, with a causal explanation like any other. A belief without rational grounds is irrational, so the naturalist's position, Lewis concludes, is self-undermining.

'What I shall discuss', Elizabeth continued, is this argument's central claim, that 'a belief in the validity of reason' is inconsistent with the idea 'that human thought can be fully explained as the product of non-rational causes'. She addressed Lewis again: 'This seems to me to be a mistake founded on various confusions you commit about the concepts of "reason", "cause" and "explanation".'[87] An intake of breath: Miss Anscombe clearly had no intention of being deferential.

A scientist who gives a causal explanation of the physiological processes involved in an instance of someone's reasoning, she said, does not consider the content of the reasoning at all. He does not, cannot, consider those processes from the point of view of 'validity' or 'truth' or 'evidence'. For him the processes are simply physiological goings-on, and because he is considering them from this point of view, questions of 'rationality' and 'irrationality' have no bearing on his explanation.

But, says Elizabeth, this does not show that beliefs have no rational explanation. 'If we have before us a piece of writing which argues for an opinion, we can discuss the question: "Is this good reasoning?" without concerning ourselves with the circumstances of its production at all.'[88] We can consider the validity of the argument without knowing whether it was written with a typewriter, on a metro ticket or sung in the bath. Our question 'Why?' has different applications – sometimes we are looking for a causal explanation, sometimes a rational one. So, 'a belief in the validity of reason' is perfectly consistent with the idea that there can be a causal explanation of human thought.

Elizabeth's point that evening was not anti-science, nor anti-naturalist. Indeed, part of what was at stake in her dispute with Lewis was the meaning of 'natural'. Lewis supposed that human reason could be natural only if it is reducible to causal explanation. But Elizabeth countered that 'natural' does not mean 'reducible to causal explanation'. Nothing is more natural for animals like us than to think and reason, to question and explain. It is part of our nature to do so. We are the sort of creatures who draw conclusions from evidence, and who ask: 'Why did that happen?', 'Why do you think that?', 'What are your reasons?' It is part of our way of being, our nature, to make these enquiries and seek out these patterns. Lewis is right to note that we cannot explain the rationality of human thought and action using the scientific tools we have developed to explain brain waves; but this does not show that brain waves are natural and reason is not.

Mary Glover would surely have approved of her former student's argument, and of the account of human action that Elizabeth would go on to develop in *Intention*. When we are interested in reasons, validity and grounds for human thought and action, Elizabeth would show, we do not look for causal chains, but for large-scale patterns. These are not patterns of cause and effect, nor of constant conjunction, but patterns which locate what H.W.B. Joseph had called 'bits of living' within a rational order.

In her book Elizabeth Anscombe displays that pattern in a striking example, featuring Nazis, murder and a conspiracy. A man is pumping water into a cistern that supplies the drinking water of a house (she was perhaps thinking back to the Blitz – stirrup pumps, water tanks, hoses). Someone has contaminated the source with a toxic substance the effects of which are cumulative. The house is occupied by Nazis. 'The man who contaminated the source has calculated that if these people are destroyed some good men will get into power who will govern well, or even institute the Kingdom of Heaven on earth and secure a good life for all the people'. This man has 'revealed the calculation, together with the fact about the poison, to the man who is pumping'. This man's arm 'is going up and down, up and down'.[89]

Elizabeth Anscombe then uses our ordinary question 'Why?' (as in 'Why are you doing that?') to uncover the rational order in the man's pumping action. The descriptions that he would give if he gave honest answers to the question 'Why?', she says, could be arranged to form a series.[90]

> Why are you moving your arm up and down?
>> I'm operating the pump. (A)
> Why are you operating the pump?
>> I'm replenishing the water supply. (B)
> Why are you replenishing the water supply?
>> I'm poisoning the inhabitants. (C)
> Why are you poisoning the inhabitants?
>> To bring about the kingdom of Heaven on Earth. (D)

The descriptions 'operating the pump', 'replenishing the water supply', and 'poisoning the inhabitants' are linked because of what they mean and the way the world is structured. In this situation, operating the pump is a way to replenish the water supply, which is a way to poison the inhabitants. Some aspects of this situation have been set up by the conspirators: they have poisoned the supply. Others were already there: the pump has always been the means to replenish the house's water supply. Others still are facts of human nature: poisons are harmful to animals like us.

In Elizabeth's example, the man who is operating the pump knows all this: he knows how the pump works, he is in on the plan, he knows about poison and the Nazis. (His position is not like that of a dupe whom the conspirators have tricked into pumping while keeping the poison and the murderous plot from him.) Knowing all that he does, Elizabeth Anscombe says, this man can operate the pump *in order* to replenish the water supply *in order* to poison the inhabitants. Though, from his position at the pump, he cannot see the causal process by which the poison gets into the men, he knows ('without observation', as she puts it), that that is what he is doing.

The rationality of the pumper's action, Elizabeth says, does not imply an explicit reasoning process, but is a matter of his 'knowing one's way about'[91] and putting what he knows into action, to secure his end. To see his action as rational, as done for a reason, there is no need to posit any 'actual mental process', she argues. He might simply, knowing what he does, begin to pump without any further thought. To say that he acts *for a reason* is not to posit some inner mental episode, a hydraulic push, that causally explains his movements in the world, where what occurs after those movements is merely an effect of what he has done. Rather, it is to acknowledge that this 'bit of living' – movement of arm on handle – has a place in a pattern that we can recognise, an ordering of the world that he is bringing about by moving his arm here and now.

The day after her encounter with Lewis, Elizabeth wrote to Wittgenstein to tell him how it had gone. Lewis was 'much more decent in discussion than I expected', she wrote, 'though he was glib and played all sorts of tricks to obscure the issue – but he wasn't really objectionable'. Yorick Smythies had helped her to prepare the paper 'by writing "Shit!" against my remarks' in a draft version.[92] She had found an ally in the club secretary, Frank Goodridge, who though Lewis's pupil was Elizabeth's friend.[93] Having heard and been convinced ('probably much too easily') by her argument, Frank 'started going for Lewis, who had said something about having written the book "at a fairly popular level"'. Frank 'reproached him almost in moral terms, that one should not, for the sake of popularizing, put up a bad argument'. The letter ends with a 'P.S. I find public discussion very difficult indeed. I am in a frightened hurry to reply to what's said to me; if I try to check this and pause to think about it, my mind goes blank. So I say a lot that is no use.'[94]

Folklore records the 'Anscombe Affair', or the 'Anscombe–Lewis debate', rather differently.[95] The 'formidable' Miss Anscombe 'attacked' Lewis, who, 'painfully humiliated' and 'deeply disturbed', thereafter turned away from theological argument to devotional writing and children's fiction; Miss Anscombe 'obliterated' him as an apologist. Elizabeth was 'inclined to construe the odd accounts of the matter by some of his friends – who seem not to have been interested in the actual arguments or the subject-matter – as an interesting example of the phenomenon called "projection"'.[96]

Though Elizabeth found C. S. Lewis confused about cause and reason, she sympathised with his motivation. He thought that it was only by defeating naturalism that a place for miracles could be found in human life. But

Elizabeth saw no conflict. She and Peter were teaching Barbara, aged five, and John, nearly three, about transubstantiation – they believed it should be taught as early as possible. The children were too young for the word 'transubstantiation' but were learning its place, the ritual of speech and action into which the use of that word would later be woven. They were being taught to see a pattern in the ritual to which the description 'changing the wine into Jesus' blood' could later be applied.

'Look! Look what the priest is doing,' Elizabeth would whisper to her children from St Aloysius' pews. 'He is saying Jesus' words that change the bread into Jesus' body. Now he's lifting it up. Look! Now bow your head and say "My Lord and my God"', and then 'Look, now he's taken hold of the cup. He's saying the words that change the wine into Jesus' blood. Look up at the cup. Now bow your head and say "We believe, we adore your precious blood, O Christ of God."' Elizabeth maintained that her narrative 'need not be disturbing to the surrounding people', but we can imagine the odd disapproving stare. The teaching was so successful that one day when Elizabeth returned from the communion rail, Barbara asked her reverently, 'Is He in you?' 'Yes,' she said, and to her amazement and delight the child prostrated herself before her.[97]

Aristotle Comes to Life

On Thursday nights, in the New Bodleian, Mary joined Elizabeth in Richard Walzer's 'particularly exciting' Aristotle classes. During the war, David Ross had helped Walzer by making him a member of Oriel College and employing him to teach. In 1945 he had been appointed Lecturer in Medieval Philosophy and he was teaching Aristotle's *Metaphysics*, *De Anima* and *Dialogues*. Yorick Smythies, Peter Strawson and Peter Geach were sometimes there too. Aquinas mixed with Wittgenstein mixed with Aristotle.[98]

Wittgenstein was proud to relate: 'Here I am, a one-time professor of philosophy who has never read a word of Aristotle!'[99] Iris, Mary and Elizabeth had. Mary recalled Elizabeth's patient explanation in which she compared Wittgenstein's interest in human life to Aristotle's: 'The special importance of language does not, then, flow from its being a particularly grand isolated phenomenon. It arises because speech is a central human activity, reflecting our whole nature – because language is rooted, in a way that mathematics is not, in the wider structure of our lives.' This is why studying language is 'an investigation of our whole nature'.[100] The order Elizabeth had found in human action, using Wittgenstein's method, turned out to be the 'same order' described by Aristotle.[101] Elizabeth said that before she had known Wittgenstein 'the great philosophers of the past had appeared to her like beautiful statues', but 'knowing him had brought them alive for her'.[102]

Throughout that year, Iris and Mary both worked their way through the 'blue book' and Elizabeth brought further fragments of Wittgenstein from Cambridge to Oxford; scraps of paper, snippets of conversation. Her German was now good and she was reading his newest, untranslated writing. Wittgenstein had been amazed at the speed with which she'd mastered the language, and she had been amazed at his amazement: 'I was struck by the incongruousness of his admiring the exercise of so elementary a skill, which I thought a very slight display of intelligence, when one could get into fearful trouble in his lectures for not grasping something which I was sure needed great powers and hard thought to grasp.'[103]

By 1948, Wittgenstein's thought had infused Elizabeth's dissertation. In 1944, a few months before the pair met, she had written of her plan to take an 'objective approach' to the question 'What is a human individual?' She would start from the question 'What is *that*?', and go on to describe the organising principles she found in human beings she observed. At the time she had worried: 'Is there any work here for a philosopher or only for an experimental psychologist?' She could now answer this question with the tools Wittgenstein had given her. The philosopher does not aim to describe particular humans, their individual psychology or mental processes. Rather, she describes the form or pattern of human life as a whole. Her goal is to chart the 'grammar' of that life, to understand which practices and concepts matter, which ways there are of going on, how nature, instinct, reason and language are shaped by and give shape to human life. The feat of observation required is also a feat of self-observation, and self-transcendence – the philosopher is studying the form of life that she herself shares. As Mary was learning from Plotinus: the macrocosm without is mirrored in the microcosm within.[104]

In her journals Iris continued to brood on 'E's' paper on the past. In late spring 1948, she wrote in her journal: 'There is no memory past <u>unsupplemented</u> (any more than there are sense data unsupplemented). There is only the woven texture . . . the interweaving of pasts of testimony & deduction with one's own past of memory.' Poised over the page, she worried about the implications of E's picture. 'Problem: to find a theory of historic past wh. doesn't make it "ghostly".' Then she adds: '<u>isn't</u> it ghostly save to historian? . . . Much of past <u>is</u> ghostly to me . . . Parts of my <u>own</u> past may seem ghostly?'[105] She discussed it repeatedly with Wasfi and Kanti, and revisited it in her notes almost a year to the day after it was first delivered. 'All this has a <u>bite</u> for me. It <u>engages</u>. Wherein does the bite lie?'[106]

One of the things that Iris took away from Elizabeth's paper was the idea that to have a concept is to have an ability. By speaking of linguistic or conceptual abilities, Elizabeth pointed Iris away from the surface features of language (of the kind that J. L. Austin and his Kindergarten were busy gathering and analysing) and towards '<u>facts</u> about how we learn use of words (hence concepts.)'.[107] This allowed Iris to make a new connection between Wittgenstein's ideas and those of Martin Buber: 'Witt's epistemological revolution is paralleled by Buber's psych/moral revolution. We are, from the start, not alone.'[108] We learn our use of words from the people with whom we share our life. A conceptual ability, just like the ability to do maths or to cook, is something acquired over time, through practice and repetition, and by being helped and corrected by those around. In the beginning, as with all abilities, a person's competence will be limited and simple: 1+1, 4 × 10, bad omelettes and tinned spaghetti. But if she keeps practising, and listens to those around her, she will get better, more competent, more sophisticated. $c=\sqrt{a^2+b^2}$, soufflé and *ravioli alla calabrese*.

Each person's concepts have their own individual history. A trip to France, the challenges of wartime rationing, living near Mrs Palm's *Delikatessen* – these things give a person's cooking a particular and individual flavour. So too the passage of their life gives their concepts their own unique character. Each time I fall in love, repent, feel remorse, forgive, hate, trust, my understanding of these words changes, becomes more personal, more tied to me, and to the particular circumstances of my life. As my concepts alter, I may even come to see my past in a different light. Iris gives an example close to herself. Suppose I'm converted to Marxism, might I not then see my past as so much bourgeois self-deception? And now again with ampersands: but if 'I am continually learning & revising & creating & recreating my language', is not rethinking my past a constant responsibility?[109] '"You mustn't hate so & so" – you "have" so & so stuck in yr past – & you can, in a way, un-hate them in your past too. After reconciliation you re-think the past in light of what's followed.'[110]

*

In her 1947 fellowship proposal, Iris had written of the need for a logical framework to understand our real relationships to others; love, promising, the body; the mysterious realm of being and feeling. The approach that Elizabeth had drawn from Wittgenstein, with its emphasis on practice and life, began with that important insight that 'we are, from the start, not alone'; that we are born into a shared world. But Iris was not convinced that she had understood the character of the rules that Elizabeth described. ('Logic is not a super-physics. (As Plato, Aristotle thought?) What the blazing hell is it then?'.)[111] She worried that in making everything public, exposable, Wittgenstein had destroyed the realm in which she wanted to locate the mysterious creative loyalty that binds two concrete historical individuals together through a promise. 'Crystallise around these considerations one's feeling that Witt. takes the body out of things – out of emotion etc.'[112] In places, she is trenchant. 'Witt's fight against the epistemological, psychological. This goes against all my instincts . . . What's wrong with the idea of phenomenology? Fight Witt. at every step!'[113]

Iris's ambitions that year were vast. Even so, she managed a broad summary in a pen sketch. She planned to bring the phenomenology of Edmund

Husserl (what little she knew of it – no one in Cambridge had even heard of Husserl)[114] into meditative harmony with the austere logicism of Wittgenstein: *Ideen* and the *Tractatus*. Lurking on the margins: Søren Kierkegaard, the ubiquitous SK of her journals. This amphibious creature gave a new 'twist' to European philosophy, her fellowship proposal had explained. He had shown that 'philosophical speculation is worthless unless it concerns itself with the concrete existing individual'[115] – and that was her own concern. The mysterious, the inexposable, the real. What logical framework might be adequate to this? By May 1948, her investigations for her thesis would require a thirty-five-word title to capture their scope. 'Some post-Hegelian theories of consciousness: a study in phenomenological and existential philosophy (Husserl, Sartre and others) with reference to Hegel's "Phenomenology of Mind" and to the work of Kierkegaard, also to the work of Wittgenstein'.[116]

Elizabeth sometimes intervened to slow her friend down. 'Elizabeth is right – one must keep on plodding like the old fashioned philosophers.'[117] But though Iris listened to and admired Elizabeth, she was not prepared to be flattened by her – in conversations with Elizabeth, Iris was just as likely to be driving the steamroller as under it. Elizabeth was also acquainted with the marshy forests; she knew Kierkegaard well. Yes, SK speaks to the individual, Elizabeth conceded. But it is 'a betrayal if we systematise his thought'. As for E herself, she said she no longer had a 'yearning for system, for unity'. 'Thought seeks a system,' Iris countered.[118] The pair talked regularly past midnight, drinking wine and smoking long after Shah, Wasfi and Kreisel had headed home. They met by daylight and took long walks together at both ends of the Varsity Line: 'Conversation on Monday with Elizabeth about the immortality of the soul (walking round Christ Church Meadow) & about memory (in her room). Also about analogies & metaph. theories (in Radcliffe Square.)'[119] Peter, Barbara and John rarely appear in Iris's (often nocturnal) journals. There is one exception. Iris accompanied the family on a spring trip to the Gog Magog, a ridge of low chalk hills six miles south of Cambridge. 'A very blue darkening evening & the branches of blackthorn in flower. A sad wonderful day.'[120]

In April 1948, an advertisement appeared in the *Oxford Gazette* for a 'Tutor to teach Philosophy' at St Anne's Society, Oxford. St Anne's had a reputation for being the 'most exciting' of the women's colleges, a place where undergraduates who married or became pregnant would not be sent down.

But academically it was 'the Cinderella of Oxford Colleges'.[121] This would change under the bold principalship of Mary Ogilvie, a Somerville historian whose nine young dons were said to be the most beautiful – and brilliant – of any at Oxford.[122]

Pip cut out the advert and posted it to the Pightle. Iris should apply, though Mary was planning to as well, she cautioned. A reply from Iris dropped through the letterbox of Number 16 three days later:

> My dear, thanks so much for the further St Anne's details. I feel very sick at the idea of competing with Mary. But I think I shall apply all the same. She is much more likely to get it – has teaching experience, is a Latinist etc – so I shall try not to think too much about the job. But I find myself wanting it very much indeed.[123]

Isobel Henderson and Donald MacKinnon each wrote a reference for both women. 'As to their general intrinsic ability, I cannot choose between the two', wrote Isobel, in a two-page letter that displays her ambivalence: 'Miss Scrutton is the more genuinely academic'; 'Miss Murdoch is perhaps more likely to produce interesting philosophical work'; Miss Scrutton is the 'better scholar'; Miss Murdoch 'is a person of unlimited enterprise'; 'Miss Scrutton strikes me as a better Oxford don'; Miss Murdoch 'is the more original'; Miss Scrutton is 'more brilliant and subtle than Miss Murdoch, if less powerful and unconventional'. For Donald MacKinnon, Mary is 'unquestionably the better scholar of the two'; but Iris is 'the better <u>philosopher</u>'. Mary is 'always alert and genuinely interested. She is genuinely curious and prepared to read widely'; Iris 'makes a very strong impact on people and can easily, without knowing it, influence them a great deal'. Mary is the sensible choice ('the general level of her intelligence and the soundness of her character obviously make her a very strong candidate'); Miss Murdoch is 'a very different person' and they would be 'taking a chance' ('She was an active Communist'). Isobel Henderson signs off: 'I wish you could appoint them both.'[124]

In July, Iris got the job. Mary was disappointed. With witty melodrama she consoled herself by ceremonially decapitating irises in the Foots' garden.[125] Philippa, whose loyalties were torn, consoled Mary while also being overjoyed that Iris would be making a permanent home in Oxford. She wrote to congratulate her, and invited her to move into 16 Park Town with her and Michael. Iris replied:

About the flat – thank you so much! . . . I felt, as you can imagine, some terror about this, but now I feel better about the idea which is from almost every point of view a <u>wonderful</u> one. I hope that truly truly in the depths of his heart Michael won't be offended by my presence in the house. Forgive this. If I could be utterly sure of <u>this</u> I should be so <u>happy</u> about the whole plan. Sorry. I expect I have much more of a 'complex' here than either you or M. And anyway I feel nervous about coming back to Oxford – forgive the nerves. This is rather 'daring' this notion of living with you . . .[126]

CHAPTER 6

Back to Life

OXFORD, CAMBRIDGE, DUBLIN & VIENNA
OCTOBER 1948–JANUARY 1951

*Elizabeth Gives Her First Lecture – A Crisis for Elizabeth &
Iris – Large-Scale Metaphysics & a New Start for Mary – Philippa
Gives a Lecture & Elizabeth Goes to Vienna – Iris & Philippa
Fill in the Background – Wittgenstein Signs His Will*

Elizabeth Gives Her First Lecture

In Oxford, Elizabeth had a room in 27 St John Street, less than a mile from Park Town. She lodged with Miss Mary Isabel Lawson, the penultimate survivor of five spinster sisters who had leased it from St John's College after the First World War.[1] Nearly eighty, Miss Lawson was struggling to keep up the house. Her charwoman, the excellent Mrs Colter, helped with the housework and washing, cleaned the windows and peeled potatoes,[2] but the house was falling into disrepair. At some point, the ceiling had collapsed in one of the rooms and no one had fixed it. There was no hot water, inside WC or heating. The window frames were rotting.[3] The interior was dark. Elizabeth slept in a tiny narrow room on the top floor.[4] Number 27 did not benefit from the low winter sun that illuminated the houses opposite. To the rear was a gloomy scullery. When Miss Lawson died at the beginning of 1949, an inspector from St John's College visited the house. He was 'disquieted' by its condition. The bursar was 'horrified'. 'The place is dirty and in every way discreditable to the College.'[5] The house would need to be 'thoroughly cleaned', 'equipped with proper sanitation and lighting', have heating installed and the collapsed ceiling reinstated.[6] Elizabeth asked whether, while they were at it, she might have picture rails in all the rooms.[7] 'In these circumstances,' the bursar recorded, 'had it not been for the kindness displayed by Miss Anscombe towards the late Miss Lawson I should have preferred to find another tenant.'[8] Such was the state of things that the college insisted the tenants move out for several months so that the house could be renovated.

A married couple, Frank and Gillian Goodridge (it was Frank who had leapt to Elizabeth's defence at the Socratic Club) were also tenants, as was an art student and inventor, Barry (Thomas Barrington) Pink.[9] These impoverished lodgings reflect Elizabeth and Peter's continuing hardship. Her fellowship was badly paid and Peter – who remained in Cambridge

with the children – was still without a stable job. He did a little tutoring in Cambridge to contribute to the family fund. They sold cherished books to keep afloat.[10] Wittgenstein, on discovering during a rain storm that Elizabeth did not own a Macintosh, nor have money to buy one, purchased her a white cape. Later, when he saw her sparse lodgings, two chairs and a wastepaper basket followed. ('You are a <u>writer</u>, you have to have a waste-paper basket.')[11]

The renovations to 27 saw Elizabeth's box-room turned into an indoor bathroom, and when she moved back in as leaseholder, Elizabeth occupied a larger room on the first floor, with the Goodridges taking on the ground floor. She often held tutorials in her room, at the top of the dark stairs at the back of the house. She was now helping to translate Wittgenstein's new work and the floor was covered by tiny heaps of paper.[12] These were piles of *Zettel*, the scraps of paper on which Wittgenstein had written his philosophical remarks, laid out in some navigable arrangement known only to Elizabeth. She was trying to get them into some kind of order and, as usual, cigarettes helped. In the middle of the floor, like a baptismal font, was a huge, hollow column she used as an ashtray. Elizabeth and Wittgenstein were working together over the fragments, with new *Zettel* appearing all the time to add to the piles she had brought back from her summer in Cambridge.[13] Typescript by typescript they were progressing towards the version that would later be published as the *Philosophical Investigations*. Elizabeth sometimes read parts of her translation aloud to her students, among them Mary Wilson from the 'Things' class, whom Elizabeth had determined to wean off the Ordinary Language Philosophy of J. L. Austin. She picked out various linguistic, grammatical or substantial topics in an attempt to bring her round. Mary Wilson found the whole 'inconclusive' approach 'wonderful!'[14] but largely because it reminded her of Coleridge, whose notebooks she had been reading. Elizabeth lent her part of the most recent typescript, now called '*Spätfassung*' (late version),[15] and Mary Wilson cycled off from St John Street with a few sheets in her basket to copy out; they concerned the meaning of sensation words and, obscurely, a beetle. 'So it happened that before many people in Oxford had seen any of the later work of Wittgenstein, I saw some of it directly. I was deeply grateful to Elizabeth for this,' she later wrote.[16]

On the morning of Tuesday 12 October 1948, Elizabeth was not to be found in her study. She had descended the stairs and stepped out of Number 27's blue front door and into the cold autumn air. She was dressed, as usual, in a shapeless pair of brown trousers – provenance unknown – her dark hair long and loose. Only her black gown gave her away: she was on the way to give a lecture. Her first lecture.

She arrived at the Examination Schools building, on the High Street, just before 10 a.m. Iris, Philippa and Mary may well have been there to greet her, the trio walking together from Park Town, across University Parks. Iris had modified her skirts, augmenting them with extra panels of fabric in imitation of the New Look – a Parisian post-war fashion that scandalised patriotic French women by its wasteful excess at a time when clothes rationing was still in force.[17] Philippa, as ever, immaculately turned out in a tailored skirt and blouse. Mary was beginning to find her own sense of style; later she would settle on a trademark hat and beads. The quartet perhaps smoked a cigarette or two on the pavement, huddled close for protection against the October wind and the Undergraduate Eyes, students streaming past them into the building. It was fitting that Elizabeth, the oldest and (all agreed) most brilliant of the four, was to be the first to step up to the lectern.

If any building is designed to make a novice lecturer tremble, it is Schools. Completed in 1881, its front face is complete with Venetian window motifs, five grand arches and a turret. Inside are columns of marble, busts of eminent men (an earl, a priest, a duke), and ornate friezes of beasts and birds. Each year, anxious undergraduates sit their examinations under its vaulted ceilings, 'puny' beneath its architecture.[18] During both wars, it had been used as a military hospital. Entering, the four women would have passed an obsolete but unnerving sign: 'Resuscitation Room'.

Between Elizabeth's arrival as an undergraduate at St Hugh's College and her first lecture in 1948, only four women philosophers had made it on to the *Gazette*'s pored-over pages – Mrs Martha Kneale, Miss Lucy Sutherland, Miss Margaret MacDonald and Miss Mary Glover. Of the sixty-six philosophy lecturers since the war, only two had been women. That day, in October 1948, the room was packed with young men who were prepared to bear the 'humiliation' of listening to a female don, as well as a sprinkling of young women. Miss Anscombe's lectures would later become legendary for the beauty of her voice, the foulness of her language and the depth of her thought. Once when asked for an example of an intrinsically pleasurable activity she said: 'shitting'.[19] It was said that you could see her visibly thinking during long pauses.[20] She spoke carefully and deliberately, almost oblivious to the audience. 'Now this is *very* interesting', she would say, standing by the blackboard and writing, slowly, '*v e r y*'.[21]

Elizabeth's topic that term was 'Some Problems in the Theory of Knowledge'. In her report to the Mary Somerville Research Fund Committee earlier in the year, she had written that she was working on the subject of 'phenomenalism' with Plato's *Theaetetus* as a starting point. She was interested in '[t]he refutation of phenomenalism by the consideration that every statement and every concept has a logic; including the names of sensible qualities and the epistemologically primitive propositions announced as data by phenomenalism'. 'This work, together with much on the problem of false belief, will go towards the preparation of lectures on the *Theaetetus* for next term', she had explained to the committee.[22] That dialogue made visible, she said, a connection between phenomenalism – 'The only beliefs you can have are whatever it is that you experience; and what you experience is always true' (167a4)[23] – and Protagoras' doctrine that 'man is the measure of all things' – 'I am the judge of the things that are for me, that they are; and of the things that are not for me, that they are not' (160c2).[24] Elizabeth had been working on these passages in the light of the remarks in Wittgenstein's typescript that would later be known as 'the private language argument'. (It was these pages that Mary Wilson had lately cycled off with.) She was now ready to share the thinking that had been the topic of many nocturnal arguments with Iris over the last year. ('E. was saying how Witt. & Plato had the same problem – how can false propositions have meaning?'[25] Iris had recorded in her diary the previous June.)

For the Protagorean phenomenalist, perception is infallible ('what you experience is always true'), so how things are is however they seem to the perceiver to be. This means that when 'the same' wind blows and one person feels it to be cool and another to be warm, it cannot be said that the wind is cool or warm 'in itself'.[26] Objective fact evaporates. The warmth or coolness of the wind depends on the perceiver. For the Protagorean each individual man is the measure of all things, 'the measure of white things, heavy things, light things . . . there is nothing of these sorts that he is *not* the measure of' (178b1).[27] All is flux.

In his *Theaetetus*, one of Plato's objections to this idea is that if each man carries the measure (*kritérion*) within him, then each person will be the measure not only of how things are, but of how things will be. And this can't be right. A wine-maker's judgement that his grapes will yield sweet wine is better than a lyre-player's; a cook's discernment is more prophetic of future pleasure than that of the feast-goer who cannot cook.[28] '[T]here is such a thing as competence here', Elizabeth will later write. Doctors match blood samples on a scale to judge how anaemic someone is – but one doctor may ask another to check if her judgement is correct, 'without any feeling of absurdity'.[29] But if Protagoras were correct, we humans would not do these things. If he were correct, there would be no sense in talking of 'right' and 'wrong' at all. 'One would like to say', as Wittgenstein put it, 'whatever is going to seem right to me is right. And that only means that here we can't talk about "right".'[30] Like Plato, Wittgenstein argued that the rule for going on with a word, for applying it to novel cases, must come from outside the individual if there is to be such a thing as meaning at all.

After her maiden lecture the women conducted a brief post-mortem. Elizabeth said, 'I would like to write upon the board "I may be as wrong as hell!".' Philippa followed, 'I should like to hold up a banner saying "we are imbeciles".' Iris was 'touched by this modesty on both sides!'[31] Later, in lectures that were preparation for her book *Intention*, Anscombe indulged something like this impulse and wrote 'I am a fool' on the blackboard. She did it with her eyes closed, in order to demonstrate that a person can usually say what she is doing (intentionally) without having to look to see what is happening.[32]

Elizabeth's first lecture drew the attention of the university authorities. They were concerned that young women undergraduates might be corrupted by her example. The issue was not her attack on phenomenalism, but her trousers. Within forty-eight hours of the lecture, news of Miss Anscombe's attire reached George White, the Clerk of the Schools. White wrote to the Senior Proctor: 'A new-comer to the Schools as a lecturer, lectured to an audience of about 120 persons today wearing trousers and the gown of a Master of Arts . . . Women who lecture at the Schools are very much in favour of as much as is possible being done to ensure that women undergraduates comply with the regulations.'[33] The clerk wrote to Elizabeth insisting that she come appropriately dressed, in a skirt. Trousers would not become an acceptable part of women's academic dress at Oxford until the 1970s.

The records are silent on Elizabeth's response, but the incident acquired mythical proportions in the annals of Somerville College, perhaps fuelled by Elizabeth's conspicuous fearlessness in the face of authority. (The following year she would tell a concerned Iris that she had been arrested 'for wandering about with her hair down at 5 a.m., & refus[ing] to give her name!').[34] The official history of Somerville College records that the two parties became entrenched, the clerk lying in wait for Miss Anscombe at 10 a.m. each Tuesday and Thursday and refusing to let her past to give her lecture if she was wearing trousers. Eventually, the legend continues, a compromise was reached: Schools provided her with a changing room, stocked with a skirt and a decanter of sherry. She would be permitted entrance to Schools in her trousers but would appear before her students in a skirt. Often, so it goes, she wore the skirt over the trousers.[35]

Whatever the outcome of the initial skirmish, it was not the end of the matter. Two years later, the Clerk of the Schools was once again compelled to write to the Senior Proctor, enclosing the previous missive as evidence of a repeat offender. Elizabeth's dry reply, dictated to a scribe and complete with a scrawling left-handed signature, expresses her hope that her 'indecency is not too great'.

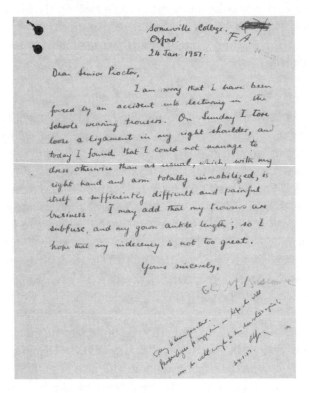

Elizabeth's success in getting into the *Gazette* may have helped Philippa to see a future for herself. At the end of the previous academic year she had been exhausted and threatened to 'give up philosophy'. Iris had prescribed complete rest: 'If you gave it up completely for say three weeks (and you can do that in the summer) that would surely do the trick. I know how sick one can get – I hope you have less teaching next term. Take it gently, old sweetheart – carry on with Nothing if possible. (Not meaning *néant* of course which is a *serious* matter, but just old-fashioned Nothing).'[36] That summer, July 1948, Philippa and Michael had taken a holiday to Cahors, in southern France. They were among the first tourists to enter the caves at Lascaux.[37] A stone cathedral of palaeolithic artistry some 17,000 years old: black stags, horses, bulls, aurochs and lions, swabbed, sprayed and incised in red and yellow. Hunting humans shrunk to the margins, tiny fragments in a landscape teeming with animal life.

A Crisis for Elizabeth & Iris

Iris enjoyed teaching, but Oxford 'society' sometimes got her down (this invariably required underlining). 'The donnishness of people, the cleverness – all the bleeding intellectuals. What a relief to board the London train & see those damn spires disappearing.'[38] When she had arrived at Oxford in 1938, St Anne's was still the Oxford Society for Home Students, and had neither college accommodation nor a dining room. Most tutors taught in their own living rooms. That was still the case a decade later when Iris invited Mother Grant, a nun in the Sacred Heart Order, dressed in habit and veil, to sit on Philippa's sofa ('Ivan the Divan', as Mary called it[39]). Iris sat on the hearthrug, her augmented skirts spread around her. The subjects of their discussions were not just Mother Grant's Thomist-inflected essays on individuation, but Iris's troubled soul. Mother Grant confided that as a child she had worried about the interminable number of people to pray for; Iris was soon to be added to her list.[40]

The trouble for Iris's soul lay in her friendship with Elizabeth. Many years later, Elizabeth would tell Peter Conradi, Iris Murdoch's biographer: 'I don't think we ever quite managed to work out what we meant to each other.'[41] This neutral phrase obscures the difficulties into which, by the middle of that Michaelmas Term 1948, their friendship had fallen.

They were still seeing each other almost daily: at Elizabeth's, at Philippa's, after a lecture, before a class, at Somerville College, at St Anne's, at White's Bar,[42] in Radcliffe Square, on Christ Church Meadow,[43] in the Clarendon Arms,[44] the Chequers Inn,[45] the Jowett Society, the Socratic Club. Their conversations ranged wide: memory, truth, meaning, Plato, Descartes, Wittgenstein, Kierkegaard.[46] They discussed Elizabeth's paper on calculating in one's head.[47] Both were avid readers of Kafka.[48] Iris waited every week outside Schools, as if Elizabeth were 'the Queen'. Iris would 'flush for pleasure when she came out', the pair walking away together, back on to Oxford's busy pavements and in search of somewhere to warm up.[49] They saw each other alone and also in company. They often went about with Yorick Smythies, who had moved to Oxford when Wittgenstein left Cambridge, and sometimes with his wife Polly (Diana Pollard).[50] Iris's journals from this time are filled with 'E.' in a way that suggests she is in the grip of something like an obsession. Polly was convinced that Elizabeth was in love with Iris.[51] The struggle to find some kind of equilibrium – philosophical and personal – is marked in Iris's journal.

> All is flux. I felt uneasy at Elizabeth's saying – we take this as physics or epistemology. (She apologized for the phrase 'metaphysical flux.') I thought of Hegel, & said to her afterwards: you omit possibility of the epistemological flux being an ontological flux. She said impatiently 'That's the Q. of which way round you make the internal relation work.'[52]

Conversations, when they took place in Park Town in the company of Mary and Philippa, fizzed with jokes. Iris asked Pip: 'Is [Spinoza] a moment in God's self consciousness?' Pip, mock-serious: 'I can't remember if he's that . . .'[53] But these topics somehow became fraught when they were transported to the dark, smoky interior of St John Street. Iris was there often; Elizabeth would telephone St Anne's or Somerville to summon her. She stayed until the early hours of the morning, the pair drinking wine and brandy. Iris smoking. Elizabeth resisting (she was seeing a hypnotist to try to quit: the sessions left her in a queer state of mind).[54] They took to arguing about good and evil, different interlocutors weaving in and out of days-long conversations. Dostoevsky romanticises good and evil, so does Graham Greene. Shakespeare is romantic by comparison with the Greeks, but he is unromantic by comparison with Dostoevsky. With the Greeks there are cosmic forces – an objective good and evil that is outside man. With Shakespeare there are such forces too. But with

Dostoevsky it's interiorised. Elizabeth opposed the romanticisation of good and evil. 'E. took Stavrogin as great example of romanticized goodness-badness – Dostoevsky being also the dupe here – the <u>poison</u> in him. (She mentioned "Notes from Underground" as least poisonous of D's works.) . . . E. is right in a way but is bearing away something of value too when she objects to this romanticization of good.'[55]

Iris's journal entries show her growing increasingly troubled as the nights drew in. On 4 November: 'How much there is about life that [one] doesn't understand. Speaking with E. this morning about the opaqueness of others' lives.'[56] Iris had a need to be seen and heard directly by Elizabeth but (perhaps thinking back to her arctic coldness in the Lyons' tea rooms) she also feared 'that what E is <u>dealing with</u> is not me but my image'. Was she, too, relating to an image of Elizabeth?[57] Iris's journals are full of self-castigation. E. lacks 'smallness', Iris writes, whereas she has 'some will to please which is on [her] face like a birthmark'.[58]

Iris seems to have been in awe too of what she codes as Elizabeth's 'high coldness', a description she derived from a folk theory of her own invention, and according to which she sorted her friends. Pip and Donald were 'high' and 'warm'; Mary was 'low' and 'cold'. She provided an interpretative cue: 'Cruces are attitude to the psychological (Mary), and the question of sentimentality/charity (Elizabeth).' The sane Mary is not sentimental (so she is, like Elizabeth, 'cold'). Her approach is empirical (low). 'How very differently coloured [are] these views of the universe. (Donnish phrase E. wd say, but this <u>such</u> an all embracing diff. of view.)'. 'I can't really class myself tho' according to this', she admitted.[59]

On Sunday 14 November, Elizabeth hosted a party and things came to a head. Drunk on cheap wine, the room foggy with cigarette smoke, Iris reached for Elizabeth, touching her arm.[60] Something was communicated. Iris and Elizabeth each recorded the secret that passed between them in their journals. Elizabeth showed Iris what she had written;[61] later, Iris would tear out the pages in hers.

The morning after the party, Elizabeth telephoned Iris at Somerville to discuss 'Sunday's party at 27 John St, <u>and then other things</u>'.[62] A week passed, then Elizabeth came to visit Iris one evening, and again the next morning after her lecture.[63] Iris reflected in her journal on sin and repentance. 'If one does something, even tho' one has some sort of repentance, it is almost impossible to regard it as one would have if one had not done it.' Once one has done something wrong the pleasure in having done it gets mixed up with its wrongness. The repentance then is shallow, for one's recognition of the wrong involved is tempered by the pleasure – and perhaps by the comfort that it all worked out in the end, or that no one found out. 'It's not a repentance comparable to the idea I shd have had of the importance of avoiding it if I had not done it.' This seems paradoxical but she goes on. 'That is the trouble: the true goods are what one has no comprehension of unless one is very near them, while the false goods are always alluring. I sometimes have the thought that I have denied myself something so inexpressibly delightful & got nothing in exchange but a hopeless struggle . . .'. She then records St Augustine's words: 'cast yourself onto God, you will not be jumping into empty space'.[64]

After this, there is more empty space in Iris's journal. Seven ripped-out pages.

During that whole month, London had been enveloped in a dense smog, and the rest of the country in freezing fog. Iris returned to her journal as the fog cleared: 'Was it only yesterday E. went away? It seems years ago.'[65] and '[C]ould I ever be prepared for instance to express my love for E. in a coldness & casualness to her which should last all my life?'[66]

On 10 December, Elizabeth had left Iris for Dublin, to visit Wittgenstein.[67] Yorick told Iris that Elizabeth did not go to bed all night after the party: she stayed awake and prayed. He said her getting away as she did was the result of prayer.[68] Iris went to Mass: she too prayed, 'continually for E, & for myself that I may really desire her well-being'.[69] She composed a sonnet.

> The dear & detailed dream of your carved head
> Fills all the dim dimensions of my pain.
> Your most intent desiring lips and eyes
> Brim from the mirror where I ask my name.
> This sudden sweet complicity, the Greek
> Verse that you told me, all our dear illusion
> Turns black between us when we speak
> Or act or move to a conclusion.
> For I could wish to possess you forever so,
> My darling, immobilized in the gesture
> Of reaching toward me. Yet I know

That this is to desire your death. Your nature
Being hard & high, you˙must be set free;
Two secret evil forms will
    lie enlaced in me.[70]

She prayed again and wondered if Elizabeth would make a confession to Wittgenstein.[71] 'I need a strong box to keep this damn diary in. Probably I ought to destroy all the entries of the last 3 weeks. Why am I unwilling to??'[72]

Elizabeth would have caught the train from Oxford to Holyhead, a six-hour journey that cuts north-west across England and Wales. With every hour the interior of St John Street receded, eventually giving way to the vast sky and coastline of Holyhead, the Welsh port and holy place – home of the sixth-century monastery founded by St Cybi. From there a three-hour ferry crossing took her to Dublin's port of Dun Laoghaire. Dublin was balmy; Elizabeth stepped off the ferry into the highest December temperature ever recorded in Ireland. She made her way along the Liffey to the riverside Ross's Hotel, on Parkgate, stripping off layers.

Intermittently unwell, Wittgenstein had left wild Rosroe in August, and arrived in Dublin via Vienna and Cambridge.[73] Now he wrote in the Palm House of the Botanic Gardens and on the tables of Bewley's oriental café on Grafton Street. *Zettel* were accumulating. Ross's Hotel, where he was staying, was a short walk from the Zoological Gardens and there he watched the giraffes, elephants, tapirs and chimpanzees, considering the enormous differences between the species.[74]

When Elizabeth arrived, Wittgenstein was ready for her. He had booked her a room at Ross's and listened to her troubles. He had been working with great intensity on notes that would later be published as *Last Writings on the Philosophy of Psychology, Volume I* (though they were not, in fact, his last writings), and material that would become part II of the *Philosophical Investigations*. The fragments, scribbled in notebooks, are wild and disordered, a record of explorations across unknown terrain. The pair went together to the zoo and Elizabeth was barked at by a crocodile; she leapt back but Wittgenstein remained unmoved (this example would later turn up in her book, *Intention*).[75] They pored over the fragments together in Wittgenstein's top-floor room overlooking Phoenix Park.[76]

A picture story. In one of the pictures there are ducks, in another rabbits; but one of the duck heads is drawn exactly like one of the rabbit heads. Someone looks at the pictures, but he doesn't notice this. When he describes them he describes this shape first as the one, then as the other, without any hesitation. Only after we have shown him that the shapes are identical is he amazed.[77]

Earlier that year Elizabeth had written of her plan to refute phenomenalism 'by the consideration that every statement and every concept has a logic; including the names of sensible qualities'.[78] Now, she could replant those statements in their proper soil, and locate them against a background that would show their place in human life. When she returned to Oxford in mid-December, she was cheerful. She credited Wittgenstein's company, a few nights' good sleep, and nicotine: she had resumed smoking (and quit hypnotism).[79]

We have in our language, Elizabeth would write in *Intention*, many descriptions for 'picked-out' sets of movement ('signing one's name'; 'jumping'; 'laughing'; 'pumping'; 'reaching'). The movements that these descriptions pick out are minute and complex, just as complex as the movements of a tree's leaves when it waves in the wind, for which we have no description.[80] That we have the descriptions that we do in our language reflects our shared human interests in other living creatures, in each other, in nature and artefact.

'Posting a letter'. 'Paying the bus fare'. 'Replenishing the water supply'. Many descriptions of actions are only intelligible – and the actions they describe only possible – in a world that also contains vast structures, shared institutions, conventions and tools: transport and postal services, money, promising, pumps and hoses. For human beings, growing up is coming to act and see under the descriptions that our language contains.[81]

*

In 1965, Elizabeth would publish a reply to J. L. Austin which finally laid to rest her café war with herself.[82] Austin thinks that he is on the opposite side to the sense-data philosophers H. H. Price and Freddie Ayer when it comes to the question 'What do I really see?' But, Elizabeth argues, he and they make precisely the same error. They all take it that an 'object of sight' is a kind of thing. White triangles or baths, black patches or cats. Elizabeth points out that there is another use of the word 'object' in which it does not mean 'thing' at all. To bring this out, she compares the verbs 'to see' and 'to aim', and the object of sight to the object aimed at.

Suppose, she says, a hunter in the forest aims at a stag and shoots. But the thing he took for a stag was his father, and so he shoots his father. At the man's trial a witness testifies: 'He aimed at his father.' The witness report, says Elizabeth, is true, but may also be misleading. Though 'his father' is a true description of the object (thing) the hunter in fact aimed at, it does not give 'the description under which' the hunter took aim – it does not give his object of aiming. If we had asked the hunter: 'What are you aiming at?' his truthful answer would have been: 'A stag.' This answer, which gives 'the description under which' he aims, gives the object of his aiming. In most cases, the object of the hunter's aiming will also be a true description of an object (thing) at which he aims, but in some cases, like this one, it is not. The hunter's father (thing) is not a stag (object of aiming).

Elizabeth says: 'to aim' is an *intentional verb*, because it takes as its grammatical object the 'description under which' I aim. It is a mark of intentional verbs that the person doing the thing – aiming, worshipping, desiring – has a certain kind of authority. If the hunter is honest, then his answer 'a stag' gives his object of aiming, even if there is no thing in the situation that falls under that description.

She argues that 'to see' is also an intentional verb. As with aiming, the description under which I see (given by an honest answer to the question 'What do you see?') is usually a description that is true of a thing at which I am looking; but in some cases, it is not. 'I see a stag', cries the tragic hunter.

With this idea, Elizabeth was able to acknowledge two kinds of use we make of the verb 'to see', where the ordinary language philosopher (Austin) and the sense-data theorist (Price and Ayer) can acknowledge only one. She calls them the *material* use and the *intentional* use. Most of the time we use the verb 'to see' materially, to describe what is there to be seen by anyone. When we use the verb materially, a certain kind of mistake is possible: the hunter is mistaken when he says truthfully: 'I see a stag', even though 'a stag' gives his object of sight. We use 'to see' materially to tell each other about our shared world, to give witness reports and descriptions to those who were not present or who are not in a position to see what is happening. But we can also use the verb purely intentionally, with no aim of describing a thing, but in order to tell another about something private or subjective or personal. (When H. H. Price, luxuriating in a mescaline-induced hallucination says: 'I see a pile of holly-like leaves on my counterpane', his intended use is purely intentional. He is describing how things appear to him. He knows no leaves are there.)

I am restricted in what I can see by my physical attributes and my location in space and time, just as I am in what I can bite, reach, kick or carry. But Elizabeth's account of perception reveals that when it comes to seeing, I am restricted – or enabled – too by my participation in human language-using life. We can say: 'The baby sees his mother posting a letter' or 'hanging out the washing', if the baby has a clear view. But 'posting a letter' is not a description under which the baby sees. Until he knows about letters and stamps and postmen, he cannot pick out this particular visual impression, give this description. And until he knows about clothes and hygiene and ideas about cleanliness and smell, he cannot see a 'washing line'. This part of what is visible to us is invisible to him. Likewise, someone may see straight off that a man is 'pumping' or (if they know what the pump is for) that he is 'replenishing the water supply'. But only those who are in on the conspiracy can add the description 'poisoning the Nazis'. Only they can place the man's action in its wider circumstances and see what he is doing in moving his arm up and down here and now. Seeing, describing and doing come together in Elizabeth's picture. The richness and variety of the human world grows and shrinks and alters as we learn to speak and act.

While Elizabeth's prayers delivered her to Wittgenstein, Iris's 'wistful seeking' led her into Eric Mascall's rooms on the first floor in Tom Quad in Christ Church.[83] She had been invited to the first meeting of a group who christened themselves 'The Metaphysicals' – a deliberately provocative name at a time when ' "metaphysical" was the rudest word in the philosopher's vocabulary'.[84] Entering just on time, she would have been the only woman present. As usual, Iris preferred to sit on the floor.[85]

Standing near the window, a group of four men. The older two, Eric Mascall and Austin Farrer, dressed in black suits and clerical collars; the younger pair, about Iris's age, were Ian Crombie and Dennis Nineham (another of MacKinnon's students). An impressive portrait of King Charles I, the Anglican Church's only saint, hung on the wall. Eric Mascall, like E. R. Dodds, had once performed an exorcism. Austin Farrer, who reminded Dennis Nineham of Iris, was an elfin mystic: 'I always felt that both he and his wife Katharine might sprout small gossamer wings at any moment and fly out through the window,' Eric Mascall would later recollect.[86] The previous term (Trinity 1948), Farrer had given a course of lectures on the 'Essay on Metaphysics' that Collingwood had written on board the *Alcinous* en route to Java. Katharine Farrer was deep into an English translation of Marcel's *Être et avoir* that would be published in 1949, with a Preface written by Donald MacKinnon. At a time 'when minuteness and subtlety of mind are too often the prerogatives of the light-heartedly destructive', MacKinnon will write, Marcel reminds us 'that a true minuteness and a true intellectual subtlety are rooted in humility and purity of heart';[87] he knows of nothing more important than Monsieur Marcel's writings on the problem of metaphysics. Not everyone agreed with him. When Gabriel Marcel had addressed Oxford's Philosophical Society in 1948, Paul Grice (the philosopher MacKinnon had beaten to the Keble post in 1936) was furious that such a 'charlatan' had been invited to speak. Iris, who had responded to Marcel's paper on that occasion – and perhaps had even arranged it – tried to mediate. But the refusal even to try to understand Marcel was obstinate. 'The air is full of inhibitions,' H. H. Price had remarked.[88]

Eric Mascall served the Metaphysicals sweet Cyprus sherry against the draughts.[89] The theologians carried the conversation, along with Basil Mitchell. Iris's age, Basil had been appointed as a tutor in philosophy at Keble by Donald MacKinnon shortly before he left for Balliol. Like MacKinnon, he was Christian, but his theism was shaped by Sufism and the teaching of Hazrat Inayat Khan. Before the war he had studied Indian philosophy and learnt Sanskrit under Sarvepalli Radhakrishnan.

Also present, though quiet, was a rather ill-looking man, Michael Foster. After he had been Freddie Ayer's tutor in 1929, teaching him Plato and Kant, the two men's lives had become curiously and unpleasantly interwoven.[90] Puritan and playboy would never get on, but circumstances kept placing Foster as a barrier to Ayer's progression – indeed, for many years

Ayer's only hope of a Christ Church fellowship lay in Foster leaving the college. Foster occasionally found himself on the end of a violent attack from the younger man, personally or philosophically (including when he had advised Trinity College that Ayer was not fit to teach the young). He met Ayer's tirades of abuse and intellectual dressings-down with 'pained and embarrassed silence'.[91] Permanently poised on the edge of deep depression, it was said that he fell short of complete sanctity only by missing the joy of the saints.[92]

In Mascall's rooms the Metaphysicals would be 'free to ask what questions [they] liked', even the ones that had been deemed unaskable by the analysts. No one in this company would arch an eyebrow or attack with an 'I don't understand!' if someone asked about God, or reality, or truth. Their aim: 'to explore how far the anti-metaphysical bias of analytic (linguistic) philosophy could be resisted'; 'make a good philosophical basis for a religious metaphysics'; and 'show that theological discourse had real metaphysical meaning'.[93] The plan: to meet three or four times a term, read papers, talk, recover metaphysics.[94] Elizabeth was known but not invited: the men feared she would either 'have moped in the corner, or have taken the whole thing over and never stopped talking'.[95]

Richard Hare's presence among the theologians attracted some suspicion. He accepted Ayer's fact-and-value distinction. He was a member too of Austin's Kindergarten.[96] Did he feel that there was a gulf between *himself* and the anti-metaphysical linguistic philosophers? he was asked. Not in substance, Hare admitted. But he distinguished between himself and J. L. Austin on the question of 'spirit'. 'In all subjects there are those who don't mind being thought to be in earnest, and those who prefer to appear less deeply concerned than they really are; this is a difference of temperament and it is frightfully important; personally I like the former sort.'[97]

Large-Scale Metaphysics & a New Start for Mary

By the beginning of 1949, Mary had found the witty and imaginative voice that would characterise her later work. Her horror of neurosis had started to find a place in her epistemology. She recommended a sharp talking-to for those whose posture of '[p]hilosophic doubt' is just 'an insatiable appetite for reassurance, a neurotic craving exposed by never gaining its object'. '[Y]ou wouldn't have to think that if you got out of a mood which there is no objective need for you to be in.' Her reply was not far from 'Oh, grow up!' To distinguish the 'self-tormenters' from the metaphysicians, 'we are driven to make some assessment of the character of each philosopher'. 'I rely here on a criterion of sanity and naturalness which can't be fully analysed,' she says, with a wink.[98]

Her explorations of reality continued. The macrocosm, for Plotinus, is 'almost wholly absorbed into the microcosm; all that has the same structure & substance as the self has been made in some sense some part of it', she had written at the end of 1948.[99] By folding reality into the self, Plotinus was able to rescue virtue in a political scene that had disintegrated: he attempted 'to make all true virtue internal', she records.[100] The contingency and formlessness of the unreal is left outside.

She was coming to understand what it is that 'differentiates a real thing from a mere existent one' in Plotinus' philosophy. 'Answer: beauty. The real is the beautiful, and as it turns out this means that it is what draws the soul because it is akin to it, because it makes the soul more really itself.'[101] As the prisoners ascend, blinking, from Plato's cave, they are drawn towards what is real and beautiful. 'What states then does desire, according to Plotinus, call on us to leave? States of formlessness, form being taken in his sense as the influence of the good.'[102] She earned money for bed and board through odd jobs at Somerville and St Hugh's. A little tutoring and a little marking. Once she stayed up all night, fuelled by black coffee, marking General Papers for the Somerville entrance; by 'three in the morning all the essays looked exactly alike'.[103] Then, towards the end of 1948, Donald McKinnon, still looking out for her, lent a hand. He invited her to take on a regular radio slot, reviewing books for the Third Programme. Her first review, broadcast at 7 p.m. on Tuesday 18 January, was of Bertrand Russell's *Human Knowledge: Its Scope and Limits*.

Though Mary found writing the radio script a trial of anxiety and effort, she discovered a talent and a taste for it. Her (by her own lights) 'savage and intolerant'[104] opening script does not survive, but we can guess she would have classed the analyst Earl Russell among those characters with an 'insatiable appetite for reassurance'. In *Human Knowledge*, Russell asks whether our everyday beliefs about the world can really be justified by our 'brief and personal and limited' experience. His detailed exploration of induction, the form of inference that empiricists, following David Hume, have traditionally employed, leads him to conclude, with regret, that it is not even *probable*, let alone *certain*, that the objective world, of baths and trains and trees, exists.[105] Everyday life depends on our blindly accepting, without evidence, the uniformity of nature and the persistence of the individual. He urges that we do so, lest we lose our minds.

In the decades that follow, Mary attacked scientific imperialism of the sort Russell had espoused – impersonal, reductive, atomistic – many times. We might imagine her voice in living rooms that January reminding listeners to keep science in its proper place. In a sense, Russell is right, she thought. As the Idealist F. H. Bradley – whose philosophy Russell rejected – had observed, it is 'a mere superstition to suppose that an appeal to experience can prove reality'.[106] But experience leaves us blind, as Russell supposes, only if we think that science and empirical observation are our only ways of finding out about reality. Bradley (like other Idealist metaphysicians, and like Wittgenstein) recognised that to discover reality, we need to turn our attention away from Russell's swirling fragments of incoming experience. We should look to the background where those fragments belong and in which they have a place as part of a whole. Russell calls the 'uniformity' of nature a hypothesis, but Mary (like the Idealists) saw that the presence of form and pattern in nature is not an empirical hypothesis but a background – a reality – against which scientific enquiry can be made. She had solved the bath-time puzzle that had been the beginning of her life in philosophy. As R. G. Collingwood noted on board the *Alcinous*: metaphysics is not an adolescent demand for reassurance, but an attempt to understand the transcendent background to human life, against which individual propositions may be verified by observation and scientific investigation. We have different methods for this study of the form of reality, its complexity, its patterns and their interrelation. Poetry, art, religion, history, literature and comedy are all the metaphysician's tools. They are how metaphysical animals explore, discover and describe what is real (and beautiful and good).

After Elizabeth returned from Dublin, she and Iris tried to put the past behind them – tried, as Iris put it, to preserve their love with a 'change of sign', in a safe form.[107] To Iris, Elizabeth seemed observably exhausted; 'pale & nervous',[108] 'more nervous & unhappy seeming than I've seen her for a long time',[109] she recorded in her journal, now an attentive observer of Elizabeth's mood. In a report to Somerville College at the end of the following year, Elizabeth would explain that she has 'suffered various accidents to health' that have impeded her work, among them the torn shoulder ligament that saw her lecturing in trousers, and problems with her sight.[110] 'My work is . . . assuming a more and more negative and destructive character.'[111] Principal Janet Vaughan may have been troubled by this news.

Elizabeth's 10 a.m. lecture on 1 March 1949 was on Plato's *Theaetetus*, but this time she was considering a later part of the dialogue and 'the problem of false belief'. Iris and Elizabeth had often discussed the question of how false belief is possible in the context of Elizabeth's talk 'The Reality of the Past' and Parmenides' puzzle: '*It is the same thing that can be thought and can be, so what is not, and cannot be, cannot be thought.*' Elizabeth was still working on the paper, preparing it as a contribution to 'a book of essays on "analytical philosophy"', where it would be published alongside papers by Alice Ambrose and Margaret Masterman.[112] 'P. rather merry in E's lecture, arguing with E', observed Iris.[113]

Iris was waiting for Elizabeth after the lecture and was delighted to see her buoyant – so much so that Iris speculated she was high on caffeine. But no – Elizabeth's mood was spiritually rather than chemically induced. She had been to St Aloysius' that morning. A woman had 'objected to her wearing <u>trousers at early mass</u>', recorded Iris in her journal, and had written a very disagreeable letter of complaint. This grievance, unlike that of the Clerk of the Schools, shook E: was there something impious, sinful, about her attire? To Iris, she had 'talked of seeing a psychiatrist', but instead she had visited her church that morning and seen a priest. She told Iris she had picked the one who 'seemed the oldest & most sober & most severe': his judgement would be safe. Happily, he reassured her: there was no objection from the Church. Iris was relieved, glad to see E. '<u>less demonridden</u>'.[114]

That afternoon, Iris went to buy crocuses for Mary, probably in the Victorian covered market. As Elizabeth was speaking of false belief, Mary was being interviewed for a lectureship at St Hugh's College. The crocuses were a post-interview good-luck gift. (Feeling joyful, Iris bought a bunch for Philippa too.) Iris and Mary met by the river and talked about joke archetypes. Mary, clutching her crocuses, suggested that the basic joke is the one where you laugh at yourself. The relief afforded moves you to a deeper level of reality – deeper self-knowledge; a clearer vision of what is artificial and trivial and, by that, of what is real and serious. Mary was perhaps feeling a little wild, high after finishing the interview and happy to laugh at her morning self, stuttering over her answers. Glad for the catharsis. There is pleasure in 'seeing the world go on', she said; whether she gets the job or not, life, reality, Mary, goes on. She waved her crocuses at the ducks, busy in March preparing their nests. 'There they bloody well go! Look at the little bastards!'[115] Year after year the ducks follow the rhythm of the university calendar: mallards pair up at the beginning of Michaelmas; they lay their eggs at the end of Hilary; the eggs hatch at the start of Trinity; ducklings and undergraduates fledge together after the summer exams.

Mary had been up against Mary Wilson for the St Hugh's job. Miss Wilson was now engaged to one of Austin's boys: Geoffrey Warnock. The Marys were interviewed by Evelyn Proctor, who had become Principal of St Hugh's in 1946, when Miss Barbara Gwyer retired. (Miss Proctor assumed Annie Rogers's title of *Custos Hortulorum*). The position went to Mary Wilson. Another disappointment. But other things were soon in store; Philippa told Mary that Herbert Hodges, at Reading, was looking for an assistant. Hodges had studied Classics at Balliol in the early 1920s; his tutor had been Sandie Lindsay. He had spent his philosophical life resisting logical positivism and the vision of philosophy that it promoted.[116] Leaving Oxford for Reading, Hodges created in miniature his vision of a collaborative, synthetic philosophy, in which lecturers and undergraduates from English, Classics and Philosophy gathered together around a cosy fire in a Victorian terrace to talk freely, and without fear of ridicule.[117] He derived this conception of philosophy, as 'an experiential science of spiritual phenomena',[118] from the German sociologist and philosopher Wilhelm Dilthey, on whom, in 1949, Hodges was writing his second book. In his review of Hodges's first book, Sandie Lindsay remarked on 'the considerable similarity between Dilthey's thought and that of the late Prof. Collingwood'. Both 'recognised that mind and body, man and Nature' are 'closely knit.'[119]

Mary applied and was offered the job. She prepared to spend a final summer in her Park Town bedsit. She did three more radio book reviews before she left, on A. C. Ewing's *Goodness and Philosophers*, Erich Fromm's *Man for Himself* and Arthur Koestler's *Insight and Outlook*. Those who tuned in were left in no doubt about Mary's evaluation: 'How far Miss Mary Scrutton ... put Arthur Koestler in his place as a philosopher I am in no place to judge', recorded one listener. 'I can only report that she brought up some formidable batteries and that the skill and confidence with which she served and fired her guns roused my admiration and stimulated my wits.'[120]

Though she was packing up her room, she was to be a regular passenger on the Great Western Railway, gazing out of the window across the familiar Chiltern hills on the 30-mile journey between Reading and Oxford. Sometimes Iris would take the train and visit her.[121] Mary's work on Plotinus continued, with trips to Oxford to visit the Bodleian, and to see E. R. Dodds, providing a welcome excuse to walk with her friends along the Cherwell.[122]

Philippa Gives a Lecture & Elizabeth Goes to Vienna

It was a week after her twenty-ninth birthday, and the start of Michaelmas Term 1949, when Philippa Foot walked across University Parks to give her first lecture, 'Some Problems in Kantian Philosophy'. As she channelled Donald MacKinnon and Heinz Cassirer, her spindly handwriting wove about the blackboard. She resisted the temptation to scrawl Elizabeth's war-cry: 'I may be as wrong as hell.' Her students would remember the sense she gave out of how hard it is to do philosophy – 'soft chuckles at the weird implications of some philosophical view'.[123]

There had been no Iris on the stairs that morning: she had moved out over the summer, taking a room at Park Town's Number 58, three doors up from Mary as she was decamping to Reading. It is possible that Iris had been finding the atmosphere at Number 16 a little stifling. Despite Pip's promise, the task of loving Iris and Michael equally was proving tough, even for tough Pip. There was much of the past that could not be revisited now that she was Mrs Foot, and the work for Pip, Iris and Michael of 'un-hating' each other was still in progress. Fifty years later he would tell Peter Conradi that reading his biography of Iris had 'cleared away the lasting bitterness left inside me since the winter of 1943–4'.[124] Iris was still living much as she had in London – her restless search for connection, love and life filled her evenings with drinks, parties, romance and drama. Perhaps the sound of her key in the door after dark, stumbling home from another adventure, was out of step with the domestic setting at the Foots'. Perhaps Iris wanted more freedom.

*

Now that she had a place of her own she could play host.

I. [I]f we dropped thing-in-itself, Witt. & Kant were working with the <u>same</u> picture. I was encouraged to say this by what Witt. says of metaphysical subject in Tractatus.

E. Q. of metaphysical subject has nothing to do with Q. of how language pictures the world.

I. What about 'the limits of my language are the limits of my world'?

E. Touché! This alone <u>would</u> seem to support a 'subjectivist' view of the Tractatus.[125]

Iris invited Elizabeth for supper often over the summer. They walked to the Victoria Arms along the river, talking of love poetry (E said: 'you can't write love poetry when you are feeling in love – it's not like a letter, it's not related to being in love like crying is to grief, it's indirect, it's a picture.' Iris disagreed).[126] Plato crops up in many places: in the Clarendon Arms, on Walton Street, in Jericho, in Iris's rooms. Sometimes Elizabeth stayed late until 2 a.m. They spoke about what one needs to look at to estimate one's own character.[127] Iris recorded a feeling of pleasure at being so fond of E. Another night Yorick came by and the three drank until 6 a.m. They discussed meaning and comparison '(<u>What is it for a meaning to have</u> a "Kernel"?)', downing four bottles of wine. Iris wrote of how happy E made her; she felt liberated and light-hearted.[128]

But the past had not quite been put to bed. 'E. said she was unhappy about me', Iris had recorded in her journal in June; 'because of past horrors there seemed to be a barrier between us, I was "reserved"'.[129] In November, Iris was still anxious about the state of their friendship. 'Rereading diaries of approx a year ago I felt some alarm. Am I being bad for E? . . . Are we only <u>now</u>, having learnt the cunning of keeping quiet, entering our own kingdom?' She determined 'Better see her less often'. But E. told her 'she would "give her ears" for an intimate friendship now',[130] and the frequency of their meetings remained undiminished. The past, Iris believed, could change if it ought to change.

On the evening of 17 November 1949, almost a year to the day since the party that had brought their friendship into crisis, Iris called on Elizabeth in the evening and the pair made the short walk along dark streets to the Chequers Inn, a fifteenth-century pub reached down a narrow alley.

They drank until closing time, then walked back to St John Street beneath a half-moon that would not have thrown much light into Elizabeth's curtainless living room. E., 'in a bad state ... read out bits from the end of the *Tractatus* & said: "[T]his means to one sheer despair. One might read this & kill oneself".'[131]

   6.41   The sense of the world must lie outside the world. In the world everything is as it is and everything happens as it does happen.

        In it there is no value – and if there were, it would be of no value.

        If there is a value which is of value, it must lie outside all happening and being-so. For all happening and being-so is accidental.

        What makes it non-accidental cannot lie *in* the world, for otherwise this would again be accidental.

        It must lie outside the world.

   6.42   Hence also there can be no ethical propositions.

        Propositions cannot express anything higher.

   6.421 It is clear that ethics cannot be expressed.[132]

In the first week of December, Elizabeth told Iris: 'Wittgenstein is dying of cancer ... If he dies like this he'll go to hell.'[133]

By now Elizabeth and Wittgenstein's task of editing and translating the work that would become the *Philosophical Investigations* was well under way. Wittgenstein's terminal diagnosis lent new urgency to their work. Elizabeth tried to persuade Wittgenstein to come and live in Oxford ('chez elle or Yorick') but he was determined to travel to Vienna.[134] The pair decided that it would be good for her to perfect her Viennese German by following him. Somerville College provided a grant[135] and Elizabeth left for Vienna on 16 January, two months pregnant. Iris saw her off.[136]

Wittgenstein had preceded Elizabeth to Vienna by three weeks, but had been too ill to write. He was resting at the family home, Alleegasse 16, along with his sister Hermine who was also dying of cancer and had less than a month to live. Elizabeth stayed with friends, visiting him two or three times a week. She met Paul Feyerabend, who invited her to speak to the Kraft Circle, an all-male student club which met in the rooms of the ageing Victor Kraft, a former member of the Vienna Circle. The Kraft Circle members, all in their early to mid-twenties, saw themselves as the inheritors of logical positivism. The group were sceptical when Elizabeth introduced them, in her slightly faltering German, to Wittgenstein's new method, and explained the importance of how language is learnt. 'What kind of primitive child psychology is this?', came their reply.[137] When Elizabeth had begun her thesis at Cambridge with the question 'What is that?', she may have been troubled by this reply, but by now she knew the answer. The child psychologist is offering an empirical hypothesis, based on observation, of the normal process of language acquisition. But Wittgenstein was describing the structure of our language-using life. He was revealing the background against which an empirical hypothesis can be formulated and tested.

A break from Oxford seems to have invigorated Elizabeth. Just before her Kraft Circle talk, she posted a much more upbeat report to Janet Vaughan:

> I am very grateful for the help I received to enable me to come to Vienna and should like to thank the Committee and Donors. My knowledge of German has enormously improved, though it is a more difficult language to master than I had realised. I am on the point of reading a philosophical paper to a discussion group here; but my German has to be extensively corrected by other people. But I shall be able to read and translate what I need for the future, so that the main aim of my visit will have been realised. In the present state of the exchange the grant which was made to me went a long way.[138]

The two philosophers worked hard through the rest of February and March, Wittgenstein recovering his appetite for philosophical conversation. His mind returned to his old friend G. E. Moore and he and Elizabeth discussed his refutation of Idealism and 'Defence of Common Sense'. The notes Wittgenstein made in those weeks became the first sixty-five remarks of *On Certainty*.[139]

Iris & Philippa Fill in the Background

At 6.50 p.m. on Sunday 26 February 1950, Iris was on the radio, her soft vaguely Irish vowels contrasting with the clipped King's English of the

BBC announcer: 'And now, "The Novelist as Metaphysician". The first of two talks by Iris Murdoch. The speaker examines the work of the existentialists Sartre, Camus and Simone de Beauvoir to discover what lies behind this rapprochement of literature and philosophy.'[140] Iris had been invited by Prudence Smith – her predecessor on the second floor of 16 Park Town – to give a talk. Prue thought Iris had 'a lovely voice'.[141]

'The free and lonely self . . . discovers the world to be full of ambiguities', came Iris's voice through the radio, describing the world in which Sartre's hero moves. 'These have to be, and are resolved by action, or by that species of action which we call inaction. That is, we are condemned to choose; we choose our religion or lack of it, our politics or lack of it, our friends or lack of them. Within the wide limits of our historical situation we choose one world or another one.'[142]

While in Brussels, Iris had been invigorated and gripped by Sartre's philosophy, she now knew that the picture that Sartre was offering, a version of which had given Richard Hare relief in the disintegrating world of a prisoner-of-war camp, was not suitable for ordinary civilian life. 'The existentialists have generalised and given a philosophical form to something which, piecemeal, most of us can recognise in the crises of our own lives' – namely, the desire to 'give a fresh meaning to [our] past experience', to create 'a new view of [our] personality' and to give 'free assent to this view'. This is something she knew of herself. But what is true and therapeutic at moments of crisis is false and harmful when taken as a general picture of the human predicament. And now, it seems, she spoke directly to Elizabeth:

> This viewpoint was strikingly expressed long ago in Wittgenstein's *Tractatus*. 'The sense of the world must lie outside the world. In the world everything is as it is and happens as it does happen. In it there is no value – and if there were it would be of no value. If there is a value which is of value, it must lie outside all happenings and being-so. For all happening and being-so is accidental.'[143]

For Sartre (in Occupied France), as for Wittgenstein (in the trenches of the First World War) and for Hare (in a prisoner-of-war camp), '[t]he fundamental moral predicament is the same'.[144] To choose and keep on choosing, where every choice creates oneself and one's world anew. Elizabeth's words echo: 'This means to one sheer despair.' And Sartre's novels show why: by 'display[ing] in detail the adventures of the beings who are in this situation of having no guarantee'.

> Meaning is suddenly seen as withdrawn . . . This is a plunge into the absurd. If indeed we confer meaning, not only upon ethical and religious systems, but upon the physical world too . . . then this meaning could in principle vanish, leaving us face to face with a brute and nameless nature.[145]

Sartre's plunge into the absurd is not a joke of the type that Mary spoke of, one that reminds you that there is something more important and which will go on whatever we choose to do. For the existentialist, 'nature' is not the name of a place that contains ducks, the lives of which have a structure and pattern and value; it is a world denatured. The existentialist denies what the Thomist – and the Marxist – affirms: that '[t]here is an intelligible unity of man and nature. Nature has its own dialectical history, and its own rationally explicable and developing interactions with the activities of man.' Where the Thomist and Marxist find nature a source of wonder and significance, the existentialist 'regards nature as the brute and meaningless scene into the midst of which man is inexplicably cast'.[146]

Iris was scheduled after a performance of Beethoven's late String Quartet in A Minor, and for that reason Richard Hare, in his St Margaret's Road home, may have missed the beginning of the broadcast. His war experience had left him with a dislike, even a distrust, of Beethoven. Before the war, he had been moved by the evocation of prayers for mercy in his *Missa Solemnis*. Now he felt it hollow, deceptive: '[t]he sort of peace we were after' is not externally gifted but comes from learning 'to still the forces of evil in ourselves'.[147] So perhaps he missed Iris's first movement towards identifying 'oddly familiar' strains of existentialism (minus the glamour and the Gauloises) in Oxford moral philosophy. Both have 'reached positions which are in some ways strikingly alike'.[148]

Iris would in time develop an account of freedom very different to Sartre's and Hare's. Moral freedom, she will argue, is not the ability to choose your own moral principles in an otherwise valueless world. True moral freedom is the ability to look steadily at reality and to see things justly. To see what matters, what things are important and good. To look again and to rethink the past. This work of looking does not involve sudden movements of the will at isolated moments of choice but is a continuous task. And as Donald

MacKinnon had seen, it requires humility and purity of heart. 'Love is the extremely difficult realisation that something other than oneself is real', she will write.[149]

Iris had spoken on the radio of the unrealistic picture of the human life that she found in both Sartre's and Hare's philosophy. Both men pictured themselves as lone subjects, facing a 'brute and nameless nature'. Philippa was ready to connect this picture with the moral subjectivist's idea of a deep contrast between statements of fact and evaluation. She would use her insights about the word 'rude', first expressed over the clatter of the Lyons' tea room on Cornmarket, to start to reinstate the connections between descriptive and evaluative language.

Hare's 'moral prescriptivism' followed Kant in holding that a principle of conduct counted as a *moral* principle when a person gave it universal and general application. I may think that I ought to kill Nazis without thinking that everyone ought to do so; but if I do think that everyone, whatever the circumstances, ought to kill Nazis, then this would make it a moral principle for me. But this created a problem, Philippa would soon be ready to tell a symposium of philosophers. If Hare's account were right, any principle of conduct, no matter how trivial or silly, could be turned into a moral principle so long as some individual held that it had universal and general application.[150] Hare's purely formal criterion ruled out any restrictions on the content of morality and so ruled out any logical connection with human life. Like the Wittgenstein of the *Tractatus*, who placed value outside 'the whole sphere of what happens' (words she had heard Iris speak on the radio), Hare thought that there is nothing in reality to ground the objectivity of moral judgement. His philosophy, like Sartre's, thus retained the formal structure of Kant's categorical imperative, but with moral principles cut free of any transcendental background.

In her symposium talk, 'When is a Principle a Moral Principle?', Philippa would point out that this cannot be right. It is not true that moral judgement floats free of our ideas about a good human life. Reality is not brute and nameless. Meaning is not withdrawn. Rather, we will only be prepared to call something a *moral* principle, she said, if we can 'fill in a certain background'. That background, she had learnt from reading Aquinas with Elizabeth, will be one that allows us to see 'a connexion, in a man's mind, with that (admittedly large) collection of virtues and vices'.[151] She illustrated this with an example. Suppose a man said that refusing to wear bright colours was one of his moral principles. We would not accept it as such, even if he thought no one ever should wear bright colours and never wore them himself, and even went around trying to prevent others from doing so. We might think it was an obsession or a phobia, but we would not accept that the injunction was part of morality. If, however, he explained that wearing bright colours was *ostentatious* and showed a surfeit of *pride* in the wearer we would begin to see how such a principle could be moral, even if we disagreed with it. Virtue terms 'connect new, and possibly surprising, applications of "good" or "bad"' and carry with them 'a special way of looking at something', Philippa would explain to her audience. They illuminate the background pattern. When Lady Bathurst thought it bad that her son should be taught by women, she used the word 'humiliating'. This word tells us about how she sees the world: it connects her judgement to her views about dignity, shame, pride, worth and status.[152] Lady Bathurst's language might help us to make sense of the Proctor's anxieties about Elizabeth's trousers, or Esther Bosanquet's concerns about Philippa wearing spectacles.

Perhaps by now Philippa was also making the connection that would find articulation in 'Moral Beliefs', published only a few years later. Although we might disagree about whether Lady Bathurst's son was humiliated, or whether wearing colourful clothes (or trousers) is ostentatious, there are nevertheless limits imposed by reality, by human life, on how these words can be sensibly used. 'It is surely clear', she would write, 'that moral virtues must be connected with human good and harm, and that it is quite impossible to call anything you like good or harm.'[153] With this insight, she found a way to put value back in the world, and to reconnect moral language to human life. The connection to virtue or vice is not a disguised appeal to a higher-order principle: 'Do not be ostentatious' or 'Always display humility'. Philippa did not think (as many contemporary 'virtue ethicists' do) that bringing an action under a virtue description implies that it ought to be done. Rather, the virtue term gives a 'way of looking at something', a way of seeing the facts in the light of ideas about the human good.

'No one believed in logical positivism any more,' Mary Wilson said later about that time, 'but we hadn't yet been able to rescue moral philosophy from its clutches. The person who really did this seriously was Philippa Foot.'[154] As their old lecturer H. H. Price had predicted in his 1945 address to the Aristotelian Society, A. J. Ayer's war cry of 'Nonsense!' was beginning to 'appear a little ridiculous'.[155]

Wittgenstein Signs His Will

Elizabeth returned from Vienna in time for her thirtieth birthday and Wittgenstein followed her. A few weeks later, on Tuesday 25 April 1950, he moved into the attic of St John Street.[156] Wittgenstein's immortal soul became a preoccupation of Elizabeth. The pair talked of religion and God, and these conversations made their way into Wittgenstein's final writings:

> Life can educate one to a belief in God. And experiences too are what bring this about; but I don't mean visions and other forms of experience which show us the 'existence of this being', but, e.g., sufferings of various sorts. These neither show us an object, nor do they give rise to conjectures about him. Experiences, thoughts, – life can force this concept on us.[157]

Wittgenstein writes that the experience of suffering, the experience of life, can force on us an attitude towards reality. Not particular, individual beliefs (verifiable one by one), but a way of seeing and being in the world. This attitude, he says, 'is that of taking a certain matter seriously and then, beyond a certain point, no longer regarding it as serious, but maintaining that something else is even more important'.[158]

It seems in those last months at St John Street, Wittgenstein's suffering brought him close to this attitude. In his *Philosophical Investigations*, he writes: 'Someone may for instance say it's a grave matter that such and such a man should have died before he could complete a certain piece of work; and yet, in another sense, this is not what matters. At this point one uses the words "in a deeper sense".'[159] At Wittgenstein's request, Elizabeth arranged for Father Conrad, a Dominican priest, to visit the house to talk about God.

On 29 January 1951 Wittgenstein signed his will, witnessed by Elizabeth's lodger Barry Pink. He bequeathed to Elizabeth one third of the copyright of his unpublished writings, to publish as she, Rush Rhees and Georg Henrik von Wright saw fit. Also, all his furniture, one third of any royalties from his work, and one third of the remainder of his estate. To his long-time companion Ben Richards, 'my French Travelling Clock my Fur Coat my complete Edition of Grimm's Fairy Tales and my book "Hernach" by W. Busch'.[160]

A week later, on 8 February, Elizabeth and Wittgenstein took the Varsity Line, travelling first class so he could lie out on the seats.[162] He had a terror of dying in hospital and so was to move into the Cambridge home of his physician Dr Edward Bevan and his wife Joan: Storey's End.

CHAPTER 7

Metaphysical Animals

NEWCASTLE & OXFORD
MAY 1950–FEBRUARY 1955

Mary Leaves Oxford – Lotte Labowsky & the Warburg School – Elizabeth Edits the Philosophical Investigations *– Iris & Mary Discuss Poetry & Paradox – Iris on Sartre, Hare & the Style of the Age – Mary Raises 'the Woman Question' & Iris Takes Lessons in Love – Back to Life*

Mary Leaves Oxford

As Elizabeth had been tending to a dying Wittgenstein in her attic, Mary was tracing out a more familiar path for a young wife. She had first seen her future husband, Geoffrey Midgley, in graduate seminars. Tall, tweedy and a pipe smoker, he had a kind and slightly mischievous face. Though he was one of Gilbert Ryle's B.Phil. boys, Geoffrey, like Mary, was trying to find a way to fit ancient philosophy into the confusing post-war scene. In the summer of 1949, a chance afternoon with a mutual friend in Mary's bedsitter, talking about philosophy over pork pie and spaghetti, left both Mary and Geoff with the desire to see more of each other. (Geoff later confessed he'd been much impressed by Mary's culinary offering, which was a good job as her cooking was to remain picnic-style.) But at the end of that summer Mary moved south to Reading and Geoff moved north to Newcastle, and they went from knee-to-knee on Mary's divan to nearly 300 miles apart.[1]

They met again the following summer at a philosophy conference in Bristol. The topic for the 1950 Joint Session of the Mind and Aristotelian Society was 'Psychical Research, Ethics and Logic'. The sun shone, and after lunch on the Sunday philosophers gathered outside with their coffee cups and cigarettes. This was a time for ambitious young men to seek out a professor and make a good impression, for the shy and awkward to gaze at their shoes and for the romantically inclined to make their move. Geoff and Mary, who were certainly in the third group, noticed 'that one of the biggest bores in the profession was going round trying to find someone to go for a walk with him' – let him remain anonymous. The pair's eyes met and Geoff said: 'Yes. Now. Quick!' They discarded their coffee cups and raced off for a walk of their own, *sans* bore. Mary, writing in her memoir, explains that 'one thing led to another, and before the end of that vacation we were engaged'.[2] The unhappy idea of herself as some sort of

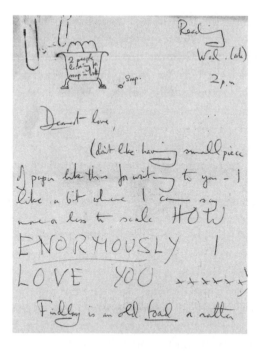

changeling, as 'ugly', 'with the needs of a woman but without the means to satisfy them', 'masculine brains thrown in as a sort of consolation', melted away.[3] Under Geoff's loving gaze she found herself transformed: ugly duckling into swan.

After some toing and froing over whether they should live in Newcastle or Reading ('I would be happy to live with you at the North Pole'),[4] it was settled: Newcastle upon Tyne. Not the North Pole, but the most northerly city in England. The wall built by Emperor Hadrian to mark the limit of the civilised world runs through it. There were benefits to being among barbarians: for Ryle's B.Phil. army, salaries increased the further one moved from 'the hub of philosophical civilization' (Oxford). Geoff's £550 was princely, though his friend Antony Flew was offered a kingly £800 to go beyond the borderlands to Aberdeen.[5] Mary and Geoff agreed on a matrimonial bed: 'It would be fun to have a big one – but don't spend your last sixpence!'[6] Leaving Oxford, Mary had bequeathed her single to Philippa. As 1950 drew to an end, and in the middle of a snowstorm in Surrey, Miss Mary Scrutton became Mrs Mary Midgley. Iris (the remaining singleton of the four) was bridesmaid.[7] Mary and Geoff honeymooned in Paris.

Mary felt at home among the coal-dusted buildings of Newcastle. As a child she had often stayed with her godmother, Bessie Callender, who told her stories of her life as one of the first female students at nearby Durham. Her grandfather David Hay (of Mott, Hay & Anderson) had been an engineer on the city's great Tyne Bridge.[8] At first, the Midgleys lived in Jesmond in a small flat that opened out from a central sitting room where Geoff took to taking apart and recomposing radios, a spillover activity from the war that Mary feared would take over the house. By late summer 1950, they had settled into a more spacious three-storey Victorian semi with a garden, and Mary's immediate attention was reoriented from Plotinus to the unruly garden and the plumbing. J. N. Findlay, the head of department at Newcastle, offered her teaching, but Mary declined: 'I really wanted to put my feet up.' They could live off Geoff's salary for now, plus a small income from her maternal grandfather's will.[9] A welcome donation of Edwardian Scrutton furniture appeared in convoy from the south, and some huge metal bookcases arrived from Geoff's uncle. As she looked out over her untamed garden Mary felt herself very fortunate to have lost out to Iris and Mary Wilson.[10]

Between January 1949 and March 1951, Mary appeared ten times on the BBC's Third Programme. BBC producer Anna Kallin liked Mary's pithy and engaging style and soon she was giving radio talks as well as reviews. In June 1951 she read an essay to mark the centenary of the anti-suffrage novelist Mary Augusta Ward. It was she who had suggested that Oxford's new institution for educating women be named in honour of scientist and polymath Mary Somerville. When the very first students had arrived at Somerville Hall in 1879, they would have been met by the twenty-eight-year-old Mary Ward, at the time eight months pregnant with her third child. For those girls, Somerville life began with a novel image of womanhood: a professional, published, educated, pregnant woman, who spoke seven languages and was at ease in Oxford's avowedly masculine world.[11]

Lotte Labowsky & the Warburg School

As Mary adapted to her life in Newcastle, new patterns were emerging in Oxford. In Trinity Term 1951, the *Oxford Gazette* included not one but two new women lecturers in philosophy. Their names, when added to 'Mrs Martha Kneale', 'Mrs Foot' and 'Miss G.E.M. Anscombe', show that for

the first time in its 850-year history, Oxford offered up five female philosophy lecturers in a single term. Vice Chancellor Lewis Farnell's worst fears
of the bewomaning of Oxford were, it seems, coming to pass. On Tuesdays
and Thursdays at 11 a.m., 'Mrs. H. M. Warnock' would be teaching 'Logic'
for Honour Moderations at Schools. This was the former Mary Wilson who,
despite Elizabeth's relentless campaigning, had now married Geoffrey Warnock. Elizabeth, Mary Wilson later recalled, 'had one mission in life which
later became two. The first was to wean me from my passion for J. L. Austin,
and try to stop me going to his lectures. This was later overtaken by a
passion to wean me from my husband to try to get me not to marry him.'[12]
But if Mary Wilson was now, by Elizabeth's lights, wholly lost to the cor-
rupting mire of Ordinary Language Philosophy and 'that Shit Geoffrey',
this did not bother Mrs Warnock. In any case she thought Elizabeth's husband, Peter Geach, 'a monster'. She had once seen him dangling a child
out of the window by its legs – punishment for failing to master some Polish
declensions.[13]

The other new name was 'Miss Labowsky', unmistakably an 'invader of
the field' on grounds of both sex and nationality. She and Miss Anscombe,
the *Gazette* announced, would be teaching a class together.

*

We have caught a glimpse of Lotte Labowsky in the background to this history several times already. Before the war, she would have been a familiar sight to Mary, Iris and Philippa among the book stacks in Somerville's library, with neat dark hair and a studious face. It was she who had smuggled Heinz Cassirer into Somerville in the aftermath of Chamberlain's Munich Agreement, past the college porters, to introduce him to Mildred Hartley. She had looked up from her book in the Senior Common Room as Elizabeth steamrollered Philippa. She lived in Summertown, and Mary's bicycle clattered past her on her daily walk to Somerville.

Dr Carlotta Labowsky was one of a dazzling array of humanist thinkers who lived in Hamburg in the first decades of the twentieth century. Their intellectual centre was the Warburg Library for the Science of Culture (Kulturwissenschaftliche Bibliothek Warburg), the former personal library of the banker-cum-scholar Aby Warburg. Warburg's esoteric vision was to curate a storehouse of the collective memory and wisdom of European civilisation, including its occult manifestations: paganism, magic, ritual. Books and manuscripts sat alongside ceramics, photographs, tapestries, mirrors and other talismanic cultural objects, and were organised under four eccentric categories: IMAGE, WORD, ACTION, ORIENTATION. Not long after he had accepted a professorship at the University of Hamburg in 1919, Ernst Cassirer, the famed Kant scholar and Heinz's father, had found on its bookshelves a concrete realisation of his abstract theory on the nature of man.[14] 'We are symbolic animals' ('*animal symbolicum*'), he wrote.[15] ('The Q. of history. Hang on to man as symbol-maker. The clue is somewhere here,' Iris had recorded in her journal in June 1947.)[16] The older Cassirer had been lecturing on Kant's moral theory when a young Donald MacKinnon, awed to be in the presence of so great a scholar, took his seat in an All Souls lecture room in Hilary Term 1934.[17] Lotte's doctoral dissertation, completed in 1932, also sprang to life among the books and artefacts of the Warburg Library. It was a study of life and art mediated by the Greek Stoic Panaetius and the Roman philosophers Cicero and Horace. A person's life can be constructed like a well-made oration or composed like a musical composition[18] and like those things it can also possess moral beauty or (after St Thomas Aquinas) radiance. Virtue can be cultivated through attention to harmonious actions and objects.[19] Two years after its completion Lotte had arrived in England penniless, excluded from university employment by the Nazis' anti-Semitic legislation. The Warburg Library preceded her by a few weeks.[20]

In 1933, just before Christmas, the steamboat *Hermia* had pulled out of Hamburg's port heading for London loaded with books and rare manuscripts and thousands of slides, photographs, art objects and pieces of furniture. Lotte's dearest friend (and one-time lover) Raymond Klibansky had master-minded the rescue by staging the evacuation as a loan.[21] He was there on the docks in London to greet these most unusual refugees. Two weeks more would have been too late. The burning of 'unGerman' literature had been under way since May and by the end of December the 'loan' would have been subject to review by Joseph Goebbels's Propaganda Ministry. More than 25,000 books had been sent up in smoke in Berlin's Bebelplatz, the square housing the State Opera and Humboldt University. Books by Plato and Aristotle, Hume, C. S. Lewis and Freud joined Brecht, Einstein and Kafka on the pyres.[22] With Warburg's treasures saved, next had come the task of gathering the archivists and scholars who could unlock their secrets. While Somerville's Principal, Helen Darbishire, made arrangements for Dr Labowsky, David Ross stepped in to secure Raymond Klibansky a fellowship at Oriel College as well as British Academy funding for his work.[23]

Lotte and Elizabeth's decision to teach a class together in Trinity Term 1951 was partly born of necessity. Lotte had been told by Classics tutor Mildred Hartley that if her name appeared on the lecture list she would be entitled to an M.A. and a small pay rise. Elizabeth was under a con-tractual obligation to teach that term, but didn't want to give proper lectures. She was pregnant again, though – Lotte told Raymond in March – 'curiously enough no one seems to have noticed it so far'. ('Eat

Ry Vita or something', Wittgenstein had advised Elizabeth when he noticed she was gaining weight; he 'seemed very startled' on learning she was pregnant.)[24] Elizabeth wanted something 'small and cosy' as the baby was due a few weeks into the term.[25] She had also been unwell: in October 1950 she needed an operation to try to save the sight in one eye: afterwards she had to rest on her back in a dark room for ten days.[26] So they offered a co-taught class in Somerville. Their choice of subject, 'Proclus' Commentary on Plato's *Parmenides* 141e10–142a8' (this amounts to ten lines and one word of text) may have begun as a scheme to ensure that 'no more than about four people' would come,[27] but both women had a serious scholarly interest in Plato's text and Proclus' commentary.

Lotte had been engaged in an ambitious translation and editorial project with Raymond Klibansky since before the war. He had discovered a complete thirteenth-century Latin translation of Proclus' commentary on Plato's *Parmenides* in the library of the fifteenth-century polymath and mystic Nicholas of Cusa. As all four extant versions of Proclus' commentary were incomplete, the discovery was staggering. The pair began working on the Latin and Greek commentaries together. Writing to Raymond to tell him about her plans with Elizabeth, Lotte affectionately referred to the recovered fragment as '"our" end bit'.[28] In 1953, this 'bit' would appear in the third volume of the *Corpus Platonicum Medii Aevi*, a compendium of all those texts that comprised the Platonic tradition in the Middle Ages. The translators of the fragment into English are named as Carlotta Labowsky and Miss G.E.M. Anscombe.[29] This volume is the first to name Labowsky (alongside Klibansky) as co-editor of the *Corpus*, but historians agree that she was 'the scholar' behind the first two volumes too – and, say some, 'the brains'.[30]

Elizabeth's interest in neo-Platonism, as well as her acquaintance with Lotte, Raymond and the Warburgians, had begun as an undergraduate. The *Gazette* gave her the pick of 'Early Medieval Philosophy', 'John of Salisbury' and 'Logic and Science in the Early Middle Ages'; all would have appealed to a new convert soaking herself in Catholic philosophy. In Hilary Term 1941, she received informal tuition from Klibanksy. Writing to Mary Glover, he reports that Elizabeth's approach to the history of philosophy was at first 'decidedly negative' – 'influenced, no doubt, by the prevailing contempt for the history of philosophy' – but he commends her effort, promise and originality. 'If her knowledge of the historical part can be brought up to the standard of her critical faculties . . . she has a good chance of getting a first', he predicted.[31] Lotte and Elizabeth became Somerville research fellows simultaneously in 1946, and Lotte would have had plenty of opportunities to join Philippa and Elizabeth's sparring in the Somerville Senior Common Room. Elizabeth, Lotte and Raymond continued to work together, along with Peter Geach, on various translation and editorial projects at least into the 1960s, when Raymond and Elizabeth co-edited A. E. Taylor's translation of Plato's *Sophist* and *Statesmen*. 'The way Forms are treated . . . would be totally acceptable to Aristotle', Taylor insisted in his introduction.[32]

The *Gazette* advised those intending to join Miss Labowsky and Miss Anscombe's class to write to Miss Labowsky by the first Monday of term. After a couple of weeks, Lotte wrote to Raymond, now at McGill University in Canada. As it turned out, her prediction of 'about four' students was wildly off:

> One good thing – very funny. E. Anscombe and I have only one candidate for our class!! It is the philosophy tutor, Philippa Foot (née Bosanquet). So we are going to spend the time discussing the Parmenides and Sophistes, etc. and I don't have to do any work for it.[33]

The class proceeded, studentless. Three brilliant women, brought together by a war, studying a manuscript that had escaped the Nazis' bonfires: a medieval Latin translation of a fifth-century Greek commentary on Plato's imagined recollection of a conversation between Socrates and Parmenides, the author of a poem written 500 years before the birth of Christ. An object of deep metaphysical structure, the past preserved over 100 generations, continuous layers of human effort, of copying and reproducing, of retelling and reimagining. 'Our weekly discussions on Parmenides are quite interesting,' wrote Lotte.[34]

Elizabeth discussed Proclus' commentary on Plato's *Parmenides* with Wittgenstein. 'Proclus', Elizabeth told him, said that '[t]he name is a logical picture of its object.' A 'logical image' or '*icon logike*'.[35] To her surprise Wittgenstein said: 'I have so often had that thought.' She was surprised because she had assumed 'that the objects, the simples, spoken of in the *Tractatus* were uniform characterless atoms'; that when Wittgenstein said that the proposition is a 'logical picture', he meant to deny that the same was true of names.[36] Later, this conversation would bear great fruit – and it would help Elizabeth see Wittgenstein's *Tractatus* in a new light.

For the Wittgenstein of the *Tractatus*, Elizabeth Anscombe would explain, objects 'can enter into some compositions and not others according to their forms', and this holds also of the names of those objects. She gives an illustration. The sentence 'Mount Everest chased Napoleon out of Cairo' does not describe a possible fact because 'Mount Everest' is the name of a mountain, and mountains, being the kinds of things that they are, do not chase. If 'Mount Everest' is the name of *a mountain*, then certain uses of the name are excluded; this is what it means to say that the name has a logical form or 'internal character'.[37] Among 'the moderns' the trend, Elizabeth complains, has been 'to deduce what could be from what could hold of thought'; but Wittgenstein had a better approach, one that he shared with Plato. '[A] thought was impossible because the thing was impossible, or, as the *Tractatus* puts it, "Was man nicht denken kann, das kann man nicht denken": an *impossible* thought is an impossible *thought*'.[38]

This idea, Elizabeth came to see, takes on new life in Wittgenstein's later work. Instead of logical form, Wittgenstein spoke of grammar. A name's internal character is revealed by the pattern of the human practices in which it is used. The piece in chess that has the name 'king' has a particular conventional shape – it is the tallest piece and has a small cross atop its head. But this word 'king' does not name this shape. It rather names a piece that in a game of chess moves according to such-and-such rules.[39] All these rules are folded into the name 'king', into what a person who uses that sign as a name can come to know and understand, just as all the practices and customs of state are folded into its homonym 'King'. This is why Wittgenstein says: '[o]ne has already to know (or be able to do) something in order to be capable of asking a thing's name'.[40] He had remarked in a lecture: 'It is a great deal of information about a word that it is a proper name, and still more, what kind of thing it is a proper name of – a man, a battle, a place etc., etc.'[41]

This Proclean insight would eventually give Elizabeth the final piece in the puzzle she had set herself in the middle of the war, boarding the Varsity Line to Cambridge. To be told the kind of thing that a name, 'n', names, she realised, is to be given the identity conditions for n. '[A]nimal, plant, peacock, man, flea, bougainvillea, banana-tree', lists Elizabeth. 'When we come to plants and animals the identity of an individual is of a different kind from the identity of a lump of lead, say. "The persistence of a certain pattern in a flow of matter" comes into our account; but the notion of a pattern, as of a shape, is here special.' When we speak of 'the shape of a horse or a human being' we mean 'shape' in a special way, she goes on. One that means that 'we don't say that someone's shape alters when he sits down'. And by 'pattern' we mean to cover '"patterns" of development over a period of life involving considerable changes, even like those from caterpillar or larva to pupa to butterfly'.[42] Our grasp of these life patterns is reflected in our use of the names of kinds of living things. A person who knows that 'Elizabeth' is the name of a *human*, uses her name in way that reflects the pattern and norms, and the considerable changes that belong to human life.

One week into Lotte and Elizabeth's class, on 29 April 1951, Ludwig Wittgenstein died at Storey's End. Elizabeth, Ben Richards and Yorick were with him, along with a Catholic priest whom Yorick had brought. They arrived too late to speak one last time – he had lost consciousness the previous day, but not before passing a message to Joan Bevan for his friends: 'Tell them I've had a wonderful life.'[43]

Many years later, Philippa Foot would come back to those words to answer the question that had hung over her since childhood: what is happiness? 'Interpreted in terms of happy states of mind it would . . . have been very puzzling indeed if a life as troubled as his had been described as a good life,' she would write. But his deathbed words 'rang true because of the things he had done, with rare passion and genius'. She contrasted Wittgenstein's happiness with that of a lobotomised patient who is 'happy all day long picking up leaves'. Despite all its anguish and misery, it is Wittgenstein's life, she says, not the patient's, that tells us more about what happiness is for human beings.[44] His great work was complete (important); in his final days he was surrounded by those who loved him (important in a deeper sense), the final scene in Storey's End.

'Elizabeth seems to be very cut up,' Lotte told Raymond.[45] Towards the end of term, Elizabeth went into labour and Mary Geach was born. Child number three. (Peter, Barbara and John were still living in Cambridge). In the weeks before, Lotte had been astonished by how little this coming event figured in Elizabeth's plans for the future, which seemed wholly oriented towards Wittgenstein's literary remains.[46] Only four days after Wittgenstein's death (and four weeks before baby Mary's birth), Elizabeth had hurried with her co-editor Rush Rhees to hand-deliver the typescript of the *Philosophical Investigations* to the head office of Blackwell Publishers. Elizabeth and Rush knew that the story of linguistic philosophy was already being written by J. L. Austin and his Kindergarten, and that they could afford no delay in making Wittgenstein's work publicly available.[47] A week later, Lotte's hands seized up, her arthritis exacerbated by an unusually cold spring. Her mother was ill and she was struggling to make ends meet: Raymond offered to send her a food parcel.[48]

Lotte, Elizabeth and Philippa's class continued, uninterrupted by death, birth or illness. 'Sometimes I feel very frivolous', Lotte confided to Raymond, 'when both the other participants look more and more worried and sit opposite each other with wrinkled brow, thinking silently and with effort.'[49] (Elizabeth later became famous for her silences. One undergraduate spent an entire hour's tutorial frantic with worry as the silence extended indefinitely into the future; years later, Elizabeth remembered the occasion as one on which they had each been too overwhelmed by the beauty of the *Philosophical Investigations* to speak.)[50] '[I]f it should turn out that I receive the M.A. by decree for this effort it would be a good joke,' Lotte confided, 'and a pleasant interlude in the history of the Parmenides interpretation (and silence ends the discourse on the One).'[51]

Iris did not attend the Proclus class, but she and Pip had gone together to at least some of Elizabeth's 'Readings on Plato' lectures the previous term. Conveniently scheduled on Tuesdays and Thursdays at noon, the timing would have been perfect for continuing the conversation over lunch in the Somerville dining hall, just like the old days.

One of the longest sustained discussions in the *Philosophical Investigations* is the section now known as the 'rule-following considerations' – paragraphs 185–242 – and in those lectures, or in their post-lecture conversations, Elizabeth presented Plato and Wittgenstein together.[52] In Plato's *Meno*, Socrates elicits from an untutored boy the geometric proof that a second square drawn on the diagonal of another square is twice the area of the first. He does so by drawing a geometric figure on the ground.

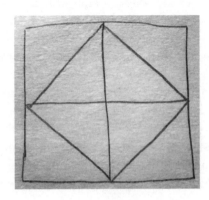

Plato argues that the only explanation of the boy's understanding is that the demonstration has awoken in the boy knowledge that his soul already possesses. In response to Socrates' questioning, the boy's soul recollects what it knew before birth.

In her journal, Iris recalled a conversation with E.

E. said to me before: there's no difference between the next application of 'blue' & the next number, from the pt of view of this problem. Or between 'proof' (the Meno example) and any concept. In all these cases we can do more than we get in the examples which teach us.[53]

Plato's Theory of Recollection, E. seemed to suggest, touches on the same phenomenon that concerns Wittgenstein in the rule-following passages of the *Philosophical Investigations*. How can a child who is shown a part of a pattern know how to 'go on'? How can we 'do more than we get in the examples which teach us'?

Suppose a teacher shows her pupils how to follow the rule '+2'. She demonstrates with series: '2, 4, 6, 8, . . .', then '11, 13, 15 . . .', then '144, 146, 148 . . .'. Now she says: 'Continue the series 1000, 1002, 1004.' These numbers are higher than any in the previous examples. And yet the child understands and does so: '1006, 1008, 1010'.[54] Is it not remarkable that such a thing is possible? How can the child do more than he gets in the teacher's examples? Plato's answer is: what the pupil gets in the examples is a reminder of the innate knowledge his soul already has – not really 'learning' at all. Wittgenstein says: what the pupil gets in the examples is just what he gets, but the pupil is a human being, and the pattern is part of human life, and creatures like us – like him – do catch on to such patterns. If we did not, our lives would not be as they are.[55] If this child does not, cannot, catch on to such patterns, there are many other parts of human life from which he will be cut off. The examples do not remind the immortal soul what it already knows, but rather we teach by showing the pupil, pencil in hand, how to go on, how we go on.

After the lecture:

P. said: aren't three things being confused? The difference between 'just doing it' (e.g. getting up in the morning, putting one foot before another) and doing it in accord with a rule. The difference between repetition and development. The difference between a finite and an infinite series.[56]

But the 'confusion' is deliberate. When Elizabeth teaches her son John the colour term 'red', John must catch on to a pattern of language use, a rhythm, that goes beyond anything that is or could be there in the teaching situation. Nothing guarantees that he will not encounter, around the next corner, an object that his learning has not prepared him for. A red face, a red sky at night, a red after-image, a red-letter day, a red rag to a bull. How do we learn to catch on to the rhythm and patterns of the complex human practices – conventional, ad hoc, ritualistic, customary – that go to make up our forms of life and that extend far beyond us? It is natural, says Wittgenstein.[57] If we did not, we would not have such practices. We just do. We bloody well go on!

Elizabeth Edits the Philosophical Investigations

Elizabeth was struggling under the weight of Wittgenstein's bequest – a *Nachlass* of over 20,000 pages,[58] much of which was at 27 St John Street, along with a newborn. The *Philosophical Investigations* now contained two parts. She and Rush Rhees had added to the first typescript a second which contained much of the work Wittgenstein and Elizabeth had discussed in Dublin's Zoological Gardens. Iris loved this material – her copy of the published book is almost black with flyleaf notes, many of which gloss those passages where Wittgenstein discusses aspect perception and the duck–rabbit. 'I meet someone whom I have not seen for years', goes one remark; 'I see him clearly, but fail to know him. Suddenly I know him, I see the old face in the altered one. I believe that I should do a different portrait of him now if I could paint.'[59] In 1947, Iris had wondered how a person might see their own past differently from the present. Now she could put this idea as Wittgenstein does. Should I not compose a different history of my past life now?

Iris and Lotte helped Elizabeth to prepare the manuscript of the *Philosophical Investigations*, combing through her translation, hunting out infelicities.[60] Elizabeth was sending improvements to the text up to the day the manuscript went to print. She 'bent over backwards to write in a pure and compressed English'. She saw in Wittgenstein's German 'a special daylight character: tough, lucid, crisp, lively and serious', and she struggled to replicate it. 'Good English, in modern times, goes in good clothes; to introduce colloquialism, or slang, is deliberately to adopt a low style. Any English style that I can imagine would be a misrepresentation of this German.'[61]

While Iris and Lotte pored over Wittgenstein's texts with Elizabeth, J. L. Austin and many in his Kindergarten waited impatiently for the work to be published. Isaiah Berlin of the Brethren pressed Denis Paul, a student he and Elizabeth shared, to show him the manuscript – but 'don't ask Miss Anscombe for permission to show me'. Isaiah's dislike of Elizabeth was deep. After the book's publication, he tried to scupper her invitation to give a radio talk, writing to Anna Kallin, the producer of the BBC Third Programme, of 'the Wittgenstein intimates – Miss Anscombe and her husband Geach and others'. 'A great deal of violent artificial neurosis, not washing etc., anyhow you can imagine – hideous stammering in place of articulate speech, perverted Catholicism, and all the other delicious attributes.' Now he told Denis Paul: 'You must not misunderstand me but I would rather not have her asked for favours on my behalf . . . I would rather you left her alone so far as I am concerned. I shall read it with great eagerness if and when it is published. If it is not, I should like to be shown it secretly, or if that is against your principles, as no doubt it should be, then not at all.'[62]

Despite the difficulties associated with being a literary executor, 1951 was the beginning of brighter, easier times for Elizabeth. Wittgenstein's legacy put an end to financial strain and in December 1951 the Rockefeller Foundation awarded Somerville College a grant to support Elizabeth in her editing and translation. By 1958, the college had received $16,200 (some £200,000 in today's money) to relieve her of undergraduate teaching and to allow her to focus on the *Nachlass*.[63] Following years of intermittent casual teaching and belt-tightening, Peter had at last secured a stable academic appointment, his wartime stint as a lumberjack finally overlooked. Still, in 1966, when he was interviewed for a professorial post at Leeds University, having already served fifteen years at the University of Birmingham, it was brought up at interview. Peter Geach glowered: 'I was rrrrrrolling logs.'[64] The children moved to St John Street and the family acquired a cat, Tibbles. From Oxford Peter commuted to Birmingham; with the help of Mrs Colter's pastries and sweeping pan, the couple would manage, in their idiosyncratic way, to perfect the art of 'telegamy'.[65] Marriage at a distance.

The publication of the *Philosophical Investigations*, beautifully translated by Elizabeth, with Lotte and Iris both thanked in the translator's note, would be hailed as one of the major turning points in twentieth-century philosophy. Anna Kallin ignored Isaiah Berlin's slander and Elizabeth recorded a 24-minute radio broadcast for the Third Programme, transmitted in July 1953. Part II of the *Philosophical Investigations* transcends everything that Wittgenstein ever wrote, she said. '[F]or compression, together with rich and sharp expressiveness; for wealth of incontestable observations and hard investigation'.[66] She ended by wondering how it would be received as a literary achievement.

Iris & Mary Discuss Poetry & Paradox

In mid-July 1951, Iris stepped off the *Flying Scotsman* and into Newcastle upon Tyne's grand Victorian station. A pregnant Mary was there on the platform to meet her, settled into her new life. Iris, in contrast, had no wish to settle. The names of stations scrawled across the right-hand corners of her letters speak of her restlessness: thoughts in a train, captured in a carriage or on a platform, in between places ('District line', 'Hammersmith Station', 'Piccadilly line', 'in the train').[67] Different lovers weave in and out of her journals. Michael Oakeshott, the Conservative political philosopher (she falls for him in October 1950. 'I hope M. doesn't break my heart anyway before Easter'[68] – but he does). Wallace Robson (he plays bridge, her mother is impressed;[69] they are briefly semi-engaged and break up in a frenzy of pain in April 1952). Arnaldo Momigliano, a Jewish Italian Warburgian and refugee scholar (they read Dante's *Rime*, and make three trips to Italy;[70] he is married). Elias Canetti, émigré novelist, future Nobel Laureate in literature (her journals record their lovemaking, his domination; he spies on her).[71] Peter Ady, her St Anne's colleague and the girl behind the 1938 Somerville marriage survey (they kiss passionately in a car after a fancy-dress party at Burcot Grange).[72]

Iris's reports of life amid philosophical civilisation would have further cemented Mary's belief that she had had a lucky escape. This time, Iris brought with her a horror story from the paper she had just given, as part of a prestigious panel with Oxford's Waynflete Professor, Gilbert Ryle, and St Andrews University Lecturer in Logic, Tony Lloyd, a former tank commander known to have 'liked nothing so much as a paper which he thought merited vigorous attack'.[73] The panel chair was H. H. Price. The four, along with a few hundred professional philosophers, had travelled to Edinburgh for that year's Joint Session. Iris had hopped off the train at Newcastle on her way back to Oxford.[74]

In her talk, 'Thinking and Language', Iris had addressed the matter at the heart of her 1947 Sarah Smithson proposal: 'thoughts and feeling that are not exposable'. Though Iris later called herself a 'Wittgensteinian',[75] her old reluctance to embrace Wittgenstein's thought wholesale was still with her (and would remain in some form).[76] Since her earliest conversations with Elizabeth, she had been sure that Wittgenstein's philosophy was leaving something out. Now she thought she'd found it – she could get out from under the net of language by attending to the experience of thinking.[77] She wanted to show that a careful, truthful description of its phenomenology did not fit the view of meaning favoured by many linguistic philosophers. On the whole, she said, we do not think in statements, expressed in inner speech that we could publicly share, make exposable, by uttering ordinary words. No. In thinking, language, if it is present, is inextricably bound with feeling and metaphor and semi-sensible image.[78] The phenomenology of thinking shows us that there is more to meaning than the use of public signs. Some thoughts cannot be communicated in the plain words of the plain man; their expression depends on there being another, a *Thou*, who is willing to attend, closely, to stuttering word and gesture, and who is close enough to 'catch on' to a meaning only partly expressed. Such communication, Iris said, 'is often only possible in limited societies, sometimes only in societies of two', a pair whose life together illuminates ways of going on that would be invisible to others.[79]

Iris wanted to show her audience of analytic philosophers, of plain-speaking linguistic analysts, that this sort of communication, ineffable, mysterious, personal, is of deep importance to human life. It is so important, she said, that we create and preserve objects that facilitate this fragile understanding. A 'public object which we can all handle', and to which we can jointly attend, can begin to expose an otherwise inexpressible thought, she explained. She offered up a fragment of a poem by John Clare:

> Frail brother of the morn,
> That from the tiny bents and misted leaves
> Withdraws his timid horn
> And fearful vision weaves.[80]

She tried to convey to her fellow symposiasts what she herself experienced as she read John Clare's description of a snail on a summer hedgerow: the feeling of 'a smooth delicate suspense followed by an enormous sense of chaotic expansion at the last line' – this was her attempt to make the inexposable exposable, to illustrate one way in which we grasp reality with the help of language, through metaphor.[81] Iris wanted to show that inner experience evades the logical techniques of the analysts – and that to ask what someone's experience was *really* like makes no sense. The inner world, like the outer, alters as our concepts deepen, and as new metaphors and images allow us to see new connections.

Tony Lloyd was first to respond. He could not agree and spoke for twice as long as Iris had to hammer home his point. Iris seemed to be suggesting, like the old Idealists, that the mind can construct the world. '[M]ight I not then change the facts about my garden by learning languages instead of doing gardening? . . . The answer to the lazy gardener is no'.[82] Gilbert Ryle, who was (unfairly) rumoured to have no inner life at all, was next in line and was another non-ideal interlocutor for Iris.[83] No lazy gardener himself, Ryle's awareness of snails had perhaps hitherto extended only to their status as pests, as outlined in his well-thumbed copy of Robinson's *English Flower Garden*.[84] We 'naturally use a metaphorical mode of speech', Iris had said to him, and 'yet we can understand each other and even come to influence what the other experiences'.[85] A metaphor can point to a new way to go on together, a new pattern in our lives. But Ryle missed her meaning altogether, and thought that Miss Murdoch's subtle phenomenology was of little philosophical – or indeed practical – interest. 'If we ask a soldier to tell us about a battle we . . . do not care which of his boots he wore, when he had a cigarette, over what tussocks of grass he walked . . . We want to know how the battle went . . . Detail is negligible.'[86]

Price, in his closing comments as chairman, was moved by Iris's description to risk a little introspection himself: 'What nonsense this sounds!', he remarked as he, like Iris, struggled to catch the phenomenology of thought in words. 'I know it does, and I know how naughty it is to use the word "feel" at all.' But he couldn't resist: 'Now I am really going off the deep end', he continued, risking the suggestion that when thinking '[i]t is almost as if one were consulting a daemon or an oracle'.[87]

To Iris, overlooking the usual Scrutton mess as she perhaps narrated the vaguely humiliating experience of not being understood by a room of (almost entirely male) philosophers, Mary's life must have seemed a picture of stability, safety and comfort. They arranged themselves in old configurations transposed to a new place. Miss Murdoch sitting cross-legged on Mrs Midgley's hearthrug. Novels, books of poetry, philosophy and life everywhere; bits of radio; a pair of cats. Geoff, hands full of radio parts, in and out: he was building an intercom system so Mary would be able to listen to their expected newborn at a distance. Mary and Geoff were beginning to develop their own private language, as all lifelong couples eventually do. Is this a rhythm that Iris could imagine herself nudged into? ('I just want to sit by the fire and read *Woman's Own*,' she joked in a letter to Wallace Robson.)[88]

Whatever Iris's impression, Mary's life left little time for reading *Woman's Own*. Later that year, on a cold October evening, Mary was on the BBC radio's Third Programme as after-dinner listening. The title of her talk, 'The Natural History of Contradictions', might have elicited some surprise in British living rooms. Does Miss Scrutton (she was listed under her maiden name) really mean to say that contradictions have a *natural history*? Is she really suggesting that paradox might be a suitable topic for antiquarians and naturalists?

'Paradox is more or less expected of philosophers,' Mary began. 'No one is surprised to hear them saying that mind is more real than matter; that wise men can be happy on the rack, or that nothing whatsoever can be certainly known.' A scientist may think he is clever because he can 'see through an apparently solid floor and know that it is only a speckled void', but this is nothing to a philosopher, who is 'a man so wise that he sees through appearances in general (not just floors)'. The fashion among contemporary professional philosophers to reject paradox (she names Wittgenstein, Moore and Russell, but might have added Ayer, Austin and Hare) has only increased the attraction of 'paradoxical writers' like Blake, Nietzsche and Kierkegaard. 'In speculation as well as in gossip, we have some natural inclination towards the more surprising version of a story.'[89] Our interest in paradox, Mary told her listeners, belongs to our natural history; paradox has an important place in human life.

Many practical reformers, she pointed out, have used paradox to illuminate a bit of hypocrisy; the shock of a contradiction between what we say and what we do may force a change. 'Man is born free and is everywhere in chains', rails Rousseau. When a philosopher puts a contradiction to practical use, as Jean-Jacques does here, he is rather like a plumber, says Mary. He 'exposes flaws in ordinary thought like a plumber letting water spout through a leak, so as to be sure what is wrong before mending it'.[90]

While leaks are a means to an end for Jean-Jacques, for other individuals the leaks are an end in themselves; they go letting off water with no intention of mending the pipes. The poet Alexander Pope thinks that a leak will not matter to us very much 'so long as we do not try to have a bath,' and for others the joy of a watery chaos is its own reward.[91]

Mary was delighted with the plumbing metaphor. She was something of an amateur plumber herself, having learnt to master the often frozen pipes at 55 Park Town (in the basement 'a bathroom with a brown-stained bath and a temperamental geyser – a geyser that ate pennies, took a week to work and gave out far more steam than hot water').[92] She would continue to compare philosophers to plumbers throughout her life, pleased with an analogy that captured her conviction that philosophy is not a luxury good but a basic human need. '[P]hilosophy is best understood as a form of plumbing,' she wrote in her nineties. It is a 'way in which we service the deep infrastructure of our lives – the patterns that are taken for granted because they have not really been questioned'.[93] It happens underground, in the dark.

The plumbing metaphor appealed to Philippa too – it perhaps stuck in her head after Mary's talk, or maybe it came into being in a Park Town conversation about Plotinus. 'Sometimes I think a philosopher is like a plumber,' she told an interviewer in her eighties. 'If you have trouble with your pipes you call in a plumber, if you have trouble with your concepts you call in a philosopher.'[94] Trouble with concepts, like trouble with pipes, is a price we pay for having complicated, intertwined and contingent lives. It is the price we pay for our natural history, each conceptual innovation beginning a new pattern that may cause a leak elsewhere, now or in the far-off future. That is why, as Mary would oft repeat, the need for philosophy will never go away.[95]

In the final few minutes of her broadcast, Mary turned to uses of contradiction and paradox that are neither practical nor absurdist, but which reveal something serious and mystical. She was drawing now on a fragment of her unfinished dissertation. Just as Iris had offered Gilbert Ryle a poem, so Mary offered one to her listeners. She chose 'Man' by the Elizabethan poet John Davies.

> I know my soul hath power to know all things,
> Yet she is blind and ignorant in all;
> I know I'm one of Nature's little kings,
> Yet to the least and basest things am thrall.
> I know my life's a pain and but a span;
> I know my sense is mocked in everything;
> And, to conclude, I know myself a Man –
> Which is a proud and yet a wretched thing.[96]

Like the cultural objects that had made their way across the North Sea on the steamboat *Hermia*, poems belong to our shared tradition, our common background. Poetry 'makes a public object,' Iris would write in her journal.[97] For her, such objects can help us to communicate aspects of our inner lives that would otherwise remain private. For Mary, poems can show up contradictions and connections that we had not noticed, and by doing so bring us back to life, messy and complicated. Poetry, then, is another of the metaphysician's tools ('art as crystallizing points of reality'[98]). With the 'Yet's of his poem John Davies uses a contradiction to show us something real and true, and thereby illuminates a break in the pattern that we have not seen before. 'There *is* a contradiction between our ideas of man's powers and his destiny, of free-will and necessity, of our involvement and our solitude.'[99] This is the sort of contradiction that 'does not yield to the most patient academic discipline'; it is an 'and' that cannot be resolved into an 'or'; a mystery that does not resolve into a problem. Yet . . . this is precisely where we bump up against what is real. And it is here that philosophers, along with poets, artists and novelists, do their work. Where metaphysical animals ask their questions.

Iris lost the journal that contains her entries between March and August 1951. She picked up an old one on 11 August, and recorded a new thought.

Poetry: a jazzed up version of the making of the extended intelligible which we do all the time by naming.[100]

The following month Miss Murdoch would be lecturing on 'Concepts and Images'.

Iris on Sartre, Hare & the Style of the Age

On 25 October 1951, Winston Churchill rode back into power when a snap election called by Labour to increase their slim parliamentary majority backfired. Despite Labour polling almost a quarter of a million more votes than the Conservatives and their allies combined, Churchill gained a majority of twenty-six seats. The Labour Party was said to have 'lost mainly in the queue for the butchers and the grocers'.[101] The Conservatives had promised to end rationing, which was still in place on meat, butter and sugar: 'Socialism Thrives upon Scarcity', Churchill's party had told voters.[102] Depending on where you looked in Oxford, the atmosphere was either doleful or gleeful.

It was in this political scene that Iris finished 'a trivial thing on Sartre'.[103] This 'trivial thing' was the manuscript for *Sartre: Romantic Rationalist*, the first book about the existentialist hero to be published in English.

'To understand Jean-Paul Sartre is to understand something important about the present time,' the book begins. Sartre is wholly contemporary; 'he has the style of the age'.[104] Like Richard Hare's work, Sartre's is also a response to the loss of the background to our moral and political thinking. This background includes the ideas that some values are common to all thinking beings; that individuals are held in a larger ethical and metaphysical structure that transcends them; that human culture stands as a bulwark against depravity. This background was taken away from Sartre and Hare through a combination of their own individual experiences (of resistance and imprisonment) and the general pressures of modernity.

This is how to understand Sartre's slogan of *existence* before *essence*: Sartre is offering up a new image to replace the one that has been lost, a new picture to fill in the gap. But, says Iris, the picture he gives us is no use. With the background scorched, 'good' can no longer be the name for an objective quality. Similarly, without such a background, 'democracy' cannot identify the form of a good society, but is something that we can only recommend with our shouts. Speaking perhaps as her past self, she detects in existentialism the ideology of the European bourgeois intellectual: '[T]his is the mythology of those who reject capitalism, with its materialist values and its deadening of human activity', but 'who are yet afraid to embrace socialism'. Instead, those 'who are morally sensitive and intelligent enough not to be taken in by capitalism now embrace a solipsistic and nihilistic individualism'.[105] They are left lonely, empty, nothing.

'This presentation may seem to an English audience utterly unreal,' Iris admitted when she voiced these ideas at the Socratic Club in Hilary Term 1952.[106] Among those listening in the audience would have been the one-time 'Oxford reds' of her Communist youth, now 'posh labour' dons. (Perhaps some confusion? *Mauvaise foi? Moi?*) The Dixieland band was long gone, replaced at grown-up dinner parties by radiograms and babysitters, MPs and lurid cocktails and, as was usual in Iris's case, marriage proposals.[107] But, insisted Iris, you dancing economists, whether you recognise it or not, have 'the style of the age'. She pressed upon her audience: we must ask what it is that 'the rejection of Marxism condemns us to'.[108]

By the time of the next general election – held in May 1955 and leading to a greatly increased Conservative majority – Iris had a much clearer idea. 'The socialist movement in England is suffering a loss of energy,' warns her essay 'A House of Theory'[109], written for a collection that advertised itself on the dustjacket as being by a dozen 'Thoughtful Young Men'.[110] The Welfare State has put paid to the severest forms of deprivation, 'the most obvious injustices', '[t]he sense of exploitation has faded'. So 'how are we to keep *thought* about socialism and *moral concern* about socialism alive in a Welfare State?'[111]

The energy that had carried her and the reds optimistically through the Oxford by-election in 1938 had dissipated. Socialist theory, she observes, has never been at home in academic institutions, but rather lives with the socialist movement, a political, radical, progressive section of society pushing for change. Socialist thinking has been 'nourished' on the factory floors by philosophical ideas, concepts and visions borrowed from Utilitarianism, Marxism and Utopianism, and then animated by a practical demand for change. While the British philosophical tradition has always been sceptical of large-scale theorising, it has fed socialism with concepts and visions of human life, welfare, politics and labour. But now things are different. It is almost half a century since philosophers began to withdraw into the technical task of linguistic analysis and 'the invention of what one might call "logical gadgets"'. The 'stream of philosophical ideas' that feeds the socialist movement has dried up.[112] The concepts that the socialist movement needs – equality, work, freedom – have stagnated, cut off from the philosophical visions that sustained them. Meanwhile, in an increasingly positivistic scene, practical economics has become technologised and efficiency has become the benchmark of success. Experts who know the technique are divided from those who do not. Without a socialist vision, there is no 'house of theory' to provide refuge from the advance of bureaucracy and efficiency. The struggle for equality and education has become the struggle for higher wages. Without a socialist vision, workers are left without a means of orientating themselves in a world in which things are done to them and in which they don't play a part. 'There is a certain moral void in the life of the country', her warning continued.[113]

Elizabeth would have sympathised with this thought. In the year that 'A House of Theory' was published, she would record a radio broadcast in which she complained of the way in which the 'procedure in making moral decisions' that is 'taught in the university' manifested in the new, post-war welfare system.[114] The goals of 'justice' and 'benevolence' – which require a metaphysical account of the human goodness – had been dispensed with in favour of metaphysically empty ideals like 'fairness', 'efficiency', 'general welfare'. The 1948 National Assistance Act obliged local authorities to provide the elderly or infirm with suitable accommodation should they be found unable to look after themselves. What sort of injustices, Elizabeth asked, might be committed in pursuit of a benign policy of improving general welfare? 'A frequent occurrence . . . is the removal by authority of elderly widows from their dwellings, which anyone can see they are not keeping in accordance with the standards of hygiene which are desirable for their own end and general welfare.' She was perhaps thinking of Miss Lawson, whom she had once cared for at 27 St John Street. 'The tender mercies of the wicked are cruel,' Elizabeth would gloss her tale.[115]

A few months after Iris's talk, she and Elizabeth almost found themselves caught up in a much more practical and concrete attack on the 'dancing economists'. It began when Elizabeth rang Iris at her flat: she was going to Paris with Georg Kreisel (he, along with Iris and Lotte, is thanked in the translator's note of the *Philosophical Investigations*) and his friend Gabriel Dirac (son of the physicist Paul Dirac). Could Iris join them?

Elizabeth and Georg had lately been in Iris's bad books, after the pair's antics had seen her thrown out of her lodgings and forced to take two unfurnished, if central, rooms at 13 King Edward Street (£7 a month, landlady 'destined to be killed with a hatchet').[116] Georg was a good cook, and he and Elizabeth often prepared 'banquets' at St John Street.[117] Elizabeth had challenged him to recreate a tiny pocket of central Europe through the production of a perfect herring soup. Iris was out of town, and for reasons now lost to history, they decided to do so on the gas ring in her Park Town room, roping in her blue chiffon scarf (a birthday present from her mother) as an ersatz sieve.[118] The soup had been a great success but the pair failed to clear up, and Iris returned home after the weekend to be greeted by a furious landlady and an unholy stink. The scarf was ruined, the landlady had taken the soup challenge for an orgy, and Iris found herself back on the pavement with her suitcase. She had been terribly upset but was quick to forgive.

Not wanting to miss out on a trip to Paris, Iris rejigged tutorials and took the 9.50 a.m. train to London to get her passport.[119] Elizabeth was to ring her the following morning with instructions, but when the phone call came at 9.30 a.m. it was not Elizabeth but her student Denis Paul: Elizabeth had flu and could not travel. A little digging by Iris, and it emerged that Elizabeth had 'received a letter from K with the phrase "Of course you know the purpose of this trip?"' whereupon she had panicked. Iris, interpreting the message as Elizabeth had, returned to Oxford, indignant on her friend's behalf. She confronted Kreisel: were the conditions as they had inferred, namely 'going to bed'?[120] (Iris had once described Kreisel to a friend as a 'sexmaniac mathematician'.[121]) Kreisel replied scornfully: 'nothing like that. But you would be expected to carry something.'[122]

It transpired that Dirac, a committed Communist, had for some years been smuggling gold sovereigns out of England to the Continent, where they could be sold at great profit. Fifty pounds was still the maximum that could be taken abroad by a traveller, but Dirac was paying friends and contacts to take out thousands. A few years later, one of his recruits, Anna Bernard, would be caught on her third such trip with £1,653 strapped to her back (£45,000 in today's money).[123] She served time in Holloway prison.

When Iris and Elizabeth discovered the truth they were shocked but, it seems, not outraged. 'Chez E. I find out that the dark phrases refer to what Dirac calls the cunt carriage of sovereigns. Helpless with laughter.'[124] This reaction, and the fact that Dirac had assumed that they would be happy with their cargo, suggests that 'bourgeois intellectual' was not a description that could have been applied to either of them.

Mary Raises 'the Woman Question' & Iris Takes Lessons in Love

For Mary, her new habitat and role were generating questions about women. She had noticed a leak in the conceptual plumbing. It was perhaps only then, far from Oxford, that she was struck by the peculiar absence of women, and thinking about women, in the philosophy she had learnt. Even on the rare occasion that a woman stood at a lectern, it was always a man she was talking about. Mary Glover: Aristotle, Locke. Martha Kneale: Locke, Berkeley, Hume, Descartes, Spinoza, Leibniz. Lucy Sutherland: Edmund Burke. And when the men who were the subjects of those lectures spoke of the 'rights of man', of 'man's nature' and of 'man's freedom', more often than not 'man' picked out that half of the species whose lives took place in the public realm of politics, law, commerce and education. Males, not humankind. 'Nobody can be attentive about everything,'

Mary would later observe. 'This is usually not fatal, because it is the job of the next philosopher to point out the lapses. But the distinctive thing about the woman question is that nobody did this. Negligence just continued. The vested interest involved was, until recently, too strong for any real attention to be possible.'[125]

In February 1952, four days after Elizabeth Windsor was proclaimed Queen, and four weeks after the birth of her baby, Tom, Mary wrote a letter to her future self and read it over the airwaves. 'My dear Posterity, I am here to give you the Woman's Point of View,' begins Mary, with typical drama. She is hopeful: the days have passed when 'women have a different language from the men, distinct traditions, distinct stories and beliefs, a whole separate culture in mute opposition to the official one'. Now, women 'have been admitted to a thousand masculine mysteries, from classical scholarship to engineering. They don't have to keep dropping out of the conversation. They can make an honest living.'[126] Women are no longer treated as 'men who have accidentally come out the wrong shape' but are seen as one half of a species, with ways of looking, thinking and writing that may illuminate human life in different ways. She writes her scripts between feeds, shopping trips and cooking (badly). Books piled on baby clothes. 'I wish I could remember who it was that compared the flow of Virginia Woolf's prose to the thoughts of a woman telling children a story, while all the time she knits and keeps an eye on the fire, and never forgets that there are cakes baking in the oven.'[127]

Not all Mary's musings on the 'women question' met with Anna Kallin's approval. 'Rings & Books', tapped out on the old typewriter, began with an observation: 'Practically all the great European philosophers have been bachelors.'[128] Men who lived semi-monastic lives that excluded one half of the adult species and all of the species' young. Mary asks: might philosophy written by people who spent their days in a mixed community, among men, women and children, who wrote while babies slept upstairs – nocturnal philosophers like herself – be a little different from what we actually find in the European tradition? After all, that two people can be in the same place at the one time is not at all illogical from the point of view of a pregnant woman. And the problem of other minds can't really arise for a breastfeeding mother who worries whether it is something *she* has eaten that has upset her baby. Isn't the European tradition's obsession with solipsism and freedom all a bit ... adolescent? Mary asked.[129] Kallin was horrified. Not by the thought that the European philosophic tradition was almost entirely made up of bachelors or that poets marry ~~badly~~ madly, but

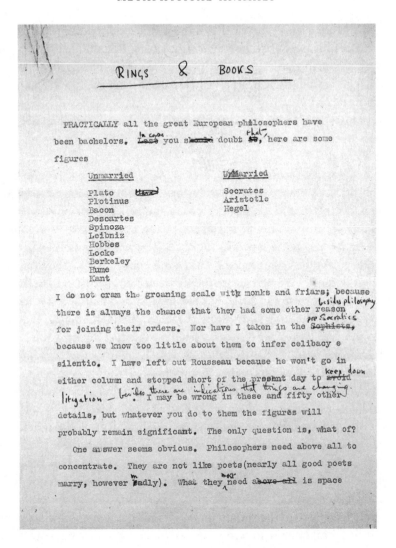

RINGS & BOOKS

PRACTICALLY all the great European philosophers have
been bachelors. *In case* Lest you should doubt it *that*, here are some
figures

Unmarried	Unmarried
Plato	Socrates
Plotinus	Aristotle
Bacon	Hegel
Descartes	
Spinoza	
Leibniz	
Hobbes	
Locke	
Berkeley	
Hume	
Kant	

I do not cram the groaning scale with monks and friars; because
there is always the chance that they had some other reason *besides philosophy*
for joining their orders. Nor have I taken in the Sophists, *pre Socratics*
because we know too little about them to infer celibacy e
silentio. I have left out Rousseau because he won't go in
either column and stopped short of the present day to avoid
keep down litigation — *besides there are indications that things are changing.* I may be wrong in these and fifty other
details, but whatever you do to them the figures will
probably remain significant. The only question is, what of?

One answer seems obvious. Philosophers need above all to
concentrate. They are not like poets(nearly all good poets
marry, however *madly*). What they *most* need above all is space

by the 'trivial, irrelevant intrusion of domestic matters into intellectual life'.[130] The script was never broadcast.

Had Iris cast her eye over Mary's heaving column of philosopher bachelors, she might have noticed a different pattern, one less radical than Mary's but perhaps more attuned to the deep source of the unreality of philosophy that Mary complains of. Iris too had noted the respect in which the café-dwelling Sartre 'eschews intimate bonds'.[131] But a life without dependants, even lived in isolation, need not be unreal and disconnected, she thought; not if it is lived with love.

Iris's lifelong philosophical and literary love affair with love began in earnest in 1951 when she agreed to give a series of radio talks on the work of the French philosopher Simone Weil, a Christian Jewish mystic and political activist who had died in 1943.[132] Middle-class and educated at L'École Normale Supérieure, after graduating Simone had chosen to join the multitude of unskilled women eking out an existence on the factory floors of Paris. Like Somerville's Mary Glover, she too hoped to develop a lived understanding of the proletarian struggle, and she too experienced directly what it was to be dehumanised, to be a living cog in the wheel of a machine, the organisation of which is opaque.[133] But Simone Weil went far beyond Mary Glover. Weil did not return to her study to consider what she had learnt, but instead immersed herself deeper and deeper in the life she sought to understand. She limited herself to the starvation rations of her impoverished workmates, decreasing her food as she increased her labour to the point of literal collapse.[134] 'Nearly all of human life', she observed in her essay on the *Iliad*, 'takes place far from hot baths.'[135] Weil died at the age of just thirty-four. After her death, four of her books were published: *Waiting on God*, *La Pesanteur et la Grâce*, *L'Enracinement* and *La Connaissance Surnaturelle*.[136]

Listening to Iris's first broadcast, one Thursday night after dinner in October 1951, Mary may have recognised fragments of Park Town conversations. Simone Weil's French words, resounding in Iris's Oxford English, spoke to the difficulties that she and her friends had struggled with so often in Philippa's front room. 'Contradiction alone proves to us that we are not all', writes Simone Weil. To come up against a contradiction – a gap, a paradox – is to come up against reality, against something other. Affliction does this too, says Weil. 'The experience of suffering is the experience of reality. For our suffering is not something which we invent. It is true.'[137] Affliction forces our attention on to reality, its otherness disarming our usual attempts at consoling ourselves by invention and fantasy. The experience of contradiction, affliction (*le malheur*), resistance, illuminates the obstacles that we must overcome if we are to contemplate what is real. Iris's philosophy, and her novels, will later show in wise, witty and tragic detail how 'fantasy' – the consoling, egoistic, mechanistic part of the imagination – can veil reality and prevent us from apprehending each other and the good.[138] We can easily become locked into our personal, privately conjured worlds. What is needed to jolt us from our reverie? To force us to look again?

By now the first draft of what would become Iris's first published novel, *Under the Net*, 'a philosophical adventure story',[139] was being written into existence. Before long, she would undertake the careful, judicious work of revising, recasting, deleting, and looking again – seven notebooks in all (her reworkings appear in darker blue ink, inter-linearly or on the back of the leaf).[140] Iris was trying to do what John Clare had done for the snail – to create an aesthetic form in which we can see reality reflected, not natural-istically, but through a complex tangle of feeling and characterisation, humour and thoughtful recognition, parody and farce. Back to life. Through the lens of the novel, the great artist is able to express a moral vision which is deep and just and compassionate.[141] By attending to the world without fantasy or hope of consolation, the great artist enables us to see reality, in all its contingency, more clearly – and sometimes also to stir us to wonder, just as beauty in nature can. It is here that Iris Murdoch (drawing obliquely on her lessons on Kant with Heinz Cassirer) would locate the great human-ity of the artist, and the continuity of art and morals. 'The essence of both of them is love.'[142]

It was in this interplay between image and reality, art and truth, recol-lection and recognition that the writings of Simone Weil first spoke to Iris. Above all, they unlocked the significance of Plato for her. As a youthful Communist during the war, lectures by E. R. Dodds (Mary's future doctoral supervisor) had left Iris cold. She had read Plato's *Republic* in 1940, while busy with the Oxford reds preparing for another Bolshevik Revolution, and had been so disgusted by 'the old reactionary' that, as she joked to a friend, she took to selling the Communist *Daily Worker*.[143] She had wanted to get close to the 'thronging multitudes' whose lives 'in mines & cotton mills' were a rebuke to Plato's vision of a just aristocracy. Now in Simone Weil she confronted a red who kept the *Symposium* in her pocket: when labour-ing as a grape picker in Vichy France, she carried it with her and taught it to her fellow farmhands.[144]

In the *Symposium*, Plato no longer holds that knowledge is a matter of the immortal soul remembering what it already knows, as it was in *Meno*. Instead, through love of what is beautiful – first the bodies and souls of particular men and women, then bodies and souls in general, then laws and practices, then knowledge (science and beautiful ideas and theories; the philosopher, after all, is a lover of wisdom) – the soul can ascend as though on the rungs of a ladder, and come to gaze steadily upon the Form of Beauty as it manifests in all these beautiful things, as in the *Republic* it gazes on the Form of the Good. For Weil, Platonism, Communism and Christianity all contain the same fundamental truth: the human soul comes to know reality through love.[145] Just as Mary Glover had said.[146] '[B]eauty is the only spiritual thing which we love by instinct', Iris Murdoch will later write.[147]

Simone Weil's posthumous voice was still drifting through British living rooms as Iris spoke that October 1951. 'That is why the only organ of contact with existence is acceptance, love. That is why beauty and reality are identical. That is why joy and the sense of reality are identical.' Iris overran by a few seconds[148] – and a few words. 'She was a very brave thinker.'[149]

Iris's lessons in love coincided in her life with a relationship that had all the Weilian themes of suffering and affliction.[150] Franz Baermann Steiner was a Jewish refugee anthropologist from Prague. His last memory of his parents was from shortly before the Nazis arrived in Czechoslovakia and Chamberlain declared 'peace for our time'. He pictured them sitting on a park bench in the sunshine.[151] He knew nothing of them throughout the war; then in July 1945 he received a letter from his childhood friend Hans Günther Adler, soon to be Iris's friend too. Franz's parents had been with him in Theresienstadt from July to mid-October 1942, and Hans wrote to tell him that they had perished at Treblinka. Adler's thousand-page study of the Theresienstadt ghetto, *Theresienstadt 1941– 1945: das Antlitz einer Zwangsgemeinschaft*, completed in 1947, detailed the mechanics of the Nazi genocide – transport, accommodation, diet, administrative structures.[152]

Shortly after receiving Adler's letter, Steiner suffered a nervous breakdown. In 1948, he began to suffer severe chest pain. He had his first heart attack a year later, aged forty.[153]

Like Iris, Franz was a journal keeper:

11th May 1951
Enter Iris Murdoch[154]

That year, Iris would be teaching F. H. Bradley, the Idealist whose distinction between existence and reality was so important to Mary. It was the first time Bradley had been taught since Freddie Ayer had declared the metaphysicians extinct. Franz was meanwhile lecturing on 'Theories of Taboo' and 'The Study of Kinship'.[155] They fell in love over glasses of cheap wine in the Golden Cross and the Lamb and Flag. They talked about everything.[156] Kafka's Prague versus Joyce's Dublin; exile; the untranslatability of value;[157] Rilke; God. The Director of the Warburg Institute later described Steiner as a living bookworm – eating his way through the stacks at the British Museum.[158] Iris was somehow able to take in Franz's past. 'A cut-off past is in a way easier to convey to another than a continuous one', he told her.[159] She took his hand. She asked him if he believed in God; 'he *loved* God'.[160] She took him to 27 St John Street to introduce him to Elizabeth in her 'untidy dining room', a scruffy barefooted Barbara (now nine) wandering among them. Elizabeth's 'beautiful face looked familiar'.[161] '[P]oetry and philosophy are close after all – I see it now,' Iris explained to her journal.[162] She read Franz's poems. They spoke about magic and taboo and myth – Steiner's friend Elias Canetti would later say of him that he considered myths 'the greatest and most precious things which humanity had produced'.[163]

For Iris's birthday Franz gave her a poem and a gift.

Dieses weinglas schenk ich dir,
Trink aus ihm, trink aus mir,
Wahr das schöne gleichgewicht
Und zerbrich uns beide nicht.[164]

[This wine-glass I present to thee
Drink from it, drink from me,
Keep the handsome balance
And don't break the two of us.]

She in turn lent him a copy of her most precious thing: the manuscript of *Under the Net*.

On 18 October 1952, Franz returned to Oxford after a holiday in Spain. He saw the lights of Oxford as his train approached. Iris was waiting for him on the platform, dressed in trousers and a grey duffel jacket, smiling and serious and sweet. She was holding a bunch of gentians in her hand.[165] A month later he suffered a second, fatal heart attack. Iris registered his death; they had agreed to marry. She rang Philippa; she could not be alone.

'Sick and rent with misery. The way F's eyes gleamed through his glasses.'[166] A note on her door cancelled her tutorials for the rest of term.

Back to Life

Philippa was not averse to 'thinking silently' about the virtues. But of the four friends it was she whose goodwill was most visible and whose daily life was most conspicuously filled with good deeds. Her 'bits of living' at 17 Broad Street were, quietly and without fanfare, part of a global effort to alleviate human suffering.

1951 was a transformational year for Oxfam. The combined value of clothing, gifts and donations that year totalled about £80,000 (over £2.5 million in today's money). That amounted to a lot of sorting, folding, post-ing, minute-taking, each bit of living part of a larger structure within which actions at new scales were possible: signing one's name *in order to* write out a cheque *in order to* make a donation *in order to* send relief to Palestinian refugees. The new General Secretary, Leslie Kirkley (a Lancastrian Quaker pacifist), did not envisage the sudden dawning of a great tomorrow and he joined Philippa and the other volunteers sorting through the Shabby Unmended. Progress would be slow and would require as many tortoises as hares. But progress there would be. Early in Kirkley's stewardship, the com-mittee voted to respond to 'natural' disasters, as well as wars, and that year sent humanitarian aid to alleviate the famine in Bihar, India. The Oxford Committee received its first mention in the House of Commons.[167]

Philippa tended to think of herself as a tortoise in academic domains too. In a preface to her collected works, she remarks on her lack of pro-ductivity over many years (she thanks Somerville for its patience).[168] But in fact she was working as Wittgenstein had recommended. '[P]eople haven't learnt the truth of what he said when he said "[o]ne must do philosophy very, very slowly"', she later remarked. '[I]n philosophy it is difficult to work slowly enough.'[169] 'We must write things!' Iris had announced to her friends one afternoon in Philippa's living room, in 1948.[170] But only now was Philippa beginning to warm to the task. She tried out her latest attack on Richard Hare in a lecture course on 'Ethical Terms and Ethical Statements' in the summer of 1951, and in 1952 she published her first article, 'The Philosopher's Defence of Morality'. Her second, 'When is a Principle a Moral Principle?', followed shortly behind. Towards the end of 1953, Iris recorded a conversation: 'Talk with Philippa lately. Why rest moral philosophy on "choice"? Why call it a choice always – after all it is not like one. We learn from Witt here too: don't look for too deep a logic.'[171]

Iris, in her critique of Hare and Sartre, had pointed out that with the metaphysical background stripped away, the isolated subject can do nothing but choose. Philippa now saw that the loss of the background was also the loss of concepts that we rely on to orientate ourselves in ethical relations to others. In Trinity Term 1954, the two friends were back at Keble College, scene of their wartime tutorials with Donald MacKinnon, to explain this together to a class of graduates. Their old tutor, who had taught them of the danger that Freddie Ayer's weedkiller posed to metaphysical animals all those years ago, would have approved. They delivered the class with Basil Mitchell, last met sipping Cyprus sherry with the Metaphysicals. 'We spent a good deal of time on the study of "mixed words"', Basil later recalled.[172] Iris and Philippa explained to the class that 'good' and 'bad', 'right' and 'wrong' are *general* words. When a person uses them, we learn very little about their moral outlook, other than that they think well or badly of something. The meaning of these concepts is exhausted, as Mary Glover might have put it, by their condemnatory or commendatory content. This is why it was so easy for Ayer to turn them into 'Boo!' and 'Hooray' and for Hare to translate them into 'Don't do it!' and 'Do it!' But words like 'honest', 'sincere', 'patient', 'ostentatious', 'grateful', 'shameful', 'proud', 'humiliating': these are *specialised* words, with deep, ramifying structure that connects to the multi-patterned background of human life.[173] Iris had recently been diagnosed with partial deafness and was taking lip-reading lessons at the Radcliffe Infirmary;[174] her large eyes would have fixed intently on the moving lips of her interlocutors, Philippa, then Basil, now their students. 'Grateful', 'shameful', 'proud', 'humiliating'. A description of human goodness requires more intensity of focus – and attention – than 'Boo!' or 'Hooray!'

Back among the barbarians, Mary's typewriter had been beating out a continuous rhythm. Reviews for the *New Statesman*, mostly of new novels, flew from its hammers: *The Blessing* by Nancy Mitford; *Night Without Sleep* by Elick Moll; *No Music for Generals* by Frederick Howard.[175] In the early 1950s she was reading twelve novels every three weeks, Geoff's metal bookcases now subjected to defeat by the rising tide of books.[176] At night, when Tom was sleeping, she tried to concentrate.

Despite the distance, and the baby, Mary continued to visit Iris in Oxford, turning up at St Anne's for tea. On one such visit, towards the end of 1952, she found herself in a bookshop facing a sea of purple spines and a queue of undergraduates snatching them off the shelves.[177] Hare's *The Language of Morals*, the manifesto of Moral Prescriptivism had been published and was a great hit. Not to be judged by its 'remarkably low price' (7s 6d), Mr Hare's 'admirable little book' deserves to be pondered by all serious students of moral philosophy, wrote Richard Braithwaite in *Mind*.[178] The thought of a new generation of moral philosophers fed on Hare's moral subjectivism left Mary feeling 'thoroughly depressed'.[179] But she was on the hunt for another book that day, and of a quite different colour. Her father, pointing the way again, had recommended that she read the newly translated *King Solomon's Ring: New Light on Animal Ways*, by the Austrian ethologist Konrad Lorenz.

King Solomon's Ring was named after the biblical king who could converse with animals. It is crammed full of tales (and drawings) of the free-roaming animals that populated Lorenz's Viennese menagerie: jackdaws, greylag geese, ravens, cockatoos, lemurs and capuchin monkeys.[180] For Mary, the book was a revelation.

Before reading it, she had not noticed the way that the strange unrealistic concept of 'animal' grouped together creatures as different as fleas and gorillas, dogs and octopi, into one abstract collective, simply so that they could be contrasted with human. After reading Lorenz's book, 'animal' now seemed to Mary an absurd tool invented by our culture simply to protect a mistaken

idea of human dignity.[181] The idea that *we're not like the* <u>Beasts</u>. Yet ...
Humans, Mary realised, do belong in the class of animals, are among the
beasts of the earth; and snails are as distinct from snow leopards as humans
are from humpback whales. And with that flashing insight, the background
to Mary's thought shifted, her concepts rearranged themselves and thought
began to flow. By removing the opposition between animal and human,
Beast and Man, Mary began to see that she could start to dissolve the paradox at the heart of our self-understanding ('I know I am one of Nature's
little kings'). Our lives are animal lives that are in many ways continuous
with those of fleas, gorillas, cats and jackdaws. Even our sense of our own
dignity and importance does not distinguish us; each animal knows itself a
'little king' in its own domain, Mary thought. Later, she would write, 'the
bird's song is not just a mechanical advance indicator of the violence with
which intruders will actually be repelled.' Rather, 'The song must be primar-
ily expressive. What it says is, "Hurrah, hurrah, it's me, it's mine, I've got
it, I am the greatest"'.[182] A memory of the Scrutton family cats, rarely seen,
fixing her mother's dachshund with a look of feline superiority.[183] John
Clare's 'frail brother of the morn', horns extended.

Now parts of her life that had once seemed hopelessly separated (the
zoophilia of her childhood, her mid-dining-hall conversations with Charlotte Williams-Ellis in Somerville, her new role as a mother) fell into
sequence as part of a whole. She turned her ethological gaze on Tom, a
tiny living creature. 'Small children are so literally and unmistakably both
animals and human beings.'[184] And she began to rethink her past. Her
childhood cycle rides to Ruislip Reservoir where she and her brother Hugh
used to swim. Why hadn't she noticed the courtship displays of the great
crested grebe going on all the while as she was splashing among the geese,
the swans and the ducks?[185] And the singing dachshund, the cats, she and
Hugh and the whole Scrutton family? They were, she now saw, part of a
'mixed community',[186] a completely familiar inter-species collective, structured by social bonds of trust, friendship and care. Dogs and horses respond
to their name. During the war: *In memoriam* notices in *The Times*. Air Raid
Precautions for Animals.

And looking now at the differences between humans, Mary began to
wonder if two individuals of a single species might be as different as a
duckling from a little bull. Geoff's bursts of infectious exuberance hid a
depressive side. ('You see, I'm really a manic-depressive,' he had told her
early on); she, 'a bit of a Pollyanna'.[187] He, unable to publish any of his

numerous philosophical articles due to a combination of extreme perfectionism and a horror of criticism; she, turning out essay after essay and holding forth on the radio and television. In notes on David Garnett's 1922 novel *Lady into Fox* (which tells the tale of a lady who turns into a fox, and whose husband tries to care for her), she writes that the story moves us because 'people do entangle themselves with people who are divided from them by differences as deep as the difference of species'. They 'patch it up with grapes and blue bed-jackets and all the rituals of society'.[188] Or they spend a lifetime, as Iris had noticed, trying to see the other as they really are.

From then on, Mary raided Newcastle's city libraries, borrowing books and studies on every kind of animal: from aardvarks to zebras, ants, red deer, lemmings, baboons or whatever.[189] As she had learnt from her father: this is 'a perfectly sensible thing to do . . . if somebody mentioned hippopotamuses, you look them up, you see'.[190]

Philippa, too, was turning her thoughts to the world of plants and animals. Virtue and vice terms, she and Iris had told the class of graduates in Trinity 1954, are 'specialized descriptions' that connect with ideas of human good and harm. But though it is 'quite impossible to call anything you like good or harm',[191] it is not easy to see where the limits lie, or to get clear about the source of this impossibility. Friendship, warmth and health are good; isolation, homelessness and illness are harms; but then, some people prefer isolation, seek out the freedom of the road, find peace in suffering. Wittgenstein's life was filled with suffering, and yet it was good. Philippa's childhood had been one of privilege, and yet she had been harmed by it. Just as Elizabeth had found that it helped her to list humans with cats and turnips, Philippa found that thinking about good and harm for other kinds of living things helped to keep her thoughts about human good rooted in reality. Moral philosophers should start by thinking about plants, she once told a startled audience.[192]

For living things, Philippa began to insist in the 1950s, there is a standard of goodness and badness that is utterly independent of human choice or practices of evaluation. In his purple book, Richard Hare claimed that when the first cacti were imported into Britain, there were no standards of evaluation, no sense in which one cactus could be said to be good or bad, better or worse.[193] (The Second World War had put a temporary stop to cacti imports from America, cutting off supplies to a nascent community of British cactus-lovers. In 1947 imports had begun again, much to the delight of the newly established National Cactus and Succulent Society.)[194] With echoes of Sartre, Hare argued that it was only when people began choosing one cactus rather than another, or to introduce standards (height, colour, spikiness) that evaluative terms could begin to apply. This meant that whether one cactus was 'better' than another was based alone on human choice and preference. But, Philippa replied, a cactus is a living organism and as such its form of life sets an internal standard for the species.[195] The National Cactus and Succulent Society is free to impose its own evaluative framework for competitions and breeders, but it remains an objective matter, independent of their decisions, whether a particular cactus is healthy or unhealthy, flourishing or damaged. Nature is not brute and formless but alive and ordered, and a source of value that is quite independent of human activities. A person who knows enough about the cactus or passionflower or helianthemum will be able to see whether a specimen is flourishing, and to judge when it is harmed or helped. Annie Rogers of St Hugh's knew this when she chose a sheltered spot for her passionflowers and a shady one for her ferns.

Though more difficult to discern, there is likewise a standard internal to the species *human*, according to which a human life is going well or badly, Philippa argued. This is not the Protagorean idea that 'man is the measure' of all things. Far from each man, individually, being the measure of what is sweet or sour, warm or cool, good or bad, Philippa argued that there is such a thing as natural goodness. It is not open to us to decide what counts as human benefit or harm, or to simply choose, *ex nihilo*, what makes a good human life. Philippa knew this when she worried about her childhood. Leslie Kirkley and the volunteers at Oxfam knew this when

they sent money to Greece to support the education of young women.[196] Wittgenstein knew it when he judged his life to have been happy.

'[P]eople who bring home potted plants', Iris later wrote, 'might even be surprised at the notion that these things have anything to do with virtue.'[197]

Though 'The Philosopher's Defence of Morality' was Philippa's first published article, her first publication was a 1951 critical review of *The Philosophy of Ernst Cassirer*, a collected volume of essays by contemporary philosophers on the great Warburgian philosopher's work. '[R]eading these essays', she complained, 'I found that I could no longer recall the peculiar excellence of Cassirer's work, which immediately impressed me again when I returned to the original.'[198] Her final word in ethics, *Natural Goodness*, reveals hidden traces of Warburgian influence, woven into the fabric of her own philosophical thought. For Ernst Cassirer, each organism is surrounded by its own environment, its *Umwelt*. The world of the sea urchin is full of 'sea urchin things'. The world of the fly is full of 'fly things'. The world of the human is full of 'human things'. And among those human things is a symbolic system.[199]

What is thinkable is determined from the side of reality, as Elizabeth had said; but human reality is full of our creations. We build structures that create new ways of acting and seeing. We write histories that draw together threads of testimony and narrative to lay down new patterns. We create symbolic objects, *entia rationis*, to help us find our way: poems, words, maps, stories. And a cultural artefact like a poem or a painting or a concerto – a 'public object which we can all handle' – is as much a part of our *Umwelt* as is a turnip or a cat. (One evening at 27 St John Street, Elizabeth had played Schumann on the gramophone for Iris. 'We sat very still. The cat climbed first on her knee then on mine. Twice our eyes met. E was utterly rapt, beautiful, severe and strong with concentration. She said later: it is a kind of vice, to want to hear certain particular things again and again and again.')[200]

Little fragments from literature light up the pages of Philippa Foot's *Natural Goodness*. George Eliot, Gertrude Stein, Montaigne, Hardy, Dostoevsky, Conrad. Printed at the bottoms of the opening pages are three images of Syracusan or Carthaginian coins, one picturing a plant, one an animal and one a human. ('Hang on to man as symbol-maker', Iris had written in 1947, 'The clue is somewhere here'.)[201]

Reflecting on the task that philosophy faces, Wittgenstein wrote: 'What we are supplying are really remarks on the natural history of human beings.'[202] A Natural History of Human Beings will include facts about human nature, of the kind that would be found in a natural history of cacti or cats. *The cactus needs warm weather to survive. A kitten is born with closed eyes. The human adult has thirty-two teeth.* But we humans are metaphysical animals. We dwell in the past as well as the present. 'You should be ashamed', 'We are very proud of you', 'What you did was brave', 'You must say sorry'. Specialised descriptions – 'humiliating', 'courageous', 'disrespectful' – orientate us towards the world and to each other. We make promises and imagine our futures. It is part of our nature to question. By asking 'Why?' the child begins to draw connections – to trace the larger patterns that transcend the region of space and time in which he is situated; to relate cause and effect, purpose and goal. He can come to see the same event here and now as falling under different descriptions. He can view it against a wider background. A square of paper goes into a box in London: *I am sending a letter*; a fur coat is folded: *I am contributing to an aid programme;* a handle goes up and down: *I am poisoning the inhabitants*.

The adults help the child by naming kinds of things, each name enfolding the structure, the patterns of the practice, within which the name has its place. Names of objects: this is a peacock, man, flea; this is food, this is clothing; this is a friend, this a parent. Names of kinds of action: this is pumping; this is sitting; this is writing; this is paying. Names of virtues: doing this is generous; that action is brave; this response is truthful.[203] Poems, maps, stories reflect these words and actions and how they fit, and do not fit, together in a vast and changeable world. How they might fit. Almost miraculously, a human child must 'catch on' to the meaning of these descriptions and come to see his own actions and the actions of those around him under them. But the child must 'do more than he gets in the teacher's examples'. He must see how to go on, how to continue the pattern himself, one foot in front of the other.

Richard Hare began to be irritated. 'We are lucky', he would soon complain, 'to have in Oxford, in the women's colleges, a number of able and distinguished philosophers; and most of them spend quite a lot of their time attacking the views of their male colleagues.' He felt himself victimised: '[T]hey all, when I am the target, accuse me of paying too <u>much</u> attention to general principles and too <u>little</u> to the peculiarities of individual cases – which require to be savoured with a feminine intuition before a right moral judgment can be passed upon them.'[204] But the 'able and distinguished philosophers' of the women's colleges kept insisting: Not a matter of female intuition, but perhaps a reassertion of a kind of Realist intuitionism, now brought to life by a kind of Idealist metaphysics.

Each Saturday at noon, throughout January and February 1955, Philippa Foot was to be seen entering Examination Schools. Philosophy students faced a difficult choice those Saturday lunchtimes. There were two simultaneous lectures on Plato to pick from; or skip them both to attend a seminar on Aquinas in Oriel with Lorenzo Minio-Paluello. Or, instead, head to Christ Church to hear Michael Foster of the Metaphysicals (now at work on his book *Mystery and Philosophy*) attacking 'The Philosophy of Analysis'.

Those who picked Philippa's 'Introduction to Ethics' joined her at what felt to her like her own beginning. She was finally seeing what work there was for a moral philosopher to do. In 'The Philosopher's Defence of Morality', published in 1952, she had gently mocked those philosophers who thought that their task was to 'provide a defence against hostile theories which are said to be "undermining the foundations of morality"' – that is, the moral subjectivism of A. J. Ayer and Richard Hare.[205] 'It would be ridiculous,' she had written, somewhat in the mode of H. A. Prichard, 'to suppose that the philosopher can produce a charm against the mood of indifference in which someone asks why he should care about what is right and wrong.'[206] By 1955, she had begun to see that moral philosophy had a different role than giving a theory in defence of morality. 'Morality has a transcendent reference', Mary Glover had written on the cusp of the war. It is connected to 'an objective standard that may be progressively discovered by us'. The moral philosopher's task, Philippa may well have told her students in that lecture, is to bring our moral language back to life. After the lecture she stepped out on to High Street and turned left, heading to 17 Broad Street and Oxfam.

As Philippa was completing her series of lectures on ethics, Iris (in her new top-floor flat at 25 Beaumont Street) was completing the second draft[207] of a 'nameless novel' (it will 'probably be recognisable as mine on points of style', she later told her publisher, 'in case I forgot to write my name on it').[208] The novel was *The Flight From the Enchanter*, a dark and mesmeric fantasy whose characters are displaced, enslaved (and enslaving), blinded by their own inattention to the reality of others. Small fragments of Iris's biography had taken on new shades on the page: UNRRA, Simone Weil, Franz, his childhood friend Elias Canetti, the lover-enchanter that she had turned to after Franz's death. That term on Mondays at 10 a.m., she lectured in Schools on 'Moral Philosophy and the Ethics of Liberalism'. Philippa's spindly handwriting on the blackboard, left over from her Saturday lecture, perhaps attracted her duster. 'R.M. Hare', 'prescriptivism', 'choice', 'duty'. Iris had a new thought to add. 'Man is a creature who makes pictures of himself and then comes to resemble the picture' (these words appearing in print the following year). 'This is the process which moral philosophy must attempt to describe and analyse.'[209]

Mary's Tom had just turned three, and had been joined by a younger brother, David. A copy of Iris's first novel, *Under the Net*, had made its way northwards to Newcastle and Mary enjoyed it enormously. Like Philippa, she was delighted to discover just how witty a writer Iris was[210] and she laughed as the narrator, Jake, kept 'looking for the person who he thinks will solve his problems when he really needs to deal with them himself'.[211] It was perhaps in light of Jake's hopeless failure to take control of his future that she formed a new, tentative image of herself as novelist: 'If Iris can do it, why not?' She started work on a sci-fi novel, *Wintersault*, her own natural history of human beings. Narrated by a future historian, it is a study of human life in the 1950s, 'before the human race began to hibernate'.[212] The cold dark days of the war and the frozen pipes and inadequate heating of her Oxford bedsit receding into the past, she asked: what sort of animal would a human be, if it hibernated instead of facing the winter months head-on? How does our species's universal exposure to winter – to cold, hunger and illness – affect our habits, sensibility and character? What would human life be like if it took place only in the gentle warmth of a spring and summer in Oxford?

On 7 February, a temperature of 57°F was recorded in some parts of the Midlands. The window of the first-floor study in 27 St John Street may have been slightly ajar, glimmers of light bouncing off microfilm copies of Wittgenstein's notebooks from the First World War. Tibbles the cat stalking among the *Nachlass*. Elizabeth had been sifting through them to bring some light to certain passages in the *Tractatus*.[213] By now, her translation of Wittgenstein's *Remarks on the Foundations of Mathematics* was well under way. '*How do I know* that in working out the series +2 I must write "20004, 20006" and not "20004, 20008"? '*Wie weiß ich . . . ?*'[214]

As Elizabeth's pen moved across the page ('How do I know . . .'), half a mile from St John Street, in a long room at the Clarendon Building in Broad Street, twenty-two members of Oxford's Hebdomadal Council were voting on the proposal made by the Vice Chancellor, Alic Halford Smith, to award Harry S. Truman an honorary degree. No other room is 'so infused with solemn experience', it has been said.[215] Portraits of their august predecessors looked down as they queued up one by one to conclude the business: beside the window, an ancient voting contraption allowed members to deposit their secret tokens – right for no, left for yes.[216] They counted the tokens: 'Practically unanimous', recorded the minute-taker, '21 out of a possible 22 votes'.[217] Drawing the meeting to a close, and striding across the gravel to the Bodleian, Alic Halford Smith would have felt confident that the ancient machinery of process and custom would take care of what happened next.

Mr Truman's Degree, Again

OXFORD

MAY 1956

Someone observing the front door of 27 St John Street in early June 1956 might have suspected its occupants of being up to no good. A steady stream of visitors appeared, on foot, by bicycle, and occasionally by car. Some walked confidently up to the door and gave a firm knock, then turned the handle and pushed it open – they had clearly visited before and knew the door would be unlocked. Others were less sure, peering at the brass numerals before knocking and waiting for a rather disordered-looking woman holding a baby to open the door, the faces of one, two, three, four grubby children, toddler to teen, peering out behind her. Students came, mothers with pushchairs, dons, nuns, elderly spinsters. Scruffy-looking chaps, and women in smart suits. Anarchists, Communists, Catholics. On the doorstep a transaction: one shilling and the visitor is handed a thin envelope. Often a few words exchanged, a shake of hands. Tibbles the cat slinks out between legs. In the envelopes were copies of Elizabeth Anscombe's short, self-published pamphlet, *Mr Truman's Degree*. Inside its front cover: 'Dedicated with respect, but without permission, to the others who said "*Non placet*".'[1] As in 1939, when she and Daniel Norman had protested about the injustice of the war, she still believed that 'being a Catholic is in a sense as much a worldly, social, political affair as it is a supernatural one'.[2]

She had perhaps been encouraged to put pen to paper by the letters that began appearing on her doorstep almost as soon as she had returned from Convocation on 1 May to change out of her skirt and back into her usual trousers. 'Bravo!' came a hand-delivered note from Philippa's neighbour (the Bloomsbury potter Phyllis Keyes) at 14 Park Town: '[A]nybody who "dares to be a Daniel and dares to stand alone" on principle in our highly organised society which rewards only those who kow-tow from expediency – deserves congratulations for their moral courage. So I just felt moved to give you a pat on the back.'[3] A missive from the Women's International League for Peace and Freedom arrived the next day, inviting her to give a talk.[4] Not all contained praise: 'As an ex-P.O.W. of the "delightful" Japanese, I know possibly more about their nature than you do, and I find it galling, to say the least of it, that you consider of no account your own Country-men.'[5] 'Crank'.[6]

In her pigeonhole at Somerville was a handwritten note from Vera Farnell and a letter from Donald MacKinnon. 'Though I agreed with the point of view put forward by the Censor [Alan Bullock] this afternoon I would like to say how much I admire the dignity with which you made your protest,' wrote the woman who had warned Iris and Mary, all those years ago: 'you have to be careful how you behave'.[7] Donald MacKinnon: 'I . . . would like to write to express to you my sincere admiration for your courage and integrity in acting as you did.'[8]

After a day or two more, the postmarks became more exotic. Her protest had been reported in newspapers around the world. Several letters from the USA. 'You had the courage to tell the truth about Mr. Truman,' wrote 'An American Woman'.[9] 'How right you are,' said another.[10] A writer from Taipei expressed his deepest admiration: 'Sorry that you failed, but a lone fighter against human stupidity and hypocrisy cannot expect anything else.'[11] Jessie Street, the Australian women's rights campaigner, wrote to congratulate her on her courage. She enclosed a set of witness accounts she had gathered in Japan in 1954.

[A] single plane was sighted heading for Hiroshima. The population flocked into the street watching the plane. The man who was telling me the story said that he was out in the street and was following the plane, holding his hand up shading his eyes from the sun. Suddenly a shining object dropped, the plane made a right angle turn and flew off. He was still watching the plane wondering whether the shining object contained a message of peace. Suddenly he was struck by a blast of tremendous heat. He only had trousers on, and his body and face and arms rose into great blisters from the heat. While he was looking at these burns, a fierce blast of wind came and blew the skin that had been blistered into ribbons . . . The people were running around screaming in terror. Children could not recognise their parents and parents could not recognise their children.[12]

It was important that the pamphlet be published before 20 June, when Encaenia (the ceremony at which the degree would be awarded) would take place. Elizabeth wanted to reissue, in print, the plea she had made at

Convocation and to point out that it was not too late for others to take a stand: 'It is possible still to withdraw from this shameful business in some slight degree', she typed. It is 'possible not to go to Encaenia; if it should be embarrassing to someone who would normally go to plead other business, he could take to his bed. I, indeed, should fear to go, in case God's patience suddenly ends.'[13]

Though she was crystal clear about her own position, she was, as she settled down to write, still puzzled about precisely what had happened at Convocation that day. Alan Bullock's defence was so woeful, it 'would not have been well received at Nuremberg', she thought. He had to pretend that 'a couple of massacres to a man's credit are not exactly a reason for not showing him honour'. But such a thing was absurd. She perhaps read over Jessie Street's interviews again: the innocent were killed, and 'a very large number of them, all at once, without warning, without the interstices of escape or the chance to take shelter', she would write.[14] It baffled her that in the face of such a fact 'so many Oxford people should be willing to flatter such a man'. She looked 'round to see if any explanation is available why'.[15]

Through her enquiries, conducted by allies in the men's colleges, she discovered that many had turned up determined to oppose her even before hearing her argument. That parties had been 'whipped up to vote for the honour'. She uncovered fears that '[t]he women are up to something', and discovered that at High Table at Worcester, All Souls and New College 'consciences were greatly exercised, [until] a reason was found to satisfy them: "*It would be wrong to try to PUNISH Mr Truman!*"' Such a reason made no sense though. It is no punishment *not* to be honoured. She considered again Bullock's speech: A great many people were involved in the responsibility of the manufacture of the bomb, and we cannot select one man as being solely responsible, even if his was the signature at the foot of the order for the bomb to be dropped.[16] But *his signature was on the order*, she perhaps thought, picturing again the shining object falling through the sky above Hiroshima, children shielding their eyes against the sun, hoping for a message of peace. Then gradually the pieces began to fall into place.

'I get some small light on the subject', she writes in her pamphlet, 'when I consider the productions of Oxford moral philosophy since the First World War.' Since, that is, the ascendancy of the Realists, Prichard and Ross, over the Idealists who went before them. This time she needs no permission from the archbishop: she is not writing as a Catholic but as herself: Miss

Elizabeth Anscombe, Philosopher. 'Up to the Second World War', she writes, 'the prevailing moral philosophy in Oxford taught that an action can be "morally good" no matter how objectionable the thing done may be.' The Realists had claimed 'that "rightness" is an objective character in acts, that can be discerned by a moral sense' and that 'it might be right to kill the innocent for the good of the people'[17] – one's duty not to kill the innocent might be overridden by one's duty to save lives. They had cut duty off from the virtue.

After the war, she continues, she finds in place of this philosophy one 'whose cardinal principle is that "good" is not a "descriptive" term'.[18] Here she has Ayer and Hare in her sights. Once value is separated from fact, a man must simply choose his principles, live by them, as best he can. For such a philosophy, moral laws like 'Do not murder' can only be personal principles dressed up to look like Kant's laws. This philosophy, she said, is 'perfectly in the spirit of the time and might be called the philosophy of the flattery of that spirit'. When she repeated these claims about Oxford moral philosophy on BBC radio a few months later, a flurry of letters followed: 'tortuous sarcasm', 'bitter sneers', 'an affront to professional standards and to the decencies of controversy'.[19] Private letters to Hare were less circumspect: 'poisonous muck', 'hellfire obscurantism'; '[a]s an attack on e.g. your views, the thing is such a farce that it is difficult to know where to begin'.[20]

But Elizabeth, Iris, Philippa and Mary had looked at past debates about duty and principle, and begun to piece together the background metaphysics that was needed to see things clearly. They had set to work on an account of human life, action and perception, that could reconnect morality with what really matters.

We apply descriptions of actions, and virtue terms, at a time and place. We teach these descriptions, and their application, on the basis of *demonstrable examples*. 'He is posting a letter', 'he is operating a pump', 'that is kind', 'she is brave', 'this is humiliating'. A child who is given these demonstrations must do more than she gets in the examples. She must see how to go on. Growing up is coming to act and see under the descriptions that our language contains, and that our world and our shared forms of life make possible. This is what it is to know your way about in the world. Reality, human life, imposes limits on which descriptions can intelligibly and truly apply, but when the world changes quickly or violently, the application of descriptions can stop being a matter of course. Possibilities for acting well and badly can shift and subvert in surprising ways as new possibilities for action open up and old ones close down. In the Oxford transformed by the war, it was possible to go to the cinema to seek refuge. To set off to the library with the intention of giving blood. To aid starving people in Greece by taking a fur coat to a shop on Broad Street. Or to have your neighbour imprisoned by complaining to the authorities about her curtains. In a disintegrating or changing world, it is easy to lose sight of what really matters for human life going well, and of which kinds of harms are of serious importance.

Harry S. Truman acted in a reality that transcended him. His 'bit of living', an order written on a piece of paper, took place in a world of natural facts, human institutions, conventions and technology. A world of presidents, peace treaties, declarations of surrender. His background was the vast machinery of war: of code names and committees, reactors, laboratories; of modified B-29 aircraft, of ships loaded with uranium criss-crossing the ocean. Harry S. Truman, it is true, did not build these structures himself. He did not set up the institutions within which he acted. He did not develop the technology. But as the President of the United States he was located within this pattern in a unique way: and he knew that. The description 'ordering the bomb' applied to Harry Truman's movement only because of the circumstances in which he acted. These included new structures that made possible actions at a grand scale.

Harry S. Truman moved his hand across the page because he was signing his name (A). By signing his name, he was ordering the dropping of the atomic bomb (B). He was ordering the dropping of the bomb *in order to* secure unconditional Japanese surrender (D). Killing the people of Hiroshima was the means to that end (C). It was essential to the achievement of that end that the people die on such a scale: without it the unconditional surrender would certainly not come. That end, a worldly event, was one that Harry S. Truman, as President of the United States, was uniquely able to bring about by moving his hand across the page, signing his name, giving the order. It is true that without the scientists who had enriched the uranium, the engineers who had modified the aircraft that dropped the bomb or the pilots who flew the planes, his action would not have been possible. It is true that without the conventions of government that create the office of President he, Harry S. Truman, would not have been able to determine the end.

But those were the facts. Those were the circumstances in which he acted. Harry S. Truman did not act blindly, unwittingly setting off chains of events he did not intend. He was not in the position of the almost 200,000 people involved in the production of the atomic bomb who did not know what they were doing. No. Truman acted in a world he could see. He knew that 'the most ferocious methods of warfare' would be needed to secure unconditional surrender: yet he chose that end. He knew that if he signed his name then some time later, far away in Hiroshima, a shining object would fall from the sky. 'We are in possession of the most destructive explosive ever devised by man. A single one of our newly developed atomic bombs is actually the equivalent in explosive power to what 2000 of our giant B-29s can carry on a single mission. This awful fact is one for you to ponder and we solemnly assure you it is grimly accurate,' read the leaflets dropped by American pilots into Japanese cities. A 'rain of ruin' was how Truman glossed it to the American public. Truman knew that the targets could not be purely military. 'It occurred to me that a quarter of a million of the flower of our young manhood were worth a couple of Japanese cities,' he remarked later.[21]

'When I say that to choose to kill the innocent as a means to one's ends is murder, I am saying what would generally be accepted as correct,' wrote Elizabeth. We may wonder what 'innocent' means, but a definition here is not necessary; 'with Hiroshima and Nagasaki we are not confronted with a borderline case. In the bombing of these cities, it was certainly decided to kill the innocent as a means to an end.'[22]

The background against which placing one's name at the foot of an order *is* committing mass murder is of such scale and complexity that it was no wonder that the dons, and even Truman himself, could not see those two events in a single frame. The human scale (folded jumpers, knitting, free dinners, Picture of the Month) was entirely absent. The dons, who looked for wickedness stamped on Truman, could not see it there. Instead, they saw a man who had found himself with a difficult decision to make, and had done what he thought duty required, had applied his moral principles as best he could. But, as Mary Midgley would write, wickedness is not a character trait, like courage or aggression; it means 'intentionally doing acts that are wrong'.[23] The background to our lives can, if it is badly arranged, make wicked acts very easy for quite ordinary and friendly people. Indeed, it can make it so easy that nobody, including the person who is doing it, even notices. Given the right circumstances 'a quite mediocre person can do spectacularly wicked things'.[24]

'We had thought something like this could not happen,' said Philippa Foot on returning to Oxford after the war when the news of the concentration camps hit.

'Protests by people who have not power are a waste of time', Elizabeth had told the assembled chamber on 1 May 1956. She was not there, she had said, to make a 'gesture of protest' against atomic bombs. Rather, she had told Convocation: 'I vehemently object to *our* action in offering Mr Truman honours.'[25]

This man, Mr Truman, is famous for one act. Folded into the character of his name is the act for which he is known everywhere. To pick out this man as a symbol of what is honourable is to pick out *that action* as good and just, as brave – to put it in the archive as a clue as to how to go on. To bring us to see *such actions* under *the descriptions* 'brave' and 'just' is to lose our grip on the meaning of these concepts. To honour President Truman – 'a man . . . known everywhere for an action'[26] so terrible – is to risk losing sight of what seriously matters to our lives going well or badly.

Donald MacKinnon had told Philippa that Plato wrote 'under the guiding impetus of a conviction that in the life and death of Socrates there was to be found a concretion . . . of the way in which things ultimately are'.[27] The actions of one individual can bring reality into focus, light it up, show us new ways to go on.

Afterwards

Elizabeth, Iris, Mary and Philippa began their philosophical lives together soon after Freddie Ayer had declared metaphysics extinct. His brand of 'weedkiller' seemed to have reduced living human animals to efficient calculating machines. 'I don't understand!' had ceased to be a request for help, an appeal to another metaphysical animal for assistance to see things more clearly. Instead, it had become a tool to limit speech, crush creativity and silence speculation. We followed these four friends in dining halls and living rooms, tea shops and pubs, and by letter, as they painstakingly began to replant ethics in its proper soil, all the time growing and maturing, and trying to see for themselves what is of serious importance in human life. This task was made all the more urgent by the darkness of the reality that surrounded them: war, murder, displacement, trauma, suffering.

By telling this story about the past, we have tried to set down a pattern that suggests different threads to pick up and weave into the familiar story of twentieth-century philosophy, different questions and different ways of thinking about what philosophy is. For all four friends, what mattered most was to bring philosophy back to life. Back to the context of the messy, everyday reality of human life lived with others. Back to the deep connection that ancient philosophers saw between Human Life, Goodness and Form. Back to the fact that we are living creatures, animals, whose nature shapes our ways of going on.

Each of the four women found different ways to balance our animality with the fact that we are language-using, question-asking, picture-making creatures. As *metaphysical animals*, our inventions, symbols and artworks change our *Umwelt* and, to some degree, our very nature. The task of answering the question 'What kind of animal is a human?' is, as such, one of 'appalling difficulty'. And the fact that the answers that we give themselves then come to belong to our reality is a guarantee that no answer can ever be final. In philosophy, it is perpetually true that '[o]ne must start from scratch'.[1]

'I think I've got onto a fruitful line in moral philosophy,' Philippa Foot told Janet Vaughan in 1957.[2] She had. Between 1952 and 1961 she published 'The Philosopher's Defence of Morality',[3] 'When is a Principle a Moral Principle?',[4] 'Free Will Involving Determinism',[5] 'Moral Beliefs',[6] 'Moral Arguments',[7] 'Goodness and Choice'.[8] Her early discussions with Elizabeth by the Somerville fireside remained crucial to her philosophy; in 2000 she would write: 'I remember, as long ago as the late 1940s confidently referring to "the difference between descriptive and evaluative reasoning" in one of the many discussions that we began to have from that time on. [Elizabeth], genuinely puzzled, simply asked, "What do you mean?".'[9] Elizabeth's puzzlement was, she said, the beginning of her forty-year struggle to understand the connection between good reasoning and goodness.

In 1959, Michael ended his and Philippa's marriage ('I remained passionately interested in having children; she turned out not to be able to have any. Feeling a fearsome cad, I walked out on her').[10] She remained at Somerville until 1969, when she resigned her fellowship in order to split her time between Oxford and the USA, where she had numerous visiting professorships, most significantly at UCLA. While in America, the focus of her attention shifted from the metaphysics of morals to applied ethics, where she disagreed in print with Elizabeth over abortion and her name became associated with the famous 'Trolley Problem': would you willingly sacrifice one to save five? By the time she retired from teaching (in 1991), she had returned to her metaphysical quarrel with moral subjectivism. Her masterpiece *Natural Goodness*, written towards the end of her life, sets out in elegant detail a moral vision the seeds of which were first planted in the 1940s: an account of natural goodness and virtue that begins from thinking about plants. 'Everything is done for the first time in this different world that is without her,' reads Philippa's journal entry after Elizabeth's death in 2001.[11] 'I learnt everything from her.'[12] In parallel to her philosophical work, Philippa continued at Oxfam, eventually becoming a Trustee. 'I do think I've had a very happy life, certainly Oxfam has been one of the continuous threads.'[13] Foot is considered today to be one of the most significant analytic moral philosophers of the twentieth century.

*

Elizabeth Anscombe, who published always as 'G.E.M. Anscombe', is credited, alongside Philippa Foot, with the revival of Aristotelian virtue ethics in the twentieth century. Her 'Modern Moral Philosophy', in which she argues that moral philosophy 'should be laid aside at any rate until we have an adequate philosophy of psychology', is one of the most widely read and cited papers in ethics today.[14] Her paper 'The First Person' has changed the way in which philosophers think about self-consciousness.[15] Elizabeth remained at Somerville until 1970 when she took Wittgenstein's former Chair at Cambridge University. She and Peter had seven children. It is thanks to her translation that Wittgenstein's *Philosophical Investigations* is recognised as a literary, as well as a philosophical, masterpiece. Her collected papers are published in three volumes: *From Parmenides to Wittgenstein; Metaphysics and the Philosophy of Mind; Ethics, Religion and Politics*.[16] Her monograph *Intention* invented philosophy of action in its current form: many agree that *Intention* is 'the most important treatment of action since Aristotle'.[17]

When her students at St Anne's learnt that 'the brilliant philosopher Iris Murdoch' was '"trying to" write a novel', they thought it amusing.[18] In the 1950s she was considered one of Britain's most promising philosophers. That decade she published many important essays: 'The Novelist as Metaphysician', 'The Existentialist Hero', 'Thinking and Language', 'The Existentialist Political Myth', 'Nostalgia for the Particular', 'Vision and Choice in Morality', 'Metaphysics and Ethics', 'A House of Theory', 'The Sublime and the Good' and 'The Sublime and the Beautiful Revisited'. In 1963 she left her philosophy lectureship, moving from Oxford to the Royal College of Arts. But she did not leave philosophy. Alongside her twenty-six novels, she published three more philosophy books: *The Sovereignty of Good, The Fire and the Sun: Why Plato Banished the Artists*[19] and *Metaphysics as a Guide to Morals*. The last is dedicated to Elizabeth Anscombe. In August 1956, she married John Bayley, a tutor in English at St Antony's College. She wore a bright-blue silk dress and a mackintosh. This was not to be a conventional marriage, and having made herself a permanent home she would continue to live many lives, with many people. In 1968, she and Pip had a brief affair.[20] It is through Iris Murdoch's quest to place the concrete historical individual – and real life – at the heart of moral philosophy that the concepts of attention, love and moral psychology have re-entered analytic moral philosophy.

*

Mary Midgley stayed in Newcastle upon Tyne. In 1964 she began part-time work at the University, increasing to full-time when the last of her children left home.[21] At the University, she and Geoff created a philosophy department of rare brilliance, in which students and teachers mixed and shared ideas and lives. They kept open house, dispensing 'tea, homemade beer and good whisky' along with 'robust discussion',[22] their three boys growing up within this mixed community. When Mary Midgley published her first book, *Beast and Man*, at the age of fifty-nine, Iris Murdoch's words appeared on the back cover: 'This is a very important book.'[23] After that, eighteen more books followed. Her work is the kernel from which much of contemporary animal and environmental ethics grows. 'We are not just rather like animals; we *are* animals,' she insisted, and her work flowed from this.[24] She was never afraid to call 'Humbug!' when someone was saying something foolish or shallow.[25]

In the 1980s, as one philosophy department after another was closed under a Conservative government led by former Somervillian Margaret Thatcher, Mary led a campaign to rescue hers. Though unsuccessful, she never gave up in her mission to defend philosophy. Philosophy is not a luxury, Mary insisted. Philosophy is something we humans need in order for our lives to go well. She argued trenchantly against the mythical idea that we can entrust our future to technology and artificial intelligence. This is a comforting sedative, but when it comes to figuring out what to do next – about climate, war, environment or education – it is ultimately suicidal. She ends her final book, *What is Philosophy For?*, with a warning and an imperative:

> [W]hat actually happens to us will surely still be determined by human choices. Not even the most admirable machines can make better choices than the people who are supposed to be programming them. So we had surely better rely here on using our own Minds rather than wait for Matter to do the job.
>
> And, if this is right, I suspect that . . . philosophical reasoning – will now become rather important. We shall need to think about *how* best to think about these new and difficult topics – how to imagine them, how to visualize them, how to fit them into a convincing world-picture. And if we don't do that for ourselves, it's hard to see who will be able to do it for us.[26]

Elizabeth Anscombe
(1919–2001)

Philippa Foot (1920–2010)
Iris Murdoch (1919–1999)

Mary Midgley (1919–2018)

Notes

Abbreviations

Works frequently cited

AC: Sally Crawford et al. (eds), *Ark of Civilization: Refugee Scholars and Oxford University, 1930–1945*
EM: Iris Murdoch, *Existentialists and Mystics*
ERP: G.E.M. Anscombe, *Ethics, Religion and Politics*
FPW: G.E.M. Anscombe, *From Parmenides to Wittgenstein*
HUOVIII: Brian Harrison, *The History of the University of Oxford Volume VIII: The Twentieth Century*
IMAL: Peter Conradi, *Iris Murdoch: A Life*
IMJ: 'Iris Murdoch Journal' (IMJ1, IMJ3, IMJ4, IMJ5, IMJ6, IMJ7)
LP: Avril Horner and Anne Rowe (eds), *Living on Paper*
MPM: G.E.M. Anscombe, *Metaphysics and the Philosophy of Mind*
ODNB: *Oxford Dictionary of National Biography*
OM: Mary Midgley, *The Owl of Minerva: A Memoir*
PI: Ludwig Wittgenstein, *Philosophical Investigations*
SW: Paula Adams, *Somerville for Women*
WW: Peter Conradi, *Writer at War*

Archives frequently cited

CIAA: Collegium Institute Anscombe Archive, Philadelphia
IMC: Iris Murdoch Collections, Kingston School of Art, Kingston University, London
MGMP: Mary and Geoff Midgley Papers, Durham University Library Special Collections, Durham

Notes

NCA: Newnham College Archive, Newnham College, Cambridge University
PCA: The Peter Conradi Archive, Kingston School of Art, Kingston University, London
RKA: Raymond Klibansky Archive, Deutsches Literatur Archiv, Marbach
SCA: Somerville College Archive, Somerville College, University of Oxford
SHCA: St Hugh's College Archive, St Hugh's College, University of Oxford

PREFACE
1 Mary Midgley, 'Rings & Books' (1950s), p. 1, Mary and Geoff Midgley Papers, Durham University Library Special Collections, Durham [MGMP], MID/C/3.
2 Mary Midgley, The Owl of Minerva: A Memoir (London: Routledge, 2005) [OM], p. 181.
3 Ibid., p. 83.
4 Iris Murdoch, Sartre: Romantic Rationalist (Glasgow: Fontana Collins, 1976), introduction.
5 Donald M. MacKinnon, 'And the Son of Man that Thou Visitest Him', Christendom 8, September 1938 (part 1), pp. 186–92 and December 1938 (part 2), pp. 262–72, at part 2, p. 264.
6 Mary Midgley, 'The Golden Age of Female Philosophy', Guardian, 28 November 2013.
7 Ved Mehta, Fly and the Fly-Bottle: Encounters with British Intellectuals (New York: Columbia University Press, 1962), p. 56.
8 Midgley, 'The Golden Age of Female Philosophy'.
9 Midgley, OM, pp. 104–5.
10 Iris Murdoch, The Sovereignty of Good (London: Routledge & Kegan Paul, 1970), p. 80.
11 Mary Midgley, What is Philosophy For? (London: Bloomsbury Academic, 2018), pp. 207–8.
12 G.E.M. Anscombe, 'Cover letter for application for a Sarah Smithson Studentship', 30 April 1944, pp. 1–2, NCA, AC/5/2. © M. C. Gormally.

PROLOGUE: MR TRUMAN'S DEGREE
1 L. H. Dudley Buxton, Oxford University Ceremonies (Oxford: Clarendon Press, 1935), p. 57.
2 G.E.M. Anscombe, Mr Truman's Degree (Oxford: 1956), p. 65.
3 Buxton, Oxford University Ceremonies, p. 33.
4 Anscombe, Mr Truman's Degree, p. 65.
5 'Report of the Committee on Honorary Degrees', 7 and 11 February 1955, Central Administrative Correspondence file for the Committee on Honorary Degrees, Oxford University Archives, UR 6/HD/7, file 3.
6 Anscombe, Mr Truman's Degree, p. 65.
7 P. Adams, Somerville for Women: An Oxford College, 1879–1993 (Oxford: Oxford University Press, 1996) [SW], p. 233.
8 Anscombe, Mr Truman's Degree, pp. 65–6.
9 Ibid., p. 65.
10 J. C. Masterman, On the Chariot Wheel: An Autobiography (Oxford: Oxford University Press, 1975), p. 304.

11 'Report of the Committee on Honorary Degrees', 7 and 11 February 1955; J. Glover, *Humanity: A Moral History of the Twentieth Century* (New Haven: Yale University Press, 2001), pp. 106–7.

12 Mary Geach, 'Introduction' in G.E.M. Anscombe, Mary Geach and Luke Gormally (eds), *Human Life, Action, and Ethics* (Exeter: Imprint Academic, 2005), p. xiv.

13 Masterman, *On the Chariot Wheel*, p. 304.

14 B. Mitchell, *Looking Back: On Faith, Philosophy and Friends in Oxford* (Durham: Memoir Club, 2009), p. 230.

15 Anscombe, *Mr Truman's Degree*, p. 64 (all words spoken by Anscombe are quotes from this pamphlet. Where necessary we have changed tenses).

16 Ibid., pp. 64–5.

17 'Solitary Opponent of Mr Truman's honorary degree', *Manchester Guardian*, 2 May 1956, p. 3.

18 Masterman, *On the Chariot Wheel*, p. 304.

19 Ibid., p. 304.

20 Anscombe, *Mr Truman's Degree*, p. 70.

21 A. L. F. Beeston, letter in the *Oxford Magazine* (Michaelmas Term, 1995), quoted in Glover, *Humanity*, p. 107.

22 J. Glover, *Humanity*, p. 106.

23 As reported in Anscombe, *Mr Truman's Degree*, p. 66.

24 A. Bullock, *Hitler: A Study in Tyranny* (London: Odhams Press, 1952).

25 Anscombe, *Mr Truman's Degree*, p. 66.

26 Ibid., p. 66.

27 Masterman, *On the Chariot Wheel*, p. 304.

28 Anscombe, *Mr Truman's Degree*, p. 64.

29 Masterman, *On the Chariot Wheel*, p. 304.

30 Jenny Teichman, 'Gertrude Elizabeth Margaret Anscombe 1919–2001', *Proceedings of the British Academy* 115 (2002), p. 49.

31 'Solitary Opponent of Mr Truman's Honorary Degree', *Manchester Guardian*, 2 May 1956, p. 3.

32 M.R.D Foot, 'Degree for Mr Truman', *Manchester Guardian*, 7 May 1956, p. 6.

33 'Oxford Don Fights Honor For Truman', *New York Times*, 19 June 1956, p. 3.

34 David McCullough, *Truman* (New York: Simon & Schuster, 1992), p. 415.

35 'Gaudy Menu 1956', Christ Church Archive, University of Oxford, sxxiv.c.1/5. College Archive, 'Gaudy Menu 1956'.

36 Ibid. Segonzac Fine Champagne 1924 is a cognac, not a champagne.

37 McCullough, *Truman*, p. 957.

38 Michael Dummett, 'Address for the Somerville Philippa Foot Memorial', Somerville College Archives, University of Oxford [SCA], SC/AO/AA/FW/Foot, p. 3.

39 'Letter from Philippa Foot to Janet Vaughan', 3 November 1957, SCA, SC/AO/AA/FW/Anscombe.

40 McCullough, *Truman*, p. 348.

41 Richard Doll, 'Vaughan [married name Gourlay], Dame Janet Maria (1899–1993)', *Oxford Dictionary of National Biography* (Oxford: Oxford University Press, 2010) [ODNB].

42 Ibid.

43 'Philippa Foot letter to Janet Vaughan'.

44 Truman's speech, http://news.bbc.co.uk/onthisday/hi/dates/stories/august/6/newsid_3602000/3602189.stm, accessed 1 August 2021.

45 'Iris Murdoch Journal 4' [IMJ4], Iris Murdoch Collection, Kingston University [IMC], KUAS202/1/4, 25 July 1947, p. 25.

CHAPTER 1: ON PROBATION

1 Midgley, OM, p. 60.

2 Ibid., p. 2.

3 Ibid., p. 21.

4 Ibid., p. 77.

5 Ibid., p. 3.

6 Ibid., p. 93.

7 'Mary Midgley interviewed by Paul Merchant', *Science and Religion: Exploring the Spectrum. Life Story Interviews*, British Library C1672/05, track 2, p. 21.

8 Mary Scrutton, 'On Being Reformed', *Listener*, 1428 (1956), p. 196.

9 'Letter from Rev. Tom Scrutton to Mary Scrutton', 26 May 1936, letters from immediate family members, MGMP MID/F.

10 Midgley, OM, pp. 81–2.

11 'Jean Wilhelma Rowntree' (Oral History), Imperial War Museum sound archive, https://www.iwm.org.uk/collections/item/object/80014585, accessed 21 June 2021.

12 Midgley, OM, p. 83.

13 'Letter from Rev. Tom Scrutton', 24 April 1939, MGMP MID/F.

14 Somerville College Report and Calendar 1938–1939, SCA SC/GB/AR/RC 1938-39.

15 Anne Ridler, *Olive Willis and Downe House: An Adventure in Education* (London: Murray, 1967), pp. 81–2.

16 J. Dewey, *Experience and Education* (New York: Kappa Delta Pi, 1948), p. 28.

17 Ibid., p. 74.

18 Ibid., p. 49.
19 Jennifer Hart, *Ask Me No More* (London: Peter Halban 1998), p. 14.
20 Mary Scrutton, 'On Being Reformed', p. 196.
21 P. Smith, *The Morning Light: A South African Childhood Revalued* (David Philip, 2000), p. 221; SCA, conversation with authors.
22 Smith, *The Morning Light*. p. 221.
23 Midgley, OM, p. 77.
24 Peter J. Conradi, *Iris Murdoch: A Life* (London: HarperCollins, 2001) [IMAL], p. 59.
25 Ibid., p. 28.
26 Ibid., p. 59.
27 Jean Storry, *At Badminton with B.M.B. by Those Who Were There* (Badminton School, Bristol, 1982), pp. 7–8.
28 Dulcibel Jenkins McKenzie, *Steps to the Bar* (Itchenor: Greengate Press, 1998). pp. 31–2.
29 'Letter to Mr W. D. Howarth', 10 January [?], PCA, KUAS6/10/1/7.
30 McKenzie, *Steps to the Bar*, p. 32.
31 'Letter from Leila Eveleigh to Peter Conradi', 27 June [1998], PCA KUAS6/10/1/1/1.
32 'McKenzie, *Steps to the Bar*, p. 32.
33 'Letter from Pat Trenaman to John Bayley', 29 February 1999, PCA, KUAS6/10/1/10.
34 'Letter to Conradi from Mary Jeffery', 22 February 1981, PCA KUAS 6/10/1/3.
35 Midgley, OM, p. 86.
36 Conradi, IMAL, p. 97.
37 Ibid., p. 396.
38 Ibid., p. 83.
39 According to Peter Conradi, Iris had originally been accepted by Somerville to study English but switched to Mods and Greats sometime in the first term: ibid., p. 85.
40 For more information see Robert Currie, 'The Arts and Social Studies, 1914–1939', in *The History of the University of Oxford Volume VIII: The Twentieth Century*, ed. B. Harrison (Oxford: Clarendon Press, 1994) [HUOVIII], pp. 109–38.
41 Adams, SW, p. 224. Also IMAL, p. 83.
42 Midgley, OM, p. 86. 'East' is now 'Darbishire' after Helen Darbishire, Somerville Principal 1930–45.
43 Joyce Reynolds, conversation with authors, 2 July 2020.
44 Conradi, IMAL, p. 84.
45 Conradi, IMAL, p. 82. See also Midgley, OM, p. 86.
46 Buxton, *Oxford University Ceremonies*, pp. 42–3.

47 'Postcard from Dean of Somerville College, Oxford (Vera Farnell) concerning appropriate academic dress for women', MGMP MID/E/36.

48 Adams, SW, p. 121.

49 Colin Seymour-Ure, 'Bathurst [née Borthwick], Lilias Margaret Frances, Countess Bathurst (1871–1965)', ODNB.

50 Janet Howarth, 'Women', in HOUVIII, pp. 345–76, at p. 360.

51 Jane Robinson, Bluestockings (London: Viking, 2009), pp. 78–9.

52 B. Harrison, 'College Life, 1918–1939', in HOUVIII, pp. 81–108, at p. 101.

53 Adams, SW, p. 164 – 'Cambridge was said to be capitalizing on Oxford's image as "socialistic, weak in athletics and be-womaned"'.

54 V. Farnell, A Somervillian Looks Back (privately printed at Oxford University Press, 1948), p. 1.

55 Howarth, 'Women', p. 362.

56 Edna Healey, Part of the Pattern: Memoirs of a Wife at Westminster (London: Headline, 2007), p. 36.

57 Midgley, OM, p. 88.

58 Ibid., p. 88; also 'Friday Train to Reading', n.d., MGMP MID/F.

59 Midgley, OM, p. 131. This is Midgley's reversal of the usual order.

60 Conradi, IMAL, p. 95.

61 Adams, SW, p. 233.

62 J. Morris, Oxford (Oxford: Oxford University Press, 2001), p. 65.

63 Ibid., p. 119.

64 Calculation based on Morris, Oxford, p. 67 (St John's is about twice as wealthy as All Souls, and All Souls about 50 times as wealthy as Somerville).

65 Adams, SW, pp. 163–5.

66 J. D. Mabbott, Oxford Memories (Oxford: Thorntons, 1986), pp. 81–2.

67 Adams, SW, p. 115.

68 Mark Rowe, J. L. Austin: Philosopher and D-Day Intelligence Officer, unpublished manuscript (Oxford: Oxford University Press, forthcoming), chapter 9. With thanks to Fanny Mitchell for permission to reproduce this note.

69 Midgley, OM, p. 23.

70 Conradi, IMAL, p. 69.

71 Storry, At Badminton with B. M. B. by Those Who Were There, p. 11.

72 'Debating Society Report', Badminton School Magazine LX, Summer Term 1936, Badminton School Archive.

73 Conradi, IMAL, p. 69.

74 Storry, At Badminton with B. M. B. by Those Who Were There, p. 8, cited in Conradi, IMAL, p. 68.

75 'Christmas Holiday Lectures', Headway, March 1937, p. 48, in PCA, KUAS6/10/2/8. See also Conradi, IMAL, p. 78.

76 Iris Murdoch, 'If I were Foreign Secretary', *Badminton School Magazine*, LXXV, Autumn Term 1937, p. 16, Badminton School Archive. See also Conradi, *IMAL*, p. 78.

77 For more see Colin Carritt, 'The Oxford Carritts' (unpublished family history, 2006).

78 Iris Murdoch, 'Badmintonians at Oxford' in *Badminton School Magazine*, LXXIX, Spring and Summer Terms 1939, pp. 27–8, Badminton School Archive; cited in Conradi, *IMAL*, p. 83.

79 Conradi, *IMAL*, p. 202.

80 Ibid., p. 83.

81 Adams, *SW*, p. 220.

82 P. Griffin, *St Hugh's: One Hundred Years of Women's Education in Oxford* (London: Palgrave Macmillan, 1986), p. 107.

83 Midgley, *OM*, p. 88.

84 Conradi, *IMAL*, pp. 84–5.

85 Ibid., pp. 82–3.

86 Ibid., pp. 89–90.

87 Midgley, *OM*, p. 87.

88 Conradi, *IMAL*, p. 84.

89 Amabel Williams-Ellis, *All Stracheys are Cousins* (London: Weidenfeld & Nicolson, 1983), p. 128.

90 Midgley, *OM*, p. 94.

91 'Mary Midgley interviewed by Paul Merchant', track 2, p. 22.

92 *St Hugh's College Chronicle: 1938–39*, no. 11, p. 31.

93 Deborah Quare, 'Mordan, Clara Evelyn (1844–1915)', *ODNB*.

94 'Report by D. H. Gray, Hilary Term 1938', Elizabeth Anscombe Student File, St Hugh's College Archive, St Hugh's College, University of Oxford [SHCA], SHG/J/3/2.

95 'Photocopied documentation on GEMA's record as a pupil at Sydenham High School', the Collegium Institute Anscombe Archive at the University of Pennsylvania, Kislak Centre for Special Collections, Rare Books and Manuscripts [CIAA], Box 14, File 562.

96 Ibid.

97 Mary Geach, correspondence with authors, 28 September 2020.

98 Ibid.

99 Anne Keene, 'Gwyer, Barbara Elizabeth (1881–1974)', *ODNB*.

100 J. Howarth, 'Anglican Perspectives on Gender: Some Reflections on the Centenary of St Hugh's College, Oxford', *Oxford Review of Education* 12:3 (1986), p. 299.

101 Griffin, *St Hugh's*, p. 20.

102 A. M. A. H. Rogers and C. F. Rogers, *Degrees by Degrees: The Story of the Admission of Oxford Women Students to Membership of the University* (Oxford: Oxford University Press, 1938).

103 J. Howarth, 'Rogers, Annie Mary Anne Henley (1856–1937)', *ODNB*.
104 See https://www.st-annes.ox.ac.uk/this-is-st-annes/history/founding-fellows/annie-rogers/, accessed 26 July 21.
105 Griffin, *St Hugh's*, pp. 304–16.
106 Mary Geach, 'Introduction' in G.E.M. Anscombe, *Faith in a Hard Ground: Essays on Religion, Philosophy, and Ethics*, ed. M. Geach and L. Gormally (Exeter: Imprint Academic, 2008), pp. i–xxvi, at p. xxii.
107 G.E.M. Anscombe, 'Introduction' in her *Metaphysics and the Philosophy of Mind: The Collected Philosophical Papers of G.E.M. Anscombe Volume Two* (Blackwell, 1981) [MPM], pp. vii–x, at p. vii.
108 Ibid.
109 Anscombe, MPM, p. vii.
110 Mary Midgley, conversation with authors, September 2016.
111 Anscombe was confirmed a year later, in July 1939, in France. 'GEMA's Certificate of Confirmation', CIAA Box 10, File 373.
112 In fact, Eleonora was born in Essen and like her parents, was a German citizen. It seems most likely that her grandparents were among the many Poles who migrated there in the early 1870s, from eastern Prussia. See Michaela Bachem-Rehm, 'A Forgotten Chapter of Regional Social History: The Polish Immigrants to the Ruhr 1870–1939', in *The Economies of Urban Diversity: The Ruhr Area and Istanbul*, ed. Darja Reuschke, Monika Salzbrunn, and Korinna Schönhärl (New York: Palgrave Macmillan, 2013).
113 E. F. A. Geach and D. Wallace, *--esques* (Oxford: Blackwell, 1918). For a brief biography of Eleonora Geach see <http://desturmobed.blogspot.com/2012/10/efa-geach.html, accessed 1 August 2021.
114 Peter Geach, 'A Philosophical Autobiography', in *Peter Geach: Philosophical Encounters*, ed. Harry A. Lewis (Dordrecht: Springer, 1991), pp. 1–25, at pp. 2, 3, 5.
115 Geach, 'A Philosophical Autobiography', p. 4.
116 Anthony Kenny, 'Peter Thomas Geach, 1916–2013', *Biographical Memoirs of Fellows of the British Academy* 14 (2015), pp. 185–203, at p. 186.
117 Geach, 'A Philosophical Autobiography', p. 10.
118 https://www.bioethics.org.uk/page/about_us/about_elizabeth_anscombe, accessed 1 August 2021.
119 Kenny, 'Peter Thomas Geach, 1916–2013', p. 187.
120 Geach, 'A Philosophical Autobiography', p. 11.
121 Midgley, OM, p. 94.
122 Ibid., p. 94.
123 'PC's interviews in Oxford, Hilary 1999', notebook, IMC, KUA26/4/1/1.
124 Conradi, *IMAL*, p. 86.
125 Beatrix Walsh, 'Mildred Hartley: A Wartime Recollection', *Somerville College Annual Report 1996*, SCA, pp. 134–7, at p. 134.
126 Ibid., p. 134.

127 Drusilla Scott, *A. D. Lindsay: A Biography* (Oxford: Basil Blackwell, 1971), p. 245.

128 Conradi, *IMAL*, p. 89.

129 Midgley, *OM*, p. 85.

130 Sally Humphreys, 'Obituary: Mary Isobel Henderson, Fellow and Tutor 1933–1967; Vice Principal 1960–1967', *Somerville College Annual Report 1967*, SCA, pp. 28–31, at p. 30.

131 Adams, *SW*, p. 232.

132 Humphreys, 'Obituary: Mary Isobel Henderson', p. 30.

133 Averil Cameron, 'Past Masters', *Times Higher Education Supplement*, 27 October 1994.

134 'Marriages', *Times*, 20 June 1933.

135 A. L. Rowse, 'Mr Charles Henderson', *Times*, 2 October 1933.

136 Scott, *A. D. Lindsay*, p. 250.

137 Denis Healey, *The Time of My Life* (London: Michael Joseph, 1989), p. 28.

138 Scott, *A. D. Lindsay*, p. 250.

139 Roger Eatwell, 'Munich, Public Opinion, and Popular Front', *Journal of Contemporary History* 6:4 (1971), pp. 122–139, at p. 128.

140 Healey, *Part of the Pattern*, p. 42.

141 Conradi, *IMAL*, p. 89.

142 Ibid., pp. 631–2 (fn. 73); see 'Letter from Margaret Stanier to Peter Conradi', 29 October 1998, IMA, KUAS6/3/143/3.

143 A. Horner and A. Rowe, *Living on Paper: Letters from Iris Murdoch, 1934–1995* (London: Chatto, 2015) [*LP*], pp. 10-11.

144 Horner and Rowe, *LP*, pp. 10–11.

145 T. Snyder, *Bloodlands: Europe Between Hitler and Stalin* (London: Vintage, 2011), p. 74.

146 John Dewey et al., *Not Guilty: Report of the Commission of Inquiry into the Charges Made Against Leon Trotsky in the Moscow Trials* (New York: Harper and Brothers Publishers, 1938).

147 Midgley, *OM*, p. 111.

148 Ibid., p. 111.

149 Michael Ignatieff, *Isaiah Berlin: A Life* (London: Chatto & Windus, 1998), p. 73.

150 L. Mitchell, *Maurice Bowra: A Life* (Oxford: Oxford University Press, 2010), p. 200.

151 E. R. Dodds, *Missing Persons: An Autobiography* (Oxford: Clarendon Press, 1977), p. 131.

152 See Chris Birks, 'From Pacifism to Popular Front: the Changing Views of the Left and the Liberal Intelligentsia in Oxford, 1933–1938' (MA dissertation, University of Oxford, 2020).

153 E. Waugh, *Brideshead Revisited: The Sacred and Profane Memories of Captain Charles Ryder* (London: Penguin, 2012), p. 22.

154 P. J. Conradi, *A Very English Hero: The Making of Frank Thompson* (London: Bloomsbury, 2013), p. 46.

155 See Carritt, 'The Oxford Carritts', p. 2.

156 S. Brown and H. T. Bredin, *Dictionary of Twentieth-Century British Philosophers* (London: Bloomsbury Academic, 2005), p. 157.

157 Conradi, *A Very English Hero*, p. 113.

158 Dorothy Emmet, *Philosophers and Friends: Reminiscences of Seventy Years in Philosophy*; foreword by Bryan Magee (Basingstoke: Macmillan, 1996), p. 33.

159 Scott, *A. D. Lindsay*, p. 120.

160 Ibid., p. 106.

161 M. Grimley, *Citizenship, Community and the Church of England: Liberal Anglican Theories of the State Between the Wars* (Oxford: Oxford University Press, 2004).

162 Scott, *A. D. Lindsay*, p. 106.

163 See J. Savage, *Teenage: The Creation of Youth Culture* (London: Pimlico, 2008).

164 Healey, *The Time of My Life*, p. 27.

165 Mitchell, *Maurice Bowra*, pp. 160–2.

166 Ibid., p. 249.

167 Smith, *The Morning Light*, p. 235.

168 S. Crawford, K. Ulmschneider and J. Elsner (eds), *Ark of Civilization: Refugee Scholars and Oxford University, 1930–1945* (Oxford: Oxford University Press, 2017) [AC], p. 14. See also B. Williams, *Shame and Necessity* (Berkeley: University of California Press, 1993), pp. x–xi.

169 Crawford et al. (eds), *AC*, p. 1.

170 Jaś Elsner, 'Pfeiffer, Fraenkel, and Refugee Scholarship in Oxford during and after the Second World War', in Crawford et al. (eds), *AC*, pp. 25–49, at p. 31.

171 Crawford et al. (eds), *AC*, p. 1.

172 Humphreys, 'Obituary: Mary Isobel Henderson', p. 30.

173 Midgley, *OM*, p. 98.

174 Eduard Fraenkel, *Aeschylus: Agamemnon, Vol 1* (Oxford: Oxford University Press, 1950), p. 95.

175 See Christopher Stray, 'A Teutonic Monster in Oxford: The Making of Fraenkel's Agamemnon', in *Classical Commentaries: Explorations in a Scholarly Genre*, ed. S. Christina and Christopher Stray Kraus (Oxford: Oxford University Press, 2015), pp. 39–57.

176 See J. G. Darwin, 'A World University', in *HUOVIII*, pp. 607–38, at p. 609.

177 Midgley, *OM*, p. 97.

178 Ibid., pp. 96–7.
179 Eduard Fraenkel, *Aeschylus: Agamemnon, Vol 3* (Oxford: Oxford University Press, 1950), p. 485, quoted in Crawford et al. (eds), AC, p. 42.
180 G. R. Burton and J. F. Toland, 'Ludwig Edward Fraenkel. 28 May 1927 – 27 April 2019', *Biographical Memorials of Fellows of the Royal Society* 69 (2020), pp. 175–201.
181 Wendy Webster, *Mixing It: Diversity in World War Two Britain* (Oxford: Oxford University Press, 2018), p. 168.
182 Fraenkel, *Aeschylus: Agamemnon, Vol. 1*, p. 95.
183 Mathura Umachandran, '"The aftermath experienced before": Aeschylean Untimeliness and Iris Murdoch's Defence of Art', *Ramus* 48:2 (2019), p. 225 et passim.
184 Conradi, IMAL, pp. 121–2.
185 Ibid., p. 97.
186 Ibid., p. 93.
187 Sue Summers, 'The Lost Loves of Iris Murdoch', *Mail on Sunday*, 5 June 1988, p. 17, quoted in Conradi, IMAL, p. 96.
188 Conradi, IMAL, p. 93.
189 For a general overview, see W. J. Mander, *Idealist Ethics* (Oxford: Oxford University Press UK, 2016). Also J. H. Muirhead, 'How Hegel came to England', *Mind* 36:144 (1927), pp. 423–47; T. H. Green, *Prolegomena to Ethics* (Oxford: Oxford University Press, 2003); Bernard Bosanquet, *Some Suggestions in Ethics* (London: Macmillan, 1918); A. D. Lindsay, 'The Idealism of Caird and Jones', *Journal of Philosophical Studies* 1:2 (1926) pp. 171–82.
190 G. E. Moore, 'The Refutation of Idealism', *Mind* 12:48 (1903), pp. 433–53.
191 G. E. Moore, *Principia Ethica* (Cambridge: Cambridge University Press, 1922), chapter 2, esp. p. 40.
192 H. A. Prichard, 'Does Moral Philosophy Rest on a Mistake?', *Mind* 21: 81 (1912), pp. 21–37, at p. 37.
193 Dorothy Emmet, *Role of the Unrealisable: Study in Regulative Ideals* (London: Palgrave Macmillan, 1993), p. 64.
194 P. J. Conradi, *Iris Murdoch, A Writer at War: Letters and Diaries, 1939–1945* (Oxford: Oxford University Press, 2011) [WW], p. 251. Also, if you wish, IMAL, p. 216.
195 Ernest Nagel, 'Impressions and Appraisals of Analytic Philosophy in Europe. I', *Journal of Philosophy* 33, no. 1 (1936), pp. 5–24, at p. 9. See also Ben Rogers, A. J. Ayer: A Life (New York: Grove Press, 1999), p. 104.
196 Rogers, A. J. Ayer, p. 114.
197 Ibid., p. 58.
198 See Friedrich Stadler, *The Vienna Circle: Studies in the Origins, Development, and Influence of Logical Empiricism* (Wien, New York: Springer, 2001).

199 See https://www.psy.ox.ac.uk/about-us/120-years-of-psychology-at-oxford, accessed 1 August 2021.

200 Midgley, OM, p. 84.

201 L. Susan Stebbing, 'Moore's Influence', *The Philosophy of G. E. Moore: The Library of Living Philosophers*, ed. Paul Arthur Schilpp (La Salle, Illinois: Open Court, 1942), pp. 517–32, at p. 530.

202 Nagel, 'Impressions and Appraisals of Analytic Philosophy in Europe. I', p. 6.

203 Ibid., p. 13.

204 John Wisdom, 'L. Susan Stebbing, 1885–1943', *Mind* 53:211 (1944), pp. 283–5, at p. 283.

205 L. Susan Stebbing, *A Modern Introduction to Logic* (London Methuen, 1930/1948), p. 1.

206 Stebbing, *A Modern Introduction to Logic*, pp. 163–5.

207 L. Susan Stebbing, *Thinking to Some Purpose* (Harmondsworth: Penguin Books, 1939), p. 63.

208 Ibid. pp. 70–1.

209 S. Chapman, *Susan Stebbing and the Language of Common Sense* (London: Palgrave Macmillan, 2013), p. 126.

210 Rogers, A. J. Ayer, p. 55.

211 A. J. Ayer, *A Part of My Life: The Memoirs of a Philosopher* (Oxford: Oxford University Press, 1978), p. 122.

212 L. Wittgenstein, *Tractatus Logico-Philosophicus* (London: Routledge, 1921). First published in German in 1921 and in an English translation by Ogden and Ramsey in 1922.

213 Ibid., §4.116 and 7.

214 'Letter from A. J. Ayer to Ryle, 9 February 1933', Gilbert Ryle Collection, Linacre College, University of Oxford.

215 Ibid.

216 Ayer, *Language, Truth and Logic*, p. 86.

217 Ibid., p. 85.

218 Ayer, *A Part of My Life*, p. 144.

219 Ayer, *Language, Truth and Logic*, p. 49 (Ayer took this proposition from F. H. Bradley's *Appearance and Reality: A Metaphysical Essay*, 2nd edition (London: Swan Sonnenschein, 1908).

220 See Bertrand Russell, 'On Denoting', *Mind* 14, no. 56 (1905), pp. 479–93.

221 Ayer, *Language, Truth and Logic*, p. 60.

222 Iris Murdoch, 'Metaphysics and Ethics' (1957), in Iris Murdoch, *Existentialists and Mystics: Writings on Philosophy and Literature*, ed. P. J. Conradi (London: Chatto & Windus, 1997) [EM], pp. 99–123, p. 60.

223 Midgley, OM, p. 120.

224 Mary Midgley, *The Myths We Live By* (London: Routledge, 2011), p. 59.

225 Price, *Hume's Theory of the External World*, p. 8.

226 Ayer, *A Part of My Life*, p. 154.
227 Ayer, *Language, Truth and Logic*, p. 137.
228 Rogers, A.J. *Ayer*, p. 123.
229 See Ignatieff, *Isaiah Berlin: A Life*, p. 85.
230 MacKinnon, 'And the Son of Man that Thou Visitest Him', part 2, p. 269.
231 Ibid., p. 266.
232 Rogers, A. J. *Ayer*, p. 124.
233 Midgley, OM, p. 118.
234 Ayer, *A Part of My Life*, p. 166.
235 'H. H. Price Reference for A. J. Ayer', 8 February 1935, A. J. Ayer Archive, Trinity College, University of Oxford, quoted in Rogers, A. J. *Ayer*. p. 106.
236 Ayer, *A Part of My Life*, p. 145.
237 'D'Arcy, Martin Cyril, SJ (1888–1976)', in *The Cambridge Encyclopedia of the Jesuits*, ed. T. Worcester, SJ (Cambridge: Cambridge University Press, 2017), p. 219.
238 Quoted in Colin Wilks, *Emotion, Truth and Meaning: In Defense of Ayer and Stevenson* (Dordrecht: Kluwer Academic Publishers, 2002), p. 38.
239 R. M. Hare, 'A Philosophical Autobiography', *Utilitas* 14:3 (2002), pp. 269–305, at p. 288.
240 G. R. G. Mure, *Retreat from Truth* (London: Blackwell, 1958), p. vii.
241 Rogers, A. J. *Ayer*, p. 124.
242 R. G. Collingwood, *An Essay on Metaphysics (1940)* (Oxford: Clarendon Press, 1957), p. viii.
243 Collingwood, *An Essay on Metaphysics*, pp. 162–3, 166.
244 Ibid., p. 21.
245 A. D. Lindsay, 'What Does the Mind Construct?' *Proceedings of the Aristotelian Society* 25 (1924), pp. 1–18, at p. 11. See also Emmet, *Philosophers and Friends*, p. 16.
246 Fred Inglis, *History Man: The Life of R. G. Collingwood* (Princeton: Princeton University Press, 2011), p. 249.

CHAPTER 2: LEARNING IN WARTIME

1 See Conradi, IMAL, p. 105–8.
2 Midgley, OM, p. 102. Chamberlain's actual words, spoken on the radio on 27 September 1938, on Germany's annexation of the Sudetenland, were: 'How horrible, fantastic, incredible it is that we should be digging trenches and trying on gas-masks here because of a quarrel in a far away country between people of whom we know nothing.'
3 Webster, *Mixing It*, p. 42.
4 IMJ1, undated, p. 103, IMC, KUAS202/1/1; also Conradi, IMAL, p. 107.
5 Midgley, OM, p. 103.

6 Addison, 'Oxford and the Second World War', *HOUVIII*, pp. 167–88, at p. 169.

7 Ibid., p. 167.

8 M.R.D. Foot, *Memories of an S.O.E. Historian* (Barnsley: Pen & Sword Books, 2009), p. 52.

9 'Photocopy of letter from Noel Eldridge to his mother' [November 1939], pp. 2–3, PCA, KAUS6/11/1/16/3 (this letter is quoted in Conradi, *IMAL*, p. 156).

10 Conradi, *IMAL*, p. 106.

11 P. Warner, *Phantom: Uncovering the Secrets of the WW2 Special Forces Unit* (Barnsley: Pen & Sword Books, 1990), pp. 325–6.

12 Conradi, *WW*, p. 111.

13 Conradi, *IMAL*, p. 96.

14 Ibid., p. 100.

15 Conradi, *WW*, pp. 121 and 118.

16 'Letter from Nick Crosbie to Mary Scrutton', undated, MGMP, MID/F.

17 Iris Murdoch, 'More about Wartime Oxford' in *Badminton School Magazine*, LXXXII, 1941–2, p. 23, Badminton School Archive.

18 C. S. Lewis, 'Learning in War-Time' (22 October 1939), in C. S. Lewis, *The Weight of Glory: A Collection of Lewis's Most Moving Addresses* (London: William Collins, 2013) pp. 49–50.

19 'Letter from Iris Murdoch to Mary Scrutton', n.d., posted from Somerville, MGMP MID/F.

20 Midgley, OM, p. 106.

21 Alice Prochaska, 'Patricia Magaret Norman', https://principal2010.files.wordpress.com/2013/09/patricia-margaret-norman.pdf, (2013), accessed 1 August 2021.

22 Adams, *SW*, p. 242.

23 Horner and Rowe, *LP*, p. 14.

24 Conradi, *WW*, p. 186.

25 Ibid., p. 190.

26 'Iris Murdoch letter to Patrick O'Regan, Blackpool', n.d. [July 1940], PCA, KUAS6/1/42/12.

27 'Iris Murdoch letter to Patrick O'Regan, Blackpool', n.d. [probably March 1941], PCA, KUAS6/1/42/10.

28 Fans of Murdoch's fiction will recognise her in Paula in *The Nice and the Good*.

29 'Philippa Foot (1920–2010) – An Oxfam Tribute', p. 3, SCA, SC/AO/AA/FW/Foot.

30 Martin Gornall, 'Philippa Foot and Thoughts about Oxfam', typescript paper, SCA Philippa Foot Papers, Box 10 Oxfam Material, p. 1.

31 Among them the young philosopher and proctor H. J. Paton. See Robert Currie, 'The arts and social studies, 1914–1939'.

32 Gornall, 'Philippa Foot and Thoughts about Oxfam', p. 1.
33 Rosalind Hursthouse, 'Philippa Ruth Foot 1920–2010', *Biographical Memoirs of Fellows of the British Academy*, 11 (2012) pp. 179–96, at p. 181.
34 Currie, 'The Arts and Social Studies, 1914–1939', p. 116.
35 Letter to the Editor, *Times*, 26 May 1936.
36 'Esther Cleveland Weds Capt. Bosanquet: Late President's Daughter Marries Coldstream Guards Officer in Westminster Abbey', *New York Times*, 15 March 1918.
37 'Old Hall, sales particulars. Sanderson Townend & Gilbert', in SCA, Philippa Foot Papers, Box 1 Family Material, 1/2.
38 Jane O'Grady, 'Philippa Foot: Obituary', *Guardian*, 5 October 2010.
39 'Commonplace book', 4 January 1998, SCA, Philippa Foot Papers, Box 3 Notebooks & Commonplace books.
40 P. J. Conradi, *Family Business: A Memoir* (Bridgend: Seren, 2019), p. 177.
41 Prophecy Coles, 'Memories of Philippa Foot, 2020', correspondence with authors, p. 3.
42 'Commonplace book, 4 January 1998.
43 Conradi, *Family Business*, p. 178.
44 Foot, *Memories of an S.O.E. Historian*, pp. 16–17.
45 Gornall, 'Philippa Foot and Thoughts about Oxfam', p. 4.
46 M. Pugh, *We Danced All Night: A Social History of Britain Between the Wars* (London: Random House, 2013), p. 129.
47 Conradi, *Family Business*, p. 177.
48 Gornall, 'Philippa Foot and Thoughts about Oxfam', p. 1.
49 Peter Conradi, 'The Guises of Love: The Friendship of Professor Philippa Foot and Dame Iris Murdoch', *The Iris Murdoch Review*, 5 (2014), pp. 17–28, p. 27.
50 'Notebook 4 (Red hardback)', August 2001, SCA, Philippa Foot Papers, Box 3 Notebooks & Commonplace books.
51 Peter Conradi and Gavin Lawrence, 'Professor Philippa Foot: Philosopher regarded as being among the finest moral thinkers of the age', *Independent*, 23 October 2011.
52 'Philippa Foot (1920–1910) – An Oxfam Tribute', p. 2.
53 Jonathan Rée, 'Philosophical Lives: Philippa Foot interview', transcript, 19 September 2000, SCA, Philippa Foot papers, box 11: SC/LY/SP/PF/11, p. 5.
54 Gornall, 'Philippa Foot and Thoughts about Oxfam', p. 1.
55 Philippa Foot, 'Mildred Hartley', *Somerville College Annual Report 1996*, SCA, pp. 130–1.
56 Foot, 'Mildred Hartley', p. 130.
57 Hursthouse, 'Philippa Ruth Foot 1920–2010', p. 181.
58 Currie, 'The Arts and Social Studies, 1914–1939', p. 120.
59 *Oxford Magazine*, 5 June 1941, p. 338.

60 Ibid., 21 November 1940, p. 1.
61 Horner and Rowe, *LP*, p. 14; Farnell, *A Somervillian Looks Back*, p. 74.
62 Addison, 'Oxford and the Second World War', p. 170.
63 Adams, *SW*, p. 239.
64 Farnell, *A Somervillian Looks Back*, p. 73.
65 Midgley, *OM*, p. 109.
66 K. M. Lea, 'Elisabeth Blochmann Obituary 1892–1972', *The Brown Book: Lady Margaret Hall Magazine, 1972*.
67 Laurence Brockliss, 'Welcoming and Supporting Refugee Scholars: The Role of Oxford's Colleges', in Crawford et al. (eds), *AC*, pp. 62–76, at p. 72.
68 Valerie Purton, *An Iris Murdoch Chronology* (Basingstoke: Palgrave Macmillan, 2007), p. 16.
69 J. Gardiner, *Wartime Britain 1939–1945* (London: Headline, 2016), pp. 166–7.
70 Gardiner, *Wartime Britain 1939–1945*, p. 59.
71 V. Lynn and V. Lewis-Jones, *Keep Smiling Through: My Wartime Story* (London: Random House, 2017), p. 115.
72 Addison, 'Oxford and the Second World War', p. 171.
73 See Scott, *A. D. Lindsay*, pp. 257–87.
74 Midgley, *OM*, p. 105.
75 'TS transcript of RMH personal interview with (now Sir) Brian Harrison', 17 June 1989, p. 10, Balliol College Archive, University of Oxford, R. M. Hare papers.
76 Hare, 'A Philosophical Autobiography', p. 276.
77 John Haldane, 'Anscombe: Life, Action and Ethics in Context', *Philosophical News*, 18 (2019), pp. 45–75, at p. 65.
78 Anscombe, *The Justice of the Present War Examined*, p. 72.
79 Ibid., p. 75.
80 Ibid., p. 81.
81 'The Parish of Beguildy', p. 6.
82 Anscombe, *Collected Philosophical Papers: Ethics, Religion and Politics Vol. 3* [*ERP*], p. vii.
83 'Oxford Student Begs for Revolt in Stuart "Plot": "Party" is Serious', *New York Herald Tribune*, 7 March 1937. See also: 'Rupprecht called "King of Britain"', *New York Times*, 31 January 1937, p. 26; 'Student made "Prince" by Oxford Jacobites', *Washington Post*, 31 January 1937; 'Prince Rupprecht: Jacobite Ceremony at Oxford', *Scotsman*, 1 February 1937; 'Anti-Coronation Stunt Suppressed at Oxford', *St Louis Post*, 8 May 1937; 'Jacobite Leader', *Vancouver Sun*, 8 June 1937. With thanks to Roger Teichmann for bringing these to our attention.
84 'Oxford Clique aims at Revolt: Backs Stuart Pretender Against Reigning', *Daily Boston Globe*, 7 March 1937.

85 Geach, 'A Philosophical Autobiography', pp. 11–12; Kenny, 'Peter Thomas Geach, 1916–2013', p. 188.

86 https://www.theweatheroutlook.com/twoother/twocontent.aspx?type=tystat &id=1180&title=January+1940, accessed 1 August 2021.

87 Midgley, OM, p. 97.

88 Ibid., p. 100.

89 Ibid.

90 'Mary Midgley interviewed by Paul Merchant', track 2, p. 26.

91 Rowe, *J. L. Austin*, chapter 9.

92 C. E. M. Joad, 'Appeal to Philosophers', *Philosophy* 15:60 (1940), pp. 400–16, at p. 405.

93 Dorothy Emmet, *The Nature of Metaphysical Thinking* (London: Macmillan, 1961).

94 H. H. Price, 'The Inaugural Address: Clarity is Not Enough', *Proceedings of the Aristotelian Society, Supplementary Volumes* 19 (1945), pp. 1–31, at pp. 24, 31.

95 Christopher Stray, 'Eduard Fraenkel (1888–1970)' in Crawford et al. (eds), AC, pp. 180–200, at p. 184.

96 Conradi, *IMAL*, p. 118.

97 Elsner, 'Pfeiffer, Fraenkel, and Refugee Scholarship in Oxford during and after the Second World War', p. 29.

98 Kate Lowe, '"I shall snuffle about and make relations": Nicolai Rubinstein, the Historian of Renaissance Florence, in Oxford during the war', in Crawford et al. AC, pp. 220-233, at p. 222.

99 Conradi, *WW*, p. 187.

100 Stray, 'Eduard Fraenkel (1888–1970)', p. 184. See also 'Super Tastes at a Pioneering Shop', *Oxford Mail*, 30 March 2011.

101 *Oxford Gazette* (1939–1940), p. 536.

102 Midgley, OM. p. 114; Rowe, *J. L. Austin*, chapter 9.

103 Midgley, OM, pp. 114–15.

104 Ibid.

105 Mary Midgley, conversation with authors, September 2016.

106 Conradi, *IMAL*, p. 112.

107 Midgley, OM, p. 110. See also Nina Bawden, *In My Own Time* (London: Virago, 1994), p. 109.

108 Mary Midgley, conversation with authors, September 2016.

109 Mary Midgley, 'Park Town' (unpublished manuscript), 2016, p. 8.

110 Ibid.

111 Midgley, OM, p. 125.

112 Ibid.

113 Philippa Foot, 'The Grammar of Goodness', *Harvard Review of Philosophy* 11:1 (2003), p. 33.

114 Midgley, OM, p. 36.

115 Philippa Foot, *Natural Goodness* (Oxford: Oxford University Press, 2001), p. 1, fn. 1.

116 'Photocopy of a letter from Iris Murdoch to Rosalind Hursthouse', n.d. [late 1993], PCA, KUAS6/3/65/3. See also Hursthouse, 'Philippa Ruth Foot 1920–2010', p. 181.

117 Conradi, *IMAL*, p. 127.

118 Harold Mytum, 'Networks of Association: The Social and Intellectual Lives of Academics in Manx Internment Camps during the Second World War', in Crawford et al. AC, pp. 96–118, at p. 109; Anna Teicher, 'Jacob Leib Teicher between Florence and Cambridge: Arabic and Jewish Philosophy in Wartime Oxford', also in Crawford et al. AC, pp. 327–340, at p. 335. See also Beatrix Walsh, 'From Outer Darkness: Oxford and her Refugees', *Oxford Magazine* (1992), pp. 5–10.

119 'Wartime diaries of H.W.B. Joseph', 23 September 1940, p. 72, Bodleian Archives & Manuscripts, MSS. Top. Oxon. E. 289.

120 Addison, 'Oxford and the Second World War', p. 171.

121 'Wartime diaries of H.W.B. Joseph', 23 September 1940, p. 72.

122 Dodds, *Missing Persons*, pp. 138–9.

123 Iris Murdoch, 'News from Oxford', *Badminton School Magazine*, LXXXI, Spring & Summer Terms 1941, p. 19, Badminton School archive.

124 'Letter from IM to Patrick O'Regan, Somerville', n.d. [probably June 1940], PCA, KUAS6/1/42/7.

125 V. Brittain, *England's Hour* (London: Macmillan, 1941), pp. 209–10, quoted in Addison, 'Oxford and the Second World War', p. 174.

126 Warnock, *Mary Warnock: A Memoir: People and Places* (London: Duckworth, 2000), p. 56.

127 Jonathan Harrison, 'Henry Habberley Price, 1899-1984', *Proceedings of the British Academy*, 80, pp. 473–91, at p. 476.

128 Ibid., p. viii.

129 Ayer, *The Central Questions of Philosophy* (London: Weidenfeld, 1977), p. 23.

130 Anscombe 'Introduction', MPM, p. viii.

131 H. H. Price, *Hume's Theory of the External World* (Oxford: Clarendon Press, 1940/1963), pp. 11–12.

132 Ibid., pp. 50–1.

133 Ibid., p. 52.

134 David Hume, *A Treatise of Human Nature* (London: Penguin, 1985), Part IV, Section II, p. 249; see 'Price, *Hume's Theory of the External World*, p. 65, fn. 1.

135 Price, *Hume's Theory of the External World*, p. 81.

136 Anscombe, 'Introduction', MPM, p. viii.

137 Ibid.
138 Cf. Anscombe, 'Substance' (1964), MPM, pp. 37–43, at p. 39.
139 H. H. Price, 'A Mescaline Experience', *Journal of the American Society for Psychical Research*, 58:1 (1963), pp. 3–20, at p. 4.
140 Ibid., pp. 18–19.
141 Midgley, OM, p. 60.
142 'Letter from Iris Murdoch to Frank Thompson', early summer 1940, in Conradi, WW, pp. 95–6.
143 H. H. Price, 'Animals and the Supernatural', *Listener*, 29 April 1936, pp. 838–8, at p. 838.
144 'Letter from Iris Murdoch to Mary Scrutton, Blackpool', n.d., MGMP, MID/F.
145 'Letter from IM to Patrick O'Regan, Blackpool'. n.d. [1941?], PCA, KUAS6/1/42/4.
146 Purton, *An Iris Murdoch Chronology*, p. 19.
147 'Iris Murdoch letter to Patrick O'Regan, Blackpool', n.d. [July 1940], PCA, KUAS6/1/42/12.
148 Walsh, 'From Outer Darkness', p. 7.
149 Ibid., p. 10.
150 R. Weber, *Lotte Labowsky (1905–1991), Schülerin Aby Warburgs, Kollegin Raymond Klibanskys* (Berlin and Hamburg: Dietrich Reimer Verlag, 2012), p. 65.
151 Farnell, *A Somervillian Looks Back*, p. 70.
152 Weber, *Lotte Labowsky*, p. 70.
153 Hartley, 'A Wartime Recollection, *Somerville College Annual Report 1996*, SCA, pp. 134–7, at p. 136.
154 Webster, *Mixing It*, p. 62.
155 Mary also took Cassirer's Trinity Term 1940 course, 'General Problems in Moral Philosophy', Midgley, OM, p. 114.
156 Ibid.
157 Immanuel Kant, *Prolegomena to Any Future Metaphysics: That Will Be Able to Come Forward as Science: With Selections from the Critique of Pure Reason*, ed. Gary Hatfield, 2nd edition (Cambridge: Cambridge University Press, 2004), p. 10 (4:260).
158 Kant, *Prolegomena to Any Future Metaphysics*, p. 7.
159 G.E.M. Anscombe, 'Causality and Determinism' (1971), MPM, pp. 133–48, p. 135.
160 See H. J. Paton, *The Categorical Imperative: A Study in Kant's Moral Philosophy* (London: Hutchinson's University Library, 1946), p. 133.
161 Midgley, OM, p. 114.
162 'Letter from Iris Murdoch to Philippa Foot', 10 October 1946, IMC, KUAS100/1/2.

163 Irene Cassirer, correspondence with authors, 27 August 2021.
164 'Letter from Lotte Labowsky to Raymond Klibansky', February 1951, Raymond Klibansky Archive, Deutsches Literatur archiv, Marbach [RKA]
165 Irene Cassirer, correspondence with authors. 12 November 2020.
166 IMJ4, 8 October 1947, p. 90.
167 'Letter from A. D. Lindsay to Mrs. Gwyer', n.d. [circa. 1927], SHCA, Mary Glover Papers, [SHCA].
168 Correspondence with authors, 18 October 2020.
169 C. H., 'Mary Reaveley Glover', *St Hugh's College Chronicle*, 55 (1982–1983), p. 44.
170 Kate Price, correspondence with authors, 14 October 2020.
171 'Report from Victor White to Miss Glover, 9 June 1939', Elizabeth Anscombe Student File, SHCA, SHG/J/3/2. For discussion, see John Berkman, 'The Influence of Victor White and the Blackfriars Dominicans on a young Elizabeth Anscombe', *New Blackfriars* (2021).
172 Lesley Brown, 'Anscombe at Somerville', reminiscences presented at *Anscombe Centenary Conference* at Somerville College, 11 September 2019.
173 Mary Glover, 'Obligation and Value', *Ethics*, 49:1(1938), pp. 68–80.
174 Ibid., p. 68.
175 Ibid., p. 69. See H. B. W. Joseph, *Some Problems in Ethics* (Oxford: Oxford University Press, 1931), p. 94.
176 Joseph, *Some Problems in Ethics*, p. 45.
177 Ibid.
178 H.W.B. Joseph, 'Purposive Action', *Hibbert Journal* 32 (1933), p. 197.
179 Joseph, *Some Problems in Ethics*, pp. 102–3.
180 Glover, 'Obligation and Value', p. 71.
181 Ibid. p. 76.
182 Mehta, *Fly and the Fly-Bottle*, p. 52. For a discussion of Glover and Murdoch see Robert Audi, 'On Mary Glover's "Obligation and Value"', *Ethics* 125:2 (2015), pp. 525–9.
183 'Report on Miss Anscombe, Michaelmas Term 1939', Elizabeth Anscombe Student File, SHCA SHG/J/3/2.
184 'Report from William G. de Burgh to Miss Glover, Michaelmas Term 1940', Elizabeth Anscombe Student File, SHCA SHG/J/3/2.
185 Ibid.
186 'Report from MacKinnon, Hilary Term 1940 and Trinity Term [1940?]', Elizabeth Anscombe Student File, SHCA SHG/J/3/2.
187 'Report from Isobel Henderson to Miss Glover, Hilary Term 1941', Elizabeth Anscombe Student File, SHCA SHG/J/3/2.
188 'Report by Miss Glover, Trinity Term 1940', Elizabeth Anscombe Student File, SHCA, SHG/J/3/2.
189 Midgley, OM, p. 113.

190 Teichman, 'Gertrude Elizabeth Margaret Anscombe', p. 38; Michael Dummett, 'Obituary (G.E.M. Anscombe)', *Tablet*, 13 January 2001, p. 31.
191 'Mrs. Gertrude Elizabeth Margaret (née) Anscombe, CV, [NCA], AC/5/2. © M. C. Gormally.
192 Teichman, 'Gertrude Elizabeth Margaret Anscombe', p. 33.
193 'Peter Conradi's notes taken from a conversation with Polly Smythies', 3 February 1998, PCA, KUAS6/1/50/1.
194 Jeremy A. Crang, '"Come into the Army, Maud": Women, Military Conscription, and the Markham Inquiry', *Defence Studies* 8:3 (2008), pp. 381–95, at p. 386.
195 Given that his 'Polish' mother and grandparents were German subjects, any efforts Peter Geach made here could surely not have succeeded.
196 'Letter from Isobel Henderson to Mary Midgley', n.d. [1942], MGMP, MID/F.
197 Conradi, *IMAL*, p. 186.
198 Midgley, *OM*, p. 105.
199 Addison, 'Oxford and the Second World War', p. 170.
200 'Letter from Donald MacKinnon to M. B. Reckitt', 3 July 1940, cited in Muller, 'Donald M. MacKinnon', p. 189.
201 Midgley, *OM*, p. 117.
202 'Letter from Donald MacKinnon to Maurice Reckitt', 3 August 1940, Maurice Reckitt Papers, University of Sussex Special Collections, SxMs44/2/2/2/8.
203 'Letter from Lois MacKinnon to Peter Conradi', 24 September 1999, PCA, KUAS6/1/31/2.
204 'Letter from Donald MacKinnon to Maurice Reckitt', 3 August 1940. There is some dispute about the word 'raked' – MacKinnon's handwriting is notoriously hard to read. We take it to mean something like 'deviated from the straight and narrow'.
205 Muller, 'Donald M. MacKinnon', p. 206.
206 'Letter from H. H. Price to B. J. Kidd', 26 November 1936, cited in Muller, 'Donald M. MacKinnon', p. 76 and p. 94 (Price notes one exception in A. E. Taylor in Edinburgh).
207 'Report by Miss Glover, Michaelmas Term 1939', Elizabeth Anscombe Student File, SHCA SHG/J/3/2.
208 Conradi, *IMAL*, p. 123.
209 Midgley, *OM*, p. 116.
210 'Mary Midgley interviewed by Paul Merchant', track 2, p. 24.
211 Rogers, *A. J. Ayer*, p. 164.
212 'Mary Midgley interviewed by Paul Merchant', track 2, p. 24.
213 Conradi, *IMAL*, p. 123.
214 Ibid., p. 127.

215 Ibid., p. 123; John Jones, 'Iris, Hegel and Me', *London Review of Books*, vol. 25 no. 24, 18 December 2003.
216 'Letter from Iris Murdoch to Philippa Foot', n.d. [*c.* January 1947], IMC, KUAS100/1/9.
217 'Letter from Vera Crane to Peter Conradi', 8 October 1998, PCA, KUAS6/11/1/12.
218 Conradi, *IMAL*, p. 124. See also 'Letter from Vera Crane to Peter Conradi', PCA, KUAS6/11/1/12/1.
219 MacKinnon, 'And the Son of Man that Thou Visitest Him', part 2, p. 264. See also Donald M. MacKinnon, *A Study in Ethical Theory* (London: A. & C. Black, 1957), p. 15.
220 MacKinnon, 'And the Son of Man that Thou Visitest Him', part 2, p. 264.
221 Donald M. MacKinnon, 'Revelation and Social Justice' (1941), *Philosophy and the Burden of Theological Honesty*, p. 145.
222 Andrew Bowyer, *Donald MacKinnon's Moral Realism: To Perceive Tragedy Without the Loss of Hope* (Edinburgh: T&T Clark, 2015), p. 185, fn. 770.
223 Donald M. MacKinnon, 'And the Son of Man that Thou Visitest Him', *Christendom* 8, September 1938 and December 1938 (1938), part 1, p. 187, fn. 2.
224 Donald M. MacKinnon, 'The Function of Philosophy in Education' (1941), in *Philosophy and the Burden of Theological Honesty*, ed. John McDowell (London: T & T Clark, 2011), p. 11.
225 Ibid., p. 14.
226 See e.g. E. L. Mascall, 'The Doctrine of Analogy', *Cross Currents* 1:4 (1951). For discussion see also Emmet, *The Nature of Metaphysical Thinking*.
227 D. M. MacKinnon, 'Metaphysical and Religious Language', *Proceedings of the Aristotelian Society* 54 (1953–4), pp. 115–30, at p. 122.
228 Ibid., p. 118.
229 Donald M. MacKinnon, *The Problem of Metaphysics* (Cambridge: Cambridge University Press, 1974).
230 MacKinnon, *A Study in Ethical Theory*, p. 6.
231 Ibid., pp. 11–12.
232 Conradi, *IMAL*, p. 125.
233 Midgley, *OM*, p. 103.
234 'Letter from Donald MacKinnon', 9 May 1942 and 'Letter from Isobel Henderson', n.d. [Trinity Term 1942], MGMP, MID/F.
235 Conradi, *IMAL*, pp. 127–8.
236 Ibid., pp. 127–8.
237 Philippa Foot, 'Iris at Home in London', *Iris Murdoch News Letter*, 13 (Autumn 1999), p. 3.
238 Conradi, *IMAL*, pp. 37–8.
239 Howarth, 'Women', p. 348.
240 Conradi, *WW*, p. 191.

241 Midgley, OM, p. 113.

242 'Letter from Isobel Henderson', n.d. [summer 1942], MGMP, MID/F.

243 'Letter from Donald MacKinnon', 14 July 1942, MGMP, MID/F.

244 'Postcard from Donald MacKinnon', 10 July 1942, MGMP, MID/F.

245 'Letter from Donald MacKinnon', 14 July 1942, MGMP, MID/F.

246 'Letter from Isobel Henderson', n.d. [summer 1942], MGMP, MID/F.

247 'Letter from Iris Murdoch to Philippa Foot', n.d. [late summer 1942] IMC, KUAS100/1/1.

248 'Letter to Miss Plumer from Isobel Henderson', vi.1948, Iris Murdoch staff file, St Anne's College Archive, University of Oxford.

249 'Letter from Isobel Henderson', n.d. [July 1942], MGMP, MID/F.

250 The poet Matthew Arnold describing the area in his 1853 work 'The Scholar Gipsy'.

251 Midgley, OM, p. 126.

252 Ibid., pp. 125–6.

CHAPTER 3: DISORDER AND HARDSHIP

1 Midgley, OM, p. 125.

2 John Haffenden, 'Interview with Iris Murdoch', *Literary Review*, 58 (April 1983), pp. 31–5.

3 Midgley, OM, p. 130.

4 *Animal & Zoo Magazine*, November 1940, 5:6, p. 12.

5 Gardiner, *Wartime Britain 1939–1945*, p. 375.

6 Ibid., p. 383.

7 Alison Feeney-Hart, 'The Little-Told Story of the Massive WWII Pet Cull', BBC News Magazine, 12 October 2013.

8 Ann Sylph, 'Whipsnade during the Second World War' (6 November 2019), *Zoological Society of London* website https://www.zsl.org/blogs/artefact-of-the-month/whipsnade-during-the-second-world-war, accessed 1 August 2021.

9 *Animal and Zoo Magazine*, 5:4 (September 1940), p. 12.

10 Ibid., 5:7 (December 1940), p. 25.

11 'Letter from Myra Curtis to Barbara Gwyer', 24 June 1942, SHCA, SHG/J/3/2.

12 'Letter from Barbara Gwyer to Myra Curtis', 25 June 1942, SHCA, SHG/J/3/2.

13 Keene, 'Gwyer, Barbara Elizabeth (1881–1974)'.

14 'Letter from Barbara Gwyer to Myra Curtis', 25 June 1942, op. cit.

15 A. Phillips, *A Newnham Anthology* (Cambridge: Cambridge University Press, 1979), p. 208.

16 For more on railways during wartime, see D. Wragg, *Wartime on the Railways* (Cheltenham: History Press, 2012).

17 Gardiner, *Wartime Britain 1939–1945*, p. 233 et passim.
18 R. Monk, *Ludwig Wittgenstein: The Duty of Genius* (London: Penguin, 1991), p. 425.
19 Ibid., p. 445.
20 Wolfe Mays, 'Recollections of Wittgenstein', in *Portraits of Wittgenstein*, abridged edition, ed. F. A. Flowers III and Ian Ground (London: Bloomsbury Academic, 2018), pp. 337–42, at p. 339.
21 Bertrand Russell, 'Philosophers and Idiots', in Flowers and Ground, *Portraits of Wittgenstein*, pp. 69–71, at p. 71.
22 Monk, *Ludwig Wittgenstein*, p. 472.
23 Cambridge Moral Sciences Club Minute Book, Michaelmas 1942, University of Cambridge Archives, Min. IX. 42.
24 Emmet, *Philosophers and Friends*, p. 100.
25 See England and Wales Census Register 1939; and Donald MacKinnon, 'Philosophers in Exile', *The Oxford Magazine* (Michaelmas Term, 1992), pp. 15–16, at p. 15.
26 Gordon Baker, 'Waismann, Friedrich (1896–1959)', *ODNB*.
27 Monk, *Ludwig Wittgenstein*, p. 413.
28 Baker, 'Waismann, Friedrich (1896–1959)'.
29 Alice Ambrose, 'Ludwig Wittgenstein: A Portrait', in Flowers and Ground, *Portraits of Wittgenstein*, pp. 245–55.
30 Emily Dezurick-Badran, '"It is a person's privilege to go to hell": how Ludwig Wittgenstein and Alice Ambrose fell out', 5 August 2013, https://specialcollections-blog.lib.cam.ac.uk/?p=5219, accessed 1 August 2021.
31 Ambrose published the paper and returned to America. From Smith College, a women's liberal arts college in Massachusetts, she would go on to publish many important papers on philosophy of language (though many of her most interesting ideas would be attributed, wrongly, to her husband, the philosopher Morris Lazerowitz. See Sophia Connell, 'Alice Ambrose and Early Analytic Philosophy', *British Journal for the History of Philosophy* (forthcoming).
32 Ambrose, 'Ludwig Wittgenstein: A Portrait', pp. 252–3.
33 G.E.M. Anscombe, 'Cover letter for application for a Sarah Smithson Studentship', 30 April 1944, pp. 1–2, NCA, AC/5/2. © M. C. Gormally.
34 Ibid.
35 G.E.M. Anscombe, 'Rough Scheme for Proposed Work for a Sarah Smithson Studentship', n.d. [30 April 1944], © M. C. Gormally.
36 R. Descartes, *Philosophical Writings*, ed. G.E.M. Anscombe and P. T. Geach (London: Nelson, 1970), second meditation, p. 69.
37 G.E.M. Anscombe, 'The Principle of Individuation', *Proceedings of the Aristotelian Society, Supplementary Volumes* 27 (1953), pp. 83–96, at p. 94.
38 Descartes, *Philosophical Writings*. p. 67.

39 Ibid., p. 76.
40 G.E.M. Anscombe, 'Events in the Mind' (1963), MPM, pp. 57–63, at p. 60.
41 Aristotle, *The Complete Works of Aristotle: Two Volumes*, ed. Jonathan Barnes (Princeton: Princeton University Press, 2014).
42 See Michael Thompson, 'Apprehending Human Form', *Royal Institute of Philosophy Supplement* 54 (2004), pp. 47–74.
43 See E. L. Mascall, 'The Doctrine of Analogy', *Cross Currents* 1:4 (1951), pp. 38–57, at p. 45.
44 G.E.M. Anscombe, 'Rough Scheme for Proposed Work for a Sarah Smithson Studentship', n.d. [30 April 1944], pp. 1–2, NCA AC/5/2. © M. C. Gormally.
45 Midgley, OM, p. 133.
46 Margaret Jones, 'Ackroyd, Dame Dorothy Elizabeth', *ODNB*.
47 Midgley, OM, pp. 132–3.
48 Ibid., p. 133.
49 'Mary Midgley interviewed by Paul Merchant', track 1, p. 14.
50 'Letter from Iris Murdoch to Philippa Foot', n.d. [late summer 1942], IMC, KUAS100/1/1.
51 Ibid.
52 Conradi, IMAL, p. 139.
53 'Letter from Iris Murdoch to Philippa Foot', n.d. [late summer 1942], IMC, KUAS100/1/1.
54 Conradi, WW, p. 123.
55 Iris Murdoch, 'A Woman Don's Delight', in *Occasional Essays by Iris Murdoch*, ed. Paul Hullah and Yozo Muroya (Okayam: University Education Press, 1998), p. 17. And Dorothy Sheridan, ed., *Wartime Women: A Mass-Observation Anthology 1937–45* (London: Phoenix, 2002), pp. 196–205.
56 Conradi, WW, pp. 97 and 101.
57 Conradi, IMAL, p. 175.
58 Foot, *Memories of an S.O.E. Historian*, p. 70.
59 Ibid., pp. 72–3.
60 Gardiner, *Wartime Britain 1939–1945*, p. 466.
61 Charles Wheeler, letter to *The Times*; 'Picture of the Month' information file, National Gallery Research Centre.
62 'Picture of the Month' information file.
63 Foot, *Memories of an S.O.E. Historian*, p. 72.
64 'Picture of the Month' information file.
65 Gardiner, *Wartime Britain 1939–1945*, p. 466.
66 Conradi, WW, p. 256.
67 Conradi, IMAL, p. 174.
68 Conradi, *Family Business*, p. 176.

69 Midgley, OM, p. 133.
70 Letter from Iris Murdoch to Margorie Boulton, 16 Aug 1942, Horner and Rowe, LP, pp. 26–7.
71 Letter from Iris Murdoch to Philippa Foot, July 1942, Horner and Rowe, LP, p. 25.
72 Conradi, IMAL, p. 142.
73 Letter to Margorie Boulton, 16 August 1942, in Horner and Rowe, LP, p. 27.
74 Letter to Frank Thompson, 24 November 1942, ibid., pp. 28–30.
75 Ibid., p. 30.
76 Letter to Margorie Boulton, 16 August 1942, ibid., p. 27.
77 Midgley, OM, p. 134.
78 Letter to Frank Thompson, 22 January 1943, in Conradi, WW, pp. 124–5.
79 Ibid., p. 112.
80 Contribution to The World at War documentary series, Thames Television Ltd (1973–4), episode 8.
81 Ibid.
82 Gardiner, Wartime Britain 1939–1945, p. 87.
83 Letter to Frank Thompson, 19 October 1942, in Conradi, WW, p. 119.
84 Letter to Frank Thompson, 24 November 1942, in Horner and Rowe, LP, p. 29.
85 Conradi, WW, pp. 122–3.
86 Ibid., p. 123.
87 Conradi, WW, p. 243 and Conradi, IMAL, p. 169.
88 M. Luke, David Tennant and the Gargoyle Years (London: Weidenfeld & Nicolson, 1991); Conradi, IMAL, p. 169.
89 Conradi, '"The Guises of Love"', p. 18.
90 'Philippa Bosanquet letter to Mother', n.d., SCA, PF 1/6/k.
91 'Photocopy of a letter from Iris Murdoch to Rosalind Hursthouse', PCA, KUAS6/3/65/3.
92 'Philippa Bosanquet letter to Mother', n.d., SCA, PF 1/6/k.
93 J. Morris, The Life and Times of Thomas Balogh: A Macaw Among Mandarins (Chicago: Sussex Academic Press, 2007), p. 38.
94 'PC's interviews in Oxford, Hilary 1999', PCA, KUAS6/4/1/1.
95 'Philippa Bosanquet letter to Mother', n.d., SCA, PF 1/6/k.
96 Ibid.
97 Morris, The Life and Times of Thomas Balogh, p. 34.
98 I. W. Busbridge, 'Anne Philippa Cobbe', Bulletin of the London Mathematical Society, 5:3 (November 1973), pp. 358–60.
99 'Photocopy of a letter from Iris Murdoch to Rosalind Hursthouse', PCA, KUAS6/3/65/3, p. 3.
100 Morris, The Life and Times of Thomas Balogh, p. 166.
101 Gornall, 'Philippa Foot and Thoughts about Oxfam', p. 2.

102 Philippa Bosanquet letter to Mother, n.d., SCA, PF 1/6/c.
103 Margaret Mead, 'The Factor of Food Habits', *Annals of the American Academy of Political and Social Science*, 225 (1943) pp. 136–41.
104 Bertha Bracey, 'Europe's Displaced Persons and the Problems of Relocation', *International Affairs*, 20 (1944) pp. 225–43.
105 Bracey, 'Europe's Displaced Persons', pp. 225–6.
106 Ibid., p. 227.
107 Roy Greenslade, 'Daily Telegraph's Holocaust article in 1942 that Went Unheralded', *Guardian*, 27 January 2015.
108 'Philippa Bosanquet letter to Mother', n.d., SCA, PF 1/6/f.
109 J. J. O'Conner and E. F. Robinson, 'Anne Philippa Cobbe', April 2015, http://mathshistory.st-andrews.ac.uk/Biographies/Cobbe.html, accessed 27 January 2021.
110 Philippa Foot, 'Obituary: A Personal Memoir', pp. 12–14; also in Conradi, *IMAL*, p. 166.
111 T. Harding, *Legacy: One Family, a Cup of Tea and the Company that Took On the World* (London: Random House, 2019), p. xii.
112 Philippa Foot, 'Obituary: A Personal Memoir', pp. 12–14.
113 Conradi, *IMAL*, pp. 168–9.
114 'Photocopy of a letter from Iris Murdoch to Rosalind Hursthouse', PCA, KUAS6/3/65/3.
115 Philippa Foot, 'Iris at Home in London,' p. 3.
116 Conradi, *IMAL*, p. 123.
117 Ibid., p. 169.
118 Cambridge Moral Sciences Club Minute Book (Lent 1944), University of Cambridge Archives, Min. IV. 44; David Archibald, *Charles Darwin: A Reference Guide to His Life and Works* (Maryland: Rowman & Littlefield, 2018), p. 46.
119 Donald M. MacKinnon, 'Revelation and Social Justice' (1941), in McDowell, *Philosophy and the Burden of Theological Honesty*, p. 145.
120 Anscombe, 'Rough Scheme for Proposed Work', p. 2.
121 Ibid.
122 Ibid., p. 1.
123 See G.E.M. Anscombe, 'Modern Moral Philosophy', *Philosophy* 33, no. 124 (1958), p. 14.
124 Ibid.
125 Anscombe, 'Rough Scheme for Proposed Work', p. 2.
126 Calista Lucy, 'A Memorial to Fallen', [created by the Keeper of the Archives], Dulwich College, p. 23.
127 Arthur Foss and Kerith Trick, *St Andrews Hospital, Northampton: The First One Hundred and Fifty Years (1938–1988)* (Cambridge: Granta Editions, 1989), p. 260.

128 'The Parish of Beguildy', p. 6.
129 John Wisdom, 'Report to the Fellowship Electors Newnham College on Mrs. Geach's (Miss Anscombe) dissertation 1944', NCA, AC/5/2.
130 'Letter from Friedrich Waismann to Miss Curtis in support of G.E.M. Anscombe's fellowship application', 15 May 1944. NCA, AC/5/2.
131 MacKinnon, 'Philosophers in Exile', p. 15.
132 Conradi, *IMAL*, p. 170.
133 'Philippa Bosanquet letter to Mother', n.d., SCA, PF 1/6/f.
134 'Letter to David Hicks', 6 November 1945, Conradi, *WW*, p. 254.
135 Ibid., p. 255.
136 Conradi, *IMAL*, p. 178.
137 Foot, *Memories of an S.O.E. Historian*, p. 84.
138 Ibid.
139 Ibid., p. 84.
140 'Letter to David Hicks', 6 November 1945, Conradi, *WW*, p. 255.
141 Midgley, *OM*, p. 133.
142 Ibid., p. 19.
143 Ibid., p. 134.
144 Ibid., p. 55.
145 Ridler, *Olive Willis and Downe House*, pp. 158–61.
146 Midgley, *OM*, p. 134.
147 St Hilda's College Archives, Oxford University Matriculation Lists (Margaret Elizabeth Rhoda Torrance went up in 1941).
148 Midgley, *OM*, p. 136.
149 Mary Midgley, conversation with authors, January 2017.
150 Midgley, *OM*, p. 136.
151 Fann, *Wittgenstein*, p. 54.
152 Desmond Lee, 'Wittgenstein 1929–31', in *Portraits of Wittgenstein*, ed. Flowers and Ground, pp. 178–87, at p. 179.
153 Theodore Redpath, 'A Student's Memoir', ibid., pp. 258–72 at p. 259.
154 I. A. Richards, 'The Strayed Poet', printed in Monk, *Ludwig Wittgenstein*, pp. 289–90.
155 Ludwig Wittgenstein, *On Certainty*, ed. Anscombe and von Wright (London: Blackwell, 1969), p. 61e.
156 Theodore Redpath, 'A Student's Memoir', p. 259.
157 Gitta Deutsch Arnold, 'Recollections of Wittgenstein', in *Portraits of Wittgenstein*, ed Flowers and Ground, pp. 398–9, at p. 398.
158 Anscombe, 'Anecdotes about Wittgenstein', CIAA Box 1, File 259. © M. C. Gormally.
159 Dialogue reconstructed from L. Wittgenstein et al., *Wittgenstein's Lectures on Philosophical Psychology, 1946-47* (Chicago: University of Chicago Press, 1989), p. 24.

160 Wittgenstein, *PI*, (Oxford: Blackwell, 1953), §23.

161 'Philippa Bosanquet letter to Mother', n.d., SCA PF 1/6/e.

162 'Margaret Stanier's typed memories of Iris Murdoch', October 1998, PCA, KUAS6/11/1/31.

163 Foot, 'Photocopy of a letter from Iris Murdoch to Rosalind Hursthouse'.

164 Conradi, *IMAL*, p. 628, n. 58; and in 'Picture of the Month information file'.

165 Philippa Foot, 'Obituary: A Personal Memoir', pp. 12–14.

166 Conradi, *A Very English Hero*, pp. 318, 345 (Thompson entered Bulgaria on 27 May 1944 and was murdered on 10 June).

167 Ibid., p. 328.

168 Conradi, *IMAL*, p. 193.

169 'Letter from Iris Murdoch to Leo Pliatzky', 30 October 1945, IMC, KUAS134.

170 Conradi, *IMAL*, p. 231.

171 'Philippa Bosanquet letter to Mother', n.d., SCA, PF 1/6/h.

172 'Philippa Bosanquet letter to Mother', October 1944, SCA, PF 1/6/a.

173 Ibid.

174 A. G. Hodges and D. George, *Behind Nazi Lines: My Father's Heroic Quest to Save 149 World War II POWs* (New York: Berkley Caliber, 2015), p. 185.

175 'Philippa Bosanquet letter to Mother', n.d., SCA, PF 1/6/h.

176 Foot, *Memories of an S.O.E. Historian*, p. 97.

177 Ibid., p. 99.

178 G.E.M. Anscombe, 'Cover letter for Research Fellowship Application', 5 May 1945, NCA AC/5/2. © M. C. Gormally.

179 Ibid.

180 Anscombe, 'Anecdotes about Wittgenstein'.

181 Anscombe, 'Rough Scheme for Proposed Work', p. 2.

182 Bertrand Russell, 'Reference for Elizabeth Anscombe', 20 May 1945, NCA, AC/5/2.

183 Ludwig Wittgenstein, 'Reference for Elizabeth Anscombe', 18 May 1945, NCA, AC/5/2.

184 John Schwenkler, 'Untempted by the Consequences: G.E.M. Anscombe's Life of "Doing the Truth"', 2 December 2019, *Commonweal* (2 December 2019), https://www.commonwealmagazine.org/untempted-consequences, accessed 1 August 2021.

185 Teichman, 'Gertrude Elizabeth Margaret Anscombe', p. 37; see also Geach's preface to *Wittgenstein's Lectures on Philosophical Psychology, 1946–47: Notes by P. T. Geach, K. J. Shah, and A. C. Jackson*, (Chicago: University of Chicago Press, 1989), p. xi.

186 Mary Alvey Thomas, 'Curtis, Dame Myra (1886–1971)', *ODNB*.

187 'Mrs. Gertrude Elizabeth Margaret (née) Anscombe, CV', NCA AC/5/2. © M. C. Gormally.

188 Geach, *Wittgenstein's Lectures on Philosophical Psychology*, p. xi.
189 Gardiner, *Wartime Britain 1939–1945*, p. 668.
190 Foot, *Memories of an S.O.E. Historian*, p. 100.
191 Midgley, OM, p. 139.
192 Purton, *An Iris Murdoch Chronology*, p. 36.
193 Jean Wilhelma Rowntree, Oral History, Imperial War Museum sound archive, https://www.iwm.org.uk/collections/item/object/80014585, accessed 1 August 2021.
194 Midgley, OM, p. 96.
195 'Letter from Isobel Henderson', 18 March 1944, MGMP, MID/F.
196 Foot, *Memories of an S.O.E. Historian*, p. 102.
197 Conradi, WW, p. 254.
198 A. D. Lindsay, 'Reference for Philippa Foot', 24 May 1945, SCA, Box 5 Appointments and Appreciations.
199 Donald MacKinnon, 'Reference for Philippa Foot', 24 May 1945, SCA, Box 5 Appointments and Appreciations.
200 Heinz Cassirer, 'Reference for Philippa Foot', 28 May 1945, SCA Box 5, Appointments and Appreciations.
201 Isaiah Berlin, *Personal Impressions* (London: Hogarth Press, 1980), p. 103.
202 Morris, *The Life and Times of Thomas Balogh*, p. 34.
203 Conradi, WW, p. 203.
204 Ibid., p. 227.
205 Conradi, IMAL, p. 206.
206 'Letter from IM to Leo Pliatzky', 30 October 1945, IMC, KUAS134.
207 IMJ3, 5 August 1945, p. 20, IMA, KUAS202/1/3.
208 Brendan Sweetman, 'Introduction', *A Gabriel Marcel Reader* (South Bend, Indiana: St Augustine's Press, 2011), p. 5.
209 Foot, *Memories of an S.O.E. Historian*, p. 100.
210 Donald M. Mackinnon, 'Reflections on the Hydrogen Bomb', *The Listener* 52, 13 (1954), p. 239.

CHAPTER 4: PARK TOWN

1 New College warden, quoted in Nicola Lacey, *A Life of H.L.A. Hart: The Nightmare and the Noble Dream* (Oxford: Oxford University Press, 2004), p. 126. See also Addison, 'Oxford and the Second World War', p. 187.
2 E. L. Mascall, *Saraband: The Memoirs of E. L. Mascall* (Leominster: Gracewing, 1992), p. 246.
3 Mehta, *Fly and the Fly-Bottle*, p. 27.
4 Adams, SW, p. 254.
5 Foot, *Memories of an S.O.E. Historian*, p. 50.

6　Warnock, *People and Places*, p. 44.

7　Adams, *SW*, p. 255.

8　Price, 'Clarity Is Not Enough', p. 1.

9　Rogers, *A. J. Ayer*, p. 182.

10　Ibid., pp. 196–7.

11　Ibid., p. 138.

12　Ibid., p. 228.

13　G. J. Warnock, 'Gilbert Ryle's Editorship', *Mind* 85:337 (1976), pp. 47–56, at p. 48.

14　Warnock, 'Gilbert Ryle's Editorship', p. 48.

15　Rowe, *J. L. Austin*, chapter 7.

16　Ibid., chapter 23.

17　Mary Midgley, conversation with authors, September 2016.

18　Rowe, *J. L. Austin*, chapter 9.

19　Ibid., chapter 21.

20　Jean Austin, 'Pleasure and Happiness', *Philosophy* 43, number 163 (1968), pp. 51–62.

21　A. Biletzki and A. Matar, *The Story of Analytic Philosophy: Plot and Heroes* (New York: Routledge, 1998), p. 22.

22　C. Reaveley (Glover) and J. Winnington, *Democracy and Industry* (London: Chatto & Windus, 1947), p. vii. Mary Glover co-authored a book, and wrote a number of newspaper articles, under the pen name 'Constance Reaveley'.

23　Reaveley and Winnington, *Democracy and Industry*, p. 78.

24　Ibid., p. 141.

25　Scott, *A. D. Lindsay*, p. 293.

26　See C. H. 'Mary Reaveley Glover'; also Scott, *A. D. Lindsay*, chapters 17 and 19. The University College of North Staffordshire (established in 1949) became the University of Keele in 1962.

27　Constance Reaveley (Glover), 'Wrong Things to Teach', *Spectator*, 2 February 1945, p. 101.

28　'Letter from Donald MacKinnon to Christopher Cox', 11 September 1958, New College Archives, Oxford, Papers of H.W.B. Joseph, PAJOS Box 23/1–2.

29　'Letter from Kenneth Sisam to the Warden, Alic Smith', 11 July 1947, Papers of H.W.B. Joseph, New College Archives, University of Oxford, PAJOS Box 23/1–2.

30　'Letter from Donald MacKinnon to Christopher Cox', 11 September 1958, ibid. In 1949, Joseph's lectures on Leibniz were published, edited by J. L. Austin.

31　Quoted in Midgley, OM, p.143. Murray's gravestone, in Westminster Abbey's Poets' Corner, reads: 'while he lived the letters of the ancient Greeks lived again'.

32 G. Murray, *Gilbert Murray: An Unfinished Autobiography* (Oxford: Oxford University Press, 1960), p. 166.
33 A. Voorhoeve, *Conversations on Ethics* (Oxford: Oxford University Press, 2011), p. 91.
34 Gornall, 'Philippa Foot and Thoughts about Oxfam', p. 2.
35 Constance Reaveley (Glover), 'Could We Go Nazi', *Spectator*, 5 October 1945, pp. 307–8, at p. 307.
36 G. R. G. Mure, *Retreat From Truth* (Oxford: Blackwell, 1958), p. 4.
37 Doll, 'Vaughan [married name Gourlay], Dame Janet Maria (1899–1993)'.
38 Smith, *The Morning Light*, p. 234.
39 Voorhoeve, *Conversations on Ethics*, p. 91.
40 Ibid., p. 92.
41 Foot, *Memories of an S.O.E. Historian*, p. 102.
42 Crawford et al. (eds), AC, p. 3.
43 I. Jacoby, *My Darling Diary, Volume 1, The Girl In and Out of Love: Oxford 1944–1950* (Penzance: United Writers, 2006), cited in Anthony Grenville, 'Academic Refugees in Wartime Oxford: An Overview', in Crawford et al. (eds), pp. 50–61, at p. 60.
44 Grenville, 'Academic Refugees in Wartime Oxford', p. 60.
45 Midgley, OM, p. 148.
46 Foot, *Memories of an S.O.E. Historian*, pp. 102–3.
47 Mary Midgley, *Wickedness: A Philosophical Essay* (London: Routledge, 1984/2001), p. 4.
48 Midgley, *Wickedness*, p. 7.
49 H. Gollwitzer et al., *Dying We Live: The Final Messages and Records of the German Resistance* (Eugene, Oregon: Wipf & Stock Publishers, 2009), p. 51.
50 Philippa Foot, 'Rationality and Goodness', *Royal Institute of Philosophy Supplement* 54 (2004).
51 Barbara Harvey, 'Address Given in Commemoration of Philippa Foot in Somerville Hall', 19 March 2011, SCA, SC/AO/AA/FW/Foot.
52 Gaby Charing, 'Memorial Address', 19 March 2011', SCA, SC/AO/AA/FW/Foot.
53 Iris Murdoch wrote an undated letter to Philippa from Chiswick, expressing envy that Foot was attending MacKinnon's lectures (IMC, KUAS100/1/9).
54 'Mary Midgley interviewed by Paul Merchant', track 5, p. 64.
55 Conradi, WW, p. 237.
56 'Letter from Iris Murdoch to Leo Pliatzky', 30 October 1945, IMC, KUAS134.
57 Conradi, WW, p. 237.
58 'Letter from Iris Murdoch to Philippa Foot', 11 November 1946, IMC, KUAS100/1/7.
59 See 'Letter from Iris Murdoch to Leo Pliatzky', 30 October 1945, op. cit.

60 Iris Murdoch, *Sartre, Romantic Rationalist*, with new introduction by Iris Murdoch (London: Penguin, 1987/1989), p. 10.

61 Catherine Lanneau, *L'Inconnue française: La France et les Belges Francophones, 1944–1945* (Bruxelles: P.I.E. Peter Lang, 2008), pp. 259–60.

62 This is the equivalent of about €14 today. F. White, *Becoming Iris Murdoch* (London: Kingston University Press, 2014). p. 32. The notebook is held in the IMA, 'Notes on a lecture given by Jean Paul Sartre', IMA, IML 682.

63 All references are to Jean-Paul Sartre, 'Existentialism is a Humanism' (1946), trans. Philip Mairet, in *Existentialism from Dostoyevsky to Sartre*, ed. Walter Kaufman (London: Penguin, 1991), pp. 345–68, at p. 349.

64 Sartre, 'Existentialism is a Humanism', pp. 348–9.

65 Ibid., p. 361.

66 Ibid., p. 349.

67 Conradi, *WW*, p. 251.

68 Morris, *The Life and Times of Thomas Balogh*, p. 34.

69 Sartre, 'Existentialism is a Humanism', p. 349.

70 Ibid., p. 350.

71 Ibid., p. 353.

72 Lanneau, *L'Inconnue Française*, pp. 259–61, at p. 261.

73 IMJ6, 12 Dec. 1948, p. J.

74 'Notes on a lecture given by Jean Paul Sartre', IMA, IML 682.

75 Conradi, *WW*, p. 251.

76 'Letter to Leo Pliatzky from Iris Murdoch', 30 October 1945, IMC, KUAS0134.

77 'Letter to David Hicks from Iris Murdoch', 3 December 1945, in Conradi, *WW*, p. 264.

78 Conradi, *IMAL*, p. 203.

79 'Letter from Iris Murdoch to Hal Lidderdale', 28 February 1946, IMC, KUAS78/65; see also Conradi, *IMAL*, p. 216.

80 Conradi, *WW*, p. 269.

81 An UNRRA communication from the British Zone for September 1946 lists 1,049 refugee children, 830 of whom are with Austrian families but adds 'it is highly probable that for each child listed as being in an Austrian family, there are possibly one or two additional to be discovered'. See 'Staff Bulletin October 1946', p. 22, UN Archives, (https://archives.un.org/), United Nations Relief and Rehabilitation Administration (1943-48), Austria Mission / Monthly Narrative Reports, item ref. S-1494-0000-0106-00001.

82 Conradi, *WW*, p. 273.

83 Conradi, *IMAL*, p. 235.

84 Gornall, 'Philippa Foot and Thoughts about Oxfam', p. 9.

85 https://www.iwm.org.uk/collections/item/object/80014585, 1 August 2021.
86 Conradi, *WW*, p. 288.
87 Ibid., p. 303.
88 Horner and Rowe, *LP*, pp. 58–9.
89 Conradi, *WW*, p. 298.
90 Conradi, *IMAL*, p. 247.
91 'Letter from Iris Murdoch to Hal Lidderdale', 17 April 1946, IMC, KUAS78/66.
92 Purton, *An Iris Murdoch Chronology*, p. 45.
93 H. C. Fey, *A History of the Ecumenical Movement, Volume 2: 1948–1968* (Eugene, Oregon: Wipf & Stock Publishers, 2009).
94 M. Metod Milač, *Resistance, Imprisonment & Forced Labor: A Slovene Student in World War II* (New York: Peter Lang, 2002)
95 Horner and Rowe, *LP*, p. 71.
96 See http://www.dpcamps.org/graz.html, accessed 1 August 2021.
97 Horner and Rowe, *LP*, p. 71.
98 Ibid., pp. 68–9.
99 'Letter from Iris Murdoch to Leo Pliatzky', 4 April 1945, IMC KUAS134.
100 'Letter from IM to "Madam" (Miss Myra Curtis, Principal of Newnham College) re. Sarah Smithson Studentship', from UNRRA, Vienna, 9 April 1946, NCA AC/5/2/1, pp. 1–2.
101 Ibid., p. 1.
102 'Letter from Iris Murdoch to David Hicks', 5 January 1946, in Conradi, *WW*, p. 280.
103 Martin Buber, *I and Thou*, trans. Ronald Gregor-Smith (Edinburgh: T & T Clark, 1958), p. 25.
104 'Letter from IM to "Madam" re Sarah Smithson Studentship', op. cit., p. 2.
105 'Letter to Principal from Donald MacKinnon', 27 April 1946, NCA, AC/5/2/3.
106 Mildred Hartley's file (under her married name), SCA SC/AO/AA/FW/Taylor.
107 'Letter to Principal from Mildred Hartley', 6 June 1946, NCA AC/5/2/4.
108 For discussion, see J. Searle, 'Oxford Philosophy in the 1950s', *Philosophy*, 90(2), 2015.
109 Christian Erbacher, 'Wittgenstein and His Literary Executors', *Journal for the History of Analytical Philosophy*, 4, 3 (2016), p. 29.
110 'John Campbell memorial address', 19 March 2011, p. 1, SCA, SC/AO/AA/FW/Foot.
111 Rée, 'Philosophical Lives: Philippa Foot interview', p. 2.
112 This is Anscombe's own translation of '*je pense, doc je suis*' in Descartes et al., *Philosophical Writings*, p. 31.

113 G.E.M. Anscombe, 'Mary Somerville Research Fellow Report, May 1947', SC/AO/FS/MSRF/Fellows' Reports. © M. C. Gormally.

114 G.E.M. Anscombe, 'Rough Scheme for Proposed Work'.

115 Wittgenstein, *PI*, §244.

116 G.E.M. Anscombe, 'Mary Somerville Research Fellow Report, May 1948', SC/AO/FS/MSRF/Fellows' Reports. © M. C. Gormally.

117 Wittgenstein, *PI*, part II, p. 174.

118 L. Wittgenstein et al., *Last Writings on the Philosophy of Psychology, Volume 1* (Chicago: University of Chicago Press, 1982), §§966.

119 Rée, 'Philosophical Lives: Philippa Foot interview', p. 2.

120 'Letter from Philippa Foot to GEMA', Boston, 19 February 1964, CIAA, Box 14, 580.

121 Philippa Foot, *Virtues and Vices: and Other Essays in Moral Philosophy* (Oxford: Basil Blackwell, 1978), p. 2.

122 Foot, *Virtues and Vices*, p. xi.

123 IMJ4, 25 October 1947, p. 145.

124 Conradi, *IMAL*, p. 246.

125 'Letter from Iris Murdoch to Mary Scrutton', n.d. [circa.1941], MGMP, MID/F.

126 Midgley, OM, p. 125.

127 'Copy of letter to Principal [MC] from Donald MacKinnon', Balliol, 3 June 1947, NCA, AC/5/2/10.

128 Purton, *An Iris Murdoch Chronology*, p. 47.

129 Conradi, *IMAL*, p. 247.

130 Ibid., p. 248.

131 'Letter from Iris Murdoch to Philippa Foot', Chiswick, 10 October 1946, IMC, KUAS100/1/2.

132 'Letter from Iris Murdoch to Philippa Foot', Chiswick, n.d., IMC, KUAS100/1/4.

133 'Letter from Iris Murdoch to Philippa Foot', Chiswick, 11 November 1946, IMC, KUAS100/1/7.

134 IMJ3, 17 March 1947, p. 84.

135 Rowe, *J. L. Austin*, chapter 9.

136 G. J. Warnock, 'John Langshaw Austin: A Biographical Sketch (1963)', in *Symposium on J. L. Austin*, ed. K. T. Fann (London: Routledge & Kegan Paul, 1969), pp. 3–21, at p. 9.

137 Rowe, *J. L. Austin*, chapter 10.

138 G. J. Warnock, *J. L. Austin*, (London: Routledge, 1989), pp. 6–7.

139 J. O. Urmson, 'Austin's Philosophy', *Symposium on J. L. Austin*, ed. Fann, pp. 22–32, at p. 24.

140 G. J. Warnock, 'Saturday Mornings', *Essays on J. L. Austin: By I. Berlin [And Others]*, ed. I. Berlin (Oxford: Clarendon Press, 1973), pp. 31–2.

141 Rée, 'Philosophical Lives: Philippa Foot interview', p. 2. Later, Austin would make an exception for Mary Wilson – but only after she had become Mary Warnock by marrying Austin's favourite, Geoffrey (Warnock, *People and Places*, p. 17).

142 Urmson, 'Austin's Philosophy', p. 24.

143 Ibid.

144 J. L. Austin, 'A Plea for Excuses', *Proceedings of the Aristotelian Society*, 57 (1956–7), pp. 1–30, at p. 24.

145 Urmson, 'Austin's Philosophy', pp. 24–5.

146 Bryan Magee and Anthony Quinton, *Modern British Philosophy* (Oxford: Oxford University Press, 1971), p. 95.

147 J. L. Austin, *Sense and Sensibilia (reconstructed from the manuscript notes by G.J. Warnock)* (Oxford: Oxford University Press, 1962), p. 16.

148 Austin, *Sense and Sensibilia*, pp. 50–2.

149 Magee and Quinton, *Modern British Philosophy*, p. 116.

150 Conversation with authors, January 2016.

151 Chapman, *Susan Stebbing and the Language of Common Sense*, p. 177.

152 Warnock, *People and Places*, p. 65.

153 Ibid.

154 Warnock, 'John Langshaw Austin: A Biographical Sketch', p. 11.

155 Daniel W. Harris and Elmar Unnsteinsson, 'Wittgenstein's Influence on Austin's Philosophy of Language', *British Journal for the History of Philosophy* 26:2 (2018), pp. 371–95.

156 J. L. Austin, 'The Meaning of a Word' (1940 manuscript), *Philosphical Papers*, 3rd edn, ed. J. O. Urmson and G. J. Warnock (Oxford: Oxford University Press, 1979), pp. 55–75.

157 Warnock, *People and Places*, p. 65.

158 IMJ3, 21 February 1947, p. 54.

159 Anscombe, 'Mary Somerville Research Fellow Report, May 1947'.

160 Anscombe, 'Mary Somerville Research Fellow Report, May 1948'.

161 G.E.M. Anscombe, 'Mary Somerville Research Fellow Report, May 1949', SCA, SC/AO/FS/MSRF/Fellows' Reports. © M. C. Gormally.

162 Isaiah Berlin, 'I'm Going to Tamper with Your Beliefs a Little' (2006), transcript, *The Isaiah Berlin Virtual Library*, (https://berlin.wolf.ox.ac.uk/), pp. 19–20.

163 'Letter from Wittgenstein to Rush Rhees', 13 July 1938, *Wittgenstein in Cambridge: Letters and Documents 1911–1951* (Oxford: Wiley, 2012), p. 279.

164 'Letters regarding Oscar Wood's appointment', Worcester College Archive, University of Oxford, WOR/PRO 10/1/54.

165 Monk, *Ludwig Wittgenstein*, p. 496.

166 'Mary Midgley interviewed by Paul Merchant', track 3, p. 36.

167 Monk, *Ludwig Wittgenstein*, p. 496.

168 Warnock, *People and Places*, p. 52.
169 'Transcript of RMH personal interview with (now Sir) Brian Harrison', p. 10.
170 Midgley, OM, pp. 159–60.
171 Foot, *Natural Goodness*, p. 1.
172 Midgley, OM, p. 160.
173 Rée, 'Philosophical Lives: Philippa Foot interview', p. 3.
174 Mary Warnock, 'A Tremendous Coup', in *Portraits of Wittgenstein*, ed. Flowers and Ground, pp. 395–7, at p. 396.
175 Prichard, 'H.W.B. Joseph', *Mind*, April 1944, 53:210, pp. 189–91.
176 Emmet, *Philosophers and Friends*, p. 4.
177 Warnock, *People and Places*, p. 57.
178 For a slightly different account of the details of this exchange – though not of the outcome – see Lacey, *A Life of H.L.A. Hart*, p. 140.
179 'Transcript of RMH personal interview with (now Sir) Brian Harrison', p. 16.
180 Warnock, 'A Tremendous Coup', p. 395.
181 Mabbott, *Oxford Memories*, p. 147.
182 Midgley, OM, pp. 156–7.
183 Lacey, *A Life of H.L.A. Hart*, p. 128.
184 MacKinnon, 'And the Son of Man that Thou Visitest Him', part 2, p. 264.
185 Midgley, OM, p. 156.
186 Mary Scrutton, 'Untitled paper on theories about perception in the philosophy of Plotinus', n.d. [1948/9], MGMP, MID/E/69.
187 'Mary Midgley interviewed by Paul Merchant', track 2, p. 19.
188 F. H. Bradley, *Appearance and Reality: A Metaphysical Essay*, 2nd edition (London: S. Sonnenschein, 1908), p. 206.
189 Mary Scrutton, 'Individuation in Plotinus', n.d. [1948/9], MGMP MID/C/22, MID/E/71, p. 27.
190 Dorothy M. Emmet, 'On the Idea of Importance', *Philosophy* 21:80 (1946), pp. 234–44.
191 This idea will show up again many years later, in Mary Midgley, 'Is "Moral" a Dirty Word?', *Philosophy* 47:181 (1972), pp. 206–28.
192 Mary Scrutton, 'Self and Not-Self in Plotinus', 1 December 1948, p. 18, MGMP, MID/C/22, MID/E/68.
193 Ibid., p. 18.
194 Dodds, *Missing Persons*, p. 180.
195 IMJ3, 17 March 1946, p. 86.
196 'Letter from Iris Murdoch to Philippa Foot', n.d. [probably winter 1946/7], IMC, KUAS100/1/9.
197 'Letter to Principal from Donald MacKinnon', 3 June 1947, op. cit.
198 Iris Murdoch, 'Scheme of Work for Sarah Smithson Studentship', n.d. [May 1947], p. 4, NCA, AC/5/2/20.

199 Ibid., p .3.
200 Ibid., p. 4.
201 I. Murdoch, 'A House of Theory' (1956), *EM*, p. 174.
202 IMJ3, 27 February 1947, p. 64.
203 'Letter to Principal from Donald MacKinnon', 3 June 1947, op. cit.
204 'Letter from Lois MacKinnon to Peter Conradi', 24 September 1999, IMC, KUAS6/1/31/2.
205 IMJ4, 23 Sept 1947, p. 53.
206 Conradi, *IMAL*, p. 254; also Midgley, OM, p. 151.

CHAPTER 5: A JOINT 'NO!'
 1 Adams, *SW*, p. 259.
 2 Teichman, 'Elizabeth Anscombe', p. 34.
 3 IMJ6, 12 June 1948, p.103.
 4 Midgley, OM, p. 147.
 5 Mary Midgley, 'Then and Now' (2016), transcript, https://www.womenin parenthesis.co.uk/then-and-now/, accessed 1 August 2021.
 6 IMJ4, 8 October 1947, p. 90.
 7 Anscombe, 'Mary Somerville Research Fellow Report, 1948'.
 8 Rée, 'Philosophical Lives: Philippa Foot interview', p. 1.
 9 Midgley, OM, p. 170.
10 IMJ6, 12 June 1948, p. 103.
11 Mary Midgley, 'Sorting Out the Zeitgeist', *Changing English* 7, no. 1 (2000), pp. 89–92, at p. 89.
12 Midgley, 'Then and Now'.
13 Hare, 'A Philosophical Autobiography', p. 283.
14 'TS transcript of RMH personal interview with (now Sir) Brian Harrison', p. 8.
15 Hare, 'A Philosophical Autobiography', p. 285.
16 Ibid.
17 'TS transcript of RMH personal interview with (now Sir) Brian Harrison', p. 4.
18 Ibid., p. 2.
19 Ibid., p. 8.
20 Hare, 'A Philosophical Autobiography' p. 285.
21 Ibid., p. 281.
22 R. M. Hare, 'Moral Objectivity', n.d. MS, pp. 7–8, R. M. Hare papers.
23 Hare, 'AUTOB2', 31 May 1994, MS, p. 4, R. M. Hare papers.
24 Hare, 'A Philosophical Autobiography', p. 285.
25 Ibid., p. 288.
26 Ibid., p. 269.

27 R. M. Hare, *The Language of Morals* (Oxford: Clarendon Press, 1952), see especially chapters 2 and 3.

28 R. M. Hare papers, Balliol College archives.

29 R. M. Hare, 'Imperative Sentences', *Mind* 58, number 229 (1949) pp. 21–39; and Hare, *The Language of Morals*.

30 Hare, 'Moral Objectivity', p. 10.

31 Murdoch, 'Metaphysics and Ethics', *EM*, p. 63.

32 Conradi, *IMAL*, p. 263.

33 Monk, *Ludwig Wittgenstein*, p. 528.

34 Conradi, *IMAL*, p. 270.

35 'Letter from Iris Murdoch to Philippa Foot', Newnham, 16 November 1947, KUAS100/1/28.

36 IMJ4, 25 July 1947, p. 25.

37 'Letter from Iris Murdoch to Philippa Foot', Cambridge, 17 October [1947], KUAS100/1/8.

38 See D. Edmonds and J. Eidenow, *Wittgenstein's Poker* (New York: Ecco, Harper Collins, 2001).

39 G.E.M. Anscombe, 'The Reality of the Past' (1950), *MPM*, pp. 103–19, at p. 114 (fn. 3); all words spoken by Anscombe are quotes (or lightly adapted quotes) from this paper.

40 Anscombe, 'The Reality of the Past', p. 103.

41 Ibid.

42 Ibid., pp. 112, 113.

43 Ibid., pp. 112–13.

44 G.E.M. Anscombe, *Intention* (Oxford: Blackwell, 1957), §1.

45 Anscombe, 'The Reality of the Past', pp. 103–4.

46 G.E.M. Anscombe, 'Hume and Julius Caesar' (1973), in her *From Parmenides to Wittgenstein: Collected Philosophical Papers Volume I* (Oxford: Basil Blackwell, 1981) [*FPW*], pp. 86–92, at p. 89.

47 IMJ4, 17 October 1947, p. 129.

48 Gabriel Marcel, *The Mystery of Being, Volume 1: Reflection & Mystery* (London: Harvill, 1951).

49 IMJ4, 8 October 1947, p. 89.

50 Gabriel Marcel, *Being and Having*, trans. Katharine Farrer (Westminster, London: Dacre Press, 1949), p. 19.

51 IMJ4, 17 October 1947, p. 128.

52 IMJ4, 2 November 1947, p. 158.

53 IMJ4, 8 October 1947, p. 89.

54 See Sweetman, 'Introduction'.

55 IMJ4, 7 November 1947, p. 166.

56 'Letter from Iris Murdoch to Philippa Foot', Cambridge, 8 November 1947, IMC, KUAS100/1/11.

57 'Letter from Iris Murdoch to Philippa Foot', n.d., postmark 30 May 1947, IMC, KUAS100/1/22.
58 'Letter from Iris Murdoch to Philippa Foot', Cambridge, 15 November 1947, IMC, KUAS100/1/12.
59 Conradi, *IMAL*, p. 261.
60 Horner and Rowe, *LP*, p. 108.
61 Monk, *Ludwig Wittgenstein*, p. 497.
62 L. Wittgenstein and C. Barrett, *Wittgenstein: Lectures and Conversations on Aesthetics, Psychology and Religious Belief* (Oxford: Basil Blackwell, 1966), p. 56.
63 Edmonds and Eidenow, *Wittgenstein's Poker*, p. 9.
64 IMJ4, 4 April 1948, p. 55.
65 Wittgenstein et al., *Wittgenstein's Lectures on Philosophical Psychology, 1946–47*.
66 'Letter from Iris Murdoch to Philippa Foot', Cambridge, 24 April 1948, IMC, KUAS100/1/16.
67 Mehta, *Fly and the Fly-Bottle*, p. 55.
68 IMJ4, 23 October 1947, p. 143.
69 Prophecy Coles, correspondence with authors, 13 October 2020.
70 Midgley, *OM*, p. 115 (and conversation with authors, September 2016).
71 Harding, *Legacy*, p. 386.
72 In this scene, Philippa's words are extracted and lightly adapted from her published papers. See Philippa Foot, 'Moral Beliefs', *Proceedings of the Aristotelian Society* 59 (1958), pp. 83–104, at p. 83.
73 See Philippa Foot, 'Moral Arguments', *Mind* 67, no. 268 (1958), pp. 502–13, at p. 508.
74 Ibid.
75 Midgley, *OM*, p. 115.
76 Ibid.
77 IMJ4, 25 July 1947, p. 25.
78 Midgley, *OM*, pp. 115–16.
79 Glover, 'Obligation and Value', p. 76.
80 Joe D. Heck, ed., *Socratic Digest 1943–1952* (Austin, Texas: Concordia University Press, 2012), p. 102.
81 Iris Murdoch in her foreword to S. Aldwinckle, *Christ's Shadow in Plato's Cave: A Meditation on the Substance of Love* (Oxford: Amate Press, 1990), p. 7.
82 'Letter to Jim Stockton of Boise State University, Idaho, Department of Philosophy', 2012, MID/E/48.
83 Jim Stockton, 'Chaplain Stella Aldwinckle: A Biographical Sketch of the Spiritual Foundation of the Oxford University Socratic Club', *Inklings Forever: Published Colloquium Proceedings 1997–2016*, Vol. 8, Article 26 (2012) pp. 1–8, at p. 6.

84 Stella Aldwinkle, 'Memories of the Socratic Club', in *C. S. Lewis and His Circle: Essays and Memoirs from the Oxford C. S. Lewis Society*, ed. Roger White, Judith Wolfe and Brendan N. Wolfe (Oxford: Oxford University Press, 2015), pp. 192–6, at p. 192.

85 Michael Ward, 'Afterword: A Brief History of the Oxford', Ibid., pp. 249–56, at p. 252.

86 G.E.M. Anscombe, 'A Reply to Mr. C. S. Lewis's Argument that "Naturalism" is Self-Refuting' (1948), in her *MPM*, pp. 224–33, at p. 224.

87 Ibid, pp. 224–6.

88 Ibid., pp. 227–8.

89 Anscombe, *Intention*, §23.

90 Ibid., §23.

91 Ibid., §48.

92 'Letter from GEMA to Wittgenstein', 3 February [1948], p. 1, CIAA Box 13, file 537.

93 'Letter from Peter Daniel to Peter Conradi', 17 March 1998, PCA KUAS6/1/51/3.

94 'Letter from GEMA to Wittgenstein', op. cit.

95 http://www.lewisiana.nl/anscombe/, accessed 1 August 2021.

96 Anscombe, *MPM*, p. x.

97 G.E.M. Anscombe, 'On Transubstantiation' (1974), in G.E.M. Anscombe, *Ethics, Religion and Politics: Collected Philosophical Papers Volume III* (Oxford: Basil Blackwell, 1981) [*ERP*], pp. 107–112, at pp. 107–8. Mary Geach identifies the child as Barbara in her introduction to Anscombe, *Faith in a Hard Ground*, p. xxii.

98 Midgley, *OM*, p. 131.

99 Maurice O'Connor Drury, *The Selected Writings of Maurice O'Connor Drury: On Wittgenstein, Philosophy, Religion and Psychiatry* (London, Bloomsbury, 2017), p. 65.

100 Midgley, *OM*, p. 159.

101 Anscombe, *Intention*, §42.

102 G.E.M. Anscombe, *From Plato to Wittgenstein*, ed. Mary Geach and Luke Gormally, *St Andrews Studies in Philosophy and Public Affairs* (Exeter: Imprint Academic, 2011), p. xiii.

103 Erbacher, 'Wittgenstein and His Literary Executors', p. 29.

104 'Self and not-self in Plotinus', 1 December 1948, p. 5, MGMA MID/E/68.

105 IMJ4, 17 October 1947, pp. 126–7.

106 IMJ4, 30 October 1948, p. 154.

107 IMJ4, 17 October 1948, p. 129.

108 IMJ4, 3 November 1947, p. 161.

109 IMJ4, 18 October 1947, p. 133.

110 IMJ4, 9 November 1947, p. 180.

111 IMJ6, 24 February 1948, p. 23.
112 IMJ6, 5 March 1948, p. 39.
113 IMJ6, 24 February 1948, p. 23.
114 'Letter from Iris Murdoch to Lucy Klatschko', n.d. [1989?], PCA KUAS6/18/2/16.
115 'Scheme of work', n.d., p. 1. NCA AC/5/2/20.
116 'Letter from Iris Murdoch to Miss Curtis reapplying for Smithson Studentship', 28 May 1948. AC/5/2/27.
117 IMJ6, 24 February 1948, p. 23.
118 IMJ6, 18 February 1948, p. 12. On 1 March Iris writes '(cf. my argumt with Elizabeth about thought seeking system!)'.
119 IMJ6, 12 June 1948, p. 106.
120 IMJ6, 4 April 1948, p. 55.
121 Hart, *Ask Me No More*, p. 135.
122 Conradi, *IMAL*, p. 291.
123 'Letter from Iris Murdoch to Philippa Foot', Cambridge, 24 April 1948, KUAS100/1/16.
124 'Letter to Miss Plumer from Donald MacKinnon', 1 June 1948, and 'Letter to Miss Plumer from Isobel Henderson', vi.1948, Iris Murdoch staff file, St Anne's College Archive, University of Oxford.
125 Conradi, *IMAL*, p. 288.
126 Horner and Rowe, *LP*, p. 112.

CHAPTER 6: BACK TO LIFE

1 'Bursar to Anscombe', 6 May 1949, correspondence between solicitor, bursar and G.E.M. Anscombe re 27 St John Street, St John's College Archive, University of Oxford.
2 M. C. Gormally, correspondence with authors, 25 September 2020.
3 'Bursar to Anscombe', 6 May 1949, op. cit.
4 Anscombe, 'Anecdotes about Wittgenstein'.
5 'Note from bursar to "gentlemen"', 6 May 1949, correspondence between solicitor, bursar and G.E.M. Anscombe re 27 St John Street, p. 1.
6 'Bursar to Anscombe', 6 May 1949, op. cit.
7 'Anscombe to Mr Chick', 14 June 1949, op. cit.
8 'Note from bursar to "gentlemen"', 6 May 1949, op. cit.
9 Monk, *Ludwig Wittgenstein*, p. 567.
10 Kenny, 'Peter Thomas Geach, 1916–2013', p. 188.
11 Anscombe, 'Anecdotes about Wittgenstein'.
12 Mary Warnock, conversation with authors, 13 January 2016.
13 Anscombe, 'Anecdotes about Wittgenstein'.
14 Mary Warnock, conversation with authors, 13 January 2016.

15 Erbacher, 'Wittgenstein and His Literary Executors', p. 26.
16 Warnock, *People and Places,* p. 59.
17 'Letter from Iris Murdoch to Philippa Foot', Chiswick, 10 July 1943, IMA KUAS100/1/43; see also Conradi, *IMAL,* p. 288.
18 N. Pevsner and J. Sherwood, *Oxfordshire* (Harmondsworth: Penguin, 1974), p. 266.
19 Jane O'Grady, 'Elizabeth Anscombe', *Guardian,* 11 January 2001.
20 Teichman, 'Gertrude Elizabeth Margaret Anscombe', p. 35.
21 Adrian Moore, conversation with authors, 31 May 2021.
22 Anscombe, 'Mary Somerville Research Fellow Report, May 1948'.
23 Timothy Chappell, (since 2014, Sophia Grace Chappell), *Reading Plato's Theaetetus* (Cambridge: Hackett, 2004), p. 103.
24 Ibid., p. 83.
25 IMJ6, 9 June 1948, p. 101.
26 Chappell, *Reading Plato's Theaetetus,* pp. 56–7.
27 Ibid., p. 130.
28 Ibid., p. 130.
29 G.E.M. Anscombe, 'The Subjectivity of Sensation' (1976) in her *MPM,* pp. 44–56, at p. 44.
30 Wittgenstein, *PI,* §258.
31 IMJ6, 15 October 1948, p. 133.
32 Anscombe, *Intention,* §46.
33 'Letter from G. H. White to the Senior Proctor', 14 October 1948, Oxford University Archives, PR 1/12/4.
34 IMJ7, 31 October 1949, IMJ, KUAS202/1/7, p. 40.
35 Adams, *SW,* p. 318.
36 Horner and Rowe, *LP,* p. 105.
37 Foot, *Memories of an S.O.E. Historian,* p. 119.
38 'Iris Murdoch letter to Hal Lidderdale', 29 December [?], IMC, KUAS78/13.
39 'Mary Scrutton to Geoff Midgley', n.d. [late 1949], MGMP, MID/F.
40 IMJ7, 1 March 1949, p. 7; also in Conradi, *IMAL,* p. 297.
41 Conradi, *IMAL,* p. 285.
42 IMJ6, 12 November 1948, p. E.
43 IMJ6, 30 June 1948, p. 106.
44 IMJ7, 15 June 1949, p. 22.
45 IMJ7, 17 November 1949, p. 42.
46 IMJ6 and IMJ7, passim.
47 IMJ6, 14 May 1948, p. 84.
48 See Erbacher, 'Wittgenstein and His Literary Executors', p. 25; and IMJ4, passim.
49 IMJ7, 15 June 1949, p. 22.
50 IMJ6 and IMJ7, passim.

51 'Peter Conradi's notes taken from a conversation with Polly Smythies', 3 February 1998, PCA KUAS6/1/50/1, cited in Conradi, *IMAL*, p. 635, n 79.
52 IMJ6, 9 November 1948, p. 150/C–D.
53 IMJ6, 11 October 1948, p. 132.
54 Anscombe, 'Anecdotes about Wittgenstein', CIAA, Box 6, file 212, p. 1.
55 IMJ6, 27 October 1948, p. 150/B.
56 IMJ6, 4 November 1948, p. C.
57 IMJ6, 14 December 1948, p. P.
58 IMJ7, 30 January 1949, p. 2.
59 IMJ6, 14 December 1948, p. O.
60 IMJ9, 14 February 1959, p. 38.
61 IMJ6, 14 December 1948, p. Q.
62 IMJ6, 15 November 1948, p. G.
63 IMJ6, 23 November 1948, p. H.
64 Ibid.
65 IMJ6, 12 December 1948, p. I.
66 IMJ6, 14 December 1948, p. Q.
67 IMJ6, 12 December 1948, p. J.
68 Ibid., p. I.
69 Ibid.
70 Ibid., p. L.
71 Ibid., pp. I–K.
72 IMJ6, 13 December 1948, p. M.
73 Monk, *Ludwig Wittgenstein*, pp. 518–19.
74 Ibid., p. 535.
75 Anscombe, 'Anecdotes about Wittgenstein', CIAA, Box 12, file 212, p. 1.
76 Erbacher, 'Wittgenstein and His Literary Executors', pp. 25–6. See also Anscombe, 'Anecdotes about Wittgenstein', p. 3.
77 L. Wittgenstein, *Last Writings on the Philosophy of Psychology* (Oxford: Blackwell, 1982), §165.
78 Anscombe, 'Mary Somerville Research Fellow Reports, May 1948'.
79 Anscombe, 'Anecdotes about Wittgenstein', CIAA, Box 12, file 212, p. 1.
80 Anscombe, *Intention*, §46.
81 Ibid., §4.
82 Anscombe, 'Intentionality of Sensation' (1965) in her *MPM*, pp. 3–20.
83 Ibid., pp. 16–17.
84 Mascall, *Saraband*, p. 247.
85 Quoted in ibid., p. 254.
86 Ibid., p. 234.
87 D. M. MacKinnon, 'Preface', in Gabriel Marcel, *Being and Having*, p. 3.
88 Mitchell, *Looking Back*, p. 254.
89 Mascall, *Saraband*, p. 248.

90 Conradi, *IMAL*, p. 305.

91 Rogers, *A. J. Ayer*, pp. 66–7.

92 Ibid., pp. 114–15.

93 V. A. Demant, 'Michael Beresford Foster: Died October 15, 1959', in *Christian Scholar*, 43:1 (March 1960), pp. 3–7, at p. 5.

94 'Peter Conradi notes from conversation with Denis Nineham', 1 April 1998, p. 1, PCA, KUAS6/13/16/1.

95 Mitchell, *Looking Back*, p. 136.

96 'Peter Conradi notes from conversation with Dennis Nineham', p. 2, op. cit.

97 Hare, 'A Philosophical Autobiography', p. 296.

98 R. M. Hare, 'A Chapter of Gulfs', n.d. unpublished manuscript, p. 4, R. M. Hare papers.

99 Scrutton, 'Individuation in Plotinus', pp. 11–12.

100 Scrutton, 'Self and Not-self in Plotinus, p. 5.

101 Ibid., p. 19.

102 Scrutton, 'Individuation in Plotinus', pp. 29–30.

103 Ibid., p. 37.

104 Midgley, OM, pp. 160–1.

105 Ibid., p. 139.

106 B. Russell, *Human Knowledge, Its Scope and Limits* (London: Allen & Unwin, 1948).

107 Bradley, *Appearance and Reality*, p. 206.

108 IMJ6, 12 December 1948, p. K.

109 IMJ7, 3 February 1949, p. 4.

110 IMJ7, 26 February 1949, p. 6.

111 Anscombe, 'Mary Somerville Research Fellow Reports, May 1951', SCA. © M. C. Gormally.

112 Anscombe, 'Mary Somerville Research Fellow Reports, May 1949', SCA, p. 1. © M. C. Gormally.

113 Anscombe, 'Mary Somerville Research Fellow Reports, May 1948', SCA. © M. C. Gormally.

114 IMJ7, 1 March 1949, p. 7.

115 IMJ7, 26 February – 1 March 1949, p. 6.

116 IMJ7, 1 March 1949, p. 8.

117 https://www.giffordlectures.org/lecturers/herbert-arthur-hodges, accessed on 1 August 2021.

118 Midgley, OM, p. 167.

119 Rudolf Makkreel, 'Wilhelm Dilthey', *The Stanford Encyclopedia of Philosophy* (Spring 2021 edition).

120 A. D. Lindsay, 'Wilhelm Dilthey', *Nature* 156:3964 (1945), pp. 461–61, at p. 461.

121 Martin Armstrong, 'Critic on the Hearth', *Listener* 42:1078 (1949), p. 507.
122 Letters between Mary Scrutton and Geoff Midgley, MGMA, MID/F, passim.
123 Midgley, OM, p. 170. Cited with the permission of Mirjam Foot.
124 Sarah Broadie, 'On Philippa Foot', 18 June 2013, *LSE Podcast* with Alex Voorhoeve, https://soundcloud.com/lsepodcasts/on-philippa-foot-audio, accessed 1 August 2021.
125 'Letter from Michael Foot to Peter Conradi', 17 December 2000, PCA, KUAS6/3/40/8. Cited with the permission of Mirjam Foot.
126 IMJ6, 9 June 1948, p. 102. [We have modified the journal entry to present it as dialogue].
127 IMJ7, 10 August 1949, p. 31.
128 IMJ7, 1 June 1949, p. 13.
129 IMJ7, 4 June 1949, pp. 14–17.
130 IMJ7, 4 June 1949, p. 14.
131 IMJ7, 10 November 1949, pp. 41–2.
132 IMJ7, 17 November 1949, p. 42.
133 Wittgenstein, *Tractatus Logico-philosophicus*, §§6.41–6.421.
134 IMJ7, 7 December 1949, p. 44.
135 Ibid.
136 Anscombe, 'Mary Somerville Research Fellow Report, May 1950'. © M. C. Gormally.
137 IMJ7, 16 January 1950, p. 45.
138 'This we thought was a particularly uninspiring kind of child psychology', in P. Feyerabend, *Killing Time: The Autobiography of Paul Feyerabend* (Chicago: University of Chicago Press, 1996), p. 75.
139 Anscombe, 'Mary Somerville Research Fellow Reports, 1950'.
140 Monk, *Ludwig Wittgenstein*, p. 563.
141 *Radio Times*, 'Third Programme', Issue 1376, 26 February 1950, p. 19.
142 Conradi, *IMAL*, pp. 289–90.
143 Murdoch, 'The Novelist as Metaphysician', (1950), in *EM*, pp. 101–7.
144 Ibid., pp. 104–5.
145 Ibid., p. 105.
146 Ibid., pp. 106–7.
147 Murdoch, 'The Existentialist Hero', pp. 111–12.
148 R. M. Hare, 'Off the record' transcript, 6 September 1982, R. M. Hare papers.
149 Murdoch, 'The Novelist as Metaphysician', p. 105.
150 Iris Murdoch, 'The Sublime and The Good', *Chicago Review* 13:3 (1959), pp. 42–55, at p. 51.
151 Foot, 'Moral Arguments', p. 512.
152 Philippa Foot, 'When is a Principle a Moral Principle?', *Aristotelian Society*, Supplementary 28:1 (1954), pp. 95–110, at pp. 105 and 106.

153 Foot, 'When is a Principle a Moral Principle?', p. 108.
154 Foot, 'Moral Beliefs', p. 94.
155 Mary Warnock (née Wilson), conversation with authors, 13 January 2016.
156 Price, 'The Inaugural Address: Clarity is Not Enough', p. 31.
157 Anscombe, 'Anecdotes about Wittgenstein'.
158 L. Wittgenstein et al., *Culture and Value* (Oxford: Blackwell, 1980), p. 85, quoted in Monk, *Ludwig Wittgenstein*, p. 572.
159 Monk, *Ludwig Wittgenstein*, pp. 572–3.
160 Ibid., p. 573.
161 'Last Will and Testament of Ludwig Wittgenstein' [copy], CIAA.
162 Anscombe, 'Anecdotes about Wittgenstein'.

CHAPTER 7: METAPHYSICAL ANIMALS

1 Midgley, OM, pp. 171–2.
2 Ibid., p. 171.
3 'Letter from Mary Scrutton to Geoff Midgley', n.d. [early 1950s], MGMP, MID/F.
4 'Letter from Mary Scrutton to Geoff Midgley', n.d. [late 1949] MGMP, MID/F.
5 Midgley, OM. p. 161.
6 'Letter from Mary Scrutton to Geoff Midgley', n.d. [late 1949], MGMP, MID/F.
7 Midgley, OM, p. 172.
8 Ibid., p. 34.
9 Ibid., p. 171.
10 Ibid., p. 162.
11 Janet Penrose Trevelyan, *The Life of Mrs Humphrey Ward* (London: Constable & Co., 1923); Mrs Humphrey Ward, *A Writer's Recollections*; *Times*, 25 March 1920.
12 Conversation with authors, 13 January 2016.
13 Ibid. (this reported event took place at 19 Fitzwilliam Street, Cambridge).
14 See Mario Wimmer, 'The Afterlives of Scholarship: Warburg and Cassirer', *History of Humanities* 2:1 (2017), pp. 245–70.
15 Ernst Cassirer, *An Essay on Man: An Introduction to a Philosophy of Human Culture* (Yale: Yale University Press, 1944), p. 26.
16 IMJ4, 13 June 1947, p. 5.
17 MacKinnon, 'Philosophers in Exile', p. 16.
18 Regina Weber, *Lotte Labowsky (1905–1991) Schülerin Aby Warburgs, Kollegin Raymond Klibanskys*, p. 48.

19 Jennifer McMahon, 'Beauty as harmony of the soul: the aesthetic of the Stoics', in *Greek Research in Australia: Proceedings of the Eighth Biennial International Conference of Greek Studies.*, ed. M. Rossetto et al. (2009), pp. 54–63.

20 Weber, *Lotte Labowsky*, p. 57.

21 See Carole Gibson-Wood, 'Raymond Klibansky and the Warburg Institute', *Canadian Art Review* 27:1/2 (2000), pp. 137–9.

22 L. Noble, 'Burning Books', https://www.lib.cam.ac.uk/collections/departments/germanic-collections/about-collections/spotlight-archive/burning-books, accessed 1 August 2021.

23 Teicher, 'Jacob Teicher between Florence and Cambridge', p. 329.

24 Anscombe, 'Anecdotes about Wittgenstein'.

25 'Letter from Lotte Labowsky to Raymond Klibansky', 8 March 1951, A: RKA.

26 'Letter from Lotte Labowsky to Raymond Klibansky', 28 October 1950, A: RKA.

27 'Letter from Lotte Labowsky to Raymond Klibansky', 8 March 1951, A: RKA.

28 Weber, *Lotte Labowsky*, p. 95.

29 Paul Oskar Kristeller, 'Reviewed Work(s): Plato Latinus by Corpus Platonicum Medii Aevi and Raymundus Klibansky: Volumen II: Phaedo by Henrico Aristippo, Laurentius Minio-Paluello and H. J. Drossaart-Lulofs: Volumen III: Parmenides usque ad finem Primae Hypothesis nec non Procli Commentarium in Parmenidem by Guillelmo de Moerbeka, Raymundus Klibansky and Carlotta Labowsky', *Journal of Philosophy* 53:5 (1956), pp. 196–9.

30 Weber, *Lotte Labowsky*, p. 89.

31 Raymond Klibansky, 'Report on Elizabeth Anscombe for Miss Glover', Hilary Term 1941, SHCA, SHG/J/3/2.

32 See J. M. E. Moravcsik, 'Review: Plato's The Sophist and the Statesman by A. E. Taylor, Raymond Klibansky and Elizabeth Anscombe', *Philosophical Review* (1963), pp. 122–4.

33 Weber, *Lotte Labowsky*, p. 95.

34 'Letter from Lotte Labowsky to Raymond Klibansky', 14 May 1951, A: RKA.

35 G.E.M. Anscombe, 'Cambridge Philosophers II: Ludwig Wittgenstein', *Philosophy* 70:273 (1995), pp. 395–407, at p. 399 ('icon' as spelled in printed article).

36 G.E.M. Anscombe, 'Grammar, Structure, and Essence', *Areté. Revista de Filosofía* 12, no. 2 (2000), pp. 113–20, at p. 113.

37 Anscombe, 'Grammar, Structure, and Essence', pp. 113–14.

38 G.E.M. Anscombe, *FPW* (Oxford: Basil Blackwell, 1981), p. xi.

39 Wittgenstein, *PI*, §31.

40 Ibid., §30.
41 Anscombe, 'Cambridge Philosophers II: Ludwig Wittgenstein', p. 399.
42 Anscombe, 'Grammar, Structure, and Essence', p. 118.
43 Monk, *Ludwig Wittgenstein*, p. 579.
44 Foot, *Natural Goodness*, p. 85.
45 Weber, *Lotte Labowsky*, p. 98.
46 'Letter from Lotte Labowsky to Raymond Klibansky', 2 June 1951, A: RKA.
47 Christian Erbacher, *Wittgenstein's Heirs and Editors* (Cambridge: Cambridge University Press, 2020), p. 3.
48 'Letter from Lotte Labowsky to Raymond Klibansky', 28 October 1951, A: RKA.
49 'Letter from Lotte Labowsky to Raymond Klibansky', 14 May 1951, A: RKA.
50 Told by Lesley Brown, correspondence with authors, 1 July 2019.
51 'Letter from Lotte Labowsky to Raymond Klibansky', 14 May 1951, A: RKA.
52 Anscombe, 'Mary Somerville Research Fellow Reports, May 1949'.
53 IMJ7, 1 March 1951. p. 64.
54 Wittgenstein, *PI*, §185.
55 Ibid., §198.
56 IMJ7, 1 March 1951, p. 64.
57 Wittgenstein, *PI*, §211, et *passim*, §185.
58 Erbacher, *Wittgenstein's Heirs and Editors*, p. 2.
59 Wittgenstein, *PI*, p. 197.
60 'Letter from Iris Murdoch to Wallace Robson', 16 December 1951, in Horner and Rowe, *LP*, p. 131.
61 G.E.M. Anscombe, 'Typed Transcript of BBC Third Programme broadcast of 23 April 1953 on Ludwig Wittgenstein', pp. 2 and 5, CIAA Box 22, file W1. © M. C. Gormally.
62 Haldane, 'Anscombe: Life, Action and Ethics in Context', p. 55.
63 Ibid., pp. 50–1.
64 Christopher Coope, correspondence with authors, 3 April 2020.
65 Teichman, 'Gertrude Elizabeth Margaret Anscombe', p. 34.
66 Anscombe, 'Typed Transcript of BBC Third Programme broadcast of 23 April 1953 on Ludwig Wittgenstein'.
67 See Horner and Rowe, *LP*, passim.
68 IMJ7, 1 November 1950, p. 60.
69 Horner and Rowe, *LP*, p. 131.
70 Conradi, *IMAL*, pp. 313–14.
71 Purton, *An Iris Murdoch Chronology*, p. 63.
72 Conradi, *IMAL*, p. 294.
73 R. Sorabji, 'Tony Lloyd', *Proceedings of the British Academy*, 97 (1998), pp. 347–55.
74 Horner and Rowe, *LP*, pp. 128–9.
75 Iris Murdoch, 'Interview for Radio New Zealand', 1978, printed in *The Iris Murdoch Review*, 1:3, p. 8.

76 IMJ6 IMA 24 February 1948, p. 23.
77 Iris Murdoch, 'Symposium: Thinking and Language', *Proceedings of the Aristotelian Society* 25 (1951), pp. 25–34.
78 Ibid., p. 32.
79 Ibid., p. 29.
80 John Clare, 'Summer Images'.
81 Ibid., p. 29.
82 A. C. Lloyd, 'Symposium: Thinking and Language', pp. 35–65, at p. 63.
83 Charlotte Vrijen, 'The Philosophical Development of Gilbert Ryle: A Study of his Published and Unpublished Writings' (PhD dissertation, Groningen, 2007), p. 25.
84 His copy is now in the Ryle Archive, Linacre College, Oxford.
85 Murdoch, 'Thinking and Language', p. 29.
86 Gilbert Ryle, 'Symposium: Thinking and Language', pp. 65–82, at p. 75.
87 H. H. Price, 'Symposium on Thinking and Language. Remarks by the Chairman', *Proceedings of the Aristotelian Society* 51 (1951), pp. 334–5.
88 Horner and Rowe, *LP*, p. 134.
89 Midgley (Scrutton), 'The Natural History of Contradictions', p. 589.
90 Ibid.
91 Ibid.
92 Midgley, OM, p. 148.
93 Midgley, *What is Philosophy For?*, p. 64; see also Mary Midgley, 'Philosophical Plumbing', *Royal Institute of Philosophy Supplement* 33 (1992), pp. 139–51.
94 Rée, 'Philosophical Lives: Philippa Foot interview', p. 4.
95 Midgley, OM, p. xii.
96 Midgley (Scrutton), 'The Natural History of Contradictions', p. 590.
97 IMJ7, 13 March 1951, p. 66.
98 IMJ3, 21 Feb 1947, p. 54.
99 Midgley (Scrutton), 'The Natural History of Contradictions', p. 590.
100 IMJ7, 11 August 1951, p. 67.
101 'Labour Party Women's Organisation, Annual Conference Report, April 1952', p. 12, quoted in M. Pugh, *Women and the Women's Movement in Britain, 1914–1959* (London: Macmillan, 1992), p. 291.
102 Ina Zweiniger-Bargielowska, 'Rationing, Austerity and the Conservative Party Recovery after 1945', *Historical Journal* 37:1 (1994), pp. 173–97, at p. 186.
103 'Letter from Iris Murdoch to Hal Lidderdale', 29 June 1951, in Horner and Rowe, *LP*, p. 128.
104 Murdoch, *Sartre* (1953/1976), p. 7.
105 Iris Murdoch, 'The Existentialist Political Myth', *Socratic Digest* 5 (1952), pp. 52–63, p. 236.
106 Murdoch, 'The Existentialist Political Myth', p. 239.
107 Conradi, *IMAL*, p. 294.

108 Murdoch, 'The Existentialist Political Myth, p. 239.
109 Murdoch, 'A House of Theory', p. 171.
110 Justin Broackes, *Iris Murdoch, Philosopher* (Oxford: Oxford University Press, 2012), p. 30.
111 Murdoch, 'A House of Theory', pp. 172 and 182.
112 Ibid., pp. 171–4.
113 Ibid., p. 171.
114 G.E.M. Anscombe, 'Does Oxford Moral Philosophy Corrupt the Youth?', *Listener*, 14 February 1957, pp. 226–71, at p. 267.
115 Ibid.
116 Conradi, *IMAL*, p. 317.
117 'Peter Conradi's notes taken from a conversation with Polly Smythies'.
118 Kenny, *Brief Encounters*, p. 176.
119 IMJ7, 5 March 1952, p. 104.
120 Ibid., pp. 104–5 (see also Conradi, *IMAL*, p. 315).
121 'Letter from Iris Murdoch to Hal Lidderdale', n.d., IMC KUAS78/17.
122 IMJ7, 5 March 1952, p. 105.
123 See Graham Lord, *Just the One: The Wives and Times of Jeffrey Bernard (1932–1997)* (London: Headline, 1997); also Conradi, *IMAL*, p. 316.
124 IMJ7, 5 March 1952, pp. 104–5.
125 These were co-written with Judith Hughes in Mary Midgley and Judith Hughes, *Women's Choices: Philosophical Problems Facing Feminism* (London: Weidenfeld & Nicolson, 1983), p. 41.
126 Mary Midgley (Scrutton), 'Letter to Posterity', *Listener*, 27 March 1952, pp. 510–11.
127 Ibid., p. 511.
128 Mary Midgley (Scrutton), 'Rings & Books', n.d. [195?], p. 1, MGMP, MID/C/3.
129 Ibid., p. 3.
130 Midgley, OM, p. 181.
131 Iris Murdoch, 'The Image of Mind' (1951), in EM, pp. 125–9, at p. 129.
132 Justin Broackes, 'Iris Murdoch's First Encounters with Simone Weil', *Iris Murdoch Review* 8, pp. 17–20.
133 Simone Weil, *Oppression and Liberty*, trans. Arthur Wills and John Petrie (London: Routledge Classics, 2001), pp. 9–10.
134 See Lawrence A. Blum and Victor J. Seidler, *A Truer Liberty: Simone Weil and Marxism* (London: Routledge, 2009).
135 S. Weil and J. P. Holoka, *Simone Weil's The Iliad, Or, The Poem of Force: A Critical Edition* (Oxford: Peter Lang, 2003), p. 3.
136 Iris Murdoch, '"Waiting on God": A Radio Talk on Simone Weil' (1951), *Iris Murdoch Review* 8 (2017), ed. Justin Broackes, pp. 9–16, at p. 10. See fn. 1. Also Justin Broackes, '"Waiting on God": Prefatory note on the text' in *The Iris Murdoch Review* (2017).

137 Murdoch, '"Waiting on God"', p. 11.
138 See Iris Murdoch, *The Sovereignty of Good* (London: Routledge Classics, 2001), p. 52 and *passim*.
139 Conradi, *IMAL*, p. 384.
140 Billie Batchelor, 'Revisions in Iris Murdoch's *Under the Net*', *Books at Iowa*, 8 (1968), pp. 30–36, at p. 30.
141 S. B. Sagare and Iris Murdoch, 'An Interview with Iris Murdoch', *Modern Fiction Studies* 47:3 (2001), pp. 696–714, at p. 697.
142 Murdoch, 'The Sublime and the Good', p. 51.
143 Purton, *An Iris Murdoch Chronology*, p. 40.
144 See A. Rebecca Rozelle-Stone and Benjamin P. Davis, 'Simone Weil', *Stanford Encyclopedia of Philosophy* (Fall 2020).
145 See Rozelle-Stone and Davis, 'Simone Weil'.
146 Glover, 'Obligation and Value', p. 75.
147 Murdoch, *The Sovereignty of Good*, p. 85.
148 Broackes, 'Prefatory note', p. 9.
149 Iris Murdoch, ' "Waiting on God", A Radio Talk on Simone Weil' (1951), pp. 15 and 16.
150 For more on Steiner and Iris, see J. Adler and R. Fardon, *Franz Baermann Steiner: A Stranger in the World* (New York: Berghahn, 2022).
151 Conradi, *IMAL*, p. 319.
152 See Peter Filkins, *H. G. Adler: A Life in Many Worlds* (Oxford: Oxford University Press, 2019).
153 Jeremy Adler and Richard Fardon, eds, *Taboo, Truth and Religion: Franz Baermann Steiner Selected Writings*, Vol. 1 (Oxford: Berghahn Books, 1999), p. 88.
154 Conradi, *IMAL*, p. 317.
155 Adler and Fardon, *Taboo, Truth and Religion*, pp. 92–3.
156 Conradi, *IMAL*, p. 317.
157 Adler and Fardon, *Taboo, Truth and Religion*, p. 89.
158 Ibid., p. 18.
159 Conradi, *IMAL*, p. 318.
160 Adler and Fardon, *Taboo, Truth and Religion*, p. 89.
161 Franz Steiner's journal, 31 October 1952, *Deutsches Literaturarchiv Marbach*, Zugangsnummer HS.1996.0151.00892, Mediennummer HS001523034.
162 Conradi, *IMAL*, p. 325.
163 Elias Canetti, 'Franz Steiner', *Akzente*, 3, June (1995), p. 205, quoted in Adler and Fardon, *Taboo, Truth and Religion*, p. 80.
164 F. B. Steiner and J. D. Adler, *Am Stürzenden Pfad: Gesammelte Gedichte*, (Goettingen: Wallstein, 2000). p. 326 (lower case 'w' and 'g' correspond to the original), trans. Mara-Daria Cojocaru.
165 Quoted in Adler and Fardon, *Taboo, Truth and Religion*, p. 97.
166 Conradi, *IMAL*, p. 337.

167 Maggie Black, *A Cause for Our Time: Oxfam, the First Fifty Years* (Oxford: Oxford University Press, 1992), pp. 37–40.
168 See for example the 1977 preface to Foot, *Virtues and Vices*.
169 Rée, 'Philosophical Lives: Philippa Foot interview', p. 3.
170 Mary Midgley, conversation with authors, September 2016.
171 IMJ8, 12 November 1953.
172 Mitchell, *Looking Back*, p. 257.
173 Murdoch, *Sovereignty of Good*, p. 22. Bernard Williams, who attended the class, uses 'thin' and 'thick' instead of Murdoch's 'general' and 'specialized'; see B. Williams, *Ethics and the Limits of Philosophy* (Cambridge, MA: Harvard University Press, 1985), pp. 217–18, fn. 7.
174 Purton, *An Iris Murdoch Chronology*, p. 67.
175 Mary Scrutton, 'Review', *New Statesman and Nation*, 1951.
176 Midgley, OM, p. 182.
177 'Mary Midgley interviewed by Paul Merchant', track 2, p. 28.
178 R. B. Braithwaite, 'Hare, R. M. – The Language of Morals', *Mind* 63, (1954), pp. 249–62.
179 Mary Midgley, conversation with authors, September 2016.
180 See Konrad Lorenz, *King Solomon's Ring: New Light on Animal Ways* (London: Routledge Classics, 2002).
181 Midgley, OM, p. 6.
182 Mary Midgley, *Beast and Man: The Roots of Human Nature* (London: Routledge, 2002), p. 235.
183 Midgley, OM, p. 30.
184 Ibid., p. 189.
185 Ibid., p. 31.
186 Mary Midgley, *Animals and Why They Matter* (Athens, Georgia: University of Georgia Press, 1998), pp. 112–24.
187 Midgley, OM. pp. 202 and 208.
188 Mary Midgley (Scrutton), 'Untitled Essay', [n.d.], MGMP, uncatalogued essay, p. 9.
189 Midgley, OM, p. 188.
190 'Mary Midgley interviewed by Paul Merchant', track 1, p. 8.
191 Foot, 'Moral Beliefs', p. 94.
192 Philippa Foot, 'Interview with Rick Lewis', in *Philosophy Now*, 41, May/June 2003.
193 Hare, *The Language of Morals*, pp. 96–7.
194 'Editorial', *Cactus and Succulent Journal of Great Britain* 8, no. 3 (1946).
195 Philippa Foot, 'Goodness and Choice', *Aristotelian Society Supplementary Volume* 35, no. 1 (1961), pp. 45–60, at p. 55.
196 Black, *A Cause for Our Time: Oxfam, the First Fifty Years*, pp. 36–7.
197 Murdoch, *The Sovereignty of Good*, p. 85.

198 Philippa Foot, 'Review: *The Philosophy of Ernst Cassirer: The Library of Living Philosophers Vol. VI*, ed. Paul Arthur Schilpp', *Philosophy* 26:98 (1951), pp. 273–4. Quote at p. 274.

199 Cassirer, *An Essay on Man*, pp. 23–6.

200 IMJ8, 12 March 1953.

201 IMJ4, 13 June 1947, p. 5.

202 Wittgenstein, *PI*, §415.

203 G.E.M. Anscombe, 'The Moral Environment of the Child', n.d., manuscript, in *Faith in a Hard Ground: Essays on Religion, Philosophy and Politics by G.E.M. Anscombe*, ed. Mary Geach and Luke Gormally (Exeter: Imprint Academic, 2008), pp. 224–33, at p. 230.

204 R. M. Hare, 'An Apology for Being a Philosopher', n.d. typescript, R. M. Hare papers, Balliol College Archives, p. 2.

205 Philippa Foot, 'The Philosopher's Defence of Morality', *Philosophy* 27:103 (1952), pp. 311–28, at p. 311.

206 Ibid., p. 319.

207 Purton, *An Iris Murdoch Chronology*, p. 70.

208 'Letter from Iris Murdoch to Mrs Smallwood', 2 May 1955, in Horner and Rowe, *LP*, pp. 170–1.

209 Murdoch, 'Metaphysics and Ethics', p. 75.

210 Conradi, *IMAL*, p. 385.

211 Midgley, *OM*, p. 183.

212 Mary Midgley (Scrutton), *Wintersault*, n.d. manuscript, MGMP MID/C/22.

213 Erbacher, *Wittgenstein's Heirs and Editors*, p. 13.

214 L. Wittgenstein, *Remarks on the Foundations of Mathematics* (London: Blackwell, 1956), part 1, section 3.

215 Morris, *Oxford*, p. 42.

216 Ibid.

217 'Report of 11 February 1955', Central University Administrative Correspondence File for the Committee on Honorary Degrees, Oxford University Archives, UR6/HD/7/3.

EPILOGUE: MR TRUMAN'S DEGREE, AGAIN

1 G.E.M. Anscombe, 'Mr. Truman's Degree', pamphlet, published by author (1956), CIAA, Box 531.

2 G.E.M. Anscombe, 'I Am Sadly Theoretical', *Catholic Herald*, 8 July 1938, p. 7; see John Berkman, 'Justice and Murder: The Backstory to Anscombe's "Modern Moral Philosophy",' in *The Oxford Handbook of Elizabeth Anscombe*, ed. Roger Teichmann (Oxford: Oxford University Press, 2021).

3 'Letter from 14 Park Town', 2 May 1956, CIAA, Box 394.

4 'Letter from Women's International League for Peace and Freedom', 4 May 1956, ibid.

5 'Letter from General E. C. O. Murphy', 2 May 1956, ibid.

6 'Letter from General E. C. O. Murphy', 8 May 1956, ibid.

7 'Letter from Vera Farnell', n.d., ibid.

8 'Letter from Donald MacKinnon', 2 May 1956, ibid.

9 'Letter from An American Woman', 4 May 1956, ibid.

10 'Letter from Carrie Packinton[?]', 4 May 1956, ibid.

11 'Letter from Ordnance Research Institute, Taipei', 3 May 1956, ibid.

12 'Letter from Jessie Street'. 5 May 1956, ibid.

13 Anscombe, *Mr Truman's Degree*, p. 71.

14 Ibid., pp. 64–5.

15 Ibid., p. 70.

16 Ibid., pp. 65–6.

17 Ibid., pp. 70–1.

18 Ibid., p. 71.

19 Anscombe, 'Does Oxford Moral Philosophy Corrupt the Youth?' pp. 266–7 and p. 271; letters from R. M. Hare and P. H. Nowell-Smith in Issue 1456; letter from Anthony Flew in Issue 1458; letter from P. H. Nowell-Smith in Issue 1459; letter from Anthony Flew in Issue 1460; letter from R. M. Hare in Issue 1461.

20 Letter to R. M. Hare from Bernard Williams, 26 January 1957, R. M. Hare Archive, Hare 2018, Box of Letters. Cited with the permission of Patricia Williams. See also letters from Patrick Nowell-Smith and Anthony Flew.

21 McCullough, *Truman*, p. 439.

22 Anscombe, *Mr Truman's Degree*, p. 64.

23 Midgley, *Wickedness*, p. vii.

24 Anscombe, *Mr Truman's Degree*, p. 64.

25 Ibid., p. 70.

26 Ibid., p. 64.

27 MacKinnon, *The Problem of Metaphysics*, p. 110.

AFTERWARDS

1 IMJ4, 25 July 1947, p. 25.

2 Somerville College Archive, Oxford, Philippa Foot letter to Janet Vaughan, 3 November 1957.

3 Foot, 'The Philosopher's Defence of Morality'.

4 Foot, 'When is a Principle a Moral Principle?'

5 Philippa Foot, 'Free Will Involving Determinism', *Philosophical Review* 66, no. 4 (1957), pp. 439–50.

6 Foot, 'Moral Beliefs'.
7 Foot, 'Moral Arguments'.
8 Foot, 'Goodness and Choice'.
9 Philippa Foot, 'Does Moral Subjectivism Rest on a Mistake?', *Royal Institute of Philosophy Supplement*, 46:107 (2000), pp. 107–23, at p. 107.
10 Foot, *Memories of an S.O.E. Historian*, p. 130.
11 'Green hardback notebook, with diary entries from August 1996', entry 15 January 2001, SCA, Philippa Foot papers, Box 3.
12 Rée, 'Philosophical Lives: Philippa Foot', p. 2.
13 Gornall, 'Philippa Foot and Thoughts about Oxfam', p. 10.
14 Anscombe, 'Modern Moral Philosophy', p. 1.
15 G.E.M. Anscombe, 'The First Person', in *Mind and Language.*, ed. Samuel D. Guttenplan (Oxford: Oxford University Press, 1975).
16 Anscombe, *FPW*; Anscombe, *MPM*; Anscombe, *ERP*.
17 Donald Davidson on cover of G.E.M. Anscombe, *Intention* (Harvard: Harvard University Press, 2000).
18 Smith, *The Morning Light*, p. 240.
19 Iris Murdoch, *The Fire and the Sun: Why Plato Banished the Artists* (Viking, 1990).
20 Horner and Rowe, *LP*, p. 357.
21 Midgley, *OM*, p. 183.
22 Jane Heal, 'Mary Midgley Obituary', *Guardian*, 12 October 2018.
23 Midgley, *Beast and Man*.
24 Midgley, introduction to the first edition, *Beast and Man*.
25 Mary Midgley, 'The Objection to Systematic Humbug', *Philosophy* 53, no. 204 (1978), pp. 147–69.
26 Midgley, *What is Philosophy For?* pp. 207–8.

Bibliography

Cited Works by the Quartet

Anscombe, G.E.M. 'I Am Sadly Theoretical'. *Catholic Herald*, 8 July 1938, 7.
———. (with Norman Daniel). *The Justice of the Present War Examined*. Oxford, 1939.
———. 'A Reply to Mr. C. S. Lewis's Argument That "Naturalism" is Self-Refuting'. *Socratic Digest* 4, no. 2 (1948): 7–16.
———. 'The Reality of the Past'. In *Philosophical Analysis*, edited by Max Black. Ithaca, NY: Cornell University Press, 1950, pp. 36–56.
———. 'The Principle of Individuation'. *Proceedings of the Aristotelian Society, Supplementary Volumes 27* (1953): 83–96.
———. 'Mr Truman's Degree'. Self published, 1956.
———. 'Does Oxford Moral Philosophy Corrupt the Youth?' *Listener*, 14 February 1957, pp. 266–71.
———. *Intention*. Cambridge, MA: Harvard University Press, 1957/2000.
———. 'Modern Moral Philosophy'. *Philosophy* 33, no. 124 (1958): 1–19.
———. 'Hume and Julius Caesar'. *Analysis* 34, no. 1 (1973): 1–7.
———. *Causality and Determinism*. Cambridge: Cambridge University Press, 1971.
———. 'The First Person'. In *Mind and Language*, edited by S. Guttenplan, Oxford: Oxford University Press, 1975, pp. 45–65.
———. *From Parmenides to Wittgenstein: Collected Philosophical Papers Volume I*. Oxford: Basil Blackwell, 1981.
———. *Metaphysics and the Philosophy of Mind: Collected Philosophical Papers Volume II*. Oxford: Basil Blackwell, 1981.
———. *Ethics, Religion and Politics: Collected Philosophical Papers Volume III*. Oxford: Basil Blackwell, 1981.
———. 'The Intentionality of Sensation: A Grammatical Feature'. In *MPM*. Oxford: Basil Blackwell, 1965/1981, pp. 3–20.

――――. 'The Subjectivity of Sensation'. In *MPM*. Oxford: Basil Blackwell, 1976/1981, pp. 44–56.

――――. 'Events in Mind'. In *MPM*. Oxford: Basil Blackwell, 1963/1981, pp. 57–63.

――――. 'On Transubstantiation'. In *ERP*. Oxford: Basil Blackwell, 1974/1981, pp. 107–12.

――――. 'Cambridge Philosophers II: Ludwig Wittgenstein'. *Philosophy* 70, no. 273 (1995): 395–407.

――――. *Human Life, Action, and Ethics: Essays by G. E. M Anscombe*, edited by M. Geach and L. Gormally, *St Andrews Studies in Philosophy and Public Affairs*. Exeter: Imprint Academic, 2005.

――――. *Faith in a Hard Ground: Essays on Religion, Philosophy, and Ethics*, edited by M. Geach and L. Gormally. Exeter: Imprint Academic, 2008.

――――. 'The Moral Environment of the Child'. In *Faith in a Hard Ground: Essays on Religion, Philosophy and Politics by G.E.M. Anscombe*, edited by M. Geach and Luke Gormally. Exeter: Imprint Academic, Undated/ 2008.

――――. *From Plato to Wittgenstein: Essays by G. E. M Anscombe*, edited by M. Geach and L. Gormally. Exeter: Imprint Academic, 2011.

――――. 'Grammar, Structure and Essence'. *Areté. Revista de Filosofía* 12, no. 2 (2000): 113–20.

Foot, P. Review of *The Philosophy of Ernst Cassirer*. Edited by Paul Arthur Schlipp. Volume VI in *The Library of Living Philosophers*. *Philosophy* 26, no. 98 (1951): 273–4.

――――. 'The Philosopher's Defence of Morality'. *Philosophy* 27, no. 103 (1952): 311–28.

――――. 'When is a Principle a Moral Principle?' *Aristotelian Society Supplementary Volume* 28, no. 1 (1954): 95–110.

――――. 'Moral Arguments.' *Mind* 67, no. 268 (1958): 502–13.

――――. 'Free Will Involving Determinism'. *The Philosophical Review* 66, no. 4 (1957): 439–50.

――――. 'Moral Beliefs'. *Proceedings of the Aristotelian Society* 59 (1958): 83–104.

――――. 'Goodness and Choice'. *Aristotelian Society Supplementary Volume* 35, no. 1 (1961): 45–60.

――――. *Virtues and Vices. And Other Essays in Moral Philosophy*. Oxford: Basil Blackwell, 1978.

――――. 'Does Moral Subjectivism Rest on a Mistake?' *Royal Institute of Philosophy Supplement* 46 (2000): 107–23.

――――. *Natural Goodness*. Oxford: Oxford University Press, 2001.

――――. 'Rationality and Goodness'. *Royal Institute of Philosophy Supplement* 54 (2004): 1–13.

Midgley (Scrutton), M. 'Letter to Posterity'. *Listener*, 27 March 1952, pp. 510–11.

———. 'The Natural History of Contradictions'. *Listener*, 11 October 1951, pp. 489–90.

———. 'On Being Reformed'. *Listener*, 9 August 1956, pp. 196–97.

———. 'The Objection to Systematic Humbug'. *Philosophy* 53, no. 204 (1978): 147–69.

———. 'Philosophical Plumbing'. *Royal Institute of Philosophy Supplement* 33 (1992): 139–51.

———. *Animals and Why They Matter*. Athens, GA: University of Georgia Press, 1983/1998.

———. *Beast and Man: The Roots of Human Nature*. London: Routledge, 1978/2002.

———. *Wickedness: A Philosophical Essay*. London: Routledge, 1984/2001.

———. *Heart and Mind. The Varieties of Moral Experience*. London: Routledge, 1981/2003.

———. *The Myths We Live By*. London: Routledge, 2011.

———. *The Owl of Minerva: A Memoir*. London: Routledge, 2005.

———. 'Park Town'. 2016. MGMP.

———. 'Rings & Books'. 1950s. MGMP.

———. 'Sorting out the Zeitgeist'. *Changing English* 7, no. 1 (2000): 89–92.

———. 'Then and Now'. 2016. MGMP.

———. *What Is Philosophy For?* London, Bloomsbury Academic, 2018.

———. (with J. Hughes). *Women's Choices: Philosophical Problems Facing Feminism*. London: Weidenfeld & Nicolson, 1983.

Murdoch, I. 'Thinking and Language'. *Proceedings of the Aristotelian Society* 25 (1951): 25–34.

———. 'The Existentialist Political Myth'. *Socratic Digest* 5 (1952): 52–63.

———. *Sartre: Romantic Rationalist*. Glasgow: Fontana Collins, 1953/1976.

———. *Sartre: Romantic Rationalist*. London: Penguin Books, 1987/1989.

———. 'Metaphysics and Ethics'. In *The Nature of Metaphysics*, edited by D. F. Pears, pp. 99–123. London: Macmillan, 1957.

———. 'The Sublime and the Good'. *Chicago Review* 13, 3 (1959): 42–55.

———. *The Sovereignty of Good*. London: Routledge & Kegan Paul, 1970.

———. *Existentialists and Mystics: Writings on Philosophy and Literature*, edited by P. J. Conradi, with a foreword by G. Steiner. London: Chatto & Windus, 1997.

———. 'The Novelist as Metaphysician'. In *EM*. London: Chatto & Windus, 1950/1997, pp. 101–7.

———. 'The Existentialist Hero'. In *EM*. London: Chatto & Windus, 1950/1997, pp. 108–15.

———. 'The Image of Mind'. In *EM*. London: Chatto & Windus, 1951/1997, pp. 125–9.

————. 'A House of Theory'. In *EM*. London: Chatto & Windus, 1956/1997, pp. 171–86.

————. 'Salvation by Words'. In *EM*. London: Chatto & Windus, 1972/1997, pp. 235–42.

————. *The Fire and the Sun: Why Plato Banished the Artists*. London: Chatto & Windus, 1977.

————. 'A Woman Don's Delight'. In *Occasional Essays by Iris Murdoch*, edited by P. Hullah and Y. Muroya: Okayam: University Education Press, 1998, pp. 193–6.

————. *Metaphysics as a Guide to Morals*. London: Chatto & Windus, 1992.

————. '"Waiting on God": A Radio Talk on Simone Weil (1951)'. *Iris Murdoch Review* 8 (2017): 9–16.

Select Bibliography

(Publication details of cited material that is not listed here are given in the notes.)

Adams, P. *Somerville for Women: An Oxford College, 1879–1993*. Oxford University Press, 1996.

Addison, P. 'Oxford and the Second World War'. In *The History of the University of Oxford Volume VIII*: edited by B. Harrison. Oxford: Clarendon Press, 1994, pp. 167–88.

Adler, J., and R. Fardon (eds) *Taboo, Truth and Religion: Franz Baermann Steiner, Selected Writings Vol. 1*. New York and Oxford: Berghahn Books, 1999.

Aldwinckle, S., and I. Murdoch. *Christ's Shadow in Plato's Cave: A Meditation on the Substance of Love*. Oxford: Oxford University Press, 1990.

Audi, R. 'On Mary Glover's "Obligation and Value"'. *Ethics* 125, no. 2 (2015): 525–9.

Austin, J. L. 'The Meaning of a Word'. In *Philosophical Papers*, edited by J. O. Urmson and G. J. Warnock, Oxford: Oxford University Press, 1979, pp. 55–75.

————. *Sense and Sensibilia* (Reconstructed from the Manuscript Notes by G. J. Warnock). Oxford: Oxford University Press, 1962.

Austin, Jean. 'Pleasure and Happiness'. *Philosophy* 43, no. 163 (1968): 51–62.

Ayer, A. J. *Language, Truth and Logic*. Harmondsworth: Penguin Books, 1936/1972.

————. *A Part of My Life: The Memoirs of a Philosopher*. Oxford: Oxford University Press, 1978.

Beaney, M., *The Oxford Handbook of the History of Analytic Philosophy*. Oxford: Oxford University Press, 2013.

Beaney, M., and S. Chapman. 'Susan Stebbing'. In *The Stanford Encyclopedia of Philosophy*, edited by Edward N. Zalta. 2017.

Berkman, J. 'Justice and Murder: The Backstory to Anscombe's "Modern Moral Philosophy"'. In *The Oxford Handbook of Elizabeth Anscombe*, edited by Roger Teichmann: Oxford University Press, 2021.

————. 'The Influence of Victor White and the Blackfriars Dominicans on a young Elizabeth Anscombe. An Essay accompanying the Republication of Elizabeth Anscombe's 'I am Sadly Theoretical: It is the Effect of Being at Oxford' (1938)', *New Blackfriars*, September 2021.

Berlin, I. (ed.). *Essays on J. L. Austin*. Oxford: Clarendon Press, 1973.

Berlin, I. *Personal Impressions*. London: Hogarth Press, 1980.

Biletzki, A., and A. Matar. *The Story of Analytic Philosophy: Plot and Heroes*. New York: Taylor & Routledge, 1998.

Birks, C. 'From Pacifism to Popular Front: The Changing Views of the Left and the Liberal Intelligentsia in Oxford, 1933–1938'. Master of Studies in Historical Studies dissertation, University of Oxford, 2020.

Black, M. *A Cause for Our Time: Oxfam, the First Fifty Years*. Oxford: Oxford University Press, 1992.

Blum, L. A., and V. J. Seidler. *A Truer Liberty: Simone Weil and Marxism*. London: Routledge, 2009.

Bowyer, A. *Donald MacKinnon's Moral Realism: To Perceive Tragedy Without the Loss of Hope*, Edinburgh: T&T Clark, 2015.

Broackes, J. (ed.). *Iris Murdoch, Philosopher*. Oxford: Oxford University Press, 2011.

————. 'Introduction'. In *Iris Murdoch, Philosopher*, edited by J. Broackes. Oxford: Oxford University Press, 2012, pp. 1–92.

————. 'Iris Murdoch's First Encounters with Simone Weil'. *The Iris Murdoch Review*, no. 8 (2017): 17–20.

————. 'Waiting on God': Prefatory Note on the Text. *The Iris Murdoch Review*, no. 9 (2017): 9.

————. *Sovereignty of Good: A Philosophical Commentary*. Oxford: Oxford University Press (2022).

Brown, S., and H. T. Bredin. *Dictionary of Twentieth-Century British Philosophers*. London: Bloomsbury Academic, 2005.

Browning, G., *Why Iris Murdoch Matters*. London: Bloomsbury, 2018.

Buber, M. *I and Thou*, trans. Ronald Gregor-Smith. Edinburgh: T&T Clark, 1958.

Bullock, A. *Hitler: A Study in Tyranny*. London: Odhams Press, 1952.

Cassirer, E. *An Essay on Man: An Introduction to a Philosophy of Human Culture*. New Haven: Yale University Press, 1944.

Chapman, S. *Susan Stebbing and the Language of Common Sense*. London: Palgrave Macmillan UK, 2013.

Collingwood, R. G. *An Essay on Metaphysics* (1940). Oxford: Clarendon Press, 1957.

Connell, S.M. and F. Janssen-Lauret, 'Lost Voices: Women in Philosophy 1880–1970'. *British Journal for the History of Philosophy*, 2022.

Conradi, P. J. *Iris Murdoch: A Life*. London: HarperCollins, 2001.

————. *Family Business: A Memoir*. Brigend: Seren, 2019.

———. '"The Guises of Love": The Friendship of Professor Philippa Foot and Dame Iris Murdoch'. *The Iris Murdoch Review*, no. 5 (2014): 17–29.

———. *Iris Murdoch, a Writer at War: Letters and Diaries, 1939–1945*. Oxford: Oxford University Press, 2011.

———. *A Very English Hero: The Making of Frank Thompson*. London: Bloomsbury, 2013.

Crawford, S., K. Ulmschneider, and J. Elsner. *Ark of Civilization: Refugee Scholars and Oxford University, 1930–1945*. Oxford: Oxford University Press, 2017.

Currie, Robert. 'The Arts and Social Studies, 1914–1939'. In *The History of the University of Oxford Volume VIII: The Twentieth Century*, edited by B. Harrison. Oxford: Clarendon Press, 1994, pp. 109–38.

Darwin, J. G. 'A World University'. In *The History of the University of Oxford Volume VIII: The Twentieth Century*, edited by B. Harrison. Oxford: Clarendon Press, 1994, pp. 607–38

Descartes, R., G.E.M. Anscombe, P. T. Geach, and A. Koyré. *Philosophical Writings*. Middlesex: Nelson, 1954/1970.

Dewey, J. *Experience and Education*. New York: Touchstone, 1997.

Dodds, E. R. *Missing Persons: An Autobiography*. Oxford: Clarendon Press, 1977.

Dudley Buxton, L. H. *Oxford University Ceremonies*. Oxford: Clarendon Press, 1935.

Edmonds, D., *The Murder of Professor Schlick: The Rise and Fall of the Vienna Circle*, Princeton: Princeton University Press, 2020.

Edmonds, D., and J. Eidenow. *Wittgenstein's Poker*. New York: Ecco, Harper Collins, 2001.

Emmet, D. 'On the Idea of Importance.' *Philosophy* 21, no. 80 (1946): 234–44.

———. *The Nature of Metaphysical Thinking*. London: Macmillan, 1945/1966.

———. *Philosophers and Friends: Reminiscences of Seventy Years in Philosophy*, with a foreword by Bryan Magee. Basingstoke: Macmillan, 1996.

———. *Role of the Unrealisable: Study in Regulative Ideals*. London: Macmillan, 1993.

Erbacher, Christian. 'Wittgenstein and His Literary Executors'. *Journal for the History of Analytical Philosophy* 4, 3 (2016): 1–40.

———. *Wittgenstein's Heirs and Editors*. Cambridge: Cambridge University Press, 2020.

Fann, K. T., and L. Wittgenstein. *Ludwig Wittgenstein: The Man and His Philosophy*. Atlantic Highlands, NJ: Humanities Press, 1967.

Farnell, V. *A Somervillian Looks Back*. Privately printed at the University Press, 1948.

Feyerabend, P. *Killing Time: The Autobiography of Paul Feyerabend*. Chicago: University of Chicago Press, 1996.

Filkins, P. H. G. *Adler: A Life in Many Worlds*. Oxford: Oxford University Press, 2019.

Flowers III, F. A., and I. Ground. *Portraits of Wittgenstein*. London: Bloomsbury Academic, 1999/2018.

Foot, M.R.D. *Memories of an S.O.E. Historian*. Barnsley: Pen & Sword Books, 2008.

Fraenkel, Eduard. *Aeschylus: Agamemnon, Vol 1: Prolegomena, Text, Translation*. Oxford: Oxford University Press, 1950.

Gardiner, J. *Wartime Britain 1939–1945*. London: Headline, 2016.

Geach, P. 'A Philosophical Autobiography'. In *Peter Geach: Philosophical Encounters*, edited by Harry A. Lewis. Dordrecht: Springer Netherlands, 1991, pp. 1–25.

Gibson-Wood, C. 'Raymond Klibanksy and the Warburg Institute'. *Canadian Art Review* 27, no. 1/2 (2000): 137–9.

Glover, J. *Humanity: A Moral History of the Twentieth Century*. New Haven: Yale University Press, 2001.

Glover, M. 'Obligation and Value'. *Ethics* 49, no. 1 (1938): 68–80.

———, C. Reaveley and J. Winnington. *Democracy and Industry*. London: Chatto & Windus, 1947.

———, and C. Reaveley. 'Wrong Things to Teach'. *Spectator*, 2 February 1945, pp. 101–2.

———, and C. Reaveley. 'Could We Go Nazi'. *Spectator*, 5 October 1945, p. 175.

Griffin, P. *St Hugh's: One Hundred Years of Women's Education in Oxford*. London: Palgrave Macmillan, 1986.

Grimley, M. *Citizenship, Community and the Church of England: Liberal Anglican Theories of the State between the Wars*. Oxford: Oxford University Press, 2004.

Hacker-Wright, J., *Philippa Foot on Goodness and Virtue*, Cham: Springer International Publishing, 2018

———. *Philippa Foot's Moral Thought*, London: Bloomsbury, 2013.

Haddock, A., and R. Wiseman, *The Anscombean Mind*, London: Routledge, 2022.

Haldane, J. 'Anscombe: Life, Action and Ethics in Context.' *Philosophical News* 18 (2019): 45–75.

Hämäläinen, N., and G. Dooley. *Reading Iris Murdoch's Metaphysics as a Guide to Morals*. Cham: Springer International Publishing, 2019.

Hare, R. M. 'Imperative Sentences.' *Mind* 58, no. 229 (1949): 21–39.

———. 'A Philosophical Autobiography: R. M. Hare.' *Utilitas* 14, no. 3 (2002): 269–305.

———. *The Language of Morals*. Oxford: Clarendon Press, 1952.

Harris, D., and E. Unnsteinsson. 'Wittgenstein's Influence on Austin's Philosophy of Language'. *British Journal for the History of Philosophy* 26, no. 2 (2018): 371–95.

Harrison, B. 'College Life, 1918–1939.' In *The History of the University of Oxford Volume VIII: The Twentieth Century*, edited by B. Harrison. Oxford: Oxford University Press, 1994, pp. 81–108.

————. *The History of the University of Oxford: Volume VIII: The Twentieth Century.* Oxford: Clarendon Press, 1994.

Heck, J. D. (ed.) *Socratic Digest 1943–1952.* Austin, Texas: Concordia University Press, 2012.

Hopwood, M., and S. Panizza. *The Murdochian Mind,* London: Routledge, 2022.

Horner, A, and A. Rowe (eds.). *Living on Paper: Letters from Iris Murdoch.* London: Chatto & Windus, 2015.

Howarth, J. 'Anglican Perspectives on Gender: Some Reflections on the Centenary of St Hugh's College, Oxford'. *Oxford Review of Education* 12, no. 3 (1986): 299–304.

————. 'Women'. In *The History of the University of Oxford: Volume VIII: The Twentieth Century,* edited by B. Harrison. Oxford: Clarendon Press, 1994, pp. 345–76.

Ignatieff, M. *Isaiah Berlin: A Life.* London: Chatto & Windus, 1998.

Inglis, F. *History Man: The Life of R. G. Collingwood.* Princeton: Princeton University Press, 2011.

Joad, C. E. M. 'Appeal to Philosophers'. *Proceedings of the Aristotelian Society* 40, no. 1 (1940): 27–48.

Joseph, H.W.B. 'Purposive Action'. *Hibbert Journal* 32:2 (1933): 213–26.

————. *Some Problems in Ethics.* Oxford: Oxford University Press, 1933.

Kenny, A. 'Peter Thomas Geach 1916-2003'. *Biographical Memoirs of Fellows of the British Academy,* XIV (2015): 185–203.

Kidd, I. J., and L. McKinnell, *Science and the Self: Animals, Evolution, and Ethics: Essays in Honour of Mary Midgley,* London: Routledge, 2015.

Lanneau, C. *L'Inconnue Française: La France et les Belges Francophones, 1944–1945.* Bruxelles: Peter Lang, 2008.

Leeson, M. *Iris Murdoch: Philosophical Novelist,* London: Bloomsbury, 2011

Levine, E. J. 'The Other Weimar: The Warburg Circle as Hamburg School'. *Journal of the History of Ideas* 74, no. 2 (2013): 307–30.

Lindsay, A. D. 'What Does the Mind Construct?'. *Proceedings of the Aristotelian Society* 25 (1924): 1–18.

————. 'The Idealism of Caird and Jones'. *Journal of Philosophical Studies* 1, no. 2 (1926): 171–82.

————. 'Wilhelm Dilthey'. *Nature* 156, no. 3964 (1945): 461–61.

Lipscomb, B. *The Women Are Up to Something: How Elizabeth Anscombe, Philippa Foot, Mary Midgley, and Iris Murdoch Revolutionized Ethics.* Oxford: Oxford University Press, 2021.

Loner, J. D. 'Wittgenstein and his Students, 1912–1968'. PhD thesis, University of Cambridge, 2018.

Lorenz, Konrad. *King Solomon's Ring: New Light on Animal Ways.* London: Routledge, 2002.

Lynn, V., and V. Lewis-Jones. *Keep Smiling Through: My Wartime Story*. London: Random House, 2017.

Mabbott, J. D. *Oxford Memories*. Oxford: Thorntons of Oxford, 1986.

MacKinnon, D. M. 'And the Son of Man That Thou Visitest Him'. *Christendom* 8, September 1938 and December 1938 (1938): 186–92 and 260–72.

———. 'The Function of Philosophy in Education (1941)'. In *Philosophy and the Burden of Theological Honesty*, edited by John McDowell. London: T & T Clark, 2011, pp. 11–14.

———. 'Revelation and Social Justice (1941)'. In *Philosophy and the Burden of Theological Honesty*, edited by John McDowell. London: T & T Clark, 2011.

———. 'Preface'. In *Being and Having* (by Gabriel Marcel, translated by Katharine Farrer). London. Westminster: Dacre, 1949, pp. 1–3.

———. 'Metaphysical and Religious Language'. *Proceedings of the Aristotelian Society* 54 (1954): 115–30.

———. 'Reflections on the Hydrogen Bomb'. *The Listener* 52, no. 13 (1954): 239–40.

———. *A Study in Ethical Theory*. London: A & C Black, 1957.

———. 'Philosophers in Exile'. *The Oxford Magazine*, 1992, pp. 15–16.

———. *The Problem of Metaphysics*. Cambridge: Cambridge University Press, 1974.

Magee, B. and A. Quinton. *Modern British Philosophy*. Oxford: Oxford University Press, 1971.

Mander, W. J. *Idealist Ethics*. Oxford University Press UK, 2016.

———. *British Idealism: A History*, Oxford: Oxford University Press, 2014.

Marcel, Gabriel. *Being and Having*, Trans. Katharine Farrer. Westminster, London: Dacre Press, 1949.

———. *The Mystery of Being Vol 1: Reflection & Mystery*. London: Harvill, 1951.

Mascall, E. L. 'The Doctrine of Analogy'. *Cross Currents* 1, no. 4 (1951): 38–57.

———. *Saraband: The Memoirs of E. L. Mascall*. Leominster: Gracewing, 1992.

Masterman, J. C. *On the Chariot Wheel: An Autobiography*. Oxford: Oxford University Press, 1975.

Matherne, S., *Cassirer*. London: Routledge, 2021.

McCullough, D. *Truman*. New York: Simon & Schuster, 1992.

McElwain, G. *Mary Midgley: An Introduction*, London: Bloomsbury, 2019.

McGuinness, B. (ed.). *Wittgenstein in Cambridge: Letters and Documents 1911–1951*. Oxford: Wiley-Blackwell, 2012.

Mehta, Ved. *Fly and the Fly-Bottle: Encounters with British Intellectuals*. New York: Columbia University Press, 1962.

Mitchell, B. *Looking Back: On Faith, Philosophy and Friends in Oxford*. Durham: Memoir Club, 2009.

Mitchell, L. *Maurice Bowra: A Life*. Oxford: Oxford University Press, 2010.

Monk, R., *Ludwig Wittgenstein: The Duty of Genius*. London: Vintage, 1992.

Moore, A. W., *The Evolution of Modern Metaphysics: Making Sense of Things*. Cambridge: Cambridge University Press, 2012.

Moore, G. E. 'The Refutation of Idealism'. *Mind* 12, no. 48 (1903): 433–53.

———. *Principia Ethica*. Cambridge: Cambridge University Press, 1922.

Morris, Jan. *Oxford*. Oxford: Oxford University Press, 2001.

Morris, June. *The Life and Times of Thomas Balogh: A Macaw among Mandarins*. Eastbourne: Sussex Academic Press, 2007.

Muirhead, J. H. 'How Hegel Came to England.' *Mind* 36, no. 144 (1927): 423–47.

Muller, A. 'Donald M. MacKinnon: The True Service of the Particular, 1913–1959'. PhD dissertation, University of Otago, 2010.

Mure, G. R. G. *Retreat from Truth*. Oxford: Blackwell, 1958.

Murray, G. *Gilbert Murray: An Unfinished Autobiography*. Oxford: Oxford University Press, 1960.

Nagel, E. 'Impressions and Appraisals of Analytic Philosophy in Europe. I'. *The Journal of Philosophy* 33, no. 1 (1936): 5–24.

Paton, H. J. *The Categorical Imperative: A Study in Kant's Moral Philosophy*. London: Hutchinson's University Library, 1946.

Pevsner, N., and J. Sherwood. *Oxfordshire*. Harmondsworth: Penguin, 1974.

Phillips, A. *A Newnham Anthology*. Cambridge: Cambridge University Press, 1979.

Price, H. H. 'The Inaugural Address: Clarity is Not Enough.' *Proceedings of the Aristotelian Society*, Supplementary Volumes 19 (1945): 1–31.

———. 'The Permanent Significance of Hume's Philosophy'. *Philosophy* 15, no. 57 (1940): 7–37.

———. *Hume's Theory of the External World*. Oxford: Clarendon Press, 1963.

Prichard, H. A. 'Does Moral Philosophy Rest on a Mistake?'. *Mind* 21, no. 81 (1912): 21–37.

———. *Moral Obligation: Essays and Lectures*. Oxford: Clarendon Press, 1949.

Pugh, M. *We Danced All Night: A Social History of Britain between the Wars*. London: Random House, 2013.

———. *Women and the Women's Movement in Britain, 1914–1959*. Basingstoke: Palgrave Macmillan, 1992.

Purton, V. *An Iris Murdoch Chronology*. Basingstoke: Palgrave Macmillan, 2007.

Ridler, A. *Olive Willis and Downe House: An Adventure in Education*. London: Murray, 1967.

Robinson, J. *Bluestockings*. London: Viking, 2009.

Rogers, A. M. A. H., and C. F. Rogers. *Degrees by Degrees: The Story of the Admission of Oxford Women Students to Membership of the University*. Oxford: Oxford University Press, 1938.

Rogers, Ben. *A. J. Ayer: A Life*. New York: Grove Press, 1999.

Ross, W. D. *The Right and The Good*, edited by Philip Stratton-Lake, Oxford: Clarendon Press, 1930/2002.

Rowe, Mark. *J. L. Austin: Philosopher and D-Day Intelligence Officer* (unpublished manuscript, forthcoming, Oxford University Press).

Rozelle-Stone, A. Rebecca, and Benjamin P. Davis, 'Simone Weil', *The Stanford Encyclopedia of Philosophy* (Fall 2020 Edition), edited by Edward N. Zalta, URL = <https://plato.stanford.edu/archives/fall2020/entries/simone-weil/>.

Russell, B. *Human Knowledge, Its Scope and Limits*. New York: Simon & Schuster, 1948.

———. 'On Denoting'. *Mind* 14, no. 56 (1905): 479–93.

Sagare, S. B., and I. Murdoch. 'An Interview with Iris Murdoch'. *Modern Fiction Studies* 47, 3 (2001): 696–714.

Sartre, J-P. 'Existentialism is a Humanism' (1946), trans. Philip Mairet. In *Existentialism from Dostoyevsky to Sartre*, edited by Walter Kaufman. London: Penguin, 1991, pp. 345–69.

Savage, J. *Teenage: The Creation of Youth Culture*. London: Pimlico, 2008.

Schwenkler, J., *Anscombe's Intention: A Guide*. Oxford: Oxford University Press, 2019.

Scott, D. A. *D. Lindsay: A Biography*. Oxford: Basil Blackwell, 1971.

Searle, J. 'Oxford Philosophy in the 1950s'. *Philosophy* 90. no. 2 (2015): 173–93.

Sheridan, D. (ed.). *Wartime Women: A Mass-Observation Anthology 1937–45*. London: Phoenix, 2002.

Smith, P. *The Morning Light: A South African Childhood Revalued*. Cape Town: David Philip, 2000.

Stadler, F. *The Vienna Circle: Studies in the Origins, Development, and Influence of Logical Empiricism*. Wien–New York: Springer, 2001.

Stebbing, S. L. *Thinking to Some Purpose*. Harmondsworth: Penguin Books, 1939.

Stray, Christopher. 'A Teutonic Monster in Oxford: The Making of Fraenkel's Agamemnon'. In *Classical Commentaries: Explorations in a Scholarly Genre*, edited by Christina S. Kraus and Christopher Stray. Oxford: Oxford University Press, 2015.

Teichman, J. 'Gertrude Elizabeth Margaret Anscombe 1919–2001', *Proceedings of the British Academy* 115 (2002): 31–50.

Teichmann, R. *The Oxford Handbook of Elizabeth Anscombe*. Oxford: Oxford University Press, 2022.

———. *The Philosophy of Elizabeth Anscombe*. Oxford: Oxford University Press, 2008.

Thompson, M. 'Apprehending Human Form'. *Royal Institute of Philosophy Supplement* 54 (2004): 47–74.

Umachandran, Mathura. '"The Aftermath Experienced Before": Aeschylean Untimeliness and Iris Murdoch's Defence of Art'. *Ramus* 48, no. 2 (2019): 223–47.

Urmson, J. O. 'Austin's Philosophy'. In *Symposium on J. L. Austin*, edited by K. T. Fann. London: Routledge & Kegan Paul, 1969.

Voorhoeve, A. *Conversations on Ethics*. Oxford: Oxford University Press, 2011.

Vrijen, C. 'The Philosophical Development of Gilbert Ryle: A Study of His Published and Unpublished Writings'. PhD dissertation, Groningen, 2007.

Walsh, B. 'From Outer Darkness: Oxford and Her Refugees'. *Oxford Magazine*, 1992, 5–7.

Warnock, G. J. 'Gilbert Ryle's Editorship'. *Mind* 85, no. 337 (1976): 47–56.

———. 'John Langshaw Austin: A Biographical Sketch (1963)'. In *Symposium on J. L. Austin*, edited by K. T. Fann. London: Routledge & Kegan Paul, 1969.

Warnock, M. *A Memoir: People and Places*. London: Duckworth, 2000.

Weber, R. *Lotte Labowsky (1905–1991): Schülerin Aby Warburgs, Kollegin Raymond Klibanskys*. Berlin and Hamburg: Dietrich Reimer Verlag, 2012.

Webster, W. *Mixing It: Diversity in World War Two Britain*. Oxford: Oxford University Press, 2018.

Weil, S., and J. P. Holoka. *Simone Weil's the Iliad, or, the Poem of Force: A Critical Edition*. London: Peter Lang, 2003.

———. *Oppression and Liberty*, translated by A. Wills and J. Petrie. London: Routledge, 2001.

White, F. *Becoming Iris Murdoch*. London: Kingston University Press, 2014.

White, R., J. E. Wolfe, and B. N. Wolfe. *C. S. Lewis and His Circle: Essays and Memoirs from the Oxford C. S. Lewis Society*. Oxford: Oxford University Press, 2015.

Williams, B. *Ethics and the Limits of Philosophy*. Cambridge, MA: Harvard University Press, 1985.

———. *Shame and Necessity*. Berkeley, CA: University of California Press, 1993.

Wimmer, M. 'The Afterlives of Scholarship: Warburg and Cassirer'. *History of Humanities* 2, 1 (2017): 245–70.

Winch, P. *Simone Weil: 'The Just Balance'*. Cambridge: Cambridge University Press, 1989.

Wiseman, R. *Routledge Philosophy Guidebook to Anscombe's Intention*. London: Routledge, 2016.

Wittgenstein, L., and G.E.M. Anscombe. *Philosophical Investigations: The German Text, with a Revised English Translation*. Oxford: Blackwell, 2001.

Wittgenstein, L. *Wittgenstein: Lectures and Conversations on Aesthetics, Psychology and Religious Belief*, edited by C. Barrett. Oxford: Basil Blackwell, 1966.

———. *On Certainty* (ed. Anscombe and Von Wright). New York Harper Torchbooks, 1969/1972.

———, P. T. Geach, K. J. Shah, and A. C. Jackson. *Wittgenstein's Lectures on Philosophical Psychology*, 1946–47. University of Chicago Press, 1989.

———, C. G. Luckhardt, G. H. von Wright, and H. Nyman. *Last Writings on the Philosophy of Psychology, Volume 1*. Chicago: University of Chicago Press, 1982.

———, and C. K. Ogden. *Tractatus Logico-Philosophicus*. London: Routledge, 1921.

———, G. H. Wright, G.E.M. Anscombe, and R. Rhees. *Remarks on the Foundations of Mathematics*. London: Blackwell, 1956.

Wragg, D. *Wartime on the Railways*. Stroud: The History Press, 2012.

Further Reading

There is a rich and growing literature on the philosophy of these women. Here is some further reading that we have benefited from while researching for *Metaphysical Animals*.

For general overviews, we recommend Teichmann, *The Philosophy of Elizabeth Anscombe*; Hacker-Wright, *Philippa Foot's Moral Thought*; McElwain, *Mary Midgley: An Introduction*; Broackes, *Iris Murdoch, Philosopher*. For accessible guidebooks to key texts, see Schwenkler, *Anscombe's Intention: A Guide*; Wiseman, *Routledge Philosophy Guidebook to Anscombe's Intention*; Broackes, *Sovereignty of Good: A Philosophical Commentary*; Hämäläinen and Dooley, *Reading Iris Murdoch's Metaphysics as a Guide to Morals*. *The Stanford Encyclopaedia of Philosophy* is a helpful open-access resource.

There are some excellent recent edited collections, including Teichmann, *The Oxford Handbook of Elizabeth Anscombe*; Haddock and Wiseman, *The Anscombean Mind*; Hacker-Wright, *Philippa Foot on Goodness and Virtue*; Kidd and McKinnell, *Science and the Self: Animals, Evolution, and Ethics: Essays in Honour of Mary Midgley*; Broackes, *Iris Murdoch, Philosopher*; Hopwood and Panizza, *The Murdochian Mind*.

For more biographical detail, see Warnock, *A Memoir: People and Places*; Kenny, *Brief Encounters: Notes from a Philosopher's Diary*; Lipscomb, *The Women Are Up to Something: How Elizabeth Anscombe, Philippa Foot, Mary Midgley, and Iris Murdoch Revolutionized Ethics*; Haldane, 'Anscombe: Life, Action and Ethics in Context'; Teichman, *Elizabeth Anscombe*; Midgley, *Owl of Minerva: A Memoir*; Conradi, *Iris Murdoch: A Life*; White, *Becoming Iris Murdoch*. For work that looks at Iris Murdoch's novels philosophically, see Browning, *Why Iris Murdoch Matters*, and Leeson, *Iris Murdoch: Philosophical Novelist*.

Other historical philosophical works that help to piece together the contours of 20th Century Philosophy, and the lives of key thinkers are: Beaney, *The Oxford Handbook of the History of Analytic Philosophy*; Blum and Seidler, *A Truer Liberty: Simone Weil and Marxism*; Chapman, *Susan Stebbing and the Language of Common Sense*; Connell and Janssen-Lauret, 'Lost Voices. Women in Philosophy 1900–1970'; Edmonds, *The Murder of Professor Schlick: The Rise and Fall of the Vienna Circle*; Loner, *Wittgenstein and his Students, 1912–1968*; Mander, *British Idealism: A History*, and also his *Idealist Ethics*; Monk, *Ludwig Wittgenstein: The Duty of Genius*; Moore, *The Evolution of Modern Metaphysics: Making Sense of Things*; Sweetman, *A Gabriel Marcel Reader*; Matherne, *Cassirer*; Rogers, *A.J. Ayer: A Life*; Muller, *Donald M. MacKinnon: The True Service of the Particular, 1913–1959*; Rowe, *J. L. Austin: Philosopher and D-Day Intelligence Officer*; Stadler, *The Vienna Circle: Studies in the Origins, Development, and Influence of Logical Empiricism*; Weber, *Lotte Labowsky (1905–1991): Schülerin Aby Warburgs, Kollegin Raymond Klibanskys*; Winch, *Simone Weil: 'The Just Balance'*.

Contemporary interpreters and scholars whose work we've found especially illuminating include: Hannah Altorf (Murdoch); David Bakhurst (Murdoch); Paul Bloomfield (Anscombe, Foot, Murdoch); Justin Broackes (Murdoch); Sophie Grace Chappell (Anscombe and Murdoch); Sophia Connell (Anscombe and Midgley); Alice Crary (Murdoch); Anton Ford (Anscombe); Jennifer Frey (Anscombe and Foot); Anil Gomes (Murdoch); Mark Hopwood (Murdoch); Nikhil Krishnan (Foot); Katherine Nieswandt (Foot and Anscombe); Evgenia Mylonaki (Anscombe and Murdoch); Gavin Lawrence (Foot); Kieran Setiya (Anscombe and Murdoch); Roger Teichmann (Anscombe).

Senior philosophers who use these women's work today, many of whom studied with them are: Lawrence Blum (Murdoch); Cora Diamond (Anscombe and Murdoch); Rosalind Hursthouse (Foot); Anthony Kenny (Anscombe); Sabina Lovibond (Murdoch); Alisdair MacIntyre (Anscombe); John McDowell (Anscombe and Murdoch); Martha Nussbaum (Murdoch); Charles Taylor (Murdoch); Michael Thompson (Anscombe and Foot); Candace Vogler (Anscombe).

List of Illustrations

List of Illustrations

List of Illustrations

Every effort has been made to trace and contact all holders of copyright in illustrations. If there are any inadvertent omissions or errors, the publishers will be pleased to correct these at the earliest opportunity.

Acknowledgements

We wrote this book during the Covid-19 pandemic. When, in February 2020, we said farewell to Somerville College's incredible archivists, Anne Manuel and Kate O'Donnell, we assumed we'd just made our first visit of many. It would be two years (and a complete draft) later before we could return. For this reason, our first and loudest thanks go to the archivists. Throughout the pandemic, working in conditions that were new and frightening and unpredictable, they responded to our strange questions, speculative enquiries and unending requests for scans and copies with kindness and enthusiasm. We *literally* couldn't have written this book without them. In Oxford: Amanda Ingram (St Hugh's), Oliver Mahony (Lady Margaret Hall and St Hilda's), Bethany Hamblen and Amy Boylan (Balliol), Fiona Richardson (Linacre), Peter Monteith (Keble), Judith Curthoys (Christ Church), Jennifer Thorp (New College), Emma Goodrum (Worcester), Michael Riordan (Queen's), Alice Millea, Anne Petre, Nicola O'Toole and many others (Oxford University Archives). In Cambridge: Frieda Midgley (Newnham) and Jonathan Smith (Trinity). Kate O'Donnell and Anne Manuel (at Somerville), Andrew Gray (at the Mary and Geoff Midgley Archive, Durham) and Dayna Miller (at the Iris Murdoch Archive, Kingston) were heroic in their efforts to help us, as was Janet Dilger (at the Klibanksy and Steiner archives, Marbach). Daniel Cheely and Terrence and Jessica Sweeney (at the Collegium Institute Anscombe Archive, University of Pennsylvania) stepped in to assist when Covid cancelled our trip to the USA. That unmade trip and, importantly, the period of sabbatical leave during which we wrote the book, was funded by an Arts and Humanities Research Council Grant. We are also grateful for grants received from the

Acknowledgements

Collegium Institute, the British Academy, the Royal Institute of Philosophy, the British Society of Aesthetics, and Durham and Liverpool Universities, and to the academics who supported our applications, including Nancy Cartwright, Jenny Saul and Matthew Soteriou.

Our debt to our colleagues is enormous. David Bakhurst, Ana Barandalla, Justin Broackes, Lesley Brown, Gary Browning, Siobhan Chapman, Alix Cohen, Peter Conradi, Andy Hamilton, Miles Leeson, André Müller, Mark Rowe and Robert Stern read the entire manuscript and between them saved us too many blushes to count. John Berkman, Chris Birks, Colin Carritt, John Haldane, André Müller, Mark Rowe and Ron Tacelli all shared unpublished research and in many cases were happy to enter into months-long email correspondence with us. Paul Bryers generously sent the script of his brilliant 1988 drama-documentary *A Vote for Hitler* and painstakingly transferred the film in small sections over our unstable internet. We have received ideas, inspiration and practical help from all of the members of the 'Women In Parenthesis' network: particular thanks to the brilliant Rachel Bollen, Ana Barandalla (whose immaculate and incisive copy-editing is truly a wonder), Mara-Daria Cojocaru (who translated the Steiner poem in the text), Amber Donovan, Eva-Maria Düringer, Sasha Lawson-Frost, David Loner, Annie MacCallion, Amber Perera, Sally Pilkington, Ellie Robson, Anne Sterle and Amy Ward. Hannah Altorf, Luna Dolezal, Liza Thompson and Dawn Wilson were early friends of 'Women In Parenthesis'. *All* of our colleagues at Durham and Liverpool have supported and encouraged us in innumerable ways: special mentions to Chiara Brozzo, Simon Hailwood, Michael Hauskeller, Daniel Hill, Ian James Kidd, Liz McKinnell, Joe Saunders, Vid Simoniti, Ben Smith, Richard Stopford, Sara Uckelman, Yiota Vassilopoulou; and at University College Dublin, Áine Mahon and Danielle Petheridge. We have relied on the encouragement and expertise of too many others to name (we hope you know who you are), so we limit ourselves to some of the women who have been mentors or inspirations: Maria Baghramian, Nancy Cartwright, Cora Diamond, Susan Frenk, Jane Heal, Jennifer Hornsby, Marie McGinn, Sarah Richmond, Christine Sypnowich, Gabrielle Taylor, Mary Warnock and Alison Wiley.

One of the great joys of writing this book has been meeting people who knew and loved the characters who appear in its pages. The families, friends and literary executors of Elizabeth Anscombe, Philippa Foot, Mary Midgley and Iris Murdoch have been generous in giving us time, tales and permissions. Audi Bayley gave us permission to use Iris's letters to Mary, now held

Acknowledgements

at Durham. Mary and Luke Gormally shared stories, photos and Anscombe family history, and gave generous permission to reproduce and quote from numerous unpublished sources. Francis and Penelope Warner let us into their home (27 St John Street). Lesley Brown helped us to build a picture of the (terribly private) Philippa Foot, and gave permission to use unpublished material from the Somerville Archive. Lawrence Blum, John Campbell, Prophesy Coles and Martin Gornall shared crucial stories. Joyce Reynolds helped us to reconstruct something of 1930s Somerville. Mary and her family – her three sons, grandchildren, and numerous friends and former colleagues – have all become friends through this process: Gillian Allnutt, Mike Bavidge, Jessica and Sheridan Few, Ian Ground, Tenzin Haarhaus, Judith Hughes and David, Martin and Tom Midgley. Miles Leeson, Anne Rowe and Francis White have shared so much wisdom on Iris Murdoch. We are also thankful to the friends and families of Heinz Cassirer (and Iona Hine), Michael Foot, Mary Glover, R. M. Hare, Lotte Labowsky, Donald MacKinnon, H. H. Price, Franz Steiner, Jessie Street, Frank Thompson, Victor White and Bernard Williams (and to Adrian Moore). Peter Conradi's book, *Iris Murdoch: A Life*, has been an invaluable resource for our work, and Peter has become a friend and mentor. As well as all the help with the book, and many stories of Iris and Philippa, we are grateful for a much-needed post-submission sauna and swim at his and Jim's idyllic home.

We have been so lucky to work on this book with an amazing team of women. Our agent Zoë Waldie (of RCW) is a phenomenon. It is due to her enthusiasm, encouragement and careful management that we have stayed (roughly) on track for the last three years. Clara Farmer (at Chatto & Windus, UK) and Kris Puopolo (at Doubleday, USA) loved our four heroines as much as we do, have made the most timely and perfectly judged editorial interventions and have remained calm when we ran amok. All three women work with incredible teams, which include Mary Chamberlain, Tom Atkins, Ryan Bowes, Becky Hardie and Natasia Patel.

Our whole families, but very especially Joseph, Rob, Penelope and Ursula, have put up with us with love, patience and kindness as we tried to co-author a book through a series of lockdowns, home-schooling episodes, false finishes, calamities and dramas. They have read drafts, helped with research, sung songs, drawn pictures, cooked dinners and told us when it was time to stop! We love them and are happy to declare the book is (now, this time, *really*) finished.

Index

EA = Elizabeth Anscombe; PF = Philippa Foot; MM = Mary Midgley; IM = Iris Murdoch
Figures in *italics* refer to illustrations.

Index

Index

Index

Index

Index

moral psychology 297

moral reality 42–3, 50, 150, 185–6

moral subjectivism 50, 145, 277, 284, 296

Mordan, Clara Evelyn 25

motive *see* action

Muirhead, J. H. (John Henry) 41

Mundle, Clement 168

murder xvi, xvii, 4–5, 8, 200–1, 291, 293, 295

Murdoch, Hughes 15, 162

Murdoch, Iris xi, xii, xiii–xiv, *xviii*, 8, *299*; birth and childhood 15; at Badminton School 15–16, 21–2; wins League of Nations essay competition 22; character and personality 22, 23, 30, 34, 151; arrives at Somerville 16, *16*, 22–3, 24, 51–2; friendship with MM 24; receives proposals of marriage 28; struggles over Greek verse and prose 30; joins political scene 30–31, 33–5, *34*, 52; as a Communist 33–4, 41, 92, 112, 149, 163, 208, 265; attends Fraenkel's *Agamemnon* classes 38–9, 40–1; and Frank Thompson 41, 57–8, 89, 107, 110–11, 128, 129; and Ayer 50, 51, 182; tours with Magpie Players 56; as a guest of the Brüderhof 56; gathers up the 'literary remains of her friends' 57; made his literary executor by Michael Foot 57; and the departure of male undergraduates 58, 59; thinks it lunacy for women to join up 59; in wartime Somerville 65, 69–70, 71, 73–4; meets EA 24, 71–2; friendship with PF 62, 73, 92, 112; and H. H. Price 76, 78, 170; her indifference to Hume 78, 80; in Blackpool 79; troubled by arrest of German scholars 79; taught Kant by Heinz Cassirer 80, 81–2; and Plato 85, 272–3; tutored by Donald MacKinnon 87–8, 89, 93; with MM at graduation dinner party 93–4, 182; at work on her first novel 96, 128; moves to London with MM 96, 97, 98, 106–7, 108–9; at the Treasury 96, 106, 111, 112; and Michael Foot 107, 120, 121; her infatuation with MacKinnon 108; leases 5 Seaforth Place 109–110, *110*; and London nightlife 111–12; and PF's arrival in London 114; invites her to move in 116–17, 120–21, 128; has affair with Thomas Balogh 120, 135, 148; on VE Day 134; with UNRRA 135–6, 148, 151, 155–6; takes to French literature xii, 136, 173, 177–8; in Belgium 148–9, 237; and

Sartre 149–50, 151, 237–8, 239, 265, 270, 276; and Queneau 151, 156, 157, 163; and David Hicks 120, 121(n140), 152, 156; in Innsbruck 151, 152, *153*; visits Austria 156–7; decides to return to philosophy 157, 174, 177; applies for three scholarships 157–8, 160–61; her references from MacKinnon and Mildred Hartley 158; withdraws from Sarah Smithson Studentship 162, *162*; her Communist past catches up with her 162–3; reunited with PF 161, 163–5, 170, 196; her Newnham application successful with MacKinnon's help 177–8; her Sarah Smithson proposal 206–7, 259; in France with MM 178–9; and Richard Hare 186–7, 239, 276; at Cambridge 187, 188; and EA's paper, 'The Reality of the Past' 188, 192, 204–6, 231; meets Gabriel Marcel 192–3; spends time with Wasfi Hijab and Kanti Shah 194; and Wittgenstein 194–5, 203, 204, 205, 206–7, 259; in Lyons' tea rooms with PF, MM and EA 195–6; offends EA 196–7; becomes friends with Stella Aldwinckle 198; and EA 206–7, 216, 219–23, 230, 231, 234–5, 282; beats MM to post of Philosophy Tutor at St Anne's 208–9; invited by PF to move in 208; and EA's first lecture 214, 217; Oxford 'society' gets her down 219; composes sonnet for EA 222–3; invited to meeting of The Metaphysicals 226–7; buys flowers for MM and PF 231; moves out of the Foots' to Park Town 233–4; gives radio talk 236–7; as MM's bridesmaid 245; and Lotte Labowsky 248, 256, 257, 258; at EA's 'Readings on Plato' lectures 254; helps her prepare manuscript of *Philosophical Investigations* 256, 257, 258; her various lovers 259; gives her paper 'Thinking and Language' 259–61; discusses paradox and poetry with MM 261–4; speaks at the Socratic Club 265; further ideas on socialist theory 266; and EA's trip to Paris 267–8; her love affair with love 270–72, 273; gives radio talks on Simone Weil 271; affair with Franz Steiner 273–5; talks with PF on moral philosophy and choice 275–6; suffers from partial deafness 276; important essays published in the 1950s 297; leaves lectureship; 297; marriage 297; has brief affair with PF 297

393

Index

Parmenides 189, 190, 231, 250, 251, 254

past xiv–xvi, 39, 76–8, 134, 143, 164; reality of 187–94, 204–5, 231, 237–8, 251, 256, 274 , 278, 282

Pasternak, Leonid 146

Pasternak, Lydia 146

Paton, H. J.: *Kant's Metaphysic of Experience* 79, 80

Paul, Denis 257, 267

Pax (Catholic peace movement) 66, 88

Penrose, Emily 18, 37

perception 77–8, 167–8, 170, 216, 225–6, 256; as seeing as, aspect perception 256; object of 255; and clarity 8–9; and concepts 8, 81, 83; and sense data 12, 49, 72, 76–8, 166–8, 170, 204, 225; and observation 42, 46, 49, 53, 190, 230; moral 42

phenomenalism 49, 51, 70, 189–90, 215–17, 224

Philosophy (journal) 176

Pickard-Cambridge, William Adair 70

Pindar 110

Pink, Barry (Thomas Barrington) 212, 241

Plamenatz, Jovan 146

Plato xvi, 27, 28, 41, 72, 84, 85, 99, 123, 124, 132, 144, 159, 168, 170, 176, 187, 188, 206, 216, 220, 227, 229, 234, 249, 250, 252, 254–6, 272–3, 283, 294

  Meno 254–5

  Parmenides 250, 251

  Republic 17, 41, 176, 272

  Sophist 251

  Statesmen 251

  Symposium 272–3

  Thaetetus 215, 216, 231

  Theory of Ideas 41

Plotinus 176–7, 185, 187, 192, 204, 229, 233, 246, 263

poetry x–xi, 42, 50, 91, 112, 127, 143, 167, 176, 230, 234, 258–4

Pope, Alexander 262

  The Dunciad 93

Popper, Karl 146, 188

Porson, Richard 134

Port Meadow, Oxford 69

Price, H. H. (Henry Habberley) xiv, xvi, xviii, 70, 176, 225, 226, 227; a felinist 78, 102, 187; lectures on 'Some Points in Hume's Theory of Knowledge' 76–7, 126; on Ayer 52, 166, 240–41; writes references for Grice and MacKinnon 89; addresses the Aristotelian Society (1945) 139, 240–41;

chairs panel at Edinburgh Joint Session 259, 261; as president of the Society for Psychical Research 168, 177

  Hume's Theory of the External World 76, 77, 80

  preface to *Matter, Mind and Meaning* (Carrington) 170

Prichard, H. A. (Harold Arthur) xviii, 42; a Realist 42, 43–4, 186, 290; his 'moral intuitionism' 42, 43–4, 50, 66, 84, 185, 187, 284; and Ayer 52; disliked by IM 151; and Wittgenstein's attendance at the Jowett Society 172, 173–4; death 174

  'Does Moral Philosophy Rest on a Mistake?' 43, 83, 173

  'The Idea of Moral Obligation' (lectures) 41, 51

Proclus: commentary on Plato's *Parmenides* 250, 251

Proctor, Evelyn 232

promising 178, 193, 206, 282

Protagoras 12, 215–16

Przeworska, Zuzanna 24

psychology 43, 48, 71, 158, 170, 192, 204, 236; and philosophical psychology 160, 194, 223, 297

Quakers 13, 66, 154

Queneau, Raymond 156, 157, 179

  Pierrot Mon Ami 129, 151–2, 156, 163

Radcliffe Infirmary, Oxford 64, 276

Radhakrishnan, Sarvepalli 227

Realism xvi, xviii, 42–4, 46, 49–50, 52, 66, 70, 140, 141, 169, 173, 176, 185, 186, 187, 283, 290, 291

refugees xiii, 31, 79–80, 112, 115, 152–3; in Oxford 57, 74–5, 146; and Oxford Refugee Committee 79; and Oxford University Refugee Appeal Fund 56, 80; Jewish 38–40, 51, 115, 157, 194, 259, 273; scholars xiii, 40, 70–1, 79–80, 101, 149, 194, 259, 273; and United Nations Relief and Rehabilitation Administration (UNRRA) 155; and German Jewish Aid Committee 40; and Friends Committee for Refugees and Aliens 115; and Central Department for Interned Refugees 115

Rembrandt van Rijn 135

  Portrait of Margaretha de Geer 107

Rhees, Rush xix, 241, 253, 256

Rhine, Joseph Banks 170

Index

Index